BEYOND CHUTZPAH

Beyond Chutzpah

On the Misuse of Anti-Semitism
and the Abuse of History

NORMAN G. FINKELSTEIN

UNIVERSITY OF CALIFORNIA PRESS   Berkeley   Los Angeles

University of California Press
Berkeley and Los Angeles, California

© 2005 by Norman G. Finkelstein

Library of Congress Cataloging-in-Publication Data

Finkelstein, Norman G.
  Beyond chutzpah : on the misuse of anti-semitism
and the abuse of history / Norman G. Finkelstein.
    p.   cm.
  Includes bibliographical references and index.
  ISBN 0-520-24598-9 (cloth : alk. paper)
    1. Arab-Israeli conflict. 2. Palestinian Arabs—
Crimes against.   3. Dershowitz, Alan M. Case for
Israel.   4. Zionism.   5. Human rights—Palestine.
I. Title.
DS119.7.F544   2005
323.1192'7405694—dc22   2005000117

Manufactured in the United States of America

14 13 12 11 10 09 08 07 06 05
10 9 8 7 6 5 4 3 2 1

To Musa Abu Hashhash and
his fellow human rights workers,
Palestinian and Israeli,
preserving the truth from falsifiers

The world is full of evil people and it is important to stand up to evil.

Alan M. Dershowitz, *Letters to a Young Lawyer*

Contents

Acknowledgments

While writing this book, I accumulated a large number of debts. Those who gave generously of their time include Rudolph Baldeo, Degaulle Adili, Nimrod Amzalak, Joshua Becker, Belabbes Benkredda, Sara Bershtel, Ruth Bettina Birn, Regan Boychuk, Diana Buttu, Roane Carey, Noam Chomsky, Chris-Gerald Ferguson, Carolyn Fialkow, Rohit Goel, Camille Goodison, Maren Hackmann, Nader Hashemi, Eliot Hoffman, Niels Hooper, Zaineb Istrabadi, Joanne Koslofsky, Wilma Kwit, Victor Lang, Darryl Li, Roy Mash, Jessica Montell, Gylfe Nagel, Nina Nazionale, Mouin Rabbani, Wafa Abdel Rahman, Colin Robinson, Sara Roy, Marilyn Schwartz, Feroze Sidhwa, Daniel Song, Shifra Stern, Rafal Szczurowski, Mark Tinsley, Jack Trumpbour, Cyrus Veeser, H. Aram Veeser, and Mary Wilson. If this book finds an audience, it will be due to a collective effort, the most satisfying kind.

Introduction

IN THE COURSE of writing this book, I passed a small milestone in my life. Twenty years ago, while researching my doctoral dissertation on the theory of Zionism, I came across a newly published book on the Israel-Palestine conflict: *From Time Immemorial: The Origins of the Arab-Jewish Conflict over Palestine* by Joan Peters.[1] Promising to revolutionize our understanding of the conflict, the book was adorned on the back cover with glowing praise from the Who's Who of American Arts and Letters (Saul Bellow, Elie Wiesel, Barbara Tuchman, Lucy Dawidowicz, and others), and it went on to garner scores of reviews in the mainstream media ranging from ecstasy to awe. Its first edition, eventually going into seven hardback printings, became a national best seller. The central thesis of Peters's book, apparently supported by nearly two thousand notes and a recondite demographic study, was that Palestine had been virtually empty on the eve of Zionist colonization and that, after Jews made the deserted parts of Palestine they settled bloom, Arabs from neighboring states and other parts of Palestine migrated to the Jewish areas and pretended to be indigenous. Here was the, as it

1. New York: Harper and Row, 1984.

were, scientific proof that Golda Meir had been right after all: there was no such thing as Palestinians.

As it happened, *From Time Immemorial* was a colossal hoax. Cited sources were mangled, key numbers in the demographic study falsified, and large swaths plagiarized from Zionist propaganda tracts. Documenting the hoax and the rather more onerous challenge of publicizing these findings in the media proved to be a turning point for me. From then on, much of my life has, in one fashion or another, centered on the Israel-Palestine conflict.[2]

Looking back after two decades of study and reflection, I am struck most by how *un*complicated the Israel-Palestine conflict is. There is no longer much contention among scholars on the historical record, at any rate for the foundational period from the first Zionist settlements in the late nineteenth century to the creation of Israel in 1948.[3] This wasn't always the case. For a long time two acutely divergent narratives on the Israel-Palestine conflict coexisted. On the one hand, there was the mainstream, or what one might call, with considerable accuracy, the *Exodus* version of the past—basically the heroic, official Zionist tale immortalized in Leon Uris's best-selling historical novel.[4] On the other hand, beyond the margins of respectable opinion, a small dissenting body of literature challenged prevailing wisdom. To take one indicative example, the mainstream Israeli account maintained that Palestinians became refugees in 1948 because Arab radio broadcasts had instructed them to flee. Yet already by the early 1960s, Palestinian scholar Walid Khalidi and Irish scholar Erskine Childers, after examining the archive of Arab radio broadcasts from the 1948 war, concluded that no such

2. For background on the Peters affair, see esp. Edward Said, "Conspiracy of Praise," in Edward Said and Christopher Hitchens (eds.), *Blaming the Victims: Spurious Scholarship and the Palestinian Question* (New York, 2001); for extensive documentation of the Peters fraud, see Norman G. Finkelstein, *Image and Reality of the Israel-Palestine Conflict*, 2nd ed. (New York, 2003), chap. 2; for recent developments in the fraud, see ibid., p. xxxii.

3. A few pockets of scholarly dispute remain: e.g., whether or not the Zionist leadership intended from early on to "transfer" the Palestinians out of Palestine. Arguments over the June 1967 war and its aftermath spring mostly from two sources: the main Israeli archives are still closed, and more important, the political repercussions of the June war—notably Israel's occupation—are still with us. The only more or less live political issue from the foundational period is the Palestinian refugee question, which is perhaps why some, albeit limited, controversy still surrounds it.

4. Putting aside its apologetics for Zionism, the sheer racism of Uris's blockbuster bears recalling. The Arabs, their villages, their homes—to the last, they're "stinking" or engulfed in "overwhelming stench" and "vile odors." Arab men just "lay around" all day "listless"—that is, when they're not hatching "some typical double-dealing scheme which

official Arab exhortations had been given.[5] But revelations such as these had little or no impact on mainstream opinion. Beginning in the late 1980s, however, a steady stream of scholarly studies, mostly by Israelis, dispelled much of the Zionist mythology enveloping the origins of the conflict.[6] Thus, it was now conceded by all serious scholars that the "Arab radio broadcasts" were a Zionist fabrication and that the Palestinians had been ethnically cleansed in 1948, and scholarly debate now focused on the much narrower, if still highly pertinent, question of whether this cleansing was the intentional consequence of Zionist policy or the unintentional by-product of war. Ultimately, on this and related issues, the dissenting narrative, proving closer to the truth, displaced the official Zionist one while, after heated polemics, a broad scholarly consensus on the historical record crystallized.

A similar process of displacement and simplification occurred, coincidentally at just about the same time, on human rights questions. Up until the late 1980s, two fundamentally conflicting claims were put forth regarding Israel's human rights record in the Occupied Territories. The official Israeli contention, echoed by mainstream media, was that Palestinians in the West Bank and Gaza benefited from the most "liberal" and "benign" of occupations. However, a handful of dissidents, mostly Israeli and Palestinian human rights activists like Israel Shahak, Felicia Langer, Lea Tsemel, and Raja Shehadeh, charged, for example, that Israel systematically ill treated and tortured Palestinian detainees. Only a small number of independent human rights organizations existed back then, and these few either whitewashed or maintained a discreet silence on Israel's egregious human rights violations. It was

---

seemed perfectly legitimate to the Arab," or resorting to "the unscrupulous ethics of the Arab . . . the fantastic reasoning that condoned every crime short of murder," or "becom[ing] hysterical at the slightest provocation." As for Palestine itself before the Jews worked wonders, it was "worthless desert in the south end and eroded in the middle and swamp up north"; "a land of festering, stagnated swamps and eroded hills and rock-filled fields and unfertile earth caused by a thousand years of Arab and Turkish neglect. . . . There was little song or laughter or joy in Arab life. . . . In this atmosphere, cunning, treachery, murder, feuds and jealousies became a way of life. The cruel realities that had gone into forming the Arab character puzzled outsiders. Cruelty from brother to brother was common." Truth be told, not much has changed in official Zionist propaganda (Leon Uris, *Exodus* [New York, 1959], pp. 181, 213, 216, 227, 228, 229, 253, 334, 352–53).

5. Walid Khalidi, "Why Did the Palestinians Leave?" *Middle East Forum* (July 1959). Erskine Childers, "The Other Exodus," *Spectator* (12 May 1961).

6. Apart from the scholarship itself, a voluminous secondary literature commenting on it has proliferated. As good a place as any to begin is "The New Historiography: Israel and Its Past," in Benny Morris, *1948 and After: Israel and the Palestinians* (Oxford, 1990), pp. 1–34.

notable—indeed, a scandal of sorts—that Israel's torture of Palestinian detainees first became known to a wider public (if still largely ignored), not on account of a human rights organization like Amnesty International but due to an investigative study published by the London *Sunday Times*.[7] At the end of the 1980s, as I said, things started changing.[8] Israel's brutal repression of the largely nonviolent first intifada, which erupted in late 1987, proved impossible to conceal or ignore, while new human rights organizations, both local Israeli and Palestinian as well as international, started springing up, and older, established ones stiffened resistance to external pressures.

In the course of preparing the chapters of this book devoted to Israel's human rights record in the Occupied Territories, I went through literally thousands of pages of human rights reports, published by multiple, fiercely independent, and highly professional organizations— Amnesty International, Human Rights Watch, B'Tselem (Israeli Information Center for Human Rights in the Occupied Territories), Public Committee Against Torture in Israel, Physicians for Human Rights– Israel—each fielding its own autonomous staff of monitors and investigators. Except on one minor matter, I didn't come across a single point of law or fact on which these human rights organizations differed. In the case of Israel's human rights record, one can speak today not just of a broad consensus—as on historical questions—but of an *unqualified* consensus. All these organizations agreed, for example, that Palestinian

---

7. See Chapter 6 of this book.

8. To be sure, the first big blow inflicted on Israel's radiant image—its first public relations debacle—was the June 1982 Lebanon invasion. The reason Israel's actual practices finally came to light then merits attention. Although the sheer brutality and density of Israel's crimes during the 1982 invasion were undoubtedly contributing factors, the main reason, according to veteran Middle East correspondent Robert Fisk, was apparently that, unlike during previous wars, neither the Arab dictatorships nor the finely tuned public relations machinery of Israel could fully control, or manipulate, the reportage: "For the Lebanese government was too weak and its security authorities too divided to impose censorship upon the Western journalists based in Beirut.... Reporters travelling with Israeli troops were subject to severe restrictions on their movements and sometimes to censorship, but their opposite numbers in Beirut could travel freely and write whatever they wished. For the very first time, reporters had open access to the *Arab* side of a Middle East war and found that Israel's supposedly invincible army, with its moral high ground and clearly stated military objectives against 'terrorists,' did not perform in the way that legend would have suggested. The Israelis acted brutally, they mistreated prisoners, killed thousands of civilians, lied about their activities and then watched their militia allies slaughter the occupants of a refugee camp. In fact, they behaved very much like the 'uncivilised' Arab armies whom they had so consistently denigrated over the preceding 30 years. The reporting from Lebanon ... was a new and disturbing experience for the Israelis. They no longer had a monopoly on the truth." Here is yet another indication of just how disastrous the numbing repression in the Arab world has been for the Arab peoples (Robert Fisk, *Pity the Nation* [New York, 1990], p. 407; emphasis in original).

detainees have been systematically ill treated and tortured, the total number now probably reaching the tens of thousands.

Yet if, as I've suggested, broad agreement has been reached on the factual record, an obvious anomaly arises: what accounts for the impassioned controversy that still swirls around the Israel-Palestine conflict? To my mind, explaining this apparent paradox requires, first of all, that a fundamental distinction be made between those controversies that are real and those that are contrived. To illustrate real differences of opinion, let us consider again the Palestinian refugee question. It is possible for interested parties to agree on the facts yet come to diametrically opposed moral, legal, and political conclusions. Thus, as already mentioned, the scholarly consensus is that Palestinians were ethnically cleansed in 1948. Israel's leading historian on the topic, Benny Morris, although having done more than anyone else to clarify exactly what happened, nonetheless concludes that, morally, it was a good thing—just as, in his view, the "annihilation" of Native Americans was a good thing—that, legally, Palestinians have no right to return to their homes, and that, politically, Israel's big error in 1948 was that it hadn't "carried out a large expulsion and cleansed the whole country—the whole Land of Israel, as far as the Jordan" of Palestinians.[9] However repellent morally, these clearly can't be called *false* conclusions. Returning to the universe inhabited by normal human beings, it's possible for people to concur on the facts as well as on their moral and legal implications yet still reach divergent political conclusions. Noam Chomsky agrees that, factually, Palestinians were expelled; that, morally, this was a major crime; and that, legally, Palestinians have a right of return. Yet, politically, he concludes that implementation of this right is infeasible and pressing it inexpedient, indeed, that dangling this (in his view) illusory hope before Palestinian refugees is deeply immoral. There are those, contrariwise, who maintain that a moral and legal right is meaningless unless it can be exercised and that implementing the right of return is a practical possibility.[10] For our purposes, the point is not who's right and who's wrong but that, even among honest

---

9. Ari Shavit, "Survival of the Fittest," interview with Benny Morris, *Haaretz* (9 January 2004). For perceptive commentary, see Baruch Kimmerling, "Is Ethnic Cleansing of Arabs Getting Legitimacy from a New Israeli Historian?" *Tikkun* (27 January 2004); for Morris's recent pronouncements, see also Finkelstein, *Image and Reality*, pp. xxix–xxx.

10. See, e.g., Salman Abu Sitta, "The Implementation of the Right of Return," in Roane Carey (ed.), *The New Intifada: Resisting Israel's Apartheid* (New York, 2001), pp. 299–319.

and decent people, there can be real and legitimate differences of political judgment.

This having been said, however, it bears emphasis that—at any rate, among those sharing ordinary moral values—the range of political disagreement is quite narrow, while the range of agreement quite broad. For the past quarter century, the international community has held to a consensus on how, basically, to resolve the Israel-Palestine conflict: a two-state settlement based on full Israeli withdrawal from the West Bank and Gaza and full recognition of Israel within its pre–June 1967 borders. Apart from the United States, Israel, and, usually, this or that South Pacific atoll, the United Nations General Assembly, in a rare and consistent display of near unanimity, annually reaffirms this formula. A 1989 General Assembly resolution, *Question of Palestine*, effectively calling for a two-state settlement and "[t]he withdrawal of Israel from the Palestinian territory occupied since 1967" passed 151 to 3, the only dissenting vote apart from those of the United States and Israel being cast by the island state of Dominica. Fifteen years later and notwithstanding sweeping geopolitical changes—an entire social system disappeared in the interim while many new states were born—the consensus continued to hold. A 2004 General Assembly resolution, *Peaceful Settlement of the Question of Palestine*, that stresses "the necessity for a commitment to the vision of the two-State solution" and "the withdrawal of Israel from the Palestinian territory occupied since 1967" passed 160 to 6, the dissenting votes apart from the United States' and Israel's being cast by Micronesia, the Marshall Islands, Palau, and Uganda.[11] Were debate to focus solely on real areas of disagreement, the conflict could probably be resolved expeditiously—if not to the liking of Israeli and American elites.

Most of the controversy surrounding the Israel-Palestine conflict is, in my view, contrived. The purpose of contriving such controversy is transparently political: to deflect attention from, or distort, the actual documentary record. One can speak of, basically, three sources of artificial disagreement: (1) mystification of the conflict's roots, (2) invocation of anti-Semitism and The Holocaust,[12] and (3) on a different plane,

11. U.N.G.A. Resolution 44/42, *Question of Palestine* (6 December 1989); U.N.G.A. Resolution 58/21, *Peaceful Settlement of the Question of Palestine* (22 January 2004). For more on these U.N. votes, see Finkelstein, *Image and Reality*, pp. xvii–xviii.
12. In this text "Nazi holocaust" denotes the actual historical event whereas "The Holocaust" denotes the ideological instrumentalization of that event. See Norman G. Finkelstein, *The Holocaust Industry: Reflections on the Exploitation of Jewish Suffering*, 2nd ed. (New York, 2003), p. 3 and chap. 2.

the vast proliferation of sheer fraud on the subject. In this introduction I will briefly discuss each of these in turn. The bulk of this study focuses on the second and third points.

The Israel-Palestine conflict is often said to pose questions of such unique profundity or complexity as to defy conventional analysis or resolution. It's been variously cast as a cosmic clash of religions, cultures, civilizations. Even normally sober observers like Israeli writer Meron Benvenisti used to contend that its essence was a "primordial, irreconcilable, endemic shepherd's war."[13] In fact, such formulations obfuscate rather than illuminate. No doubt, the conflict raises thorny theoretical and practical problems, but not more so than most other ones. It is also perfectly amenable to comparative analysis, bearing in mind, as always, the limits to any historical analogy. The obvious reason Israel's apologists shun such comparisons and harp on the sui generis character of the Israel-Palestine conflict is that, in any of the roughly comparable cases—the Euro-American conquest of North America, the apartheid regime in South Africa—Israel comes out on the "wrong" side in the analogy.[14]

Serious analysis of the Israel-Palestine conflict rarely makes resort to ponderous explanations, if for no other reason than because its origins are so straightforward. In 1936 a British royal commission chaired by Lord Peel was charged with ascertaining the causes of the Palestine conflict and the means for resolving it. Regarding the aspirations of Palestinian Arabs, its final report stated that "[t]he overriding desire of the Arab leaders . . . was . . . national independence" and that "[i]t was *only to be expected* that Palestinian Arabs should . . . envy and seek to emulate their successful fellow-nationalists in those countries just across their northern and southern borders." The British attributed Arab anti-Jewish animus to the fact that the Jewish claim over Palestine would deny Arabs an independent Arab state, and to Arab fear of being subjugated in an eventual Jewish state. It concluded that there was "*no doubt*" the "underlying causes" of Arab-Jewish hostilities were "first the desire of the Arabs for national independence; secondly their antagonism to the establishment of the Jewish National Home in Palestine,

---

13. Meron Benvenisti, "Two generations growing up in Jerusalem," *New York Times Magazine* (16 October 1988); for similar formulations, see his *Intimate Enemies: Jews and Arabs in a Shared Land* (Berkeley, 1995), pp. 9 ("a primeval contest, a shepherds' war"), 19 ("its endemic intercommunal nature").

14. For comparison with the Euro-American conquest of North America, see Norman G. Finkelstein, *The Rise and Fall of Palestine: A Personal Account of the Intifada Years* (Minneapolis, 1996), pp. 104–21; for comparison with apartheid, see Finkelstein, *Image and Reality*, p. xxvii and chap. 7.

quickened by their fear of Jewish domination." Eschewing airy formulations like Benvenisti's "primordial, irreconcilable, endemic shepherd's
war" and, again, pointing up the manifest sources of the turmoil in
Palestine, the commission wrote:

> Nor is the conflict in its essence an interracial conflict, arising from any
> old instinctive antipathy of Arabs towards Jews. There was little or no fric-
> tion . . . between Arab and Jew in the rest of the Arab world until the strife
> in Palestine engendered it. And there has been precisely the same political
> trouble in Iraq, Syria and Egypt—agitation, rebellion and bloodshed—
> where there are no "National Homes." *Quite obviously*, then, the problem
> of Palestine is political. It is, as elsewhere, the problem of insurgent nation-
> alism. The only difference is that in Palestine Arab nationalism is inextrica-
> bly interwoven with antagonism to the Jews. And the reasons for that, it is
> worth repeating, are *equally obvious*. In the first place, the establishment
> of the National Home [for Jews] involved at the outset a blank negation of
> the rights implied in the principle of national self-government. Secondly, it
> soon proved to be not merely an obstacle to the development of national
> self-government, but apparently the only serious obstacle. Thirdly, as the
> Home has grown, the fear has grown with it that, if and when self-govern-
> ment is conceded, it may not be national in the Arab sense, but government
> by a Jewish majority. That is why it is difficult to be an Arab patriot and
> not to hate the Jews.[15]

The injustice inflicted on Palestinians by Zionism was manifest and,
except on racist grounds, unanswerable: their right to self-determination, and perhaps even to their homeland, was being denied. Several
sorts of justification were supplied for the Zionist enterprise as against
the rights of the indigenous population, none of which, however, with-
stood even cursory scrutiny. Belief in the cluster of justifications put
forth by the Zionist movement presumed acceptance of very specific
Zionist ideological tenets regarding Jewish "historical rights" to Palestine and Jewish "homelessness." For example, the "historical rights"
claim was based on Jews having originated in Palestine and resided
there two thousand years ago. Such a claim was neither historical nor
based on any accepted notion of right. It was not historical inasmuch as
it voided the two millennia of non-Jewish settlement in Palestine and
the two millennia of Jewish settlement outside it. It was not a right
except in mystical, Romantic nationalist ideologies, implementation
of which would wreak—and have wreaked—havoc. Reminding fellow

---

15. *Palestine Royal Commission Report* (London, 1937), pp. 76, 94, 110, 131, 136,
363; emphases added.

Zionists that Jewry's "historical right" to Palestine was a "metaphysical rather than a political category" and that, springing as it did from "the very inner depths of Judaism," this "category . . . is binding on us rather than on the Arabs," even the Zionist writer Ernst Simon was emphatic that it did not confer on Jews any right to Palestine without the consent of the Arabs.[16]

Another sort of justification conjured away the injustice inflicted on the indigenous population with the pretense that Palestine was (nearly) vacant before the Jews came.[17] Ironically, this argument has proven to be the most compelling proof of the injustice committed: it is a backhanded admission that, had Palestine been inhabited, which it plainly was, the Zionist enterprise was morally indefensible. Those admitting to the reality of a Palestinian presence yet functioning outside the ideological ambit of Zionism couldn't adduce any justification for Zionism except a racist one: that is, in the great scheme of things, the fate of Jews was simply more important than that of Arabs. If not publicly, at any rate privately, this is how the British rationalized the Balfour Declaration. For Balfour himself, "we deliberately and rightly decline to accept the principle of self-determination" for the "present inhabitants" of Palestine, because "the question of the Jews outside Palestine [is] one of world importance" and Zionism was "rooted in age-long traditions, in present needs, in future hopes, of far profounder import than the desires and prejudices of the 700,000 Arabs who now inhabit that ancient land." For Cabinet Minister (and the first British high commissioner of Palestine during the Mandate period) Herbert Samuel, although denying the indigenous population majority rule was "in flat contradiction to one of the main purposes for which the Allies were fighting," it was nonetheless permissible because the anterior Jewish presence in Palestine "had resulted in events of spiritual and cultural value to mankind in striking contrast with the barren record of the last thousand years." And for Winston Churchill, testifying before the Peel Commission, the indigenous population had no more right to Palestine than a "dog in a manger has the final right to the manger, even though he may have lain there for a very long time," and no "wrong has been done to these people by the fact that a stronger race, a higher grade race, or at any rate, a more worldly-wise race, to put it that way, has

16. Yosef Gorny, *Zionism and the Arabs, 1882–1948: A Study of Ideology* (Oxford, 1987), p. 197. For analysis of these Zionist rationales, see Finkelstein, *Image and Reality*, pp. 101–2.

17. For background and discussion, see Finkelstein, *Image and Reality*, pp. 89–98.

come in and taken their place."[18] The point is not so much that the British were racists but rather that they had no recourse except to racist justifications for denying the indigenous population its basic rights. Pressed to justify what was done, they became racists not from predilection but from circumstance: on no other grounds could so flagrant a denial be explained.

If only because of its eminent provenance and frequent quotation, one last argument merits consideration. The Marxist historian Isaac Deutscher put forth, in the form of a parable, less a justification than a largely sympathetic ex post facto explanation for Zionism's trampling of Palestinian rights:

> A man once jumped from the top floor of a burning house in which many members of his family had already perished. He managed to save his life; but as he was falling he hit a person standing down below and broke that person's legs and arms. The jumping man had no choice; yet to the man with the broken limbs he was the cause of his misfortune. If both behaved rationally, they would not become enemies. The man who escaped from the blazing house, having recovered, would have tried to help and console the other sufferer; and the latter might have realized that he was the victim of circumstances over which neither of them had control. But look what happens when these people behave irrationally. The injured man blames the other for his misery and swears to make him pay for it. The other, afraid of the crippled man's revenge, insults him, kicks him, and beats him up whenever they meet. The kicked man again swears revenge and is again punched and punished. The bitter enmity, so fortuitous at first, hardens and comes to overshadow the whole existence of both men and to poison their minds.[19]

This account gives Zionism both too little and too much credit. The Zionist denial of Palestinians' rights, culminating in their expulsion, hardly sprang from an unavoidable accident. It resulted from the systematic and conscientious implementation, over many decades and despite vehement, often violent, popular opposition, of a political ideology the goal of which was to create a demographically Jewish state in

18. Isaiah Friedman, *The Question of Palestine: British-Jewish-Arab Relations, 1914–1918* (London, 1992), pp. 13–14 (Samuel), 325–26 (Balfour); cf. 331. Clive Ponting, *Churchill* (London, 1994), p. 254. Most versions of the non-Zionist justification synthesized the "empty land" thesis with the racist one: namely, Palestine had remained sparsely populated and barren in Arab hands, while Jews, as the bearers of civilization and progress, would—or, after the fact, had—put the land to productive use, thereby earning title to it.

19. Isaac Deutscher, *The Non-Jewish Jew and Other Essays* (New York, 1968), pp. 136–37; for similar formulations, see pp. 116, 122.

Palestine. To suggest that Zionists had no choice—or, as Deutscher puts it elsewhere, that the Jewish state was a "historic necessity"[20]—is to deny the Zionist movement's massive and, in many respects, impressive exertion of will, and the moral responsibility attending the exertion of this will, in one rather than another direction. The expulsion of Palestinians did not come about on account of some ineluctable, impersonal objective force compelling Palestinians to leave and Jews to replace them. Were this the case, why did the Zionists conscript, often heavy-handedly, the Jewish refugees after World War II to come to Palestine and oppose their resettlement elsewhere? Why did they stimulate, perhaps even with violent methods, the exodus of Jews from the Arab world to Palestine? Why did they call, often in deep frustration and disappointment, for the in-gathering of world Jewry after Israel's establishment? If Zionist leaders didn't make the obvious amends after the war of allowing Palestinians to return to their homes and sought instead to fill the emptied spaces with Jews, it's not because they behaved irrationally, but rather, given their political aim, with complete rationality.

Deutscher, of course, knows all this. Indeed, he acknowledges that "[f]rom the outset Zionism worked towards the creation of a purely Jewish state and was glad to rid the country of its Arab inhabitants."[21] To claim that Zionist leaders acted irrationally in refusing to "remove or assuage the grievance" of Palestinians,[22] then, is effectively to say that Zionism is irrational: for, given that the Palestinians' chief grievance was the denial of their homeland, were Zionists to act "rationally" and remove it, the raison d'être of Zionism and its fundamental historic achievement in 1948 would have been nullified. And if seeking to "rid the country of its Arab inhabitants" was irrational, how can the "positive" flipside of this goal, a Jewish state, have been a "historic necessity"? It's equally fatuous to assert that Palestinians act irrationally when they "blame" the Zionists "for their misery" and not accept that they were "the victim of circumstances over which neither of them had control." It's only irrational if Zionists bore no responsibility for what happened. Yet Deutscher is nearly breathless in his praise for the achievements of the Zionists in Palestine: "The emergence of Israel is indeed . . . a phenomenon unique in its kind, a marvel and a prodigy of

20. Ibid., p. 112.
21. Ibid., p. 137.
22. Ibid., pp. 137–38.

history, before which Jew and non-Jew alike stand in awe and amazement."[23] Isn't it pure apologetics to sing paeans to the summoning of material and moral energy that made possible such undoubtedly real accomplishments, yet deny, in the name of "historic necessity" and "fortuitous" "circumstances," that any real responsibility is incurred for the dark underside of them?[24] The selfsame concentrated will, meticulous attention to detail, and lucid premeditation that created Israel also created its victims.

Although in violation of the indigenous population's elementary right and in contradiction of avowed international principle, a second socioeconomic entity (in addition to the native Palestinian Arabs) came into existence in Palestine and, inevitably, demanded *its* right to self-determination. Unlike the prior Zionist claim to Palestine, based on an imaginary "historical right," this one seemed to be grounded in generally accepted criteria of right: the Jewish settlements now comprised a vital, organic, distinct community. The creation of this community, however, had been contingent on the resort to force: without the "steel helmet and the gun's muzzle" (Moshe Dayan) of the Zionist settlers, crucially supplemented by the "foreign bayonets" (David Ben-Gurion) of the British Empire in the form of the Mandate, a proto-Jewish state could never have come into being.[25] The question of at what point a claim acquired by might becomes one anchored in right is complicated, indeed probably insoluble on an abstract level. The intuitive argument that a moral-legal threshold has been crossed when a new generation, born on the land, stakes its claim on the basis of birthright poses as many questions as it resolves. Doesn't this give incentive to hold out as long as possible in defiance of international law and public opinion? This, of course, was the essence of the Zionist approach: if sufficient facts were created on the ground and sufficient time elapsed, hard reality could not be reversed.

23. Ibid., p. 118.
24. In fact, Deutscher's reflections on Zionism, although remarkable in their acuteness—not a single page passes without another novel insight or uncannily accurate prediction—are nonetheless marred, at any rate before his scathing denunciation of Israel after the June 1967 war, by typical Zionist and racist apologetics: the kibbutzim were "Jewish oases scattered over the former Arabian desert" (p. 99); prior to Zionist settlement "no established society existed in the Palestine desert" (p. 100); the Zionist claim that "Palestine is and never ceased to be Jewish" is on a par with the Arab claim that "Jews are . . . invaders and intruders" (p. 116); and so on.
25. Benny Morris, *Israel's Border Wars, 1949–1956* (Oxford, 1993), p. 380 (Dayan). See Finkelstein, *Image and Reality*, pp. 98–110, for discussion (Ben-Gurion at p. 106).

This brings to the fore a related consideration. The United Nations crowned the Zionist movement with legal title to more than half of Palestine some thirty years after Zionist settlers began in earnest, in the wake of the Balfour Declaration and despite overwhelming indigenous opposition, to create, "dunum by dunum, goat by goat," facts in Palestine. Yet more than thirty-five years have elapsed since Jewish settlers began creating facts in the West Bank and Gaza. Haven't these by now acquired legitimacy as well? In any event, when the Peel Commission first proposed in 1937 partitioning Palestine on the ground that a distinct Jewish entity had crystallized, Palestinian Arabs rejected the legitimacy of a Jewish claim founded on force over and against the rights of the indigenous population, as they did in 1947 when the United Nations General Assembly ratified the partition resolution. (Although officially opposing the Peel recommendation and officially accepting the U.N. recommendation, in fact the Zionist movement was rather more ambivalent in both instances.)[26] It's not hard to see the argument on their side,[27] although in hindsight it's also not hard to see the imprudence of rejecting partition.

Complex as this conflict over rights emerging out of forcible Zionist settlement is at the abstract level, it found practical resolution after resurfacing in modified form following the June 1967 war. Confronted by the inescapable reality of Israel's existence and lacking viable political options, Palestinians cut the theoretical Gordian knot in the mid-1970s by effectively conceding legal title to some 80 percent of their historic homeland. Apart from the refugee question, the only truly complicated element of the Israel-Palestine conflict was thus overcome. Yet this resolution remains provisional and fragile. If Israel has created new facts on the ground in the Occupied Territories that preempt a two-state settlement, a new complication of the conflict will have arisen. But it won't be on account of a "primordial, irreconcilable, endemic shepherd's war" or "historic necessity" or "fortuitous" "circumstances." Just as the prior conflict originated in conscious, willful Zionist denial of basic Palestinian rights, so the intractability of a new conflict will originate in this same premeditated injustice, indeed, in denial of even a severely attenuated form of Palestinian rights.

26. See Appendix III to this book.
27. For a forceful restatement of the reasons behind the Palestinian rejection of the partition resolution, see Walid Khalidi, "Revisiting the UNGA Partition Resolution," *Journal of Palestine Studies* (autumn 1997), pp. 5–21.

Benny Morris, although approving the ethnic cleansing of Palestine and nearly pathological in his hatred of Palestinians,[28] nonetheless anchors Palestinian opposition to Jewish settlement in a perfectly rational, uncomplicated motive: "The fear of territorial displacement and dispossession was to be the chief motor of Arab antagonism to Zionism."[29] What's remarkable about this formulation isn't so much what's said but, rather, what's not said: there's no invoking of "Arab anti-Semitism," no invoking of "Arab fears of modernity," no invoking of cosmic "clashes." There's no mention of them because, for understanding what happened, there's no need of them—the obvious explanation also happens to be a sufficient one. Indeed, in any comparable instance, the sorts of mystifying clichés commonplace in the Israel-Palestine conflict would be treated, rightly, with derision. In the course of resisting European encroachment, Native Americans committed many horrendous crimes. But to understand why doesn't require probing the defects of their character or civilization. Criticizing the practice, in government documents, of reciting Native American "atrocities," Helen Hunt Jackson, a principled defender of Native Americans writing in the late nineteenth century, observed: "[T]he Indians who committed these 'atrocities' were simply ejecting by force, and, in the contests arising from this forcible ejectment, killing men who had usurped and stolen their lands. . . . What would a community of white men, situated precisely as these Cherokees were, have done?"[30]

To apprehend the motive behind Palestinian "atrocities," this ordinary human capacity for empathy would also seem to suffice. Imagine the bemused reaction were a historian to hypothesize that the impetus behind Native American resistance was "anti-Christianism" or "anti-Europeanism." What's the point of such exotic explanations—unless the obvious one is politically incorrect? Of course, back then, profound explanations of this sort weren't necessary. The natives impeded the wheel of progress, so they had to be extirpated; nothing more had to be said. For the sake of "mankind" and "civilization," Theodore Roo-

---

28. He's called the Palestinian people "sick, psychotic," "serial killers" whom Israel must "imprison" or "execute," and "barbarians" around whom "[s]omething like a cage has to be built." See the *Haaretz* interview and the pages on Morris's recent pronouncements in *Image and Reality* cited above.

29. Benny Morris, *Righteous Victims: A History of the Zionist-Arab Conflict, 1881–1999* (New York, 1999), p. 37.

30. Helen Hunt Jackson, *A Century of Dishonor* (New York, 1981), p. 265.

sevelt wrote, it was "all-important" that North America be won by a "masterful people." Although for the indigenous population this meant "the infliction and suffering of hideous woe and misery," it couldn't have been otherwise: "The world would probably not have gone forward at all, had it not been for the displacement or submersion of savage and barbaric peoples." And again: "The settler and pioneer have at bottom justice on their side: this great continent could not have been kept as nothing but a game preserve for squalid savages."[31]

It was only much later, after the humanity of these "squalid savages" was ratified—in any event, formally—that more sophisticated rationales became necessary. In the case of the United States, the "hideous woe and misery" inflicted could be openly acknowledged because the fate of the indigenous population was, figuratively as well as literally, in large part a dead issue. In the case of Palestine it's not, so all manner of elaborate explanation has to be contrived in order to evade the obvious. The reason Benny Morris's latest pronouncements elicited such a shocked reaction is that they were a throwback to the nineteenth century. Dispensing with the ideological cloud making of contemporary apologists for Israel, he justified dispossession on grounds of the conflict between "barbarians" and "civilization." Just as, in his view, it was better for humanity that the "great American democracy" displaced the Native Americans, so it is better that the Jewish state has displaced the Palestinians. "There are cases," he baldly states, "in which the overall, final good justifies harsh and cruel acts that are committed in the course of history." Isn't this Roosevelt speaking? But one's not supposed to utter such crass things anymore.[32] To avoid outraging current moral sensibilities, the obvious must be papered over with sundry mystifications. The elementary truth that, just as in the past, the "chief motor of Arab antagonism" is "[t]he fear of territorial displacement and dispossession"—a fear the rational basis for which is scarcely open to question, indeed, is daily validated by Israeli actions—must, at all costs, be concealed.

To evade the obvious, another stratagem of the Israel lobby is playing The Holocaust and "new anti-Semitism" cards. In a previous study,

---

31. For these and similar formulations, see Theodore Roosevelt, *The Winning of the West* (New York, 1889), 1:118–19, 121; 4:7, 54–56, 65, 200, 201.

32. In fact, one isn't even allowed to remember that Roosevelt said them: one searches recent Roosevelt biographies in vain for any mention of the pronouncements of his just cited, or scores of others like them pervading his published writings and correspondence.

I examined how the Nazi holocaust has been fashioned into an ideological weapon to immunize Israel from legitimate criticism.[33] In this book I look at a variant of this Holocaust card, namely, the "new anti-Semitism." In fact, the allegation of a new anti-Semitism is neither new nor about anti-Semitism. Whenever Israel comes under renewed international pressure to withdraw from occupied territories, its apologists mount yet another meticulously orchestrated media extravaganza alleging that the world is awash in anti-Semitism. This shameless exploitation of anti-Semitism delegitimizes criticism of Israel, makes Jews rather than Palestinians the victims, and puts the onus on the Arab world to rid itself of anti-Semitism rather than on Israel to rid itself of the Occupied Territories. A close analysis of what the Israel lobby tallies as anti-Semitism reveals three components: exaggeration and fabrication; mislabeling legitimate criticism of Israeli policy; and the unjustified yet predictable "spillover" from criticism of Israel to Jews generally. I conclude that if, as all studies agree, current resentment against Jews has coincided with Israel's brutal repression of the Palestinians, then the prudent, not to mention moral, thing to do is end the occupation. A full Israeli withdrawal would also deprive those real anti-Semites exploiting Israeli policy as a pretext to demonize Jews— and who can doubt they exist?—of a dangerous weapon as well as expose their real agenda. And the more vocally Jews dissent from Israel's occupation, the fewer will be those non-Jews who mistake Israel's criminal policies and the uncritical support (indeed encouragement) of mainline Jewish organizations for the popular Jewish mood.

I began this introduction recalling the *From Time Immemorial* hoax, since a main reason so much controversy swirls around the Israel-Palestine conflict is the vast proliferation of sheer fraud masquerading as serious scholarship. Although imperfect, a mechanism for quality control nonetheless exists in intellectual life. In practice it usually takes the form of a sequence of skeptical questions. If someone quotes a book putting forth an altogether aberrant thesis, he or she is usually asked, "Where does the author teach?" or "Who published the book?" or "Who blurbed the book?" or "What sorts of reviews did it receive [in the main professional journals]?" The answers to these questions generally provide a more or less accurate gauge of how much credence to put in the publication. It is one of the egregious features of the Israel-Palestine conflict, however, that these mechanisms of quality control

33. Finkelstein, *Holocaust Industry*.

function barely, if at all.[34] The book's author can teach at a first-rank university, and the book itself can be published under a prestigious imprint, receive lavish blurbs as well as reviews in prominent mainstream publications, and yet still be complete nonsense. The most recent addition to this genre and the subject of the second part of this book is the best seller *The Case for Israel* by Harvard law professor Alan Dershowitz.[35] It can fairly be said that *The Case for Israel* surpasses *From Time Immemorial* in deceitfulness and is among the most spectacular academic frauds ever published on the Israel-Palestine conflict. Indeed, Dershowitz appropriates large swaths from the Peters hoax. Whereas Peters falsified real sources, Dershowitz goes one better and cites absurd sources or stitches evidence out of whole cloth. The core chapters of the present book juxtapose the findings of all mainstream human rights organizations about Israel's human rights record in the Occupied Territories against Dershowitz's claims. I demonstrate that it's difficult to find a single claim in his human rights chapters or, for that matter, any other chapter of *The Case for Israel* that, among other things, doesn't distort a reputable source or reference a preposterous one. The point, of course, is not that Dershowitz is a charlatan. Rather, it's the *systematic institutional bias* that allows for books like *The Case for Israel* to become national best sellers. Were it not for Dershowitz's Harvard pedigree, the praise heaped on his book by Mario Cuomo, Henry Louis Gates Jr., Elie Wiesel, and Floyd Abrams,[36] the favorable notices in media outlets like the *New York Times* and *Boston Globe*,[37] and so on, *The Case for Israel* would have had the same shelf life as the latest publication of the Flat-Earth Society.

34. Revealingly, this caveat applies to the field of "Holocaust studies" as well. For pertinent criticism by Raul Hilberg, dean of Nazi holocaust scholars, see Finkelstein, *Holocaust Industry*, p. 60.

35. All references in this book are to the first hardback printing of *The Case for Israel*, published in August 2003 by John Wiley and Sons, Inc. Almost immediately after publication of *The Case for Israel* I publicly charged, and provided copious evidence, that it was a fraud (see www.NormanFinkelstein.com under "The Dershowitz Hoax"). In the first paperback edition of his book, published in August 2004, Dershowitz entered some revisions.

36. See their laudatory comments for the book posted on www.Amazon.com.

37. In the *New York Times Sunday Book Review*, Ethan Bronner praised Dershowitz for his "intelligent polemic" and ability "to construct an argument" and for being "especially effective at pointing to the hypocrisy of many of Israel's critics" ("The New New Historians," 9 November 2003). Bronner sits on the *Times*'s editorial board, where he's its "expert" on the Israel-Palestine conflict. In the *Boston Globe*, Jonathan Dorfman waxed rhapsodic about how Dershowitz "goes after Israel's enemies . . . with the punch and thrust of courtroom debate" and praised the author for having "restated some obvi-

The purpose of *Beyond Chutzpah* is to lift the veil of contrived controversy shrouding the Israel-Palestine conflict. I am convinced that anyone confronting the undistorted record will recognize the injustice Palestinians have suffered. I hope this book will also provide impetus for readers to act on the basis of truth so that, together, we can achieve a just and lasting peace in Israel and Palestine.

---

ous truths about Israel—truths its friends need to convey, its enemies need to confront, and the chattering classes need to learn before they venture forth with pronouncements about Israel that are simple, easy—and wrong" ("Dershowitz makes the 'Case,'" 26 November 2003). Both these reviews appeared *well after* evidence had been widely disseminated demonstrating that Dershowitz's book was rubbish.

PART I

THE NOT-SO-NEW "NEW ANTI-SEMITISM"

> We currently face as great a threat to the safety
> and security of the Jewish people as the one
> we faced in the 1930s—if not a greater one.
>
> Abraham Foxman, National Director,
> Anti-Defamation League

1

From *Jesus Christ Superstar* to *The Passion of the Christ*

THE LATEST PRODUCTION of Israel's apologists is the "new anti-Semitism." Just as Palestinians renewed their resistance to occupation and Israel escalated its brutal repression of the revolt, there was a vast proliferation of books, articles, conferences, and the like alleging that—in the words of Anti-Defamation League (ADL) national director Abraham Foxman—"we currently face as great a threat to the safety and security of the Jewish people as the one we faced in the 1930s—if not a greater one."[1] As it happens, the allegation of a new anti-Semitism is neither new nor about anti-Semitism. Thirty years ago, ADL national leaders Arnold Forster and Benjamin R. Epstein published to great fanfare a study entitled *The New Anti-Semitism*, and less than a decade later ADL national leader Nathan Perlmutter (with his wife, Ruth Ann Perlmutter) put out *The Real Anti-Semitism in America*, alleging yet again that the United States was awash in a new anti-Semitism.[2] The main

---

1. Abraham H. Foxman, *Never Again? The Threat of the New Anti-Semitism* (San Francisco, 2003), p. 4.

2. Arnold Forster and Benjamin R. Epstein, *The New Anti-Semitism* (New York, 1974); Nathan Perlmutter and Ruth Ann Perlmutter, *The Real Anti-Semitism in America* (New York, 1982). For background and discussion, see Norman G. Finkelstein, *The Holocaust Industry: Reflections on the Exploitation of Jewish Suffering*, 2nd ed. (New York, 2003), pp. 32–38.

purpose behind these periodic, meticulously orchestrated media extrav-
aganzas is not to fight anti-Semitism but rather to exploit the historical
suffering of Jews in order to immunize Israel against criticism. Each campaign to combat the "new anti-Semitism" has coincided with renewed
international pressures on Israel to withdraw from occupied Arab territories in exchange for recognition from neighboring Arab states.

Forster and Epstein's *The New Anti-Semitism* came to serve as a tem-
plate for subsequent productions. A few chapters of this book are given
over to the anti-Semitic ravings of mostly marginal, right-wing extremists in the United States, while a larger space is devoted to deploring
anti-Semitism in the African American community. To highlight the
pervasiveness of this new anti-Semitism, mainstream institutions are
also subject to random, more or less preposterous accusations—newspapers like the *Washington Post* and *New York Times* for being soft on
anti-Semites, and the film industry for producing animated features like
"X-rated *Fritz the Cat*... which had a tasteless synagogue sequence,
and *The Crunch Bird*, which used Jewish dialect and ethnic caricature
for a vulgar joke and which won an Academy Award in 1972."[3]

The periodic brouhahas over the new anti-Semitism show continu-
ities even in fine details. A main item in Forster and Epstein's bill of
indictment was Norman Jewison's just-released cinematic version of
Jesus Christ Superstar. "From an anti-Semitic stage production he created an even more anti-Semitic film," they charged. The "anti-Semitic"
stage production was cowritten by Andrew Lloyd Webber, who went
on to create such scandalously anti-Semitic Broadway musicals as
Cats (a coded allusion to Katz?), while Jewison had just produced and
directed the screen adaptation of *Fiddler on the Roof*. Webber and Jewison are castigated for perpetuating the lie that "the Jews, collectively,
killed Christ" and ignoring "the new, ecumenical interpretation of the
Crucifixion," instead following "'the old, primitive formulation of the
Passion play, the spirit of which was discarded by Vatican II.'" The
biased rendering of the biblical protagonists is said to be irrefutable
proof of the film's anti-Semitic thrust: "*Superstar* represented, after all,
a very free adaptation of the New Testament story.... The malevolent
image of the street mobs of Jerusalem and of the priests was preserved
intact and once again they were assigned major blame for the Crucifixion. At the same time, the authors of *Superstar* chose to whitewash the

---

3. Forster and Epstein, *New Anti-Semitism*, pp. 56 (*Post*), 113 (*Fritz the Cat*), 300
(*Times*).

character of Pontius Pilate, exonerating Pilate of blame in the condemnation and trial of Jesus and thereby heightening the responsibility
assigned to the Jewish priesthood." Fast forward to 2004. The assault
on Mel Gibson's *Passion of the Christ* struck identical notes, Frank
Rich of the *New York Times*, for example, charging: "There is no question that it rewrites history by making Caiaphas and the other high
priests the prime instigators of Jesus' death while softening Pontius
Pilate, an infamous Roman thug, into a reluctant and somewhat con-
science-stricken executioner."[4]

Abraham Foxman was said to have been appalled at the potential
anti-Semitic fallout of Gibson's film. But the primary target audience of
Passion was exactly those Christian fundamentalists with whom ADL
has been aligned for years. For instance, Ralph Reed of the Christian
Coalition frequently addressed ADL meetings. Why the selective indig-
nation against Gibson? Apart from the obvious fact that, as "faithful
supporters" of Israel, the Christian Coalition gets a partial pass,[5] could
it be that ADL's national director almost literally stole a page from
an old book, seizing on *Passion* to whip up hysteria about the new anti-
Semitism? Foxman, who fired the first salvos against Gibson's *Passion* and thereafter dominated this theater of war, is prominently listed
on the acknowledgments page of Forster-Epstein's *The New Anti-
Semitism*. The crisis of *Passion* was a win-win situation: if Gibson
caved in, it would broadcast the message not to mess with Jews; and if
he didn't, it would prove the omnipresence of anti-Semitism. Already
before the film's release, Foxman was capitalizing on it for his accusations of anti-Semitism. The 2003 ADL "Audit of Anti-Semitic Incidents" highlights: "In early 2003 Mel Gibson announced the making of
his forthcoming film, 'The Passion of the Christ.' What followed was a
nearly year-long controversy that elicited hateful anti-Semitic e-mails
and letters to ADL and other Jewish organizations, as well as journalists, religious leaders and those who commented critically on the film"
and "'the hate mail was an indication of the anti-Semitic feelings
that were stirred as a result of the Jewish concerns about the film.'"[6]

---

4. Forster and Epstein, *New Anti-Semitism*, pp. 91 ("created," "killed"), 93–94
("represented"), 97 ("ecumenical" and, quoting *New York Times*, "primitive"). Frank
Rich, "Mel Gibson Forgives Us for His Sins," *New York Times* (7 March 2004).
    5. Foxman, *Never Again?* pp. 147–51 (Christian fundamentalists and "supporters"
at 149).
    6. "ADL Audit Finds Anti-Semitic Incidents Remain Constant; More Than 1,500
Incidents Reported across U.S. in 2003" (ADL press release, 24 March 2004; internal
quote is from ADL head Abraham Foxman).

Plainly, Foxman's confidence wasn't misplaced that journalists, ever on the lookout to expose yet new manifestations of anti-Semitism, would take the bait; and pundits and columnists, ever on the lookout for causes to champion but only if against a phantom enemy, would fearlessly lead the charge. Each of them—the *New Republic*'s Leon Wieseltier, the *New York Times*'s Frank Rich, *Vanity Fair*'s Christopher Hitchens, the *Washington Post*'s Charles Krauthammer—elbowed the next, vying for the title of chief slayer of the Gibson dragon. Even if one believes the worst accusations leveled against *Passion* by ADL—that it's every bit as anti-Semitic as *Superstar*—how much courage did it take to denounce Gibson in these publications, and for their audiences? Reversing cause and effect and feigning wounded innocence, Rich piously accused Gibson, not ADL and its media adjuncts, of firing the "opening volley" and "looking for a brawl." It was testament to the sheer idiocy of this "controversy" that the heart of it was Gibson's biblical scholarship. Before *Passion*, who ever thought that Gibson had even the clue of an idea in his head? The punditry was on a par with periodic learned disputations on the deeper meaning of Michael Jackson's latest lyrics.[7]

The principal—indeed, the *real*—target of Forster and Epstein's *New Anti-Semitism* was criticism directed at Israel after the October 1973 war, when new pressures were exerted on Israel to withdraw from the Egyptian Sinai and to reach a diplomatic settlement with the Palestinians. This "hostility" against Israel, it was alleged, "is the heart of the new anti-Semitism." It was said to both spring from anti-Semitism and constitute its "ultimate" form: "The only answer that seems to fit is that Jews are tolerable, acceptable in their particularity, *only* as victims, and when their situation changes so that they are either no longer victims or appear not to be, the non-Jewish world finds this so hard to take that the effort is begun to render them victims anew" (their emphasis).[8] The possibility that criticism of Israel might have sprung from Israel's intransigence—its refusal to withdraw despite Arab offers of peace—was too absurd even to consider. Apart from the usual bogies like the United Nations, the Soviet Union, and the Arab world,[9] the

---

7. Frank Rich, "The Greatest Story Ever Sold," *New York Times* (21 September 2003).

8. Forster and Epstein, *New Anti-Semitism*, pp. 16 ("only answer"), 17, 152 and 219 ("ultimate"), 323–24 ("hostility," "heart").

9. Forster and Epstein's *New Anti-Semitism*, like its clones, includes expansive chapters on anti-Semitism in the Communist and Arab worlds. It bears mentioning, especially

alleged proof of a resurgent anti-Semitism was that even Israel's traditional allies in Western Europe and the United States were given to Jew-
hating outbursts. For example, in the United Kingdom fewer people
agreed that "Israel should hold all or most of the territory it occupied in
June 1967," and a British *Guardian* article reported that Israel was
using "ignoble subterfuges" to confiscate Palestinian land. In Germany
a *Stern* magazine article alleged that "terror and force were used by
the Jews in the compulsory founding of their state in 1948." In Latin
America the danger of a new anti-Semitism was particularly "worri-
some" in Argentina, where a "left-wing spokesm[a]n" called for "a just
peace [in the Middle East] based on the evacuation of all the occupied
territories," and his supporters were "proclaiming 'the right of the
Palestinians to self-determination.'" [10]

In the United States the threat of a new anti-Semitism emanated,
according to Forster and Epstein, from the "Radical Left," such as the
Trotskyist Socialist Workers Party, the Stalinist American Communist
Party, and the Maoist Progressive Labor Party—even if their combined
constituency could have comfortably fit into a telephone booth. In
addition, it was alleged that sectors of the religious and peace community had succumbed to the anti-Semitic temptation. For example, "the
line had been crossed" when a liberal Protestant clergyman sermonized
that "now oppressed become oppressors: Arabs are deported; Arabs
are imprisoned without charge"; and when the National Council of
Churches called for "the recognition of the right of Palestinian Arabs to
a 'home acceptable to them which must now be a matter of negotia-
tion.'" A publication of the American Friends Service Committee (Quakers) had also crossed the line when asserting "that Egypt and Israel
were equally guilty for the outbreak of the June 1967 war" (which, if
anything, demonstrates a bias *in favor of* Israel); that Israel should "as
a first step commit itself to withdraw from all the occupied territory—
a strictly Arab reading of the U.N. Security Council's resolution of

---

since ADL and kindred studies on anti-Semitism never do, that both the Soviet bloc and
Arab states officially supported the international consensus for resolving the Israel-Arab
conflict. This first, Forster-Epstein production of the new anti-Semitism coincided with
the campaign to "free Soviet Jewry." For the American Jewish establishment, the campaign served the double purpose of vilifying the Soviet Union, thereby currying favor with
U.S. ruling elites, and freeing up Jewish immigrants for Israel, thereby staving off the
Arab "demographic bomb."

    10. Ibid., pp. 255 ("hold"), 260 (Germany), 264 (United Kingdom), 273 ("worri-
some"), 275 ("left-wing spokesm[a]n").

November 22, 1967" (in fact, this reading of Resolution 242 was the consensus of the international community, including the United States); and that American Jews should—horror of anti-Semitic horrors— "reject simplistic military solutions, and . . . encourage calm and deliberate examination of all the issues."[11] The occasional public mention of an American Jewish lobby mobilizing support for Israel or, even more rare, of U.S. hypocrisy in the Israel-Arab conflict was likewise adduced by Forster and Epstein as prima facie evidence of anti-Semitism; for example, a *Washington Post* story claimed that "the influence of American Jews on American politics is quite disproportionate to their numbers in the electorate" and that "[t]hey lobby on Capitol Hill and often they have had direct access to the White House," and a CBS News commentary "accused the United States of a 'double standard' in regard to Middle East terror."[12] In the face of this overwhelming accumulation of evidence, who, except a diehard Jew-hater, could doubt the lethal danger of a new anti-Semitism?

By the time Nathan and Ruth Ann Perlmutter published *The Real Anti-Semitism* (1982), American Jewish elites had gravitated yet further to the right end of the political spectrum. Accordingly, as compared to *The New Anti-Semitism*, the space in *The Real Anti-Semitism* given over to anti-Semitism on the right contracted, while that devoted to anti-Semitism on the left—a label that designated not *the* left but anyone to *their* left—expanded. For Forster and Epstein, the radical left "today represents a danger to world Jewry at least equal to the danger on the right." But for the Perlmutters, the danger emanating from the left loomed much larger, and, it bears repeating, not just the radical but even the moderate left, reaching well into the mainstream. "[W]e have not discussed the Right, not because it is not of concern to Jews," they explained at one point, "but rather because that danger is so well known by Jews."[13] Yet the likelier reason for this relative silence on the right was that American Jewish elites had now aligned themselves with—indeed, more and more *belonged to*—the right, apart from its

11. Ibid., pp. 80–81 (liberal Protestant clergyman), 86–88 (American Friends), 125 (Radical Left), 323 (National Council of Churches). For Israel's refusal to withdraw from the Sinai after Egyptian President Sadat offered Israel full peace in February 1971, see Norman G. Finkelstein, *Image and Reality of the Israel-Palestine Conflict*, 2nd ed. (New York, 2003), chap. 6; for Israel's responsibility for the outbreak of the June 1967 war, and the meaning of U.N. Resolution 242 of November 1967, see chap. 5 and the appendix of *Image and Reality*.

12. Forster and Epstein, *New Anti-Semitism*, pp. 117–24 (*Post* at 122, CBS at 123).

13. Ibid., p. 7 (cf. p. 12); Perlmutters, *Real Anti-Semitism*, p. 139.

lunatic fringe. Domestically, as institutionalized anti-Semitism all but vanished and American Jews prospered, the bonds linking Jews to their erstwhile "natural" allies on the left and among other discriminated-against minorities eroded. American Jewish elites increasingly acted to preserve and protect their class, and even "white," privilege. Internationally, as Israel's political intransigence and brutal occupation alienated public opinion and its alignment with the right in the United States (as elsewhere) deepened, American Jewish elites found themselves increasingly at odds with the political center and in league with the right. The Perlmutters charted these developments with remarkable, if morally repugnant, candor.

Classical anti-Semitism of the type that targeted Jews simply for being Jewish, according to the Perlmutters, no longer posed a potent danger in the United States: "The Klansmen and the neo-Nazis are today no more than socially scrawny imitations of their once politically meaningful forebears, while uptown, the very fact of whispered anti-Semitism is testimony to its low estate." A new type of anti-Semitism, however, had replaced it. This "real" anti-Semitism was defined by the Perlmutters as any challenge inimical to Jewish *interests*. If not subjectively driven by animus toward Jews, it was nonetheless objectively harmful to them: "Essentially, this book's thesis is that today the interests of Jews are not so much threatened by their familiar nemesis, crude anti-Semitism, as by a-Semitic governmental policies, the proponents of which may be free of anti-Semitism and indeed may well—literally—count Jews among some of their best friends." Practically, this meant pinning the epithet "anti-Semitic" on domestic challenges to Jewish class privilege and political power as well as on global challenges to Israeli hegemony. American Jewish elites were, in effect and in plain sight, cynically appropriating "anti-Semitism"—a historical phenomenon replete with suffering and martyrdom, on the one hand, and hatred and genocide, on the other—as an ideological weapon to defend and facilitate ethnic aggrandizement. "Unchallenged and unchecked," real anti-Semitism, the Perlmutters warned, "can loose once again classical anti-Semitism." In fact the reverse comes closer to the truth: it is the mislabeling of legitimate challenges to Jewish privilege and power as anti-Semitism that breeds irrational resentment of Jews, more on which later.[14]

14. Perlmutters, *Real Anti-Semitism*, pp. 9 ("Essentially"; cf. pp. 105–7), 231 ("Klansmen," "Unchallenged").

Given that the domestic power of American Jewish elites was firmly entrenched, the club of anti-Semitism was mainly wielded to assail Israel's critics. Israel, according to the Perlmutters, was "indisputably the overriding concern of Jewry," "the issue central to our beings"— but only if it was a Sparta-like Israel in thrall to the United States.[15] From the mid-1970s *this* Israel was coming under attack. When the Palestine Liberation Organization (PLO) joined the international consensus supporting a two-state settlement, pressures mounted on Israel to follow suit—or, in the Perlmutters' twisted logic, Israel had been "cornered in the public-relations cul de sac of 'peace.'" To head off this PLO "peace offensive" (Israeli strategic analyst Avner Yaniv's phrase), Israel invaded Lebanon in June 1982.[16] The Perlmutters were at pains to acknowledge that, although nonetheless "murder's accomplices," Israel's critics were mostly *not* motivated by anti-Jewish animus. If they took exception to Israeli policy, it was on account of their being either misguided dupes of "trendy" Third World ideologies (like opposition to "racism," "sexism," and "imperialism") or grubby opportunists anxious about the price of Arab oil.[17] One possibility the Perlmutters didn't entertain was that Israel might be in the wrong. Real anti-Semites didn't just include usual suspects like the National Council of Churches, which "called on Israel to include the PLO in its Middle East peace negotiations," and the United Nations, which "has become an arena for vicious assaults on Jewish interests"—such as supporting a two-state settlement. Rather, defined by the damage, however indirect, they might inflict on Israel, *anti-Semites,* in the Perlmutters' lexicon, was a catchall for, among others, those wanting to "scuttle the electoral college" in the name of democracy, which would diminish the clout of American Jews (concentrated in swing states) and concomitantly diminish Jewish influence over Middle East policy; those calling for peaceful resolution of conflicts and cuts in the military budget, on account of which "nowadays war is getting a bad name and peace too favorable a press"—plainly a disaster for Israel; those opposing nuclear power, which would increase "the West's dependency on OPEC oil and . . . our economy's thralldom to recycling petrodollars"; and on

15. Ibid., pp. 80 ("indisputably"), 154 ("central"). For American Jewry's support of a militarized and dependent Israel, see Finkelstein, *Holocaust Industry*, chap. 1.

16. Perlmutters, *Real Anti-Semitism*, p. 262. Avner Yaniv, *Dilemmas of Security* (Oxford, 1987), p. 70.

17. Perlmutters, *Real Anti-Semitism*, pp. 32–33, 107–8, 163–64 ("trendy"), 230–44 ("murder's accomplices" at 244).

and on. Scaling the peaks of absurdity, the Perlmutters suggest that "even the *New York Times* is guilty," if not of outright anti-Semitism then of . . . Holocaust denial.[18]

Like the Forster-Epstein study, *The Real Anti-Semitism* focused obsessively on anti-Semitism in the black community. The worst of Jewish sins, according to the Perlmutters, was that they "have tended to care more for mankind than the world has cared for [Jews]," a disposition arising from "God's disproportionately generous gifting of Jews with brimming empathy." The problem, in short, was that Jews were too wonderful for their own good. And nowhere had the generosity of Jewry been more manifest than "its doting role in the nourishment of the infant NAACP and Urban League, its lawyers, strategists and activists in behalf of racial justice." Except for black ingratitude, how then to account for poll data cited by the Perlmutters showing an escalation of African American hostility toward Jews?[19] In fact, as even *The Real Anti-Semitism* suggests (if obliquely), black-Jewish tensions sprang in part from class conflict over initiatives supporting the disadvantaged, like affirmative action, which American Jewish organizations prominently opposed; in part from a lack of lockstep support for Israel in the black community; and in part from the uncorking of an ugly, just barely repressed, racism among many Jews.[20] On the last point, consider the Perlmutters' explanation that New York Jews had grown conservative because their Upper Manhattan neighborhoods were no longer safe from criminals after dark: "Fear and filth, it seems, grow thick where music, art, theater, libraries and liberal constituencies thrive." "Fear and filth"—to whom could that be referring? In order to make amends and return to the good graces of Jews, according to the Perlmutters, it was incumbent upon "the Black" to lend—no surprises here—Israel greater support: "Loud, clear, repeated condemnations of

18. Ibid., pp. 61–62 (*Times*), 108–9 (electoral college), 116 ("war is getting"), 159 ("include the PLO"), 248 (United Nations), 282 (nuclear power).

19. Ibid., pp. 86ff. (poll data), 186 ("doting"), 211 ("God's"), 251 ("tended to care"). As it happens, American Jewish support for the Civil Rights Movement reaped significant benefits for Jews as well. "The highly visible alliance between Jews and blacks during the civil rights demonstrations of the 1950s and 1960s made Jews the target of renewed hatred by many right-wing racists," Harvard law professor Alan Dershowitz observes. "But in the end, the civil rights period brought with it an end to much of the social and economic discrimination suffered by the Jews" (Alan M. Dershowitz, *Contrary to Popular Opinion* [New York, 1992], p. 366).

20. Perlmutters, *Real Anti-Semitism*, pp. 182–203, 264–77; for Jewish organizations opposing affirmative action and for Jewish racism, see Finkelstein, *Holocaust Industry*, p. 36.

the United Nations' offenses against the Jewish people; loud, clear, repeated contradictions of the National Council of Churches' skewed reports on the Middle East; delegations to Washington supportive of Israel's security."[21] Repellent as they were, the Perlmutters plainly couldn't be faulted for lack of consistency.

And by this reckoning, the religious right no longer figured as anti-Semitic, because it had pledged support for the Holy State: "Fundamentalist intolerance is currently not so baneful as its friendship for Israel is helpful." How little the "real" anti-Semitism had to do with the genuine article and how much with criticism of Israeli policy could be gleaned from the Perlmutters' preference for the Christian right, which was steeped in anti-Jewish bigotry but "pro"-Israel, as against liberal Protestantism, which was free of anti-Jewish bigotry but "anti"-Israel:

> Why then do we feel more comfortable today with the Reverend Bailey Smith, leader of the Southern Baptist Convention, who has seriously declared, "With all due respect to those dear people, my friends, God Almighty does not hear the prayer of a Jew," than we do with the socially conscious National Council of Churches? After all, the Southern Baptists have yet to disclaim the charge of deicide against me, while member organizations of the National Council of Churches acquitted me even while the Vatican Council II's jury was still out. The answer lies not in their measures of anti-Semitism, but in their political postures. Christian-professing religious attitudes, in this time, in this country, are for all practical purposes, no more than personally held religious conceits, barely impacting the way in which Jews live. Their political action, as it relates to the security of the state of Israel, impacts us far more meaningfully than whether a Christian neighbor believes that his is the exclusive hot line to "on high."

On this criterion, Jerry Falwell of the Moral Majority and Pat Robertson of the Christian Broadcasting Network likewise passed muster. Although their fundamentalist theology reeked of anti-Semitism, it was of no account so long as they gave backing to a militarized Israel. "[L]et's praise the Lord," the Perlmutters counseled, borrowing the title of a World War II hit, "and pass the ammunition." Indeed, they didn't just praise the Christian right but exonerated it as well: "[R]arely has a religious persuasion been as broadly smeared as have fundamentalists. As excoriations of Zionism have served to camouflage raw anti-Semitism, so have swollen hyperboles descriptive of the Moral Majority and

---

21. Perlmutters, *Real Anti-Semitism*, pp. 114 ("Fear and filth"), 203 ("Loud, clear"), 206 ("the Black").

the Religious Roundtable beclouded the image of fundamentalists." Little as can be said for the claims of this analogy, the Perlmutters do deserve credit for clearly and accurately aligning, in the analogy's terms, Zionism (at any rate, their brand of it) with the Moral Majority.[22]

Finally, apart from lavishing praise on Israel, in order to get on the Perlmutters' A-list of fighting anti-Semitism, one had to be tough on crime ("our violence-ridden times are ripe for considering as a priority the defense of the victim"); oppose affirmative action ("That reverse discrimination has been arbitrarily punitive of individual whites is self-evident"); and favor an aggressive U.S. military posture as well as a sharp increase in the military budget ("to more credibly deny expansionist [Soviet] threats to world peace"). On this last point, the Perlmutters took note of the seeming irony that ADL sounded more like "a conservative defense organization than ... a Jewish human-rights agency."[23] It wasn't at all ironic: reflecting its elite Jewish constituency, ADL had in fact become a bastion of reaction.

Like *The New Anti-Semitism*, the foreword to *The Real Anti-Semitism* acknowledged the input of Abraham Foxman. By the time he succeeded Nathan Perlmutter as head of ADL, Foxman was a veritable impresario of "new anti-Semitism" productions. As Israel headed toward a new crisis in fall 2000, he knew exactly which strings to pull and what buttons to press.

22. Ibid., pp. 155–56 ("helpful" and Bailey Smith), 172 ("[L]et's praise"), 176 ("[R]arely").

23. Ibid., pp. 228 ("violence-ridden"), 254–58 (military budget; "more credibly" and "defense organization" at 254), 264–77 (affirmative action; "reverse discrimination" at 269).

2

Israel
The "Jew among Nations"

"WHAT EACH THING is when fully developed," Aristotle observed in *The Politics,* "we call its nature." In this sense, the latest revival of the new anti-Semitism reveals its true essence. Although Abraham Foxman's *Never Again? The Threat of the New Anti-Semitism* (2003) included standard props, like chapters on right-wing loonies ("Danger on the Right: Violence and Extremism in the American Heartland") and African Americans ("Troubled Alliance: The Rift between American Blacks and Jews"), as the production hit the road, all pretenses were dropped that it was about anything except Israel. In addition, the distinction between "real" and "classical" anti-Semitism was discarded. In *The Real Anti-Semitism,* the Perlmutters had de-demonized anti-Semites, making of them merely Gentiles with contrary "interests." But as Israel's illegal and immoral policies came under closer scrutiny, the only defense available was to re-demonize critics, claiming they were classical Jew-haters. Finally, whereas in the original *New Anti-Semitism* marginal left-wing organizations like the Communist Party and the Socialist Workers Party were cast as the heart of the anti-Semitic darkness, in the current revival Israel's apologists, having lurched to the right end of the political spectrum, cast mainstream organizations like Amnesty International and Human Rights Watch in this role.

The dominant trope of the new "new anti-Semitism" is that Israel has become the "Jew among nations": "Israel has fast become the Jew of the world" (Phyllis Chesler, *The New Anti-Semitism*); "Israel, in effect, is emerging as the collective Jew among nations" (Mortimer B. Zuckerman, "The New Anti-Semitism"); "If classical anti-Semitism was anchored in discrimination against the Jewish religion, the new anti-Jewishness is anchored in discrimination against the Jews as a people— and the embodiment of that expression in Israel" (Irwin Cotler, "Human rights and the new anti-Jewishness"); "The state of Israel . . . has been transformed into 'the "Jew" of the nations'" (Gabriel Schoenfeld, *The Return of Anti-Semitism*).[1] As with the "new anti-Semitism," Israel's apologists have merely recycled this representation of Israel as the collective Jewish victim of anti-Semitic prejudice. In their 1982 study the Perlmutters pointed up the "transformation . . . from anti-Semitism against Jews to anti-Semitism the object of which is the Jews' surrogate: Israel," while in his 1991 autobiography Harvard Law School professor Alan Dershowitz, decrying the "newest form of anti-Jewishness," explained that "[i]t is impossible to understand why Israel receives the attention—most particularly the criticism—it does receive without recognizing that Israel is the 'Jew' among the nations."[2] In any event, the reasoning is that, since Israel represents the "Jew among nations," criticism of Israel springs from the same poisoned well as anti-Semitism and therefore is, by definition, anti-Semitic. And since the last major outbreak of anti-Semitism climaxed in The Holocaust, those currently criticizing Israel are fomenting a new Holocaust. "Very quickly," Foxman portends in *Never Again?* "the actual survival of the Jewish people might once again be at risk." The transparent motive behind these assertions is to taint any criticism of Israel as motivated by anti-Semitism and—inverting reality—to turn Israel (and Jews), not Palestinians, into the victim of the "current siege" (Chesler).[3]

---

1. Phyllis Chesler, *The New Anti-Semitism: The Current Crisis and What We Must Do about It* (San Francisco, 2003), p. 4; Mortimer B. Zuckerman, "The New Anti-Semitism," *U.S. News & World Report* (3 November 2003); Irwin Cotler, "Human rights and the new anti-Jewishness," *Jerusalem Post* (5 February 2004) (Cotler is currently Canada's Minister of Justice); Gabriel Schoenfeld, *The Return of Anti-Semitism* (San Francisco, 2004), p. 147.

2. Nathan Perlmutter and Ruth Ann Perlmutter, *The Real Anti-Semitism in America* (New York, 1982), pp. 162–63; Alan M. Dershowitz, *Chutzpah* (Boston, 1991), pp. 121, 210 (cf. p. 4).

3. Abraham H. Foxman, *Never Again? The Threat of the New Anti-Semitism* (San Francisco, 2003), p. 39; Chesler, *New Anti-Semitism*, p. 180.

The chief political and ideological advantage of playing the anti-Semitism card, however, was succinctly (if unwittingly) put by one of Israel's most vigorous apologists, Harvard professor Ruth Wisse. "In the case of the so-called Arab-Israel conflict," she explained, "to permit the concept of anti-Semitism into the discussion is to acknowledge that the origins of Arab opposition to the Jewish state are to be located in the political culture of the Arabs themselves, and that such opposition can end only if and when that political culture changes."[4] It displaces fundamental responsibility for causing the conflict from Israel to the Arabs, the issue no longer being Jewish dispossession of Palestinians but Arab "opposition" to Jews, and fundamental responsibility for resolving it from Israel ending its occupation to the Arab world ending its irrational hostility toward Jews. Although Israel's apologists claim to allow for criticism of the occasional Israeli "excess" (what is termed "legitimate criticism"), the upshot of this allowance is to delegitimize the preponderance of criticism as anti-Semitic—just as Communist parties used to allow for criticism of the occasional Stalinist "excess," while denouncing principled criticism as "anti-Soviet" and therefore beyond the pale. In fact, belying all the hysterics, in places like the United States and Germany, Israel receives virtually no sustained criticism. The allegation of a new anti-Semitism is being used to silence the tiny percentage of media coverage that manages to escape ideological control. In places like Britain, where coverage of the conflict is clearly better, for all the complaints of its being pro-Arab and anti-Semitic, serious media analysis still shows a very pronounced bias in favor of Israel.[5]

For her part, Phyllis Chesler, in The New Anti-Semitism, barely disguises that alleging a new anti-Semitism is simply the pretext for defending Israel. Copying "pro"-Israel websites, she devotes eight pages to "A Brief History of Arab Attacks against Israel, 1908–1970s" but nary a word to Israeli attacks against Arabs, and four pages to "Recent Arab Terrorism against Israel" but nary a word to Israeli terrorism against Arabs. There have been "nine major Israeli wars of self-defense in the last fifty-five years," according to Chesler, but apparently none in which the Arabs were defending themselves from Israeli attack, even though her count includes, among multiple dubious examples, the

4. Ruth R. Wisse, "On Ignoring Anti-Semitism," in Ron Rosenbaum (ed.), Those Who Forget the Past: The Question of Anti-Semitism (New York, 2004), p. 200.
5. See Greg Philo and Mike Berry, Bad News from Israel (London, 2004).

1956 Israeli invasion of Sinai, the 1982 Israeli invasion of Lebanon, and the 1987 and 2000 Palestinian revolts against Israel's occupation. Reaching to the outer limits of "legitimate criticism," she does allow that "perhaps, it may be argued, Jews or individual Israelis ought to bear some moral responsibility" for the Sabra and Shatila massacres. Although confessedly "not a military insider and expert," Chesler concludes that "Israeli control of the borders, checkpoints, and roads right down to the sea and to the river in the West Bank and in Gaza" are "possibly—probably—now essential for Israel's safety"; yet she fails completely to consider what the Palestinians might require for *their* safety, or just to survive.[6]

A contrived scandal erupted in November 2003 after the European Monitoring Centre on Racism and Xenophobia (EUMC) was accused of suppressing an incendiary report on anti-Semitism in the European Union. World Jewish Congress president Edgar Bronfman declared the European Commission "guilty" of "Anti-Semitism" for its having "censored" the report, although the EUMC is institutionally autonomous. In its defense the EUMC maintained that the report it had commissioned but didn't distribute, *Manifestations of Anti-Semitism in the European Union*, was "biased" and "lacking in empirical evidence." E.U. foreign policy chief Javier Solana concurred that it "did not meet the criteria of consistency and quality of data."[7] In fact, the data assembled in the *Manifestations* report, the standards it used to measure anti-Semitism, and the conclusions it reached barely rose to the comical. It was, nonetheless, by far the most intensive, minute cataloging of the new anti-Semitism to date, which was one reason Israel's apologists touted it. Especially because it focused on the peak period of this new anti-Semitism, the claim that Jew-hatred was running rampant in Europe effectively stood or fell on the report's findings. A product of the Center for Research on Anti-Semitism (Zentrum für

6. Chesler, *New Anti-Semitism*, pp. 19 ("wars"), 31 (Sabra and Shatila), 44–52 ("Arab Attacks"), 82–85 ("Arab Terrorism"), 168 ("insider," "Israeli control," "essential"), 225 (wars).

7. Bertrand Benoit, "EU racism group shelves anti-Semitism study," *Financial Times* (22 November 2003) ("biased"); Bertrand Benoit and Silke Mertins, "Brussels urged to publish report on anti-Semitism," *Financial Times* (25 November 2003) ("criteria"); Bertrand Benoit, "Shelved EU study of anti-Semitism goes on net," *Financial Times* (3 December 2003); Cobi Benatoff and Edgar M. Bronfman, "Europe's moral treachery over anti-Semitism," *Financial Times* (5 January 2004) ("Anti-Semitism," "censored"); George Parker, "Prodi shelves plan for anti-Semitism conference," *Financial Times* (6 January 2004) ("lacking"); Raphael Minder, "Racism talks revived as Jews support Prodi," *Financial Times* (8 January 2004).

Antisemitismusforschung [ZfA]) at Berlin's Technical University, *Manifestations* bore the typical earmarks of Germany's public culture on all matters regarding Jews and Israel. If Germany was once the European hotbed of anti-Semitism, it has now become the hotbed of philo-Semitism: on the one hand, "politically correct," utterly cynical public officials and media ferret out anti-Semites where a smattering are to be found, resembling nothing so much as the medieval witch hunts; and on the other, Israel's apologists, holding Germany in thrall, exploit the Nazi horrors to strike down any criticism of Jewish leaders or Israel, stifling public discourse and stoking private resentment.[8]

This isn't the first time German public opinion has been manipulated into fighting a phantom "new anti-Semitism." In 1981, as pressures mounted on Israel to negotiate a two-state settlement with the Palestinians, the Union of Jews and Christians issued a declaration entitled "On the Danger of a New Anti-Semitism" at the German Evangelical Churchday. It cautioned that "signs of a relapse into hostility towards Jews are currently on the rise," alleging in particular that "[b]ehind the criticism of the Israeli government, . . . the old anti-Semitism is visible."[9] Likewise, the red thread running through the German-authored *Manifestations* report was the equating of criticism of Israel with anti-Semitism: "[T]he tradition of demonising Jews in the past is now being

8. See Norman G. Finkelstein, "Counterfeit Courage: Reflections on 'Political Correctness' in Germany," in Alexander Cockburn and Jeffrey St. Clair (eds.), *The Politics of Anti-Semitism* (Oakland, Calif., 2003). A recent act in this never-ending German passion play was the public outcry against a resurgent Nazism when the hometown speech (to 120 people) of the obscure conservative German politician and CDU representative Martin Hohmann was belatedly unearthed. Never mind that he never said what he was repeatedly accused of, first in Germany, then echoed internationally. Prefacing his remarks with the acknowledgment that "[w]e all know the devastating and unique deeds done at Hitler's bidding," and heaping contempt on Hitler's contemporary followers ("brown offal"), Hohmann then went on to object to the Goldhagen thesis that the "whole [German] people" were "murderers from birth onwards." In this context, he argued that *if* Germans were a "perpetrator people" because the Nazi leadership was German, then Jews must be considered a "perpetrator people" because the Bolshevik leadership, which also committed heinous crimes, was preponderantly Jewish. In fact, he dismissed both propositions as false, concluding (as befits a religious fundamentalist) that the real "perpetrator people" are "the Godless." But this didn't prevent the lunatic public German denunciation of Hohmann (and, later, his expulsion from the CDU parliamentary faction) on the grounds that he called Jews a "perpetrator people"—which is what he emphatically did not do. For an English translation of Hohmann's speech, and perceptive commentary, see "The Case of Martin Hohmann," *Labor and Trade Union Review* (December 2003).

9. Hans-Jochen Luhmann and Gundel Neveling (eds.), "Erklärung der Arbeitsgemeinschaft Juden und Christen beim Deutschen Evangelischen Kirchentag: Zur Gefahr eines neuen Antisemitismus," *Deutscher Evangelischer Kirchentag Hamburg 1981—Dokumente* (Stuttgart and Berlin, 1981), p. 626.

transferred to the state of Israel." And the "sharp criticism of Israeli politics across the entire political spectrum" was adduced as proof of the "threatening nature" of the new anti-Semitism. Consider this convoluted example listed under "Forms of anti-Semitic prejudice": "While the historical victim status of Jews continues to be acknowledged, for many Europeans it no longer transfers to support of Israel. Israeli policies toward the Palestinians provide a reason to denounce Jews as perpetrators, thereby qualifying their moral status as victims that they had assumed as a consequence of the Holocaust. The connection between anti-Semitism and anti-Israeli sentiment lies in this opportunity for a perpetrator-victim role reversal." In other words, although Europeans recognize Jewish suffering in the Nazi holocaust, they are still anti-Semitic because, believing that Jews can also be perpetrators, they won't automatically support Israel. In addition, the report tabulated under the heading "Prevalent anti-Semitic prejudices" the "assumption of close ties between the US and Israel," as well as the belief that Jews have "a major influence over the USA's allegedly biased pro-Israel policies" and the belief that Israel has perpetrated "apartheid," "ethnic cleansing," and "crimes against humanity."[10]

A sampling of the study's breakdown of "anti-Semitic" incidents in European Union countries fleshes out what the new anti-Semitism really means. It should be noted that the data assembled in *Manifestations* came mainly from the period when sympathy for Palestinians and hostility toward Israel peaked, during Israel's Operation Defensive Shield (March–April 2002), which culminated in the siege of Jenin refugee camp. *Belgium*—"During a pro-Palestinian demonstration, . . . front windows were shattered and an Israeli flag burnt"; *Ireland*— "The Israeli embassy has received a number of hate telephone calls in the last month"; *Spain*—"Many young Spaniards consider support of the PLO a crucial qualification for being identified as 'progressive' or leftist"; *Italy*—"During the [Communist party] congress, a number of objects explicitly referred to Palestine: the Palestinian flag, a book by the representative of the Palestinian National Authority (PNA) in

---

10. Werner Bergmann and Juliane Wetzel, *Manifestations of anti-Semitism in the European Union* (Vienna, 2003), http://eumc.eu.int/eumc/material/pub/FT/Draft _anti-Semitism_report-web.pdf, pp. 10 ("demonising," "assumption," "major influence"), 23 ("apartheid," "ethnic cleansing," "crimes against humanity"), 23–24 ("victim status"), 29 ("threatening") (hereafter: *Manifestations*). In this and other publications on the new anti-Semitism, the use of the term *genocide* is likewise deplored. In fact, this term subsumes a broad range of destructive aims, some of which perhaps are, and some clearly not, descriptive of Israeli policy toward Palestinians.

Italy, . . . and the kefiah, the traditional Arab head gear"; *Nether-lands*—"Gretta Duisenberg, wife of European Central Bank President Wim Duisenberg, has hung a Palestinian flag from her balcony"; *Por-tugal*—"The Israel Embassy has received slanderous calls and Internet messages with offensive content"; *Finland*—"Pro-Palestine movements have distributed their leaflets on many occasions. Some of these leaflets . . . have asked people to boycott Israeli products to help attain peace in Israel."[11]

If virtually any criticism of Israel signals anti-Semitism, the sweep of the new anti-Semitism, unsurprisingly, beggars the imagination. Apart from usual suspects like Arabs, Muslims, and the Third World gen-erally, as well as Europe and the United Nations, Chesler's rogues' gallery includes "Western-based international human rights organiza-tions, academics, intellectuals"; "Western anticapitalist, antiglobalist, pro-environment, antiracist," and "antiwar" activists; "progressive fem-inists," "Jewish feminists" ("American Jewish feminists stopped fight-ing for women's rights in America and began fighting for the rights of the PLO"); "European, and left and liberal American media" like *Time* magazine, the Associated Press, Reuters, the *Washington Post, Los Angeles Times, New York Times*, British *Guardian, Toronto Star*, the BBC, NPR, CNN, and ABC, as well as many Israelis like the late "Yeshayahu Leibowitz of Hebrew University"—an orthodox Jew and one of Israel's most revered intellectuals. And "anyone who denies that this is so," Chesler throws in for good measure, is also "an anti-Semite." Small wonder that Chesler sees a world awash in "Nazi-level" anti-Semitism: "It's as if Hitler's Brown Shirts have returned from the dead, in greater numbers, and are doing their dirty Kristallnacht work everyday, everywhere." Even in the United States, the new anti-Semitism is so pervasive that those daring to criticize it "wear the yel-low star." Amid these absurd dilations Chesler juxtaposes the Eastern propensity for "hyperexaggeration" against her own "Western stan-dard of truth-telling and objectivity." To convey the amplitude of the new anti-Semitism, she lets loose a barrage of strange similes and metaphors: "There is a thrilling permissibility in the air—the kind of electrically charged and altered reality that acid-trippers or epileptics may experience just prior to a seizure"; "Doctored footage of fake Israeli massacres has now entered the imagination of billions of people;

11. *Manifestations*, pp. 41 (Belgium), 55 (Ireland), 60 (Spain), 71 (Italy), 82 (Nether-lands), 88 (Portugal), 91 (Finland).

like pornography, these ideas can never be forgotten"; "It's as if the political equivalent of the AIDS virus has been unleashed in the world"; "To be a Jew is to live dangerously, on the margins, with an open, 'circumcised' heart." "Acid-trippers," "epileptics," "pornography," "AIDS," "'circumcised' heart"—one begins to wonder whether Chesler's magnum opus, *Women and Madness*, was autobiographical.[12] The media also get chastised by Chesler for their "obsessive focus" on Israeli treatment of Palestinians, which is a "distracting luxury." Rather, she counsels that they should focus attention on the "major problems that affect the majority" of the world's population. Of course, the "obsessive focus" of America's most prosperous ethnic group on its supposed suffering and persecution isn't a "distracting luxury."[13]

Chesler is a picture of sobriety, however, next to *Commentary* editor Gabriel Schoenfeld. According to him, we are past Kristallnacht in America and well into the Final Solution. "The plain fact," he reports, "is that something unprecedented is taking place: Jews in the United States are being targeted for murder." His Black Book of anti-Semites doesn't just include the familiar "environmentalists, pacifists, anarchists, antiglobalists and socialists"; the "mainstream British and European press" (*Le Monde*, *The Economist*) as well as "French television

12. Chesler, *New Anti-Semitism*, pp. 5 ("thrilling," "pornography"), 12 ("yellow star"), 13 ("AIDS"), 18 ("'circumcised'"), 69 ("progressive feminists"), 71 (*Time*), 89 ("Brown Shirts"), 94 ("hyperexaggeration"), 96 ("Western standard"), 178 ("anyone who denies"), 181 ("antiwar"), 182 (Israeli anti-Semites), 188 ("American Jewish feminists"), 190 (Leibowitz), 219 (anti-Semitic media), 220 (CNN, NPR, *New York Times*, *Los Angeles Times*), 226 ("Nazi-level"), 245 ("anticapitalist, antiglobalist"), 246 ("human rights organizations, academics, intellectuals"), 259n5 (Associated Press, Reuters, BBC, CNN, ABC, *Washington Post*, *Toronto Star*, *Guardian*). Those wondering why the popular global movement contesting corporate dominance of the world economy is anti-Semitic can turn to the journal *Foreign Policy* for insight: "[I]t helps enable anti-Semitism by peddling conspiracy theories. In its eyes, globalization is less a process than a plot hatched behind closed doors by a handful of unaccountable bureaucrats and corporations. Underlying the movement's humanistic goals of universal social justice is a current of fear mongering—the IMF, the WTO, the North American Free Trade Agreement, and the Multilateral Agreement on Investment (MAI) are portrayed not just as exploiters of the developing world, but as supranational instruments to undermine our sovereignty. Pick up a copy of the 1998 book *MAI and the Threat to American Freedom* . . . and you'll read how '[o]ver the past twenty-five years, corporations and the state seem to have forged a new political alliance that allows corporations to gain more and more control over governance. This new "corporate rule" poses a fundamental threat to the rights and democratic freedoms of all people'" (Mark Strauss, "Antiglobalism's Jewish Problem," *Foreign Policy* (November–December 2003), reprinted in Rosenbaum, *Those Who Forget*, pp. 278–79). It's hard to make out what's more laughable, the claim that this analysis is a "conspiracy theory" or that it is anti-Semitic.
13. Chesler, *New Anti-Semitism*, p. 201.

news" and the BBC; "liberal-to-Left organizations like Human Rights Watch and Amnesty International"; *New York Times* columnist Maureen Dowd and *Hardball* host Chris Matthews; and so on. He also counts as anti-Semites those using "the term 'neoconservative,'" because it is a "thinly veiled synonym for 'Jew.'" Leaving aside the dubious assumption that use of this term carries the alleged imputation, and leaving aside that the founders of the neoconservative movement *were* overwhelmingly Jewish (proudly so), if the appellation *neoconservative* is anti-Semitic, what does that make the Jewish neoconservatives clustered around *Commentary* who appropriated it and who typically use it to distinguish themselves?[14]

But what puts Schoenfeld's account in a special class is the extraordinary spectrum of Jews he tabulates as anti-Semitic. Indeed, according to Schoenfeld, the new anti-Semitism emanates mainly from the political left, and it is Jews who dominate this anti-Semitic left. In other words, the juggernaut of the new anti-Semitism is "largely a Jewish contingent"; and again, "left-wing Jews" are "in the vanguard" of the new anti-Semitism. However absurd, it is all the same unsurprising to see Noam Chomsky classified as an anti-Semite in Schoenfeld's book; Chomsky became the bête noire of Israel's apologists after proving to be the most principled and effective Jewish critic of Israeli policy. It begins to raise eyebrows, however, when the likes of Rabbi Michael Lerner of *Tikkun* magazine and Daniel Boyarin, "a leading academic figure in Jewish studies in the United States" (Schoenfeld's description), get the same treatment. But one truly begins to worry about Schoenfeld's mental poise when he questions the bona fides of Leon Wieseltier, the fanatically "pro"-Israel literary editor of the fanatically "pro"-Israel *New Republic*. Doubting the imminence of another Final Solution, Wieseltier has committed the sin of being, if not an outright anti-Semitism denier, at any rate an anti-Semitism minimizer. It seems the revolution is devouring its children.[15]

14. Schoenfeld, *Return*, pp. 2 ("targeted"), 86 ("environmentalists"), 87–100 ("mainstream" at 89), 124 (Dowd), 125 (Matthews), 128 ("neoconservative," "synonym"), 148 ("liberal-to-Left").

15. Schoenfeld, *Return*, pp. 130–39 ("largely" at 130, "leading" at 137, "left-wing" and "vanguard" at 139), 148–49 (Wieseltier). Among those classified as an anti-Semite, as well as a self-hating Jew and "[e]ntering the terrain of outright Holocaust denial," is this writer. Schoenfeld reports, for example, that "Finkelstein echoes the revisionist historians who claim that Holocaust reparations are a 'racket' used by avaricious Jews to enrich themselves" (pp. 132, 134). Oddly, Schoenfeld seems to have forgotten what he himself wrote on the subject. In a lead September 2000 *Commentary* article entitled "Holocaust Reparations—A Growing Scandal," Schoenfeld chastised Holocaust profi-

An anthology edited and introduced by Ron Rosenbaum, *Those Who Forget The Past: The Question of Anti-Semitism*, stands on a moral and intellectual par with Chesler's and Schoenfeld's musings.[16] The journalist Alexander Cockburn once quipped about a neoconservative periodical that it arrived on the doorstep already wrapped in cobwebs. Something similar can be said about Rosenbaum's collection. Written just before or after the Iraq war, many of the book's contributions already made, on the book's mid-2004 publication date, for an embarrassing read. *Daily Telegraph* columnist Barbara Amiel sings paeans to "16,000-pound daisy cutter bombs" for giving a needful "nudge" to the "Arab/Muslim world's intransigence." *Vanity Fair* journalist Marie Brenner, adducing French opposition to the U.S. attack on Iraq as ultimate proof of a pervasive anti-Semitism—which clarifies what the hysteria about a new anti-Semitism is really about—reports that the French stubbornly disapproved "even when the citizens of Baghdad openly embraced American forces." Albeit only for a week, if that long. To demonstrate the "Nazi" mentality of Daniel Pearl's captors, writer Thane Rosenbaum focuses on the "prurient, hard-porn" qualities of the video recording his beheading, and especially the "humiliation" Pearl was made to suffer on camera. Would he now also care to ruminate on what the photographs and videos from Abu Ghraib prison tell us about the mentality of those who held Iraqis captive and those who approved the interrogation methods? Playwright and screenwriter David Mamet, another eminent authority on anti-Semitism selected for inclusion in Rosenbaum's anthology, explains that the world is in "debt to the Jews" because, "[h]ad Israel not in 1981 bombed the Iraqi nuclear reactor, some scant weeks away from production of nuclear bomb material, all New York (God forbid) might have been Ground Zero." Except that the Iraqi reactor wasn't making nuclear weapons; it was probably the Israeli bombing that induced

---

teers in incendiary prose for having "unrestrainedly availed themselves of any method, however unseemly or even disreputable." Schoenfeld also alleged that "[i]n a December 2001 lecture delivered in Beirut, Lebanon, Finkelstein likened Israeli actions to 'Nazi practices' during World War II, albeit with some added 'novelties to the Nazi experiments'" (Gabriel Schoenfeld, "Israel and the Anti-Semites," in Rosenbaum, *Those Who Forget*, p. 112n). Those wanting to compare Schoenfeld's imaginative rendering with the actual text should consult the new introduction to Norman G. Finkelstein, *Image and Reality of the Israel-Palestine Conflict*, 2nd ed. (New York, 2003), which is a footnoted version of this writer's Lebanon lecture.

16. The anthology includes a handful of token pieces by the likes of Edward Said and Judith Butler to affect balance.

Saddam to embark on a nuclear weapons program; and Iraq had nothing to do with the attack on the World Trade Center. Debt canceled. According to contributor Robert Wistrich of the Hebrew University, "Saddam's Iraq provided a sinister confirmation" of the "Nazi" outlook pervading the Arab world in its "determination to develop weapons of mass destruction and its readiness to use them," while Saddam's defeat fortunately eliminated "the specter of deadly weapons in the hands of a ruthless dictator." Except that no weapons of mass destruction were found, and such a weapons program had long been abandoned.[17]

Finally, speaking of cobwebs, fiction writer Cynthia Ozick, in the afterword to Rosenbaum's anthology, does yet another reprise of her signature role. The afterword begins on the dramatic note, "We thought it was finished. The ovens are long cooled. . . . The cries of the naked. . . . The deportation ledgers. . . . We thought it was finished. . . . Naively, foolishly, stupidly, hopefully, a-historically, we thought that the cannibal hatred, once quenched, would not soon wake again. It has awakened." She thought it was finished? Has Ozick forgotten that in the original production of *The New Anti-Semitism*, she already sang a variation of the same tune, "All the World Wants the Jews Dead"? That was the title of her widely heralded 1974 *Esquire* article. Has she forgotten that her *Esquire* article began with the same invocation of Nazi death camps; that she proceeded to castigate the Arabs who, marching in Hitler's footsteps, were out to murder all the world's Jews, including herself ("Cairo and Damascus, which hold the torches, are on the far end of the globe. Yet they mean me"); how she then roundly indicted the rest of the world (and even fellow Jews) for their complicity and silence? Has she even forgotten her outraged peroration, "Palestinian refugees, political tacticians, national liberationists, Olympic terrorists, and terrorists of the air! Destroyers of forty-nine peaceful lives in a single postwar spring! Shooters of thirteen mothers and babies at Qiryat Shemona! Murderers of . . . !" Does this ancient diva, rolled out for every new anti-Semitism production, really not remember that she's reading from a hoary script?[18]

17. Barbara Amiel, "Islamists Overplay Their Hand," p. 34; Robert S. Wistrich, "The Old-New Anti-Semitism," pp. 76–77, 88; Thane Rosenbaum, "Danny Pearl," pp. 125–26; Marie Brenner, "France's Scarlet Letter," p. 247; David Mamet, "'If I Forget Thee, Jerusalem': The Power of Blunt Nostalgia," p. 459, all in Rosenbaum, *Those Who Forget*. For Iraq's nuclear reactor, see Noam Chomsky, *Hegemony or Survival: America's Quest for Global Dominance* (New York, 2003), p. 25.

18. Cynthia Ozick, "Afterword," pp. 595–96, in Rosenbaum, *Those Who Forget*. For Ozick's earlier jeremiad, see "All the World Wants the Jews Dead," *Esquire* (November 1974).

"[T]he heart of anti-Zionist anti-Semitism," Rosenbaum maintains in his introduction, is denial of these irrefutable facts: "Jews want to live in peace, but three wars in which Arab states tried to drive them into the sea, and a terror campaign by Palestinians who reject the idea of a Jewish state, have left Israelis with the tragic choice between self-defense and self-destruction."[19] Rosenbaum takes special pride in injecting the prospect of a "Second Holocaust" in the new anti-Semitism debate. "[E]very European nation was deeply complicit in Hitler's genocide," and "[f]or the most part, Europeans *volunteered*" (his emphasis). Not only Germans but all Europeans, according to Rosenbaum, were Hitler's Willing Executioners. Now Europeans "are willing to be complicit in the murder of the Jews again." Indeed, they began plotting the second Holocaust from shortly after World War II. Imposing on Jews a state apart, Europeans conspired to "get the surviving Jews—reminders of European shame—off the continent, and leave the European peoples in possession of the property stolen from the Jews during the war." Let us put to one side the irony that it used to be an argument *against* Zionism, not one made by its defenders, to point up the common ground it shared with anti-Semitism of wanting to segregate Jews from Europe. Consider instead the central thesis. Before Rosenbaum came along, who would have guessed that the main impetus behind Israel's creation wasn't Jews longing for a homeland but Europeans longing to expel them—and to keep their stolen property, no less? The perfidy didn't end there. It wasn't Zionists but non-Jewish Europeans who sought to found the Jewish homeland in Palestine. Europeans purposely located Israel in an "indefensible sliver of desert in a sea of hostile peoples." And there's yet more. These Europeans purposely made Israel too small to accommodate Jews and Palestinians, so the Jews would expel the Palestinians, so the Palestinians would hate the Jews, so the "Semites [would] murder each other and blame the Jews." And if that weren't enough, Europeans have now embarked on covertly exterminating the remnant Jewish community on the continent as they "allow their own Arab populations to burn synagogues and beat Jews on the street *for* them" (his emphasis). Rosenbaum isn't sanguine about Israel's survival, on account of its inordinate restraint. Although he *does* "feel bad for the plight of the Palestinians," he believes that, to avert another Holocaust, not just the suicide bombers

---

19. "Introduction" to Rosenbaum, *Those Who Forget*, p. lix.

but "their families" as well should suffer "the exact same fate of the people the bombers blow up." The tragedy, alas, is that "Israelis won't do that"—that is, contrary to Rosenbaum's bidding, Israel won't indiscriminately murder men, women, and children—"and that is why there's likely to be a second Holocaust." All is not lost, however. When "a nuclear weapon is detonated in Tel Aviv," Israel will "sooner, not later," launch a "nuclear retaliation" against "Baghdad, Damascus, Tehran, perhaps all three." This time around, damn it, Jews will teach the goyim a lesson they won't soon forget: "The unspoken corollary of the slogan 'Never again' is: 'And *if* again, not us alone'" (his emphasis). It's an irony totally lost on Rosenbaum that these bedtime fantasies are interlarded in a volume edited by him ridiculing the paranoid conspiracy theories and bloodlust yearnings for revenge rife in the Arab world.[20]

Not to be outdone, in his contribution to the Rosenbaum collection, Philip Greenspun, an MIT expert on software and Web applications who has apparently never published a book or article on Israel (his essay, one of the two longest, consists almost entirely of URL references), confidently puts forth these theses: The establishment of Israel was the centerpiece of a global conspiracy to kill the Jews. Europe initially created Israel "as a concentration camp for Jews." But "[h]istorically most concentration camps for Jews have eventually turned into death camps and certainly there is no shortage of people worldwide trying to effect this transformation." In Europe these not-so-closeted Nazis prominently include academics supporting a cultural boycott of Israel, the proof being that they are "an echo of 1930s Germany in which university professors joined the Nazi party at a rate double that of the general population." In the Arab world, reality is yet more terrifying. "If we assume that the percentage of Muslims who really buy into what their leaders are telling them about Jews is equal to the percentage (33) of German voters who opted for Hitler in 1932, that works out to more than 400 million Jew-hating Muslims." If we

20. Ron Rosenbaum, "'Second Holocaust,' Roth's Invention, Isn't Novelistic," in Rosenbaum, *Those Who Forget*, pp. 170–77 passim. He traces the genesis of the phrase *Second Holocaust* back to a dialogue debating Israel's vulnerability in Philip Roth's 1993 novel *Operation Shylock* (pp. 170–71), and claims that for virtually the first time Jews are now contemplating an "existential threat" to Israel (pp. xxviii–xxix). In fact, if not always the precise phraseology, at any rate these notions haunted American Jewish life from as far back as the 1948 Arab-Israeli war and became staples of Zionist propaganda after the June 1967 war. See Peter Novick, *The Holocaust in American Life* (Boston, 1999), chap. 8, and Norman G. Finkelstein, *The Holocaust Industry: Reflections on the Exploitation of Jewish Suffering*, 2nd ed. (New York, 2003), chap. 1.

assume . . . Turning to our shores, the only reason the United States supports Israel, according to Greenspun, is from fear of being swamped by Jewish immigrants. Yet a critical mass of Americans also wants the Jews dead. This is shown by the combined facts that "about half of Americans hold some of the same beliefs about Jews espoused by the Nazi party" and that "Hitler was able to hold power in Germany with only 33 percent of the vote in 1932 and 44 percent in 1933." It is symptomatic of the paranoid mind that every event is construed as yet another link in some grand conspiracy. But paranoia has crossed a singular threshold when those calling themselves Zionists construe Israel's founding as the centerpiece of a grand anti-Semitic conspiracy. In a similar frame of mind, columnist Nat Hentoff professes that, "if a loudspeaker goes off and a voice says, 'All Jews gather in Times Square,' it could never surprise me."[21]

The consequences of the calculated hysteria of a new anti-Semitism haven't been just to immunize Israel from legitimate criticism. Its overarching purpose, like that of the "war against terrorism," has been to deflect criticism of an unprecedented assault on international law. Herein lies the greatest danger. In crucial respects, the Iraq war marked a watershed: principled refusal to participate in a war of aggression (surely a major lesson to be drawn from Hitlerism) was equated with, of all things, Jew-hatred. Thus, the global movement opposing the United States' illegal "preventive war" against Iraq, which Israel and mainstream Jewish organizations cheered on, stood accused of "anti-Semitism of a type long thought dead in the West." Even prominent American poets deploring the war and Israel's occupation were chastised for playing "on the edges of 1930s-style anti-Semitism." And, as the German people courageously refused to be browbeaten into supporting Washington's criminal aggression, the German branch of the Israel lobby, explicitly comparing Saddam Hussein to Adolf Hitler, used the occasion of Holocaust Remembrance Day to denounce German opposition to the war on Iraq, and later urged support for "necessary wars."[22]

21. Philip Greenspun, "Israel," in Rosenbaum, *Those Who Forget*, pp. 460–97 passim; Hentoff quoted in Amy Wilentz, "How the War Came Home," *New York* (6 May 2002).

22. For mainstream American Jewish support for attacking Iraq, see, e.g., "ADL Commends President Bush's Message to International Community on Iraq Calling It 'Clear and Forceful'" (Anti-Defamation League press release, 12 September 2002), and "AJC Lauds Bush on State of Union Message on Terrorism . . ." (American Jewish Committee press release, 7 February 2003). For Israel's enthusiastic support of the war, see

Likewise, the new anti-Semitism has been deployed to undermine the most basic principles of human rights. "The great moral issue facing the world at the dawn of this millennium," Alan Dershowitz declares, "is whether Israel's attempt to protect itself against terrorism will result in a massive increase in worldwide anti-Semitism." Of course, with marginal exceptions, no one contests Israel's right to defend itself against terrorism; the criticism springs from its gross violations of human rights in the name of fighting terrorism. The epithet of "anti-Semitism" is being used by Dershowitz, however, not just to deflect criticism of these gross violations but to *legalize* them. For, in the name of Israel's defense and—incredibly—"the rule of law," he has advocated a massive rollback of a century's progress in humanitarian and human rights law. Maintaining that "[h]uman rights law and rhetoric have become powerful weapons selectively aimed at Israel," Dershowitz goes on to proclaim that "[t]he time has come for the United States to insist that the international law of war be changed" and for the United States "to lead the fight to revise 'archaic' international laws and conventions"— in particular, "the Geneva Convention." Indeed, in a shocking pronouncement at an Israeli conference, he asserted that Israel isn't at all bound by international law: "Israelis are obliged to follow the rule of law that exists in the democracy called Israel the way I am obliged to follow the rule of law in the democracy called the United States. . . . Your moral obligation to comply with the letter of the rule of international law is voluntary; it is a matter of choice and a matter of tactic, not a matter of moral obligation or democratic theory." Fur-

---

Meron Benvenisti, "Hey ho, here comes the war," *Haaretz* (13 February 2003); Uzi Benziman, "Corridors of Power: O what a lovely war," *Haaretz* (18 February 2003); Gideon Levy, "A great silence over the land," *Haaretz* (16 February 2003); Aluf Benn, "Background: Enthusiastic IDF awaits war in Iraq," *Haaretz* (17 February 2003); and Aluf Benn, "The celebrations have already begun," *Haaretz* (20 February 2003). For "anti-Semitism," see Eliot A. Cohen, "The Reluctant Warrior," *Wall Street Journal* (6 February 2003) ("long thought dead"), and J. Bottum, "The Poets vs. The First Lady," *Weekly Standard* (17 February 2003) ("1930s-style"), as well as "ADL Says Organizers of Anti-war Protests in Washington and San Francisco Have History of Attacking Israel and Jews" (Anti-Defamation League press release, 15 January 2003); "Blackballing Lerner" (editorial) and Max Gross, "Leftist Rabbi Claims He's Too Pro-Israel for Anti-War Group," *Forward* (14 February 2003); and David Brooks, "It's Back: The socialism of fools has returned to vogue not just in the Middle East and France, but in the American left and Washington," *Weekly Standard* (21 February 2003). For Germany, see "Spiegel kritisiert Nein zum Irak-Krieg," *Süddeutsche Zeitung* (26 January 2003); Helmut Breuer and Gernot Facius, "'Es gibt notwendige Kriege.' Paul Spiegel, Zentralratsvorsitzender der Juden, sieht die Öffentlichkeit in einem 'Dornröschenschlaf,'" *Die Welt* (13 February 2003) ("necessary wars").

thermore, Dershowitz explicitly lends support to political liquidations ("The virtue of targeted assassination . . . is precisely that it is targeted and tends to avoid collateral damage and collective punishment"; "It strengthens civil liberties, not those of the Israelis, but those of the Palestinians"); collective punishment such as the "automatic destruction" of a Palestinian village after each terrorist attack ("home destruction is entirely moral . . . among the most moral and calibrated responses"); torture such as a "needle being shoved under the fingernails" ("I want maximal pain . . . the most excruciating, intense, immediate pain"); and ethnic cleansing ("Political solutions often require the movement of people, and such movement is not always voluntary. . . . [I]t is a fifth-rate issue analogous in many respects to some massive urban renewal"). To be sure, when *Palestinians* violate international law, Dershowitz is much more protective of it. Palestinian targeting of Israeli civilians, he opines, is "never acceptable. . . . It violates the Geneva Accords, it violates the international law of war and it violates all principles of morality"—unlike shoving a needle under someone's fingernails.[23]

The poisoning of public discourse on human rights by apologists for Israel is not confined to the United States. The most appalling and shameful example is Germany. Michael Wolffsohn, a staunch German-Jewish "supporter" of Israel and professor at the University of the German Armed Forces, maintained on German television, "As a means against terrorists, I do consider torture, or the threat of torture, legitimate, yes I do." He subsequently cited Dershowitz, whose support of torture has been widely reported in Germany, as one of his inspirations. When the German minister of defense rebuked him (as did many others),

23. Dershowitz, *Chutzpah*, p. 215 ("Political solutions"); Alan M. Dershowitz, *Why Terrorism Works: Understanding the Threat, Responding to the Challenge* (New Haven, 2002), pp. 131–63 ("needle" at pp. 144, 148), 172–81, 183–86, 221 ("time has come"); Alan M. Dershowitz, "New response to Palestinian terrorism," *Jerusalem Post* (11 March 2002), ("automatic destruction"); "Why terrorism works," an interview with Alan M. Dershowitz (12 September 2002), www.salon.com ("I want," "never acceptable"); Alan M. Dershowitz, "Alle lieben tote Juden. . ." (interview), *Die Welt* (15 June 2002) ("civil liberties"); Alan M. Dershowitz, *The Case for Israel* (Hoboken, N.J., 2003), pp. 166–72 ("home destruction" at p. 171), 173–75 ("targeted assassination" at p. 174), 231–32 ("great moral issue," "rule of law"); Alan M. Dershowitz, "Defending against Terrorism within the Rule of Law," at Herzliya Conference, Israel (18 December 2003), www.herzliyaconference.org ("human rights law and rhetoric," "Israelis are obliged"); Dan Izenberg, "Dershowitz: Speak up about Israel's positive points, too," *Jerusalem Post* (22 December 2003) ("archaic"); Alan M. Dershowitz, "Rules of War Enable Terror," *Baltimore Sun* (28 May 2004) (Geneva Convention).

Wolffsohn, as well as the main spokesman for German Jews, alleged that he was the victim of anti-Semitism. In a full page statement published in Germany's most influential newspaper and entitled "J'accuse!" Wolffsohn, invoking memory of The Holocaust and his own imagined persecution ("Members of the Federal government have thrown one of their citizens, and a Jew at that, to the wolves"), proclaimed that Theodor Herzl was right—Jews weren't safe anywhere except in a state of their own—and that whereas the main lesson of The Holocaust for Germans was "never again to be a perpetrator," the main lesson for Jews is "never again to be a victim," which for Jews signifies that any means is legitimate in the name of self-defense. Leaving aside that Zola's original "J'accuse . . . !" was in defense of a Jew *innocent* of the charges leveled against him, it's hard not to savor—or not to be revolted by—the ironies of this episode: a Jewish professor at a German war college defending the use of torture is publicly reprimanded, after which the Jewish professor, wrapping himself in the mantle of The Holocaust, accuses of anti-Semitism those Germans deploring his advocacy of torture and, explicating the lessons of The Holocaust, declares that while The Holocaust forbids Germans (and everyone else) from being perpetrators, it entitles Jews to do as they please.[24]

Things are scarcely better elsewhere. In Canada the chairman of the B'nai Brith Institute for International Affairs, acknowledging that Israel resorts to terror tactics against Palestinians, maintained they were "acceptable": "[T]error is an option to be used by states in order to prevent deaths. . . . Acts that take place in Gaza and the West Bank, you might want to classify them as terrorists sponsored by the state. But when that is being done to prevent deaths, are we going to say that that is wrong?"[25] Meanwhile, in France, an October 2004 report solicited

24. Wolffsohn's original statements approving torture were made on the N-TV program *Maischberger* (5 May 2004) (full text can be found at www.wolffsohn.de/MW/Artikel_uber_MW/Interview/interview.html). For reference to Dershowitz, see Wolffsohn's press release (19 May 2004) at www.wolffsohn.de/MW/Artikel_uber_MW/Presseerklarung/presseerklarung.html ("Presseerklärung zu meiner angeblichen Befürwortung von Foltermassnahmen"); for the German Ministry of Defense's rebuke, see "Erklärung des Sprechers des Verteidigungsministeriums" (Berlin, 18 May 2004); for a German-Jewish leader supporting Wolffsohn's charge of anti-Semitism, see Margarete Limberg, "'Hochgeachteter Politiker, geschätzter Mensch und geliebter Freund'—Paul Spiegel über den scheidenden Bundespräsidenten Johannes Rau," *Deutschlandfunk* (23 May 2004); for Wolffsohn's "J'accuse!" see *Frankfurter Allgemeine Zeitung* (25 June 2004).
25. He made these remarks on the *Michael Coren Show* on 19 October 2004. After a hailstorm of criticism, he submitted his resignation (Marina Jimenez, "B'nai Brith official quits after terrorism remark," *Globe and Mail* [3 November 2004]).

by the Interior Ministry and getting wide media play contrived a bizarre new category: "anti-Semitism by proxy" (*l'antisémitisme par procuration*). It defined proxy anti-Semites as those who haven't themselves committed, or directly manipulated or openly incited anyone to commit, an anti-Semitic act, but whose "opinions, words or sometimes simply silence lend support to such violence." The main perpetrators of such "mute" anti-Semitism are alleged to be "radical anti-Zionists" who denounce "the policy of Sharon" while favoring "dissident Jewish voices" and who believe Palestinian refugees have a "right to return" to their homes. This is a direct throwback to the darkest days of Stalinism, when those criticizing the Soviet regime were, by virtue of this fact alone, branded "objective" abettors of fascism, and dealt with accordingly. Indeed, in a truly terrifying passage, the report recommends *criminalizing* any "accusations" of "racism" or "apartheid" against Israel as well as "comparisons" thereof: "In the situation that we currently find ourselves in, they have major consequences which can, by contagion, endanger the lives of our Jewish citizens. It is legitimate to legally ensure that they won't be thrown around lightly." Apart from punitive sanctions, the report recommends more Holocaust education, in particular, emphasizing the "singular, universal and unique" character of The Holocaust. One day it's the uniqueness and universality of theological absolutism; the next day it's the uniqueness and universality of Marxism-Leninism; now it's the uniqueness and universality of The Holocaust. The one constant is the totalitarian cast of mind, and attendant stigmatizing of dissent as a disease that must be wiped out by the state.[26]

To combat the new anti-Semitism, Chesler declares, "We Must Fight the Big Lies" and "[e]ducate" the "ever-increasing crowd of naïve and misinformed students." Most of *The New Anti-Semitism* is devoted to refuting these "Big Lies." For example, Jews can justly lay "claim to the land of Israel," she asserts, because they "prayed to and for Jerusalem and Israel three times a day" while in exile. Does this mean that if Native Americans, in exile not from two thousand but a mere two hundred years ago, "prayed to and for" Chesler's home, she would forfeit title to it? In addition, "God promised the land to the patriarch Abraham and to all the other Jewish patriarchs and matriarchs." Lest there be doubts, she appends an endnote to prove this. "[M]any Palestinians

---

26. Jean-Christophe Rufin, *Chantier sur la lutte contre le racisme et l'antisémitisme* (19 October 2004).

(they, their parents, and their grandparents, too)," according to Chesler, "were actually born in Jordan, Egypt, Lebanon, and Syria." Never mind that all serious scholars dismiss this Zionist fairy tale. She reports that Hamas was launching terrorist attacks even prior to Israel's occupation of the West Bank and Gaza in 1967. Never mind that Hamas wasn't founded until the late 1980s. The Israeli army, according to Chesler, is "one of the most civilized . . . in the world." Never mind that the former head of Israel's secret police, Avraham Shalom, publicly lamented, with respect to Israeli conduct in the Occupied Territories, that "we are behaving disgracefully. Yes, there is no other word for it. Disgracefully." Israeli soldiers "have not targeted Palestinian women and children," she states, and "the majority of Palestinians who have been killed in the last three years have been armed (male) soldiers and (male) suicide bombers." Never mind the reports of respected human rights organizations copiously documenting that Israeli soldiers routinely and with impunity resort to "excessive," "disproportionate," "indiscriminate," "reckless," as well as "deliberately targeted" firepower against Palestinians posing no danger to them, "leading to many casualties," a "large proportion" of whom are children; and that the "vast majority" of Palestinians killed during the second intifada "have been unarmed civilians and bystanders." Chesler goes on to assert that, during Operation Defensive Shield in the spring of 2002, climaxing in the siege of Jenin refugee camp, Israeli soldiers neither targeted ambulances and medical personnel nor looted Palestinian property; that it was Palestinian terrorists (not Israelis) who used Palestinian civilians as human shields; and that no Israeli tank deliberately ran over a wheelchair-bound Palestinian. Never mind that, on each one of these claims, human rights organizations uniformly found contrariwise. Israel is not an "apartheid state," Chesler insists. Never mind not only that the apartheid analogy is a commonplace in Israeli political discourse but that Chesler herself cites a "most excellent colleague" from Israel stating that "We are becoming like South Africa." "What's *new* about the new anti-Semitism," according to Chesler, "is that for the first time it is being perpetrated in the name of anti-racism, anti-imperialism, and anti-colonialism" (her emphasis). Never mind that, in the same breath, she castigates the United Nations resolution from *three decades ago* that equated Zionism with "racism," "imperialist ideology," and "apartheid." She assails Noam Chomsky on the grounds that the quotations he cites from Israeli sources "do not sound right or in context to me." Case closed.[27] Lastly, Chesler silences any lingering doubts on the Arab refugee question by recalling that "[m]ore Jewish Arabs fled from Arab lands such as . . . *India*"; silences any lingering doubts on Israel's commitment to democracy by rhetorically asking, "If Israel is a racist apartheid country, why did it absorb dark- and olive-skinned Arab Jews from *India*?"; and silences any lingering doubts about her own support of Arab rights by lauding the "bravery" of "Arab and Muslim intellectuals, artists, and political dissidents" like "Aung San Suu Kyi"—who happens to be the *Buddhist* Nobel laureate from *Buddhist* Burma. Before embarking on the prodigious labors of this tome—judging from the acknowledgments, her every body part cried out in Christlike agony—shouldn't Chesler first have consulted the idiot's guide to the Middle East?[28]

Other treatises on the new anti-Semitism allege the same "Big Lies" about Israel. In a *New York* magazine cover story, Craig Horowitz decries the "grotesquely distorted" language like *apartheid* used to depict Israeli policy, as well as the "outrageous, flamboyantly anti-Israel behavior of the United Nations." For example, he points to the U.N.'s recent condemnation of Israel merely "for building a fence to keep out suicide bombers"—although eventually it might also keep *in* Israel as much as half of the West Bank. Pondering Daniel Pearl's murder on Salon.com, Columbia University journalism professor Samuel G. Freedman refers to the "dogma" of Pearl's captors that the United States has given Israel "unconditional support"—where could they have gotten such a bizarre notion?—and refers to scenes of Palestinian children killed by Israelis as "supposed" victims. Holocaust historian

27. Chesler, *New Anti-Semitism*, pp. 51 and 53 (U.N. and Zionism), 87 ("what's new"), 97 ("Israeli tanks"), 98 ("one of the most civilized," "not targeted," "majority of Palestinians who have been killed," "do not confiscate property"), 151 (Chomsky), 153 ("attacking ambulances"), 170 ("confiscate property," "majority of the Palestinians who have been killed"), 181–82 ("excellent colleague"), 199 ("actually born"), 216 ("[e]ducate," "We Must Fight"), 217 ("apartheid state"), 226 (U.N. resolution), 227 ("What's *new*"), 237 ("prayed," "God promised"), 241 ("Hamas"), 244 ("human shields"), 245 ("naïve and misinformed," "apartheid"), 249. For Zionist demographic myths regarding the Arab population of Palestine, see Finkelstein, *Image and Reality*, chap. 2; for the Shalom quote, see Alex Fishman and Sima Kadmon, "We Are Seriously Concerned about the Fate of the State of Israel," *Yediot Ahronot* (14 November 2003); for the findings of human rights organizations regarding Israeli human rights violations in the Occupied Territories generally and during Operation Defensive Shield in particular, see Part II of this book.

28. Chesler, *New Anti-Semitism*, pp. 113 ("India"—my emphasis), 174 ("Aung San Suu Kyi"), 228 ("India"—my emphasis).

Omer Bartov bewails in *The New Republic* "poisonous rhetoric" that
"portray[s] the Israeli operation in Jenin" as a "war crime"—although
that's exactly how Amnesty International and Human Rights Watch
portrayed it; and "rhetoric" that proclaims that "Zionism Is Ethnic
Cleansing"—although that's exactly what Zionism was in 1948,
according to many of Israel's leading historians. Tom Gross, a highly
touted British monitor of media anti-Semitism, likewise heaps scorn on
the "tales" of Israeli war crimes in Jenin. Claiming both to have read
the human rights reports on Jenin and to base his media criticism on
them, he asserts that Israeli destruction was limited to "one small area
of the camp"—although Amnesty and HRW both reported that four
thousand people, or more than a quarter of the camp population, were
rendered homeless by Israeli destruction, most of which was inflicted
after the fighting had already ceased. Singing the praises of the "good
and moral forces that operated in Jenin" and "our combat ethics,"
David Zangen, an IDF medical officer who served in Jenin, avows, in
testimony that Rosenbaum found "so fascinating," that "[a]t no stage
was medical care withheld from anyone"—although both Amnesty and
HRW found overwhelming evidence that Israel blocked medical and
humanitarian aid to the camp for over ten days. Meanwhile, *New
Republic* editor in chief Martin Peretz, who previously acclaimed Joan
Peters's *From Time Immemorial* as flawless scholarship destined to
"change the mind of our generation . . . and the history of the future,"
rages against "hysterical, Israel-hating lies" such as that Israelis
"destroyed homes in Jenin just for the hell of it." Except that an Israeli
bulldozer operator in Jenin afterward boasted for an Israeli newspaper:
"I wanted to destroy everything. I begged the officers . . . to let me
knock it all down: from top to bottom. . . . For three days, I just
destroyed and destroyed. . . . I found joy with every house that came
down. . . . If I am sorry for anything, it is for not tearing the whole
camp down. . . . I had plenty of satisfaction. I really enjoyed it." (After
publication of this article, the IDF awarded the bulldozer operator a
citation for outstanding service.) Schoenfeld denounces a Hizbollah
leader's "anti-Semitic" depiction of the 1948 Arab-Israeli war, according to which Israelis committed "massacres, . . . destroyed houses,
wiped out entire villages, and founded a state of their own on land
stolen through acts of slaughter, terrorism, violence, and cruelty"—
although that's exactly what Israeli historians like Benny Morris have
documented. Cynthia Ozick denounces the Hitlerian "Big Lie" that
Israel "violates international law" and the "hallucinatory notion" that

Israel colonizes the Occupied Territories and victimizes Palestinians. It's hard not to admire the mental discipline that can completely shut out reality. Media mogul Mortimer Zuckerman, in a cover story for *U.S. News & World Report,* sets straight the historical record regarding Israel. Besides deploring the fact that Israel is being accused of "ethnic cleansing and apartheid," he recycles hoary Zionist myths such as that "when the Jews arrived, Palestine was a sparsely populated, poorly cultivated, and wildly neglected land of sandy deserts and malarial marshes"; that there's "nothing to suggest that the flight of the Palestinians was not voluntary" in 1948, and that "[i]n fact, those who fled were urged to do so by other Arabs"; that "news reports, and even Palestinian testimony and writings . . . established the fact that groups like Fatah, Hamas, and Islamic Jihad used women and children as shields during the fighting" in Jenin and that "the Israelis exercised great restraint during the battle"; and on and on. Zuckerman even conjures up the laughable claim that the "Fourth Geneva Convention, drafted originally in response to the atrocities of the Nazi regime," was designed "to protect people like diplomats and visitors subjected to a military occupation," and apparently not civilian populations. Leaving to one side that the formal title of this convention is *Fourth Geneva Convention Relative to the Protection of Civilian Persons in Time of War* and that Article 4 makes explicit that its prime concern is indigenous populations, let's just consider Zuckerman's logic: that, in light of the massive Nazi atrocities committed against civilian populations during World War II, legislators convened at Geneva in 1949 to draft protections for the likes of "diplomats and visitors."[29]

29. Craig Horowitz, "The Return of Anti-Semitism," *New York* (15 December 2003); Omer Bartov, "Did Hitlerism Die with Hitler?" *New Republic* (2 February 2004); Schoenfeld, *Return,* pp. 23, 146; Zuckerman, "The New Anti-Semitism." Rosenbaum, "Introduction," p. xxiii ("fascinating"); Samuel G. Freedman, "Don't Look Away," p. 130; Tom Gross, "Jeningrad: What the British Media Said," p. 138 ("one small area"); Dr. David Zangen, "Seven Lies about Jenin," p. 149; Tom Gross, "The Massacre That Never Was," p. 152 ("tales"); Martin Peretz, "The Poet and the Murderer," p. 421; Cynthia Ozick, "Afterword," pp. 603, 613, in Rosenbaum, *Those Who Forget.* For the findings and conclusions of Amnesty and HRW regarding Jenin, see Part II of this book; for Israeli scholars concluding that Israel engaged in "ethnic cleansing" in 1948, see the various publications of Baruch Kimmerling, Ilan Pappe, and Benny Morris (Morris calls it a "partial ethnic cleansing"); for Peretz and Peters, see Finkelstein, *Image and Reality,* p. 22; for testimony of Israeli operator, see Tsadok Yeheskeli, "I made them a stadium in the middle of the camp," *Yediot Ahronot* (31 May 2002), and for IDF citation, see Human Rights Watch, *Razing Rafah: Mass Home Demolitions in the Gaza Strip* (New York, October 2004), p. 34; for the Zionist mythology recycled by Zuckerman, see Finkelstein, *Image and Reality,* passim. Bartov, Gross, and their ilk deride the media for depicting what happened in Jenin as a "massacre." Yet, as Amnesty observes in its report on Jenin,

If combating the new anti-Semitism means exposing the "Big Lies" about Israel, it also entails exposing the mainstream media, which are said to be the main purveyors of these lies. The EUMC's *Manifestations* report repeatedly alleges the anti-Semitic undercurrent of European news coverage of the Israel-Palestine conflict, pointing, for example, to "left-liberal papers" like the British *Guardian* and *Independent*, which are so "spiced with a tone of animosity, 'as to smell of anti-Semitism.'" Getting down to specifics, the study points to the depiction of "Palestinians as a people allegedly oppressed by a so-called imperialist Israeli state" as typical of the anti-Semitic "[p]artisanship" of the "left-oriented media." Leaving aside the audacious insertion of the qualifier "allegedly," how often is Israel characterized as "imperialist" in the liberal European media? The anti-Semitic bias of the German "quality press" is revealed in the fact that "reporting concentrated greatly on the violent events and the conflicts." To demonstrate scientifically the anti-Semitic bias of European reportage, the study highlights poll data showing that "those Europeans who followed media coverage of the events in the Middle East the closest were more likely to be sympathetic to the Palestinian case." That they might be more sympathetic because they are better informed is a conclusion too ridiculous—not to mention anti-Semitic—to entertain. Even if the content of coverage is not itself anti-Semitic, "[t]he intensive and consonant focus on events . . . has a clear effect on the climate of opinion." Thus, if the reality of the Israel-Palestine conflict evokes hostility to Israel, shining a too bright light on it is "objectively" anti-Semitic, even if the coverage is accurate.[30] As already noted, the notion of a pro-Palestinian bias in the Western media is sheer fantasy.

A related concern of those combating the new anti-Semitism is the Internet—an understandable worry, since it is not (yet) controlled by the likes of those who could be counted on for responsible, balanced coverage of the Middle East such as Izzy Asper, Silvio Berlusconi, Conrad Black, Rupert Murdoch, and Mortimer Zuckerman. Having plainly

---

it was primarily due to the massiveness of Israel's missile assault, its denial of media access, and its own military briefings of "hundreds killed" that rumors of a massacre spread; see also Philo and Berry, *Bad News*, pp. 192–99, refuting allegations that British media uncritically reported a "massacre" at Jenin.

30. *Manifestations*, pp. 7, 8 ("those Europeans"), 27 ("violent events"), 28 ("intensive and consonant"), 34 ("allegedly oppressed"), 97 ("smell," quoting *The Economist*), 98.

learned the lessons of totalitarianism and the importance of unfettered speech, the authors of *Manifestations* recommend that "private and state organisations should exert continuing pressure on large Internet providers to remove racist and anti-Semitic content from the net"; that "it is essential to extend the jurisdiction of European courts to include detailed provisions on the responsibility of Internet service providers"; that "a particularly intensive monitoring is required, one which in the first instance must be undertaken by state authorities"; and that "cases of police prosecution and information from state security authorities" should be publicized. To judge by their definition, if every Internet user guilty of "anti-Semitism" is to be prosecuted, they should also be calling for mass internment camps.[31]

Returning to this side of the Atlantic, Foxman also waxes ominous on the "dark underbelly" of the Internet, "where the virus of anti-Semitism is ready to be spread." Although he professes opposition to government censorship, one must take with a shaker of salt his avowal that "[t]he best antidote to hate speech, I've always maintained, is more speech." In the very same pages he boasts that "ADL has worked closely with several major Internet companies to establish and enforce clear guidelines regulating what is acceptable and unacceptable on their sites," and laments the fact that "some Internet service providers have been less willing to establish firm policies against hate speech." He cites as an egregious offender Earthlink's "acceptable use policy," which "supports the free flow of information and ideas over the Internet" and allows for the distribution of "Hitler's *Mein Kampf* and more than two dozen of Hitler's speeches. It's not illegal activity, but the message is clearly hateful." Beyond the fact that Hitler's *Mein Kampf* and speeches are primary historical sources and clearly *ought* to be studied if we are to learn from the past, it bears keeping in mind Foxman's definition of *hateful*. For example, this staunch advocate of "more speech" sought, unsuccessfully, to block publication of a study coauthored by this writer that criticized Daniel Goldhagen's *Hitler's Willing Executioners.* Although the study was strongly endorsed by a dozen eminent historians of the Nazi holocaust (including Raul Hilberg, Christopher Browning, and Ian Kershaw), Foxman protested its publication on the grounds that "[Finkelstein's] anti-Zionist stance . . . goes beyond the

31. *Manifestations*, pp. 13 ("private and state"), 31 ("European courts," "intensive," "cases"), 34–35.

pale." ADL has now "developed software . . . to block access to Internet sites that ADL believes promote hate." Columbia University professor Simon Schama conjures up harrowing accounts of an Internet replete with ghastly Nazi websites, only to then slip in that, worldwide, "estimates of regular visitors and inhabitants of these kinds of sites . . . may amount to no more than maybe 50,000 or 100,000 at most"—that is, the capacity of one ballpark. He juxtaposes the contents of these scurrilous websites against the "critical historically informed" publications of ADL. This judgment of ADL scholarship is of a piece with Schama's past cheerleading for Goldhagen's *Hitler's Willing Executioners* as an "astonishing . . . and riveting book, the fruit of phenomenal scholarship and absolute integrity," which "will permanently change the debate on the Holocaust." Dean of Nazi holocaust scholars Raul Hilberg immediately pronounced Goldhagen's book "worthless." It's not too soon to reckon who was right. Totally ignored in current scholarly debate, except as an object of derision, Goldhagen's book had a shelf life roughly equal to that of the Cabbage Patch doll.[32]

Another important method to combat the new anti-Semitism, according to *Manifestations*, is to "foster Holocaust education, remembrance and research" and "apply the lessons of the past to contemporary issues of prejudice, racism and moral decision-making." There's one crucial caveat, however: one can't learn any lessons from the Nazi holocaust applicable to Israel, for "allusions to or comparisons [of]

---

32. Foxman, *Never Again?* pp. 255–56 ("dark," "virus"), 264, 268 ("guidelines," "Earthlink"), 269–70 ("antidote," "software"). For Foxman's intercession to ban publication of this writer's book, *A Nation on Trial* (coauthored with Ruth Bettina Birn), as well as Hilberg's assessment, see Finkelstein, *Holocaust Industry*, pp. 65–67. Simon Schama, "Virtual Annihilation," in Rosenbaum, *Those Who Forget*, pp. 361 ("critical"), 363 ("estimates"). Schama's praise for Goldhagen was featured as the lead blurb on the book jacket. For further tantrums regarding the Internet, see also Harold Evans, "The View from Ground Zero," in Rosenbaum, *Those Who Forget*, pp. 39–56. To demonstrate the biases of Arab media like Al-Jazeera as against the "ruggedly independent self-critical free press" in the West, Evans cites these examples: "At the start of the Afghan campaign, [Al-Jazeera] gave twice as much air-time to Bin Laden and his supporters as the coalition"—unlike Western media, which naturally gave equal time to both; and "[a]n Arab critic of America and the coalition is always given the last word"—unlike Western media, which never give America and the coalition the last word. To prove the "Muslim world's relentless caricatures of the Jew," Evans points to fabrications like "Israeli authorities infected by injection 300 Palestinian children with HIV virus during the years of the intifada"—as against Israel apologist Alan Dershowitz, who claims falsely that Palestinian suicide bombers purposely infect Israelis with AIDS and rat poison, more on which in Part II.

Israel's actions with the behaviour of the Nazi regime have to be viewed as anti-Semitic." Does this caveat mean that those Israeli Jews drawing "allusions to and comparisons" with the Nazi regime must be viewed as anti-Semitic? Sweden gets slaps on the wrist because "Israeli politics has been compared with Nazi politics on a few occasions," while in Germany "[l]eading representatives of the Jewish community continuously expressed their view" that "allusions to or comparisons with the behaviour of the Nazi regime would be unacceptable and unjustified." However, German Jewish leaders comparing Saddam (or whoever happens to be on the U.S.-Israeli "hit list") to Hitler, and those opposing the United States' criminal aggression to appeasers of Nazism, was not only acceptable and justified but the essence of Holocaust education. And of course it's acceptable and justified—one might even say de rigueur—to compare Palestinians and their leaders to Nazis. Although urging that "[o]ne must be cautious in drawing parallels," Schoenfeld nonetheless professes not only that "[t]he parallels between Nazism and the current Arab-Muslim brand of anti-Semitism" are "striking," and not only that the fate of Israelis at the hands of Palestinians resembles "Auschwitz," but that, if anything, the Palestinians are yet *more* morally depraved than the Nazis: "If there is a difference (aside from capability) between the Nazis and the Palestinians, it is that the former kept their murderous intentions a tightly wrapped secret," whereas "the Palestinians trumpet their murderous intentions." In addition, the fact that "The Holocaust . . . is being universalized" and "enlisted in the service of a variety of contemporary causes" smacks, according to him, of anti-Semitism—so much for "learning the lessons of The Holocaust"—while yet more perverse, in his view, are those who "twist the very concept of racial prejudice in such a way as to suggest that Jews, having once been its victims, now merit the world's censure as its perpetrators." The one and only lesson of The Holocaust is its "specifically Jewish tragedy."[33] Beyond all else, such restrictions make clear that "Holocaust education" and the concomitant slogan "Never Again" are being used as ideological weapons to defend Jewish interests.

In their common loathing of Western freedoms, there is a clear "line of continuity" not only between Hitler and Islamic fundamentalists,

33. *Manifestations*, pp. 12 ("foster"), 17 ("Israel's actions"), 33 ("apply"), 47 (Germany), 93 (Sweden). Schoenfeld, *Return*, pp. 46 ("parallels"), 72 ("cautious"), 96–97 ("universalized").

according to Robert Wistrich of the Hebrew University in Jerusalem, but between these Nazi-like fundamentalists and "anti-globalist leftists" as well. And, in their mutual hatred of Jews and Israel, "Yasir Arafat, the Fatah Al-Aqsa Brigades," as well as "millions of Sunni and Shi'a Muslims, conservative Wahhabi Saudis, Iranian Ayatollahs, Al-Qaeda, Hizballah, Hamas, the Muslim Brotherhood, Islamic Jihad, and many secular Arab nationalists, despite the many differences among these groups," according to Wistrich, "display many parallels with Nazism." For there to be peace in the Middle East "and a genuine 'dialogue of civilizations,'" Wistrich concludes, these modern-day Nazis must suffer the same "comprehensive and decisive defeat" as Hitler did. Echoing Schoenfeld and Wistrich, Ruth Wisse of Harvard asserts that, compared to Nazi anti-Semitism, "the Arab variety is worse." Germans concealed their genocidal war "under cover of a wider European conflict," she explains, whereas for the "Arab nations, through the PLO," this destruction is "explicitly at the heart of their mission"; indeed, they openly boast about their murderous intentions. Wisse warns that "the West paid dearly for ignoring Hitler's war against the Jews," and "[o]ne can only hope it will not pay as dearly for having ignored or underestimated for so long the Arab war against Israel and the Jews." It merits notice that these selfsame guardians of Holocaust memory normally blanch at *any* comparisons with Nazis. "Do not compare" we're always told—except if comparison is being made with Israel's ideological enemies or those critical of its policy, which currently means most of the world. And in conflating Palestinians with Nazis, thereby dignifying the Nazis with the real, rational grievances of the Palestinians, don't these Holocaust-mongers come close to justifying, if not the Final Solution, at any rate Nazi hatred of Jews? It also bears emphasizing that the taboo on "allusions to or comparisons [of] Israel's actions with the behaviour of the Nazi regime" applies to literally *any* reference, however remote. France's leading Holocaust-monger, Alain Finkielkraut, deplores the use of terms like *roundups, internment camps,* and *watchtowers* in depictions of Israeli army actions because they "imply a comparison with Nazism." So should we say, "After an early morning get-together, Israel repositioned scores of Palestinian males on a campground surrounded by upended rectangular edifices with spotlights"?[34]

---

34. Wistrich, "The Old-New Anti-Semitism," in Rosenbaum, *Those Who Forget,* pp. 86–88; Wisse, "On Ignoring Anti-Semitism," in ibid., pp. 191–92, 207; Alain Finkielkraut, "Une croix gammée à la place de l'étoile," *L'Arche* (May–June 2002). Sur-

Finally, the best way to combat the new anti-Semitism is, unsurprisingly, to support Israel. In the climactic chapter of her book, "What We Must Do," Chesler exhorts "[e]ach Jew" to "find a way to support Israel." In its country-by-country breakdown of "[g]ood practices for reducing prejudice, violence and aggression," *Manifestations* lists these exemplary actions: *Greece*—"There was . . . an excellent treatment of Zionism as the quest for national identity and a state by . . . journalists"; *Spain*—"the Evangelical Church and the Institute for Judeo-Christian Studies in Madrid together with the Jewish communities of Madrid and Barcelona organised a demonstration of support for Israel"; *Italy*—"There are . . . websites created for the specific purpose of countering the wave of misunderstanding and of responding to media attacks against Israel"; *Finland*—"Some speakers have come from Israel to give lectures about the situation in Israel. There was also one pro-Israel demonstration."[35]

Recent events demonstrate just how little the new anti-Semitism has to do with anti-Semitism and just how much it has to do with Israel, as well as how the new anti-Semitism actually signals the open alignment of Israel and its supporters with the far right. Just after Italian prime minister Silvio Berlusconi publicly whitewashed Mussolini's Fascist regime, which had enacted anti-Semitic racial laws and in its last phase deported thousands of Jews to their death in Nazi concentration camps, ADL conferred on him its Distinguished Statesman Award. "This man is the only clear voice [of] support and understanding of Israel [in Europe]," Foxman explained, and "[h]e has spoken out that anti-Zionism is anti-Semitism." Not grasping that blanket support for Israeli crimes takes moral precedence, three Jewish Nobel laureates in economics—Franco Modigliani, Paul A. Samuelson, and Robert M. Solow—protested that the award was "bad for the Jews, bad for Italy,

veying "Muslim Anti-Semitism," Bernard Lewis, in Rosenbaum, *Those Who Forget*, pp. 549–62, points up the Arab world's depicting of "Jews as Nazis"—although his own books propagandistically tar Palestinians and Arabs with Nazism; its "rewriting" of history, which "makes Jews disappear from the ancient Middle East"—although he refused to dissociate himself from Joan Peters's hoax, which made Palestinians disappear from the modern Middle East; and its "Holocaust denial" and welcoming of such Holocaust deniers as Roger Garaudy—although he is the leading academic denier of the Armenian holocaust and, although he's careful not to mention it when rehearsing Garaudy's indictment for Holocaust denial in France, Lewis himself was indicted and convicted by a French court for denying the Armenian holocaust. On these points, see Finkelstein, *Image and Reality*, p. 48, and Finkelstein, *Holocaust Industry*, pp. 62–63, 69.

35. Chesler, *New Anti-Semitism*, p. 209; *Manifestations*, pp. 59 (Greece), 62 (Spain), 76 (Italy), 92 (Finland).

bad for the United States and even bad for Israel."[36] Soon thereafter, Israeli government officials welcomed "with pomp and ceremony" Gianfranco Fini, leader of Italy's neo-Fascist National Alliance party. Fini, who had previously acclaimed Mussolini as "the greatest politician of the 20th century," got the invitation, according to Israeli sources, because "Jerusalem looks favorably upon Fini's unwavering support of Sharon's policies" and, in particular, on account of Fini's speech "at a meeting of the B'nai Brith [parent organization of ADL] in Milan in favor of the separation fence." Unimpressed, Yossi Sarid of Israel's Meretz party called Fini a "Fascist creep," while former Israeli justice minister Yossi Beilin deplored the visit as a "disgrace to Israel."[37] To judge by Schoenfeld's account, across Europe the "far right," far from posing a mortal danger to Jews, comprises an important potential ally: "[Austria's Jörg] Haider, in particular, has made a point of stressing the importance of friendship between Austria and the state of Israel, and has made a visit to the Holocaust Memorial Museum in Washington, D.C. [France's Jean-Marie] Le Pen, for his part, has suggested that French Jews make common cause with him in containing the troubles unleashed by the Arab influx." Indeed, it is a striking fact that many of those Jews sounding alarms about the new anti-Semitism also sound alarms about the growing Arab presence in Europe.[38] In the case of California governor Arnold Schwarzenegger an additional dynamic was at play. Although Schwarzenegger had previously praised Adolf Hitler as well as former Austrian president Kurt Waldheim, his "staunchest defender" during the gubernatorial race was the Simon Wiesenthal Center, main branch of the Israel lobby on the West Coast. Apart from singing Israel's praises, Schwarzenegger took the extra precaution of, as it were, purchasing an indulgence: according to the associate dean of the Los Angeles–based operation, "Schwarzenegger is Hollywood's largest contributor to the Wiesenthal Center." Soon after taking office, Schwarzenegger announced that he

36. Eric J. Greenberg, "Standing behind Berlusconi," *Jewish Week* (19 September 2003) ("spoken out"); "A Shocking Award to Berlusconi" (letter), *New York Times* (23 September 2003) (Nobel laureates); Nathaniel Popper, "ADL Dinner for Berlusconi Causes a Stir," *Forward* (26 September 2003) ("clear voice").

37. Amiram Barkat, "Fini condemns his country's 'disgraceful past,'" *Haaretz* (24 November 2003) ("pomp," "unwavering support," "B'nai Brith," "greatest politician," "disgrace"); "On visit to Israel, Italian official denounces country's Fascist past," *International Herald Tribune* (25 November 2003) ("creep").

38. Schoenfeld, *Return*, p. 78. For French-Jewish support of Le Pen, "a matter of concern for the leaders of the Jewish community," according to a former president of the

was journeying to Israel for the ground breaking of a new $200 million Wiesenthal Center museum in Jerusalem. Rabbi Marvin Hier, head of the Los Angeles Wiesenthal Center, hailed the upcoming trip as "a statement of solidarity with the state of Israel." Not exactly. It's more likely a statement that Schwarzenegger will be seeking a second term of office.[39]

Just as Israel profited from the U.S. war against terrorism, so the United States profited from the new anti-Semitism, Israel's apologists tarring critics of U.S. policy with the "anti-Semitic" slur. And just as the Clinton administration promoted the Holocaust reparations scam to get Jewish money and Jewish votes, so the Bush administration undoubtedly supported the new anti-Semitism scam with the same calculations in mind. Working together, the Bush administration and Israel and its lobby foisted the new anti-Semitism on the international agenda. In April 2004 the Organization for Security and Cooperation in Europe (OSCE) was forced to convene a special conference in Berlin devoted to the new anti-Semitism. Secretary of State Colin Powell represented the U.S. government, while, before an audience numbering nearly a thousand, Elie Wiesel, who flew in with Powell aboard a U.S. Air Force jet, made crystal clear, notwithstanding his usual vacuous homilies, what this gathering was really about: "There are too many cities in the world plagued by vocal and violent hatred towards the Jewish people . . . extreme left-wing banners unashamedly slandering Israel . . . mass incitement to hysterical violence disguised as anti-Israeli propaganda . . . anyone expressing solidarity with victims of terrorism in Israel being scandalously branded as anti-Arab." At the conference Wiesel justified his failure to speak out on behalf of Palestinians on the ground that "I cannot associate myself with people who educate their children to wear explosives and kill"—as if this apologist for Israeli breaches of international law supported Palestinian rights before the suicide bombings.[40]

Representative Council of the Jewish Organizations of France (CRIF), see Adar Primor, "Le Pen will fight anti-Semitism, says his Jewish running mate," *Haaretz* (19 March 2004). See, e.g., Schoenfeld, "Israel and the Anti-Semites" (p. 102), and Wisse, "On Ignoring Anti-Semitism" (p. 192), in Rosenbaum, *Those Who Forget*, as well as Edgar Bronfman's comments in *Der Spiegel* ("'Es ist etwas faul'" [12 January 2004]), for anxieties about Europe's growing Arab population.

39. "Schwarzenegger Taps Wiesenthal Rabbi," *Forward* (17 October 2003); "Schwarzenegger to Visit Israel" (29 April 2004), www.CNN.com.

40. For the text of Wiesel's speech, as well as other documents from the 28–29 April 2004 Conference on Anti-Semitism, see www.osce.org/events/conferences/ antisemitism2004/; for Wiesel's remarks on Palestinians, see Tovah Lazaroff, "Wiesel:

In June 2004 the new anti-Semitism circus pitched its big tent at the United Nations, the ubiquitous Wiesel once again in the center ring. Wiesel professed bewilderment that "60 years after the worst tragedy in human history," and although he had been "convinced that anti-Semitism had died in Auschwitz," Jew-hatred was once again on the rise. In his OSCE speech, Wiesel similarly lamented that after the war he "naively thought that, for years and years to come, whenever a Jew would be seen anywhere in Europe, he or she would be carried on people's shoulders and enveloped by everyone." "Had any pessimist told me then, that in my lifetime," Jews would yet again come under attack, he continued, "I would not have believed it. But it now has become reality." Poor Elie is shocked—shocked!—by the sudden reemergence of anti-Semitism after a sixty-year respite. Indeed, consider these statements of his: "Had anyone told us, when we were liberated, that we would be compelled in our lifetime to fight anti-Semitism once more . . . we would have had no strength to lift our eyes from the ruins." And again: "What makes anti-Semitism so popular that once more our people has to be exposed to this disease of mankind? Once more in our lifetime anti-Semitism is a threat. All over the world a concentrated effort is being made once again to isolate the Jews. Israel has never been so alone. And you cannot separate the State of Israel from the people of Israel. . . . Therefore the new anti-Semitism in Europe and in the U.S. is of grave concern to all Jews." The one tiny problem with Wiesel's current shock is that the two monologues just quoted come from his 1981 performance of the new anti-Semitism, the second from an April 1981 speech entitled "The New Anti-Semitism." In his U.N. speech Wiesel called anti-Semitism "the oldest collective bigotry in recorded history," as well as one that uniquely combined all other forms of bigotry. Everything about Jews is unique: anti-Semitism, the Holocaust, Israel, Jewish nationhood and peoplehood . . . Beyond its repellent chauvinism, this intellectually hollow doctrine of uniqueness serves the useful ideological function of allowing Israel to claim unique moral dispensation: if Jewish suffering was unique, then Israel shouldn't be bound by normal moral standards.[41]

Talk anti-Semitism with Muslims," *Jerusalem Post* (online edition) (28 April 2004); for Wiesel's gross apologetics on behalf of Israel and the United States, see Finkelstein, *Holocaust Industry*, passim, and Finkelstein, *Image and Reality*, pp. xxv, 48.

41. For a record of the U.N. proceedings, see "'Jews Everywhere Must Feel That the United Nations Is Their Home, Too,' Secretary-General Tells Seminar on Anti-Semitism"

U.N. secretary-general Kofi Annan, no doubt calculating that he could score a few easy points with his patrons in Washington, played along with the charade. "Sixty years later, anti-Semitism, once again, was rearing its head," he intoned. "The world was witnessing an alarming resurgence of that phenomenon in new forms and manifestation." Annan called on "everyone to actively and uncompromisingly refute those who sought to deny the fact of the Holocaust or its uniqueness." But what should be done to those denying its uniqueness—imprisonment? the death penalty? an hour's confinement with Wiesel? One might have thought that a secretary-general coming from a continent historically decimated by colonialism would be somewhat skeptical of The Holocaust's uniqueness and, given that Africa is currently being ravaged by starvation, disease, and war, that he would have bigger priorities than mobilizing the international community to affirm Holocaust uniqueness. Predictably, the U.N. meeting quickly degenerated

---

(United Nations press release HR/4773, PI/1589), www.un.org/News/Press/docs/2004/hr4773.doc.htm. For Wiesel's 1981 speeches on the "new anti-Semitism," see Irving Abrahamson (ed.), *Against Silence: The Voice and Vision of Elie Wiesel* (New York, 1985), 1:216, 376–81; for the chauvinism and instrumental value of the Holocaust uniqueness doctrine and Wiesel's antics generally, see Finkelstein, *Holocaust Industry*, passim. The main distinction of this Nobel peace laureate has been conscripting the Nazi holocaust to justify illegal, murderous wars of aggression, those launched by either Israel or the United States and backed by both. His advocacy of the United States' "illegal" (U.N. Secretary-General Kofi Annan) invasion of Iraq in March 2003 is a recent case in point. Bob Woodward, in *Plan of Attack* (New York, 2004), reports this episode on the war's eve:

> Elie Wiesel, writer, survivor of Auschwitz and Nobel Peace Prize winner, came to see [Condoleezza] Rice on February 27 and the president dropped by her office. Rice moved to the couch so the president could take the chair closest to Wiesel. Wiesel told the president that Iraq was a terrorist state and that the moral imperative was for intervention. If the West had intervened in Europe in 1938, he said, World War II and the Holocaust could have been prevented. "It's a moral issue. In the name of morality how can we not intervene?" . . . In the face of such evils, neutrality was impossible, Wiesel said. Indecision only promoted and assisted the evil and the aggressor, not the victims. "I'm against silence." In the days after, Bush routinely repeated Wiesel's comments. "That was a meaningful moment for me," he recalled later, "because it was a confirming moment. I said to myself, Gosh, if Elie Wiesel feels that way, who knows the pain and suffering and agony of tyranny, then others feel that way too. And so I am not alone." (pp. 320–21)

As of September 2004 the respected British medical journal *Lancet* conservatively estimated the number of Iraqis killed at 100,000, mostly women and children and mostly due to U.S. air strikes. What can one say except: Gosh, Elie, job well done? (Les Roberts et al., "Mortality before and after the 2003 invasion of Iraq: cluster sample survey," www.thelancet.com).

into a U.N.-bashing free-for-all. York University professor Anne Bayef-sky accused the United Nations of being the "leading global purveyor of anti-Semitism," while Abraham Foxman called on the U.N. to finally "stop demonizing and delegitimizing the Jewish people," and Malcolm Hoenlein of the Conference of Presidents of Major American Jewish Organizations demanded that the U.N. not hold Israel "to an impossible standard against which no other nation was held." Amid these denunciations it bears recalling the U.N.'s actual record on Israel. According to former Israeli ambassador to the U.N. and foreign minister Abba Eban, "the overwhelming balance" of the U.N.'s "influence on Israel's destiny and status is dramatically positive," and "[n]o nation involved in a struggle for legitimacy . . . has received such potent support from the overall jurisprudence of an international organization" (*Jerusalem Post*, 1988). Although it is true that the U.N. keeps Israel to a double standard, it's exactly the reverse of the one Israel's apologists allege: Israel is held not to a higher but lower standard than other member states. A careful study by Marc Weller of the University of Cambridge comparing Israel and the Occupied Territories with similar situations in Bosnia and Herzegovina, Kosovo, East Timor, occupied Kuwait and Iraq, and Rwanda found that Israel has enjoyed "virtual immunity" from enforcement measures such as an arms embargo and economic sanctions typically adopted by the U.N. against member states condemned for identical violations of international law. At the U.N. anti-Semitism seminar, Hoenlein also denounced "[d]enial of the Holocaust by representatives of the United Nations." Surely he is the ideal candidate to set the historical record straight at the U.N. about The Holocaust. At an April 2004 meeting in Toronto, Hoenlein told the audience that it wasn't Hitler but the Palestinian Mufti of Jerusalem who wanted to kill the Jews and, reluctantly, "Hitler followed the wishes of the Mufti." Where was Hoenlein when the defendants at Nuremberg needed him? Finally, participants at the U.N. seminar denounced the "disgraceful" World Court deliberations on Israel's separation barrier and the Durban Declaration and Programme of Action for stating that "Palestinians were the victims of Israeli racism"; accused "anti-Semites and anti-Zionists" of holding the "twisted" belief that "Jews used the Holocaust as an excuse for disregarding the suffering of everyone else"; and wondered "if referring to the Israeli presence in Gaza and the West Bank as occupation was really helpful"—why not just call it a field trip? Dr. Ruth Westheimer, the émigré from Nazi Germany turned radio sex therapist, struck the note closest to reality when she "commended participants for discussing the problem and offered her services."[42]

42. For the Eban quote and Cambridge University study, see Finkelstein, *Image and Reality*, respectively, pp. 247n2 and xviii; for Hoenlein's Toronto speech, see Rick Kardonne, "Hoenlein: Toronto has biggest Hezbollah headquarters outside of the Mideast," *Jewish Tribune* (8 April 2004). On a related note, at the U.N. meeting Bayefsky accused Kofi Annan of a double standard for denouncing Israel's liquidation of Hamas leaders without mentioning Israeli victims of terrorism. What does the actual record show? A 22 March 2004 statement by Annan "strongly condemns Israel's assassination of Hamas spiritual leader Sheikh Ahmed Yassin" without mentioning Israeli victims of terrorism ("Statement attributable to the Spokesman for the Secretary-General on the assassination of Sheikh Ahmed Yassin")—just as a 15 March 2004 statement by Annan "strongly condemned the double suicide bombing on Sunday in the Israeli port of Ashdod" without mentioning Palestinian victims of Israel's occupation ("Annan condemns double suicide bombing in Israeli port"). The only discernible difference is that Annan also sent his "deepest condolences to the families of the victims" in Ashdod, but didn't make a comparable gesture to the families of the eight Palestinian bystanders killed with Yassin.

3

Crying Wolf

WHAT'S CURRENTLY CALLED the new anti-Semitism actually incorporates three main components: (1) exaggeration and fabrication, (2) mislabeling legitimate criticism of Israeli policy, and (3) the unjustified yet predictable spillover from criticism of Israel to Jews generally.

EXAGGERATION AND FABRICATION

The evidence of a new anti-Semitism comes mostly from organizations directly or indirectly linked to Israel or having a material stake in inflating the findings of anti-Semitism. For instance, *Manifestations* lists as a main source of data on Denmark the "Israeli Embassy in Copenhagen," on Finland the "Friends of Israel Association," on Ireland the "Israeli Embassy" as well as the "Ireland-Israel Friendship League," and so forth. The annual reports of Tel Aviv University's Stephen Roth Institute for the Study of Contemporary Anti-Semitism and Racism serve as a major source of data and analysis. Its 2000–2001 *Antisemitism Worldwide* survey highlighted this ominous development: "Prof. Norman Finkelstein's book, *The Holocaust Industry*, [was] enthusiastically welcomed, especially in Germany, and by the extreme right in particular. . . . His arguments, even though completely refuted by serious researchers and publicists, have rekindled the image of the manipulative, greedy, power-hungry Jew." None of these refutations is cited, perhaps because none exist; Raul Hilberg did praise the book's key findings as a "breakthrough." The data on anti-Semitism supplied by domestic American Jewish organizations such as ADL and the Simon Wiesenthal Center and their counterparts elsewhere in Europe are also relied upon. These organizations stand in the same relationship to their respective host countries as Communist parties once did, except that they view Israel rather than Stalin's Russia as the Motherland. And, were they not able to conjure up anti-Semitism, Abraham Foxman and Rabbi Hier of the Wiesenthal Center would face the prospect of finding real jobs. In the cases of Foxman and Hier this would be a real tragedy: both get paid nearly a half million dollars annually from their respective "charitable" organizations.[1]

Many claims of anti-Semitism prove on investigation to be wildly overblown or fabricated. A lead article in the influential American journal *Foreign Policy* entitled "Antiglobalism's Jewish Problem" alleges that "protesters at the 2003 World Social Forum (WSF) in Porto Alegre, Brazil, display[ed] the swastika," and "[m]archers . . . carried signs reading 'Nazis, Yankees, and Jews: No More Chosen Peoples!'" Yet those actually in attendance at the demonstration never witnessed this phalanx of flaming storm troopers.[2] In an article for *Mother Jones* entitled "The Rough Beast Returns," Todd Gitlin declares that "[w]icked anti-Semitism is back, . . . and if that wasn't bad enough, students are spreading the gibberish. Students!" To document this charge, he cites the email "message [that] flew around the world" of Laurie Zoloth, then-director of Jewish Studies at San Francisco State University. SFSU "is the Weimar Republic with brown shirts it cannot control," Zoloth alleged—the Nazis in this instance being "an angry crowd of Palestinians." On one spring day they allegedly coalesced into an "out of

---

1. Werner Bergmann and Juliane Wetzel, *Manifestations of Anti-Semitism in the European Union* (Vienna, 2003), http://eumc.eu.int/eumc/material/pub/FT/Draft_anti-Semitism _report-web.pdf, "Annex: Reporting institutions and data sources." For the Roth 2000–2001 survey, see www.tau.ac.il/Anti-Semitism/asw2000-1/general_analysis.htm; for "breakthrough," see Hilberg's comment on the back cover of Norman G. Finkelstein, *The Holocaust Industry: Reflections on the Exploitation of Jewish Suffering*, 2nd ed. (New York, 2003); for salaries of Foxman and Hier, see www.charitywatch.org/criteria.html.

2. Mark Strauss, "Antiglobalism's Jewish Problem," reprinted in Ron Rosenbaum (ed.), *Those Who Forget the Past: The Question of Anti-Semitism* (New York, 2004), p. 271. Interviews with attendees Noam Chomsky, Arundhati Roy, and Anthony Arnove, all of whom denied the claim (21 December 2004). For the Simon Wiesenthal Center's similar fabrication of anti-Semitism at the 2004 World Social Forum in India, see the detailed account by Jewish peace activist Cecilie Surasky, "Anti-Semitism at the World Social Forum?" www.commondreams.org/views04/0219-08.htm.

control mob," launching a "raw, physical assault" on "praying students, and the elderly women who are our elder college participants, who survived the Holocaust," while the police stood idly by. Curiously, Gitlin, who currently teaches journalism at Columbia University, doesn't seem to have checked his source. Had he done so, he might have discovered that the consensus among Jewish spokespersons in the Bay Area, including Dr. Fred Astren, current director of Jewish Studies at SFSU (and a personal witness to the alleged incident), was that Zoloth had a penchant for "wild exaggeration," born of a mindset nurtured in "Marxist-Leninist" politics—except that she's in thrall not, as in bygone days, to the Soviet Union, but to "the Jewish State of Israel, a state that I cherish." The police didn't intervene because nothing happened warranting their intervention. The reverberations of Zoloth's email, Astren dryly observes, were less a testament to the power of her truth than to the "power of the internet." Apart from the pogrom-that-never-was at San Francisco State, the only evidence Gitlin adduces that the anti-Semitic "danger is clear and present" on college campuses is that "two students of mine" wondered whether in fact Jews didn't show up for work at the Twin Towers on September 11. Truly, "the rough beast returns."[3]

The progressive American Jewish monthly *Tikkun* ran a lengthy article by Miriam Greenspan entitled "What's New about Anti-Semitism?" which sang the praises of Phyllis Chesler's opus as a "vital contribution to understanding the resurgence of this virulent new strain of anti-Semitism." The proof of this "virulent new strain" is highlighted in the lead paragraph: "A Jewish student wearing a yarmulke at Yale University is attacked by a Palestinian in his dormitory." Yet no one at Yale's Center for Jewish Life or the university administration had ever heard of such an assault. At the University of Chicago, Gabriel Schoenfeld reports, "a university-appointed preceptor told a Jewish student he would not read her BA paper because it focused on topics relating to Judaism and Zionism." Yet no one ever filed a complaint at the University of Chicago's Center for Jewish Life, while the university administration, after learning about the alleged incident (which first surfaced in the

---

3. Todd Gitlin, "The Rough Beast Returns," *Mother Jones* (May–June 2002), reprinted in Rosenbaum, *Those Who Forget*, pp. 263-66. Zoloth's email is also reprinted in Rosenbaum, *Those Who Forget*, pp. 258-61. The quoted phrases describing Zoloth and her background come from a national Jewish spokesperson who requested anonymity (Astren confirmed this Jewish leader's assessment for the record).

right-wing website *Campus Watch*), did do a thorough investigation but found no evidence to substantiate it. In early 2004 Columbia University in New York came under attack. In a film produced by a shadowy organization and privately screened for select audiences, "pro"-Israel students, using the lingo of political correctness, anguished that their "voices" in defense of Israel were being "silenced" by faculty members. Local newspapers headlined that Columbia was awash in anti-Semitism and along with local politicians called for the sacking of professors. The hysteria at Columbia was part of a much broader campaign orchestrated by a consortium of well-heeled "pro"-Israel organizations and foundations to "take back" college campuses where, in recent years, a handful of dissenters have finally broken the total stranglehold held by Israel's apologists over public debate. In December 2004 Columbia president Lee Bollinger appointed an ad hoc committee to investigate student complaints, and in March 2005 the committee released its findings. After an exhaustive investigation and despite enormous pressures for a resounding guilty verdict, the committee was able to document only one possibly culpable incident, in which a Palestinian professor, during Israel's invasion of Jenin, "became angered at a question that he understood to countenance Israeli conduct of which he disapproved, and . . . , responded heatedly." On the allegation of anti-Semitism, the report roundly concluded: "[W]e found no evidence of any statements made by the faculty that could reasonably be construed as anti-Semitic." Significantly, the most damning findings bore not on the conduct of Israel's critics but of its supporters. The report observed that unregistered "students" were disrupting and secretly filming the classes of professors critical of Israeli policy. A Columbia professor had apparently even enlisted students to report back what was being said in the class of one such professor "as part of a campaign against him." On the latter point, the committee reserved its harshest words: "We find it deeply disturbing that faculty were apparently prepared to encourage students to report to them on a fellow-professor's classroom statements," thereby turning students "into informers." Although the allegations of anti-Semitism were formally repudiated, the hysteria did cow Columbia as well as other universities into establishing endowed chairs in Israel studies—i.e., new outposts for party indoctrination, alongside chairs in Holocaust studies. Indeed, the real revelation of the Columbia episode was not that the claim of anti-Semitism was a fraud, but how de facto agents of a foreign government have, in service to their Holy State, conspired to muzzle academic freedom in the United States.[4]

A speech by Harvard president Lawrence Summers that raised the specter of a burgeoning anti-Semitism on college campuses received wide attention and won him many accolades. The main job of a university president is to raise money. Harvard Law School professor Alan Dershowitz recalls a Harvard fund-raiser telling him that in recent years "Harvard has been virtually supported by Jews." One doesn't have to be an economist of Summers's distinction to reckon that playing the new anti-Semitism card won't hurt the alumni fund-raising drive. Variations on this ploy are standard fare at Harvard. It surely didn't lose him points at Harvard when, back in 1992, entrepreneurial black professor Henry Louis Gates Jr. denounced black anti-Semitism, or what he called the "new anti-Semitism"—how often that tag line keeps popping up—in a full-page *New York Times* op-ed. Trashing powerless people, especially if they're of your "own kind," to curry favor with the powerful is called moral courage in elite circles.[5] Alleging that "something's changed," Paul Berman infers evidence of resurgent anti-Semitism from a single Egyptian panelist at New York's

4. Miriam Greenspan, "What's New about Anti-Semitism?" *Tikkun* (November–December 2003). Gabriel Schoenfeld, *The Return of Anti-Semitism* (San Francisco, 2004), p. 121 (University of Chicago); for the University of Chicago's response, see the unpublished correspondence (28 August 2002) of Larry Arbeiter, Director of Communications, University of Chicago, to the *Jerusalem Post*, made available to this writer by Seth L. Sanders, Writer for Humanities, Religion and Arts, University of Chicago News Office. Scott Sherman, "The Mideast Comes to Columbia," *The Nation* (4 April 2005) ("take back"); *Ad Hoc Grievance Committee Report* (28 March 2005), www.columbia.edu/cu/news/05/03/ad_hoc_grievance_committee_report.html; Nathaniel Popper, "Israel Studies Gain on Campus as Disputes Grow," *Forward* (25 March 2005) (endowed Israel chairs). For other documented examples of fraud regarding campus anti-Semitism, see Sara Roy, "Short Cuts," *London Review of Books* (1 April 2004), and Tom Tugend, "From Hate to Hoax in Claremont," *Jewish Journal of Greater Los Angeles* (2 April 2004).

5. Lawrence Summers, "Address at Morning Prayers," in Rosenbaum, *Those Who Forget*, pp. 57–60; Alan M. Dershowitz, *The Vanishing American Jew: In Search of Jewish Identity for the Next Century* (Boston, 1997), p. 271; Henry Louis Gates Jr., "Black Demagogues and Pseudo-Scholars," *New York Times* (20 July 1992). The targets of Gates's op-ed, a handful of "Afrocentric" demagogues trafficking in anti-Semitism, exercised roughly the same negligible influence in his own academic milieu as Holocaust deniers—denunciation of whom is also considered, in those same circles, an act of courage. Gates periodically barters a black name to "pro"-Jewish causes and publications, most recently, Dershowitz's *The Case for Israel*, his blurb for which reads: "My first visit to Israel, at the age of 19, was both a deeply mystical and a profoundly troubling experience. I quickly came to understand that Israel was a treasure of civilization for the entire human community, but a most vulnerable one . . . . *The Case for Israel* is indispensable reading for those of us who are deeply disturbed by the rise of anti-Semitism in American society, even on college campuses." It's tributes like this that give pandering a bad name.

annual Socialist Scholars Conference who "stated her approval of the suicide bombers" and a single audience member who "even spoke out in the panelist's defense." Support of suicide bombers does not in itself signify anti-Semitism, but even if it did, what would this example prove? Berman reports that the conference attendees numbered in the thousands, including "every ridiculous left-wing sect." For Berman this one panelist and one audience member reveal that "[t]he new wind is definitely blowing." If so, it wouldn't even register on the weather channel.[6]

The evidence of a new anti-Semitism often proves on inspection to be no evidence at all. A centerpiece of *Manifestations*' indictment is an "anti-Semitic" poster for a demonstration protesting Bush's impending visit to Berlin (see Figure 1). Its analysis of the poster reads: "The well-known picture of 'Uncle Sam' is showing a 'typical Jewish nose.' Also the poster implies the supposed Jewish world conspiracy because on the forefinger of 'Uncle Sam' hangs the world on a thread. Portraying 'Uncle Sam' as Jewish refers to the supposed Jewish influence on the United States policy and connects anti-Jewish and anti-American feelings." No one shown the poster by this writer could discern a Jewish nose, let alone a Jewish conspiracy, although several people did make out the vague outlines of an African American proboscis. The authors of *Manifestations* manifestly need a long vacation. Schoenfeld detects "classic" anti-Semitism in a *Tikkun* advertisement opposing the occupation (see Figure 2). Isn't the banner "Jews Aren't Bullies or Exploiters," with a peace sign, no less, affixed to it, just a dead giveaway of its anti-Semitic provenance?[7]

Similarly, Foxman sniffs anti-Semitism everywhere. It is anti-Semitic to believe that "Jews are more loyal to Israel than to this country"—although, for all anyone knows, this might be empirically true and, for many Zionists, it *ought* to be true. Indeed, Foxman himself maintains that to deny the Jewish people the right to a "homeland of their own"

6. Paul Berman, "Something's Changed," in Rosenbaum, *Those Who Forget*, pp. 15, 27. Berman also omits mention that when another panelist at the same conference session immediately condemned this approval of suicide bombings, the audience erupted in loud applause (interview with *Nation* editor Roane Carey, 21 December 2004). In response to charges of discrimination directed at Israel's Law of Return, which grants automatic citizenship exclusively to Jews, Berman maintains that the law reflects "Israel's autonomy as a state—its right to draw up its own laws on immigration" (p. 24). Would Berman offer a similar defense of U.S. immigration laws that favored Caucasians against Asians, and Western and Central Europeans against Slavs, Italians, and Jews?

7. *Manifestations*, pp. 7–8n13, 48; Schoenfeld, "Israel and the Anti-Semites," in Rosenbaum, *Those Who Forget*, p. 113.

Figure 1. The case of the elusive Semitic proboscis. Design by Uta Eickworth, Berlin.

and "independence, sovereignty" in Israel is also anti-Semitic—but doesn't this mean that, regardless of where Jews happen to reside, Israel *is* their state? And who can dispute that he acts like a loyalist of Israel—or, at any rate, its paid agent? It was "anti-Semitism pure and simple" when "Belgium, the seat of the International Court of Justice at [T]he Hague, . . . sought to indict the prime minister of the state of Israel for crimes against humanity," and also when Danes opposed the appointment by Israel of a notorious torturer as ambassador to Denmark. Foxman justifies this charge of anti-Semitism on the grounds that comparable criminals have escaped accountability. Leaving aside that The Hague is not in Belgium but the Netherlands, don't all criminals (and their apologists) cry selective prosecution? But only the likes of Foxman would claim that holding murderers and torturers accountable for their crimes is anti-Semitic as well. To allege that the American Israel Public Affairs Committee (AIPAC) targets candidates critical of Israel, Foxman asserts, "echo[es] familiar anti-Semitic slanders"—even though AIPAC boasts about doing this. Nonetheless, Foxman assures readers regarding the epithet *anti-Semitic* that "we're very careful about how and when we use it," and ADL has "given a great deal of thought to

Figure 2. "A Form of Classic Anti-Semitism." From *Tikkun* magazine. Cartoon by Khalil Bendib.

drawing appropriate distinctions among various degrees and levels of anti-Semitic speech and action." This prudence and nuance have been on full display on each of the many occasions that ADL slandered this writer as a "known Holocaust denier." "If I were reckless about accusations of anti-Semitism," Foxman continues, "I would quickly lose that credibility and therefore any effectiveness as a leader on this issue." Foxman rose to Ronald Reagan's defense when, journeying to Germany's Bitburg cemetery, Reagan declared that the German soldiers (including Waffen SS members) buried there were "victims of the Nazis just as surely as the victims in the concentration camps," and Foxman subsequently honored Reagan with ADL's "Torch of Liberty" award; Foxman oversaw a far-flung domestic U.S. spying operation with ties to Israeli intelligence and the apartheid regime in South Africa; after taking a payoff from Marc Rich—the billionaire commodities trader who fled to Switzerland before standing trial on an indictment for fifty-one counts of tax evasion, racketeering, and violating trade sanctions with

Iran—Foxman helped engineer his presidential pardon during Clinton's final hours in office. That this man retains credibility offers terrifying insight into contemporary U.S. political culture.[8]

Manifestations cites as evidence of European anti-Semitism an ADL poll of the European Union showing that nearly half of the respondents agreed with the statement "The Jews still talk too much about the Holocaust." Indeed, the wonder is that the percentage of Europeans resenting chauvinistic incantation and political instrumentalization of The Holocaust isn't much greater. In its country-by-country break-down, the *Manifestations* study also spotlighted these allegedly anti-Semitic incidents: *Denmark*—"A person with connections to the Pro-gressive Jewish Forum describes how, . . . when entering her office, a colleague said, 'you've occupied there (her chair) very well, haven't you—ha ha'"; *Greece*—"[T]wo articles . . . put forward the view that Jews have excessively used the pain resulting from the cruelty of the Holocaust"; *Italy*—"[L]arge graffiti in bold characters saying 'Jews murderers' was seen in an underground pass in the city of Prato" (but did they check the sewers in the Abruzzi?); *Netherlands*—"[A] Jewish market vendor in the centre of Amsterdam was threatened with a pistol and the words 'I'll shoot you dead'" (isn't that what robbers usually say?). No doubt aware just how flimsy—not to say risible—this evi-dence is, the authors of *Manifestations* proceed to hypothesize "deeply latent anti-Semitic and anti-Zionist prejudices in the German public," a "spiritual (or psychological) anti-Semitism" among Italians, an anti-Semitic "latent structure" among Greeks, and, as already seen, a "smell of anti-Semitism" among British.[9]

Soon after publication of *Manifestations*, the European Monitoring Centre on Racism and Xenophobia released another, more compre-hensive study entitled *Manifestations of Antisemitism in the EU 2002–2003* (hereafter: *Manifestations II*), scrutinizing a full two-year

---

8. Abraham H. Foxman, *Never Again? The Threat of the New Anti-Semitism* (San Francisco, 2003), pp. 14 ("loyal to Israel"), 17 ("homeland "), 18 ("independence"), 25 ("Belgium"), 26 ("pure and simple" and Denmark), 36 (AIPAC), 142 ("very careful"), 245 ("various degrees"), 247 ("reckless"). For the ADL's use of the "Holocaust denier" epithet, see "Anti-Defamation League (ADL) Letter to Georgetown University," www .NormanFinkelstein.com (under "The real 'Axis of Evil'"). For Foxman's defense of Rea-gan, his spying operation, and his role in Rich's pardon, see Finkelstein, *Holocaust Indus-try*, pp. 22, 30–31, 212.

9. *Manifestations*, pp. 24n63 ("talk too much"), 45 (Denmark), 51 ("deeply latent"), 56 ("latent structure"), 58 (Greece), 69–70 ("spiritual"), 72 (Italy), 81 (Netherlands).

period as against the several months of *Manifestations*.[10] Although still suffering from some of the biases and apologetics of *Manifestations*, it was nonetheless a far more rigorous and sober report.[11] No doubt because the findings of *Manifestations II* weren't the stuff of sensationalist, hysterical headlines about a rampant new anti-Semitism, it was largely ignored in the media. One unambiguous indicator of the report's relative seriousness was that Foxman expressed "disappointment" with it.[12] For the full two-year period and altogether for the fifteen E.U. countries surveyed, *Manifestations II* reports not a single anti-Semitic homicide and a handful of anti-Semitic assaults causing serious personal injury.[13] Although there were a considerable number of attacks on Jewish property, some serious, the overwhelming majority

10. European Monitoring Centre on Racism and Xenophobia, *Manifestations of Antisemitism in the EU 2002–2003* (April 2004), http://eumc.eu.int/eumc/index.php.

11. Problematically, the report classified as anti-Semitic a textbook containing the sentence "When a Palestine [*sic*] child in Jerusalem saw a Jewish soldier coming, it winced with fear" (p. 45); a website posting that stated, "It is really sad how all politicians grovel to the lobby; everyone who does not and dares to have a different opinion is denounced immediately, and is branded as antisemitic or racist" (p. 63); a couple of articles "that put forward the view that Jews have used excessively the pain resulting from the cruelty of the Holocaust" (p. 79); a "drawing of Ariel Sharon and an attached Hitler-like moustache" (p. 90); "a newspaper article with a picture of Palestinian victims of the Middle East's conflict with the word[s] 'Israeli Justice' written on top of the article" (p. 120); "banners and placards . . . against Israel and Prime Minister Sharon . . . on which the 'S' was replaced with swastikas or written the same way as Nazi SS" (p. 127); a "letter to the editor" that "accused the Israelis of being themselves responsible for the emerging anti-Semitism" (p. 156); "leaflets some of which ask for a boycott of Israeli products" (p. 178). In and of themselves, none of these examples would seem to be anti-Semitic. It is even doubtful that agreeing with the statement "[Jews have too much influence in the world" proves, as the report claims, anti-Semitism (pp. 69–71, 259)—anymore than agreeing with the statement "White people have too much influence in the world" or "Males have too much influence in the world" proves, respectively, a racist or sexist cast of mind. On the other hand, this second report is generally more cautious than *Manifestations* about conflating criticism of Israel with anti-Semitism (see esp. pp. 13–14, 228–32, 240–41).

12. "ADL Raises Questions Surrounding EUMC Report on Anti-Semitism" (ADL press release, 1 April 2004), www.adl.org/PresRele/ASInt_13/4474_13.htm. Foxman faulted the press release that announced publication of *Manifestations II* for downplaying involvement of Muslim youth in anti-Semitic acts. In fact, the press release accurately summarized the report's findings.

13. Anti-Semitic incidents amounting to "extreme violence"—i.e., "[a]ny attack potentially causing loss of life" (p. 343)—and for which details are given in *Manifestations II* include several in France (one Jewish youth "was sent to the hospital requiring many stitches"; another "was sent to the hospital with many contusions" [pp. 100–101]) and Austria ("an attack by four skinheads on a man in the Vienna underground . . . one of the skinheads beat him with a belt" and "a violent attack against an orthodox Jew in Vienna who was violently beaten to such an extent that he lost consciousness" [p. 159]). In most E.U. countries there weren't any such attacks.

of anti-Semitic incidents consisted of various kinds of verbal threat and abuse; for example, "[a]n antisemitic letter, originating in France, was sent to an individual in Belgium"; "in Paris, a man accompanied by his three children was insulted and told 'You kill a Palestinian child,'" and "[a]n Internet search revealed a report on a farmer in Upper Austria, who put up a billboard in front of his farm saying 'Jews are blackmailing the whole world' and 'Ariel Sharon is a state terrorist.'"[14] Even in France, which witnessed the greatest number of anti-Semitic incidents of the countries surveyed—for example, three arson attacks damaging Jewish communal property in 2002, although none in 2003[15]—the evidence of a pervasive anti-Semitism was nil. Rather the contrary: "surveys show that antisemitic attitudes within the general French population are declining," fully 89 percent of the respondents in one poll replying affirmatively to the question "Is a French person of Jewish origin 'as French as the others'?" And, although in the French instance Muslim youths were mostly responsible for anti-Semitic incidents, a survey found that in general "young people of North African origin are in fact even more intolerant of anti-Semitism than the average." Finally, it bears notice that "[t]he number of victims of anti-Semitism" in France was "inferior to the number of immigrant victims" of bias attacks.[16]

Right around the time *Manifestations II* was released, the highly respected Pew Research Center published the findings of its latest international survey, conducted from late February to early March 2004 in the United States and eight other countries. "Despite concerns about rising anti-Semitism in Europe," it found, "there are no indications that anti-Jewish sentiment has increased over the past decade. Favorable ratings of Jews are actually higher now in France, Germany and Russia than they were in 1991." Put simply, the claims of a rampant new anti-Semitism are a sham. A nonideologically driven political agenda would rank animus directed at Muslims as the priority concern given that "Europeans hold much more negative views of Muslims than of Jews."[17] But the hysteria over a new anti-Semitism hasn't anything to do with fighting bigotry—and everything to do with stifling criticism of Israel.

14. *Manifestations II*, pp. 40 ("letter"), 103 ("You kill"), 156 ("billboard").
15. Ibid., pp. 100–101.
16. Ibid., pp. 20, 98, 104–5 ("young people"), 109–11 (89 percent), 113 ("declining"), 273 ("immigrant victims").
17. Pew Research Center for the People and the Press, *A Year after Iraq War: Mistrust of America in Europe Ever Higher, Muslim Anger Persists. Summary of Findings* (16

MISLABELING LEGITIMATE CRITICISM OF ISRAELI POLICY

There is broad consensus among those treating the topic that the emergence of the new anti-Semitism coincided with the latest flare-up in the Israel-Palestine conflict, reaching a peak during Operation Defensive Shield and the siege of Jenin in the spring of 2002: "Ever since the new intifada began in September 2000, the incidence of anti-Semitic rhetoric and physical violence in countries around the world has escalated enormously, fueled by anti-Israeli feeling" (Foxman); "Today's virulent outbreak in Europe and (to a much lesser extent) in the United States does appear to be an epiphenomenon of the Arab-Israel conflict. Anti-Semitism unquestionably intensified greatly on both continents with the eruption of the second intifada" (Schoenfeld); "The fact that a rise in anti-Semitic activities is clearly observable in most of the EU Member States since the beginning of the so-called al-Aqsa Intifada . . . points to a connection between events in the Middle East with criticism of Israel's politics, on the one hand, and mobilisation of anti-Semitism on the other" (*Manifestations*); "[L]inkage between the number of reported anti-Semitic incidents and the political situation in the Middle East . . . can be seen by the significantly high peak of incidents in some countries during the month of April 2002, the month in which the Israeli army controversially occupied several Palestinian towns" (*Manifestations II*). The causal relationship would seem to be that Israel's brutal repression of Palestinians evoked hostility toward the "Jewish state" and its vocal Jewish supporters abroad. Accordingly, an ADL survey found that almost two-thirds of Europeans believed that "the recent outbreak of violence against Jews in Europe is a result of anti-Israel sentiment and not traditional anti-Semitic or anti-Jewish feelings," while in Italy, for example, "commentators assess that the rise in the scope of anti-Semitism is the result of Israel's governmental policy towards the Arabs since the outbreak of the intifada." Similarly, *Manifestations* found that, apart from fringe "right-wing extremists," for whom anti-Semitism has always figured as a rallying point, the animus toward and violence against Jews in Europe emanated mainly from

---

March 2004), p. 4; for statistical comparison with 1991, see Pew Research Center for the People and the Press, *A Year after Iraq War: Mistrust of America in Europe Ever Higher, Muslim Anger Persists. A Nine-Country Survey*, p. 26. For poll data confirming the decline of anti-Semitism in Germany as compared to 1991 and a similar tendency in France, see also *Manifestations II*, pp. 64–65, 111, 261. For hostility against Muslims being greater than against Jews, see also *Manifestations II*, pp. 110, 145, 283.

"young Muslims mostly of Arab descent" closely identifying with the Palestinian struggle. (*Manifestations II* cautions that "on the basis of available data and looking at the EU as a whole, it is problematic to make general statements" regarding which of these two groups bears greater responsibility for anti-Semitic acts.)[18] This explanation would also account, inversely, for the precipitate decline in antipathy to Israel and Jews when hope loomed large for a just settlement during the early Oslo "peace process" years, prompting even Dershowitz to acknowledge the marginalization of anti-Semitism not just in the United States but globally.[19]

Yet, it is precisely this causal relationship that Israel's apologists emphatically deny: if Israeli policies, and widespread Jewish support for them, evoke hostility toward Jews, it means that Israel and its Jewish supporters themselves might be causing anti-Semitism; and it might be doing so because Israel and its Jewish supporters are *in the wrong*. Holocaust industry dogma a priori rejects this hypothesis: animus towards Jews can never spring from wrongs committed by Jews. The argument goes like this: the Final Solution was irrational; the Final Solution marked the culmination of a millennial Gentile anti-Semitism; ergo, each and every manifestation of anti-Semitism is irrational.[20] Since anti-Semitism is synonymous with animus toward Jews, any and all animus directed at Jews, individually or collectively, must be irrational. "Anti-Semitism . . . resembles a disease in being fundamentally irrational," Foxman typically asserts. "[T]hose who hate Jews do so not because of factual evidence but in spite of it." Thus, according to Schoenfeld, Palestinians become suicide bombers not because of what Israel has concretely done but because it has been turned into a "diabolical abstraction." For Rosenbaum, anti-Semitism is an irrational, inexplicable, and ineluctable Gentile affliction: "The explanation of renewed anti-Semitism is anti-Semitism: its ineradicable pre-existing history—and its efficacy. It has become its own origin." Unsurprisingly, when billionaire financier George Soros, who is Jewish, suggested otherwise, telling a gathering of Jewish notables that the "resurgence of

18. Foxman, *Never Again?* p. 31; Schoenfeld, *Return,* pp. 67, 71, 152 ("epiphenomenon"); *Manifestations,* pp. 5, 6, 7 ("young Muslims"), 15, 16, 19 ("rise in anti-Semitic activities," "recent outbreak"), 24, 25, 27, 70 ("commentators"); *Manifestations II,* pp. 20–22 ("problematic"), 25 ("[L]inkage"), 239, 319.
19. This is the central thesis of Dershowitz's book *Vanishing American Jew* (1997); for his statement on the decline of anti-Semitism globally, see esp. pp. 87–89.
20. For a fuller exposition of this Holocaust industry dogma, see Finkelstein, *Holocaust Industry,* chap. 2.

anti-Semitism in Europe" was largely due to Sharon's policies and the behavior of Jews, he incurred the audience's wrath. Committing the same sin, former Israeli Knesset Speaker Avraham Burg observed, "The unfavorable attitude toward Israel that exists today in the international community stems in part from the policy of the government of Israel." "Let's understand things clearly," Elan Steinberg of the World Jewish Congress retorted after Soros's speech: "Anti-Semitism is not caused by Jews; it's caused by anti-Semites." Foxman called Soros's remarks "absolutely obscene." If it's "obscene" for a Jew to say that Jews might be causing anti-Semitism, for a non-Jew to say it is—surprise, surprise —anti-Semitic. *Manifestations* deplores a Dutch newspaper article entitled "Israel abuses the anti-Semitism taboo" because "the author used the classical anti-Semitic stereotype that the Jews themselves are to blame for anti-Semitism," as well as a letter to an Austrian newspaper because it "accused the Israelis of being themselves responsible for the emerging anti-Semitism."[21]

Two exceptions are allowed to this dogma of anti-Semitism as a Gentile pathology that—to quote Holocaust industry guru Daniel Goldhagen—is "divorced from actual Jews," "fundamentally *not* a

---

21. Foxman, *Never Again?* p. 42; Schoenfeld, *Return*, p. 45; "Introduction," in Rosenbaum, *Those Who Forget*, p. lxii; Uriel Heilman, "In rare Jewish appearance, George Soros says Jews and Israel cause anti-Semitism," *Jewish Telegraphic Agency* (9 November 2003) (Soros, Steinberg, Foxman); Ari Shavit, "On the eve of destruction," *Haaretz* (14 November 2003) (Burg); *Manifestations*, pp. 82, 85. Compare Roman Bronfman, a member of Israel's left-leaning Meretz party, on the real roots of the "new anti-Semitism":

> How can this hatred toward us be explained, particularly in the developed European states? And why is it being expressed specifically now, and with such intensity? . . . [W]hen the waves of hatred spread and appeared on all the media networks around the world and penetrated every home, the new-old answer surfaced: anti-Semitism. After all, anti-Semitism has always been the Jews' trump card because it is easy to quote some crazy figure from history and seek cover. This time, too, the anti-Semitism card has been pulled from the sleeve of explanations by the Israeli government and its most faithful spokespeople have been sent to wave it. But the time has come for the Israeli public to wake up from the fairy tale being told by its elected government. The rhetoric of the perpetual victim is not a sufficient answer for the question of the timing. Why all of a sudden have all the anti-Semites, or haters of Israel, raised their heads and begun chanting hate slogans? Enough of our whining, "The whole world is against us." . . . The time has come to look at the facts and admit the simple but bitter truth—Israel has lost its legitimacy in the eyes of the world and we are guilty for what has happened. . . . [I]f anti-Semitism was until now found exclusively in the extreme political fringes, Israel's continued policy of the cruel occupation will only encourage and fan the spread of anti-Semitic sentiments. ("Fanning the flames of hatred," *Haaretz* [19 November 2003])

response to any objective evaluation of Jewish action," and "*independent* of the Jews' nature and actions" (his emphases). The first exception is that anti-Semitism *can* arise from Jews doing the *right* thing: although conspicuous Jewish support for the civil rights movement undoubtedly increased anti-Semitism among southern whites in the United States, Jews would never have thought to disclaim responsibility for causing this sort of anti-Semitism; on the contrary, it was a badge of honor. And second, although irrational, this Gentile pathology does spring from an all-too-human passion: ressentiment. If, as Nietzsche maintained, "slave morality" sprang from the Jews' envy of the truly aristocratic among them, Holocaust industry dogma maintains that "anti-Semitism" springs from Gentile envy of the Jewish aristocracy: they hate us because we're so much better. "The new anti-Semitism transcends boundaries, nationalities, politics and social systems," Mortimer Zuckerman explains. "Israel has become the object of envy and resentment in much the same way that the individual Jew was once the object of envy and resentment." It won't escape notice that Holocaust industry dogma bears striking resemblance to the politically correct interpretation of the U.S. "war against terrorism." The Arabs hate us either because they're irrational fanatics or because they envy our way of life: it can't possibly be because we might have done something wrong—that's called apologetics for "Islamo-fascism." To supply the "cause of the attacks on America," Jeffrey Goldberg of *The New Yorker* digs up an Egyptian intellectual to say: "These are people who are envious. . . . Talent gives rise to jealousy in the hearts of the untalented." The reciprocal "natural" sympathy that Israel and the United States have exchanged since September 11—"Now they know how we feel" (Israel) and "Now we know how they feel" (United States)—is anchored in this chauvinistic and exculpatory ideology. Here are the anguished sighs of mutual recognition by those who imagine themselves to be not just innocent but too good for their own good.[22]

The doctrine of essential Jewish innocence, incidentally, also explains the appeal that Sartre's little book *Anti-Semite and Jew* has had for many Jews. "In his surgical exploration of classical anti-Semitism," the Perlmutters typically gush, "his work was seminal." On the face of it, the book was a most unlikely favorite—even less so Sartre, a

---

22. Daniel Jonah Goldhagen, *Hitler's Willing Executioners: Ordinary Germans and the Holocaust* (New York, 1996), pp. 34–35, 39, 42; Zuckerman, "The New Anti-Semitism"; Jeffrey Goldberg, "Behind Mubarak," in Rosenbaum, *Those Who Forget*, p. 548.

person of the left. After all, Sartre's point of departure is that Jewish peoplehood lacks any content except what anti-Semitism endows it with: "the anti-Semite," in his famous formulation, "*makes* the Jew" (his emphasis). But from this premise Sartre goes on to argue that stereotypical Jewish vices are either the invention or the fault of the anti-Semite—which means (or can be understood to mean) that Jews possess no vices or don't bear any responsibility for them. And if animus toward Jews does exist, it can't be on account of a wrong they commit: "Far from experience producing his [i.e., the anti-Semite's] idea of the Jew, it was the latter which explained his experience," and, again, anti-Semitism "precedes the facts that call it forth." Although the motive behind this philo-Semitic doctrine was surely decent, its effect has been a disaster, for what is its consequence except to breed complete moral irresponsibility? "*Jews* are not to blame for anti-Semitism," Dershowitz, echoing Sartre, asserts. "Anti-Semitism is the problem of the bigots. . . . Nothing *we* do can profoundly affect the twisted mind of the anti-Semite" (his emphases). In sum, Jews can never be culpable for the antipathy others bear towards them: it's always of *their* making, not ours.[23]

SPILLOVER

In some quarters anger at Israel's brutal occupation has undoubtedly spilled over to an animus toward Jews generally. But however lamentable, it's hardly cause for wonder. The brutal U.S. aggression against Vietnam and the Bush administration's aggression against Iraq engendered a generalized anti-Americanism, just as the genocidal Nazi aggression during World War II engendered a generalized anti-Teutonism. Should it really surprise us if the cruel occupation by a self-declared *Jewish* state engenders a generalized antipathy to Jews? "All cases in which the Jews are made collectively responsible for the policy of the Israeli government," *Manifestations* solemnly opines, "represent a form of anti-Semitism." Accordingly, Spain is reckoned anti-Semitic because "[t]he mass media often confuses Israel and the Jewish community." But if many Jews themselves repudiate any distinction between Israel

23. Nathan Perlmutter and Ruth Ann Perlmutter, *The Real Anti-Semitism in America* (New York, 1982), p. 131. Jean-Paul Sartre, *Anti-Semite and Jew* (New York, 1976), pp. 13 ("Far from"), 17 ("precedes"), 69 ("makes"). Alan M. Dershowitz, *Chutzpah* (Boston, 1991), p. 100.

and world Jewry, indeed, if they denounce such a distinction as itself anti-Semitic; if mainstream Jewish organizations lend uncritical support to every Israeli policy, however criminal, indeed, abetting the most virulent tendencies inside Israel and muzzling principled dissent outside Israel; if Israel defines itself juridically as the sovereign state of the Jewish people, and Jews abroad label any criticism of Israel anti-Jewish—the real wonder is that the spillover from antipathy toward Israel to Jews generally hasn't been greater. "Anyone who does not distinguish between Jews and the Jewish state is an anti-Semite," Chesler avows in one place, but in the same book she avows that "American and Diaspora Jews" must understand that "Israel is our heart and soul . . . we *are* family" (her emphasis). Likewise, Italian journalist Fiamma Nirenstein professes that "Jews everywhere should consider their being identified with Israel a virtue and honor" and should insist that "[i]f you're prejudiced against Israel, then, you're against the Jews." It would seem to be anti-Semitic both to identify and not to identify Israel with Jews. "Iranian anti-Semitic propagandists make a point," according to Schoenfeld, "of erasing all distinctions among Israel, Zionism and the Jews." Yet in an article for *Commentary* magazine, which Schoenfeld edits, Hillel Halkin asserted: "Israel is the state of the Jews. Zionism is the belief that the Jews should have a state. To defame Israel is to defame the Jews" ("The Return of Anti-Semitism"). So are Halkin and *Commentary*'s editor also anti-Semitic?[24]

Just as it's too simple (and convenient) to label accusations of Jewish responsibility for Israeli policy anti-Semitic, so it's too simple (and convenient) to label the notion of Jewish power anti-Semitic. Jews now rank as the wealthiest ethnic group in the United States; with this economic power has accrued substantial political power. Their leaders have wielded this power, often crudely, to mold U.S. policy regarding Israel. These leaders have also utilized this power in other realms. Under the guise of seeking "Holocaust reparations," American Jewish organizations and individuals at all levels of government and in all sectors of American society entered into a conspiracy—this is the correct word—to blackmail Europe. It was on account of "Jewish money" that the Clinton administration went along with this shakedown operation,

24. *Manifestations*, 17 ("All cases"), 61 (Spain); Chesler, *New Anti-Semitism*, pp. 192, 209–11 ("heart and soul," "family"), 245 ("Anyone"); Fiamma Nirenstein, "How I Became an 'Unconscious Fascist,'" in Rosenbaum, *Those Who Forget*, p. 302; Schoenfeld, *Return*, p. 11; Hillel Halkin, "The Return of Anti-Semitism," *Commentary* (February 2002).

providing—even to the detriment of U.S. national interests—crucial support for it at every juncture. And who can seriously believe that the pro-Jewish bias of the corporate media has nothing whatever to do with the influential Jewish presence at all levels of it? "It's undoubtedly true that there are prominent Jews among the producers, directors, studio executives, and stars in Hollywood," Foxman concedes. "It's even true that, proportionately, there has always been a relatively prominent Jewish presence in the movie, TV, and record industries." But, he continues, "[t]he Jews who work in Hollywood are there not *as Jews* but as actors, directors, writers, business executives, or what have you," concerned only with "the bottom line" (his emphasis). His proof? "This explains the paradox that no anti-Semitic conspiracy theorist has ever tackled—how it is that the supposedly Jewish-controlled movie industry has produced so few films dealing with overtly Jewish characters or themes." Is that why Hollywood has produced a mere 175 films on the Nazi holocaust since 1989? Legitimate questions can surely be posed regarding when and if Jews are acting as people who happen to be Jewish or acting "as Jews," and, on the latter occasions (which plainly do arise), regarding the actual breadth and limits of this "Jewish power," but these questions can only be answered empirically, not a priori with politically correct formulae. To foreclose inquiry on this topic as anti-Semitic is, intentionally or not, to shield Jews from legitimate scrutiny of their uses and abuses of formidable power. In an otherwise sensible treatment of the new anti-Semitism, Brian Klug maintains that "it is a form of anti-Semitism" if an accusation against Jews mimics an anti-Semitic stereotype such as the idea of Jews being "powerful, wealthy . . . pursuing [their] own selfish ends." Yet if Jews act out a Jewish stereotype, it plainly doesn't follow that they can't be committing the stereotypical act. Can't they commit a vile act even if it conforms to a Jewish stereotype? It is perhaps politically incorrect to recall but nonetheless a commonplace that potent stereotypes, like good propaganda, acquire their force from containing a kernel—and sometimes even more than a kernel—of truth. Should people like Abraham Foxman, Edgar Bronfman, and Rabbi Israel Singer get a free ride *because* they resemble stereotypes straight out of *Der Stürmer*?[25]

25. For blackmailing Europe, see esp. Finkelstein, *Holocaust Industry,* chap. 3; for the impact of "Jewish money" on Clinton, see the appendix to *Holocaust Industry.* Foxman, *Never Again?* pp. 249–50. David Sterritt, "The one serious subject Hollywood doesn't avoid," *Christian Science Monitor* (22 November 2002) (Holocaust films); Brian Klug, "The collective Jew: Israel and the new anti-Semitism," *Patterns of Prejudice* (June

In *The Holocaust Industry*, this writer posited a distinction between the *Nazi holocaust*—the systematic extermination of Jews during World War II—and *The Holocaust*—the instrumentalization of the Nazi holocaust by American Jewish elites and their supporters. A parallel distinction needs to be made between *anti-Semitism*—the unjustifiable targeting of Jews solely for being Jews—and *"anti-Semitism"*—the instrumentalization of anti-Semitism by American (or other) Jewish elites. Like The Holocaust, "anti-Semitism" is an ideological weapon to deflect justified criticism of Israel and, concomitantly, powerful Jewish interests. In its current usage, "anti-Semitism," alongside the "war against terrorism," serves as a cloak for a massive assault on international law and human rights. Those Jews committed to the struggle against the real anti-Semitism must, in the first instance, expose this specious "anti-Semitism" for the sham it is. "[T]here are no patent remedies and quick solutions available" for anti-Semitism, the authors of *Manifestations* conclude. "[I]t is not possible to formulate a once and for all strategy, which is effective everywhere."[26] This writer begs

---

2003) (an adaptation of this essay appeared in the 2 February 2004 issue of *The Nation* under the title "The Myth of the New Anti-Semitism"). The question of the extent of Jewish power comes up most often in regard to U.S. policy toward Israel. Those believing that U.S. national interests ultimately trump the power of the Jewish lobby typically point to Eisenhower's decision in 1956, despite an impending election, to rein in Israel. Yet it's also possible to adduce contrary evidence. For example, it's difficult to peruse the *Foreign Relations of the United States* volumes from the 1960s without concluding that the United States considered Israel's acquisition of nuclear weapons as in fundamental conflict with American national interests. The fear was that once Israel acquired an atomic bomb, Egypt would demand that the Soviet Union supply it with one, setting off an unconventional arms buildup in the Middle East that would culminate in a nuclear conflagration. The main leverage that successive U.S. administrations had was to deny Israel conventional weaponry unless it ceased nuclear development. But whenever the United States tried to apply this pressure, the Jewish lobby brought to bear overwhelming pressure of its own, the arms transfer going through without Israeli concessions. In recent years it has become nearly impossible to empirically test the hypothesis that U.S. national interest trumps the Jewish lobby or vice versa. This is because the degree of interpenetration, or revolving door, of personnel between the Jewish lobby and U.S. administrations effectively precludes such a test. Looking at older documents, one could see the U.S. government "here" and the Jewish lobby "there," and watch how they interacted. But now it's hard to know where "here" ends and "there" begins. How can one really know on what interest or at whose behest a Martin Indyk, Dennis Ross, Paul Wolfowitz, or Richard Perle is acting when he argues policy on the Middle East? Of course, a case can also be made that this whole question is moot: Israel has become so integral to, as well as dependent on, U.S. policy that it has ceased to exist as an autonomous actor having autonomous interests, anymore than Texas has autonomous interests (does anyone ask whose interests Bush is serving?); and the interpenetration of the Jewish lobby and U.S. administrations is more symptom than cause of this wholly internalized relationship.

26. *Manifestations*, p. 37.

to differ. Tell the truth, fight for justice: this is the time-tested strategy for fighting anti-Semitism, as well as other forms of bigotry. If, as all the important studies agree, current resentment against Jews has coincided with Israel's brutal repression of the Palestinians, then a patent remedy and quick solution would plainly be to end the occupation. A full Israeli withdrawal from the territories conquered in 1967 would also deprive those real anti-Semites exploiting Israel's repression as a pretext to demonize Jews—and who can doubt they exist?—of a dangerous weapon, as well as expose their real agenda. And the more vocally Jews dissent from Israel's occupation, the fewer will be those non-Jews who mistake Israel's criminal policies and the uncritical support (indeed encouragement) of mainline Jewish organizations for the popular Jewish mood. On the other side, the worst enemies in the struggle against real anti-Semitism are the philo-Semites. This problem typically arises on the European scene. By turning a blind eye to Israeli crimes in the name of sensitivity to past Jewish suffering, they enable Israel to continue on a murderous path that foments anti-Semitism and, for that matter, the self-destruction of Israelis. The philo-Semitic application of this special dispensation to American Jewish elites has proven equally catastrophic. As already noted, Jewish elites in the United States have enjoyed enormous prosperity. From this combination of economic and political power has sprung, unsurprisingly, a mindset of Jewish superiority. Wrapping themselves in the mantle of The Holocaust, these Jewish elites pretend—and, in their own solipsistic universe, perhaps even imagine themselves—to be victims, dismissing any and all criticism as manifestations of "anti-Semitism." And, from this lethal brew of formidable power, chauvinistic arrogance, feigned (or imagined) victimhood, and Holocaust-immunity to criticism has sprung a terrifying recklessness and ruthlessness on the part of American Jewish elites. Alongside Israel, they are the main fomenters of anti-Semitism in the world today. Coddling them is not the answer. They need to be stopped.

PART II

THE GREATEST TALE EVER SOLD

Almost all criminal defendants—including most of my
clients—are factually guilty of the crimes they have been
charged with. The criminal lawyer's job, for the most part,
is to represent the *guilty*, and—if possible—to get them off.

Alan M. Dershowitz, *The Best Defense*

Introduction

> The defense attorney comes close to being a pure
> one-sided advocate for his generally guilty client.
>
> Alan M. Dershowitz, *Letters to a Young Lawyer*

IN 2003 ALAN DERSHOWITZ, Felix Frankfurter Professor of Law at Harvard Law School, published *The Case for Israel.*[1] The book became an immediate and influential national best seller. American Jewish organizations reportedly earmarked a copy for every Jewish high school graduate and widely distributed it on college campuses, while the Israeli Foreign Ministry purchased thousands of copies for worldwide distribution, Israeli embassies stockpiled it, Israeli information officers used it as a basic text, and Israel's Mission at the United Nations distributed hundreds of copies to U.N. ambassadors and officers.[2] Dershowitz himself plainly invested a great deal in this literary undertaking. He reports having recruited a small army of research assistants and having labored on the book "since 1967" (p. vii). One might reasonably infer that *The Case for Israel* represents the summit of Dershowitz's mental powers.

"The purpose of this book," Dershowitz succinctly sets forth, "is to help clear the air by providing direct and truthful defenses to false

1. Hoboken, N.J.: John Wiley and Sons. All parenthetical page references in the body of this text refer to the first cloth edition of the book, published in August 2003.

2. Haim Handwerker, "A paragon, this Israel," *Haaretz* (12 December 2003); Stuart Winer, "Dershowitz: Use cable to fight anti-Semitism," *Jerusalem Post* (online edition) (23 December 2003); "Israeli Mission Distributes Dershowitz Book to World Leaders" (12 January 2004), www.israel-un.org/latest/un_newsletter/12jan2004.htm.

accusations" (p. 12). In his view, Israel's "supporters" have been too passive in the face of unwarranted attacks: "The time has come for a proactive defense of Israel to be offered in the court of public opinion" (p. 1). One might have thought that, whatever shortcomings Israel's "supporters" suffer from, failure to defend Israel aggressively is not one of them. Indeed, as was shown in Part I of this book, using the pretext of fighting the "new anti-Semitism," they have orchestrated a media extravaganza the past few years to fend off criticism of Israel. According to Dershowitz, he is "unique in being a senior professor who is prepared to speak out for Israel."[3] This will perhaps come as a surprise even to his Harvard colleagues,[4] let alone those familiar with academic life generally. Be that as it may, Dershowitz has set himself a formidable task: exposing not only the lies purveyed by Israel's avowed enemies but those that "[m]any Israeli peace advocates are also willing to accept" (p. 220). To achieve this goal, he tells readers, "I support [my case] with facts and figures, some of which will surprise those who get their information from biased sources," and "I do not generally rely on pro-Israel sources but primarily on objective, and sometimes to emphasize the point, overtly anti-Israel sources" (pp. 2, 7).

In reality Alan Dershowitz has concocted a threadbare hoax. It's not altogether a coincidence that the Amazon.com website typically brackets *The Case for Israel* with Joan Peters's *From Time Immemorial*. Peters's book was published in 1984, after Israel invaded Lebanon and suffered its first major public relations debacle. Dershowitz's book was published in 2003, after the second intifada, when Israel endured another public relations disaster. Both books served the same basic purpose of shoring up morale among the Zionist faithful. Their modi operandi were likewise identical: in the guise of a scholarly tract, each grossly distorts the documentary record. To be sure, in Dershowitz's case this description applies only on those rare occasions when he adduces any evidence at all: whereas Peters's forte was mangling primary documents, Dershowitz's is citing absurd sources or stitching claims out of whole cloth.[5] Leaning on his academic pedigree to wow

3. Handwerker, "A paragon."

4. See, e.g., the statements of Harvard professor Ruth Wisse quoted in Part I of this book.

5. On a related note, it is unnerving how heavily Dershowitz relies in general on Hollywood pulp films to support legal arguments. To illustrate a point in a scholarly article for *Israel Law Review*, he cites at great length "'Mississippi Burning'—which was nominated for 7 Academy Awards" ("Is It Necessary to Apply 'Physical Pressure' to Terror-

readers and in lieu of any supporting evidence, he typically clinches an argument with rhetorical flourishes like "This is a simple fact not subject to reasonable dispute" (p. 7), or "[T]here can be no reasonable disagreement about the basic facts" (p. 8), or "This is simply historical fact" (p. 75), or "These are incontrovertible historical facts not subject to reasonable dispute" (p. 77), and on and on—almost invariably signaling that the assertion in question is sheer rubbish. Regarding his lecture tour for *The Case for Israel*, Dershowitz reports, "Whenever I make a speech, the most common phrase I hear from students afterward is, 'We didn't know.'"[6] One reason perhaps is that much of what he claims never happened. During a television debate on his book, Dershowitz offered to "give $10,000 to the PLO" if his interlocutor (or anyone else) could "find a historical fact in my book that you can prove to be false."[7] The genuine challenge is to unearth *any* meaningful historical fact in *The Case for Israel*.

The core of Dershowitz's book is a defense of Israel's human rights record. "[I]t is the thesis of this book," he writes,

> that no nation in the history of the world that has faced comparable threats to its survival—both external and internal—has ever made greater efforts at, and has ever come closer to, achieving the high norms of the rule of law. Yet no civilized nation in the history of the world . . . has ever been as repeatedly, unfairly, and hypocritically condemned and criticized by the international community as Israel has been over the years. The net result is that the *gulf* between Israel's *actual* record of compliance with the rule of law and its *perceived* record of compliance with the rule of law is greater than for any other nation in history. (p. 222; emphases in original)

The gulf would appear to be substantial indeed, for in Dershowitz's opinion, Israel's record on human rights is "generally superb" (p. 204). To prove this thesis, however, he must negotiate a daunting obstacle. Since the late 1970s and even more so since the beginning of the 1987–1993 uprising, when it could no longer be ignored, Israel's human rights record in the Occupied Territories has been monitored by

ists—and to Lie About It?" [spring–summer 1989], p. 199n18), while to illustrate a point in a conference paper delivered in Israel he draws on "a great film, 'The Accused,' with Jodie Foster" ("Defending against Terrorism within the Rule of Law" [18 December 2003], www.herzliyaconference.org/Eng). The perverse results of Dershowitz's reliance on yet another "great film" and Academy Award winner are examined later.
6. Winer, "Dershowitz."
7. *Scarborough Country* (8 September 2003), www.msnbc.com/news/963879.asp.

a multitude of human rights organizations, some based in Israel itself, such as B'Tselem (Israeli Information Center for Human Rights in the Occupied Territories), the Public Committee against Torture in Israel, and Physicians for Human Rights–Israel, and others fulfilling a global mandate such as Amnesty International and Human Rights Watch. It is also subject to supervision by U.N. and other agencies charged generally with monitoring compliance with human rights law. Although each of these bodies maintains an autonomous research and field staff, their respective findings on Israel and the Occupied Territories, regarding both actual fact and legal interpretation, on substance as well as on detail, are often indistinguishable one from the next. An Amnesty International study of human rights violations during the second intifada observes: "[T]here have been numerous investigations into the situation in Israel and the Occupied Territories—by the UN . . . and international and local human rights organizations—and there has been a remarkable consensus in the conclusions and recommendations of the resulting reports."[8] The problem for Dershowitz is that these findings, which reflect the consensus of the human rights community, do not support the claim that Israel's human rights record is "generally superb"; rather the contrary. The most fundamental—and telling—fact about the chapters of *The Case for Israel* devoted to human rights issues is that *never once does Dershowitz cite a single mainstream human rights organization to support any of his claims*. It's not because he doesn't want to, but because he can't. Instead, he resorts to blatantly partisan sources or—in brazen contempt of scholarly protocol—simply invents evidence. Had he cited the findings of mainstream human rights organizations, Dershowitz would have had to title his book *The Case* against *Israel*.

Not only does Dershowitz systematically ignore their findings, but in order to justify having done so, he seeks to malign the human rights organizations themselves. On the one hand, his thesis is untenable so long as their credibility remains intact; on the other, these organizations constitute the main bulwark of human rights protections, which he staunchly opposes. This twofold concern points up Dershowitz's dilemma. "The case for Israel can and should be made not by compromising principles of justice, egalitarianism, civil liberties, and liberalism," he wrote in *Chutzpah*, but "rather by reference to those lofty

---

8. Amnesty International, *Broken Lives—A Year of Intifada* (London, 2001), p. 9.

principles."[9] Having postured as a liberal and civil libertarian, he's duty bound to defend "those lofty principles," yet as a blind supporter of Israel, he cannot but oppose them: dependent as it is on brute force, Israel's occupation would prove unsustainable if the applicability of international law were recognized and, more important, actually enforced. Accordingly, while parading as a civil libertarian in the United States and justifying Israeli policy in the name of these principles, Dershowitz has consistently defended Israel's most egregious human rights violations.

To demonstrate that "Amnesty International has failed the test of even-handedness," Dershowitz twice cites an op-ed columnist who alleges that an Amnesty representative at a U.N. conference misstated that none of the Palestinian suicide bombers were minors (pp. 130, 195). Neither Dershowitz nor the columnist cited provides the name of this spokesperson, making the claim impossible to verify. On the other hand, Amnesty's prepared remarks and formal interventions at the conference—which are what substantively count and which are available for inspection—don't contain such a statement. Even if, against the available evidence, the alleged statement was accurately reported, what would it prove except that an Amnesty representative in an informal setting made an error?[10] Dershowitz also alleges that Amnesty grossly lied about Israel's record on torture. It didn't, but he grossly misrepresented the documentary record; see Chapter 6. B'Tselem is not a "human rights" organization, according to Dershowitz, because it "investigate[s] only Israel and the territories." In *Chutzpah,* Dershowitz leveled a similar charge against Al-Haq, the respected Palestinian human rights organization. He juxtaposes such human rights organizations, whose only concern is "promoting . . . parochial interests" and "self-serving advocacy of their own rights and interest,"

9. Alan Dershowitz, *Chutzpah* (Boston, 1991), p. 212.
10. Dershowitz cites Anne Bayefsky, "Human Rights Groups Have Less Than Noble Agendas," *Chicago Sun-Times* (6 April 2003). In the column Bayefsky alleges that the statement was made by an Amnesty "representative" during a "lunchtime recess." For Amnesty's written submission to the conference, see Amnesty International, *2003 UN Commission on Human Rights: A Time for Deep Reflection* (13 March 2003); for its oral statement, see Commission on Human Rights, 59th Session (17 March–25 April 2003); "Agenda item 8: Question of the violation of human rights in the occupied Arab territories, including Palestine" (31 March 2003); for a record of the plenary discussion after Amnesty delivered its oral statement, see NGO News Center, United Nations Commission on Human Rights, 59th session, "Plenary—31 March 2003—Afternoon session" (1 April 2003).

against authentic *"human* rights organizations" such as the "Anti-Defamation League," whose concern is "the universal rights of *all* human beings" (emphases in original).[11] Leaving aside his example of an authentic human rights organization (which speaks for itself)[12] and looking strictly at his argument, this would mean that the ACLU isn't a real civil liberties organization, because its mandate covers only *American* civil liberties; and the NAACP isn't a real civil rights organization because its mandate covers only *black* people. Revealingly, Dershowitz is altogether mute on Human Rights Watch, although its salience in the human rights community matches Amnesty's, and its reports on Israel and the Occupied Territories reach the same damning conclusions as Amnesty's. The reason for this silence is not hard to find. HRW is an *American*-based organization, and many of its leading members are prominent Establishment figures. To denounce them as effectively anti-Semitic would require real chutzpah, not the cost-free—or really, highly lucrative—brand that Dershowitz peddles.

Were the purpose of Part II of this book merely to "expose" Dershowitz, its value would be rather limited. For those not willfully credulous, he has already exposed himself many times over. Rather, the substantive aim is to use *The Case for Israel* as a peg to explore crucial aspects of the Israel-Palestine conflict. Chapters 4 through 9 present a comprehensive picture of Israel's human rights record, as assembled by mainstream human rights organizations. If truth and justice are the most potent weapons in the arsenal of the oppressed, the manifold reports of these human rights organizations are the most underutilized resource of those struggling for a just resolution of the Israel-Palestine conflict. It appears that they are rarely read and almost never cited. And it is mainly because these uniquely authoritative publications lie around collecting dust that apologists can propagate so much mythology about Israel's human rights record. Were their findings widely disseminated, Israel's occupation would clearly be seen as morally indefensible.

Because Dershowitz appears to command respect as a legal scholar and civil libertarian,[13] special attention is also paid to his rendering of

---

11. Ben Zion Citrin and Shoshana Kordova, "Dershowitz comes to the defense of Appel," *Haaretz* (23 December 2003); Dershowitz, *Chutzpah*, p. 231.

12. For the Anti-Defamation League's (ADL's) wretched record of apologetics for, and quashing of any criticism of, Israel, see Part I of this book.

13. From whence Dershowitz's reputation as a civil libertarian springs is something of a mystery. Consider just his record in the U.S. context. Many of his classic courtroom cases collected in *The Best Defense* (New York, 1983) don't bear at all on civil liberties.

Israel's human rights record in comparison to the mainstream consensus. In addition, because Dershowitz's historical chapters recycle hoary myths on the Israel-Palestine conflict and also concoct new ones, a comparison between standard scholarship and his presentation is equally essential. Appendices II and III essay such a juxtaposition. Appendix I, on authorship, poses pointed questions about our cultural institutions. What does it say about intellectual life when a university chair at a leading university not only lifts material from another author's text, but does so from a book that has been uniformly discredited; when he is manifestly ignorant of the content of his own book; when the book is replete with transparent, pernicious errors; and when, despite all this, both he and the book are showered with praise?

He advocated for Jewish Defense League thugs who murdered the (Jewish) secretary of impresario Sol Hurok; for an Orthodox rabbi with a net worth of more than $100 million in the 1970s who brutally abused elderly patients in nursing homes he owned; for a notoriously corrupt megabucks attorney defending drug lords; and so on. There's only one ephemeral reference to his defense of an indigent black man. True, Dershowitz comes across as a passionate supporter of nudity and hard-core pornography. He also claims to be staunchly opposed to capital punishment, but this profession of faith rings rather hollow in the face of his equally staunch defense of extrajudicial executions. Dershowitz concludes *The Best Defense* on the exalted note that "[t]he job of the defense attorney is to challenge the government; to make those in power justify their conduct in relation to the powerless; to articulate and defend the right of those who lack the ability or resources to defend themselves," and that "[a]ttorneys who defend the guilty and the despised will never have a secure or comfortable place in any society" (pp. 415, 417). Perhaps so, but what does any of this have to do with *him*?

4

Impurity of Arms

DURING THE EARLY WEEKS of the second intifada (beginning in September 2000), the ratio of Palestinians to Israelis killed was 20:1, with the overwhelming majority of Palestinians "killed in demonstrations in circumstances when the lives of members of the [Israeli] security services were not in danger" (Amnesty International).[1] For the second intifada from September 2000 through November 2003, B'Tselem (Israeli Information Center for Human Rights in the Occupied Territories) reports the following data:

PALESTINIANS	ISRAELIS
2,236 Palestinians were killed by Israeli security forces in the Occupied Territories, including 428 minors.	196 Israeli civilians were killed by Palestinians in the Occupied Territories, including 30 minors.
32 Palestinians were killed by Israeli civilians in the Occupied	178 members of the Israeli security forces were killed by

---

1. For ratio, see Ben Kaspit, "When the intifada erupted, it was finally clear to all: Israel is not a state with an army but an army with a state," *Maariv* (6 September 2002), citing "government and security officials." Amnesty International, *Broken Lives—A Year of Intifada* (London, 2001), p. 14.

PALESTINIANS *(continued)*

Territories, including three minors.

48 Palestinians, residents of the Occupied Territories, were killed by Israeli security forces within Israel, including one minor.

ISRAELIS *(continued)*

Palestinians in the Occupied Territories.

376 Israeli civilians were killed within Israel by Palestinian residents of the Occupied Territories, including 74 minors.

77 members of the Israeli security forces were killed within Israel by Palestinian residents of the Occupied Territories.

Total = 2,316

Total = 827

The above figures considerably underestimate Palestinian deaths since, for example, they "do not include Palestinians who died after medical treatment was delayed due to restrictions of movement." For the first intifada (beginning December 1987) through May 2003, B'Tselem reports 3,650 Palestinians and 1,142 Israelis killed.[2]

NUMBERS

Challenging these figures, Dershowitz makes, and keeps repeating, three sorts of argument:

> The 3:1 ratio of Palestinians to Israelis killed during the second intifada "[i]gnored," according to Dershowitz, that "Palestinian terrorists had *attempted* to kill thousands more" in attacks thwarted by Israeli authorities (pp. 10, 123, 124; emphasis in original). Yet "in the first few days of the intifada," the Israeli newspaper *Maariv* reported, citing Israeli intelligence, "the IDF [Israel Defense Forces] fired about 700,000 bullets and other projectiles in Judea and Samaria and about 300,000 in Gaza. All told, about a million bullets and other projectiles were used"—or as one Israeli officer quipped, "a bullet for every child."[3] Should these spent shells also be tabulated as the Israeli army's attempts to kill one million Palestinian children in the first days of the intifada?

2. B'Tselem (Israeli Information Center for Human Rights in the Occupied Territories), "Total Casualties," www.btselem.org/English/Statistics/Total_Casualties.asp.
3. Kaspit, "When the intifada erupted."

The "2,000 or so Palestinians killed" in the second intifada included, according to Dershowitz, "alleged collaborators who were killed by other Palestinians" and "the suicide bombers themselves" (pp. 10, 123, 125–26). Yet the B'Tselem figure cited above does not include alleged Palestinian collaborators killed, and B'Tselem explicitly states that "the figures do not include Palestinians killed by an explosive device that they set or was on their person." Dershowitz also objects that the figure for Palestinian dead includes "armed Palestinian fighters" (p. 125), although he doesn't object that nearly a third of the figure for Israeli casualties consists of "Israeli security forces."

"When only innocent civilians are counted," according to Dershowitz, "significantly more Israelis than Palestinians have been killed" (pp. 10, 126–27, 146). The sole piece of evidence for this claim is an "internal analysis by the IDF" (p. 126). Yet, citing the same 3:1 ratio as B'Tselem of Palestinians to Israelis killed during the second intifada, Amnesty International reports: "The vast majority of those killed and injured on both sides have been unarmed civilians and bystanders."[4] Even if, for argument's sake, we assume that 51 percent of Palestinian casualties and 100 percent of Israeli casualties were civilians (which we know is not the case), many more Palestinian than Israeli civilians would nonetheless have been killed.

MOTIVE

Dershowitz repeatedly maintains that Palestinian and Israeli killings can't be compared because Israeli killings of Palestinians lacked willful intent. They were "unintended," "inadvertent," "caused accidentally," and so forth (pp. 11, 121, 124, 128, 190, 192). To demonstrate this, Dershowitz points to these pieces of evidence:

He reports that "[w]hen Israelis accidentally kill a civilian, there is internal criticism, boards of inquiry, and sometimes even punishment" (p. 128). Indeed, he points to one case in which an "Israeli soldier [was] given 49 days in jail for killing [a] Palestinian boy"

---

4. Amnesty International, "No one is safe—the spiral of killings and destruction must stop" (press release, 29 September 2003).

(p. 251n21)—which surely proves Israel's respect for Palestinian life. Dershowitz might also have cited this exemplary case: "Jerusalem District Court . . . sentence[d] Nahum Korman, a 37-year-old Israeli citizen, to six months community service for the killing of an 11-year-old Palestinian child, Hilmi Shawasheh. He was also ordered to pay 70,000 shekels to the victim's family. The punishment is in sharp contrast with the six and half year sentence given to Su'ad Hilmi Ghazal, a Palestinian from Sebastia village near Nablus who in December 1998 at the age of 15 and whilst suffering from psychological problems injured an Israeli settler by stabbing him." Or he might have cited the case of an IDF soldier "sentenced to 65 days' imprisonment for killing a 95-year-old Palestinian woman."[5] These derisory sentences were handed down in the tiny handful of Palestinian killings, mostly high-profile, actually prosecuted. Under the heading "First Conviction of Causing the Death of Palestinian in the Al-Aqsa Intifada," B'Tselem observes: "On May 3rd 2004 a Military Court sentenced Captain Zvi Kortzky to two months' imprisonment, four months' of military tasks and six months' probation. He had been convicted of shooting to death Muhammad Zid, 16. . . . This is the first time that an IDF soldier has been convicted of 'causing the death by negligence' of a Palestinian during the al-Aqsa intifada. . . . The conviction of Captain Kortzky is one of only three convictions related to the killing or wounding of civilians. . . . [Israel] has opened only seventy-two Military Police investigations that deal with killing or causing severe injury to civilians. Only thirteen of the investigations resulted in indictments, and only three convictions were obtained. The light sentence given to Kortzky, who killed a minor who was sitting in his home and did not endanger soldiers, gives a strong impression that Palestinian life is worthless."[6]

---

5. Amnesty International, "Impunity for Killers of Palestinians" (24 January 2001) (Korman); *Amnesty International Annual Report 2003*, "Israel and the Occupied Territories" (95-year-old woman).

6. B'Tselem, "First Conviction of Causing the Death of Palestinian in the Al-Aqsa Intifada," www.btselem.org/English/Special/040506_Court_Marshal.asp. See also on B'Tselem website, "Military Police investigations during the al-Aqsa Intifada," www .btselem.org/English/Open_Fire_Regulations/Jag_Investigations.asp, noting that even the few Military Police investigations "were opened only after human rights organizations, diplomats, or journalists put pressure."

Dershowitz cites an article by the editor of an Israeli periodical singing paeans to the "ethical training received by Israeli soldiers" —much like American Communists used to cite articles from Soviet Life singing paeans to the "freest country in the world"; the testimony of Professor Michael Walzer of Princeton University, "a strong critic of the Israeli occupation"—which will certainly come as news to critics of the Israeli occupation;[7] and "stories" told by "the chief of staff of the IDF" and an "Israeli infantry officer" that testify to the "tossing and turning . . . typical of Israeli soldiers who must make life-and-death decisions constrained by a rigid code of conduct"—plainly irrefutable evidence (pp. 145–47).

The consensus among human rights organizations, sampled in Table 4.1, is that Israeli security forces have resorted to reckless use of force in the Occupied Territories, showing callous disregard for human life. "[W]hen so many civilians have been killed and wounded," B'Tselem concludes, "the lack of intent makes no difference. Israel remains responsible."[8] In addition, as Amnesty International observes, Israel has at its disposal ample less violent options: "The Israeli security forces' ability to police violent demonstrations without the use of firearms is indicated in their policing of violent demonstrations by Jewish groups. . . . [N]o demonstration organized by a Jewish group has ever been fired on, even by rubber bullets."[9] Finally, another of Amnesty's conclusions bearing on U.S. responsibility for the ongoing atrocities merits mention: "The overwhelming majority of cases of unlawful killings and injuries in Israel and the Occupied Territories have been committed by the IDF using excessive force. In particular, the IDF have used US-supplied helicopters in punitive rocket attacks where there was no imminent danger to life. Israel has also used helicopter gunships to carry out extrajudicial executions and to fire at targets that resulted in the killing of civilians, including children. Many of Israel's military helicopters and spare parts have been supplied by the USA, Canada and the UK."[10]

7. For Walzer's gross apologetics for Israel, see Norman G. Finkelstein, *Image and Reality of the Israel-Palestine Conflict*, 2nd ed. (New York, 2003), pp. 1–3, 140, and sources cited on p. 207n9.

8. B'Tselem, *Operation Defensive Shield: Soldiers' Testimonies, Palestinian Testimonies* (Jerusalem, 2002), p. 5.

9. Amnesty International, *Excessive Use of Lethal Force* (London, 2000), p. 7; see also Amnesty International, *Broken Lives*, pp. 17–18.

10. Amnesty International, *Broken Lives*, p. 12.

TABLE 4.1 ISRAEL'S USE OF LETHAL FORCE
IN THE OCCUPIED TERRITORIES

Human Rights Watch, *Investigation into the Unlawful Use of Force in the West Bank, Gaza Strip and Northern Israel* (New York, 2000)	"The organization found a pattern of repeated Israeli use of excessive lethal force during clashes between its security forces and Palestinian demonstrators in situations where demonstrators were unarmed and posed no threat of death or serious injury to the security forces or to others. In cases that HRW investigated where gunfire by Palestinian security forces or armed protesters was a factor, use of lethal force by the IDF was indiscriminate and not directed at the source of the threat, in violation of international law enforcement standards" (p. 1).[a]
Amnesty International, *Excessive Use of Lethal Force* (London, 2000)	"[T]he majority of people killed were taking part in demonstrations where stones were the only weapon used. . . . A large proportion of those injured and killed included children usually present and often among those throwing stones during demonstrations. Bystanders, people within their homes and ambulance personnel were also killed. Many persons were apparently killed by poorly targeted lethal fire; others . . . appear, on many occasions, to have been deliberately targeted. In many of the locations where children were killed there was no imminent danger to life nor reasonable expectation of future danger" (pp. 5–6).[b]
B'Tselem (Israeli Information Center for Human Rights in the Occupied Territories), *Trigger Happy: Unjustified Shooting and Violation of the Open-Fire Regulations during the al-Aqsa Intifada* (Jerusalem, 2002)	"[Open-fire] regulations apparently enable firing in situations where there is no clear and present danger to life, or even in situations where there is no life-threatening danger at all" (p. 7).[c] "[T]he Military Police investigations unit has opened almost no investigations into cases where soldiers fired in violation of the Regulations. . . . The Military Police investigations that were initiated were not frank and serious attempts to reach the truth. . . . [I]n only two cases were indictments filed for unjustified shooting, and they were filed more than a year after the incidents occurred" (pp. 11–13).[d]

(continued)

TABLE 4.1 *(continued)*

B'Tselem, *Trigger Happy* *(continued)*	"During the first months of the al-Aqsa intifada, Palestinians held hundreds of demonstrations. . . . Palestinian demonstrators did not open fire in the vast majority of demonstrations. The soldiers responded to these demonstrations by using excessive and disproportionate force, leading to many casualties, including children" (p. 16). "[R]egulations . . . permit soldiers to open fire, automatically, at any Palestinian who approaches areas in the Gaza Strip referred to as 'danger zones.' . . . In effect, it constitutes a death sentence for every person who approaches, whether deliberately or by mistake, a settlement's fence, certain roads, or the fence along the border. . . . An order of this kind also completely ignores the fact that many Palestinians try to sneak into Israel to go to work and not to injure Israeli soldiers or civilians" (pp. 39–41).

[a]See also Human Rights Watch, *Center of the Storm: A Case Study of Human Rights Abuses in Hebron District* (New York, April 2001), pp. 3–4 and chap. 5.
[b]See also Amnesty International, *Broken Lives—A Year of Intifada* (London, 2001), pp. 14, 20, 23.
[c]See also B'Tselem, "The Open-Fire Regulations," www.btselem.org/english/Open_Fire_regulations/index.asp: "[t]he Regulations now state, in part, that stone-throwing is 'life threatening.'"
[d]For lack of military investigations, see also Amnesty International, *Broken Lives*, pp. 23–25, and B'Tselem, *Operation Defensive Shield: Soldiers' Testimonies, Palestinian Testimonies* (Jerusalem, 2002), p. 5, which reports: "In the first 18 months of the current intifada, soldiers have killed 697 Palestinians, but the army has launched only 21 Military Police investigations involving illegal shooting and filed only four indictments."

The following three sections titled "No Evidence," "Reducing Fatalities," and "Avoiding Civilian Casualties" refute Dershowitz's attempts to prove in specific instances Israel's benign use of force in the Occupied Territories. The subsequent sections titled "Terrorist Abortion" and "Diabolical Plots" expose Dershowitz's absurd attempts to demonstrate the unfathomable evil Israel faces, justifying its resort to lethal force.

─────────────────── NO EVIDENCE ───────────────────

To demonstrate that Israeli killings of Palestinians are unintentional, Dershowitz writes on page 126 of *The Case for Israel*, regarding the Israeli siege of Jenin in April 2002:

There is no evidence that Israeli soldiers deliberately killed even a single civilian.

In its comprehensive study *Jenin: IDF Military Operations*, Human Rights Watch found that "many of the civilian deaths" amounted to "unlawful and willful killings" by the IDF—for example, "Kamal Zgheir, a fifty-seven-year-old wheelchair-bound man who was shot and run over by a tank on a major road outside the camp on April 10, even though he had a white flag attached to his wheelchair."[11] In its comprehensive study *Shielded from Scrutiny: IDF violations in Jenin and Nablus*, Amnesty International likewise documented many cases "where people were killed or injured in circumstances suggesting that they were unlawfully and deliberately targeted"—for example, "On 6 April 2002, 33-year-old Jamal al-Sabbagh was shot by the IDF after he had been taken into their custody," although, according to a witness, "he was unarmed and had posed no threat to the soldiers who had detained him."[12]

On page 144 of *The Case for Israel*, Dershowitz further asserts that the Israeli siege of Jenin "**is regarded by many as a model of how to conduct urban warfare.**" Human Rights Watch concluded that "during their incursion into the Jenin refugee camp, Israeli forces committed serious violations of international humanitarian law, some amounting *prima facie* to war crimes," while Amnesty likewise concluded that "the IDF carried out actions which violate international human rights and humanitarian law; some of these actions amount to war crimes."[13]

REDUCING FATALITIES

To demonstrate Israel's sensitivity to Palestinian life, Dershowitz states on page 128 of *The Case for Israel*:

Israel tries to use rubber bullets and other weapons designed to reduce fatalities, and aims at the legs whenever possible.

A November 2000 study by Physicians for Human Rights (PHR) found that in Gaza "[n]early half the victims were shot in the head.

11. Human Rights Watch, *Jenin: IDF Military Operations* (New York, 2002), pp. 2–3 and esp. chap. 6 ("Civilian Casualties and Unlawful Killings in Jenin").
12. Amnesty International, *Shielded from Scrutiny: IDF Violations in Jenin and Nablus* (London, 2002), pp. 14–25 (Sabbagh at 16–17), 67 ("unlawfully and deliberately").
13. Human Rights Watch, *Jenin*, chap. 2 ("Summary"); Amnesty International, *Shielded from Scrutiny*, p. 5.

There were several victims shot in the back or from behind and in one instance, evidence indicates the victim was probably on the ground when shot. . . . In several of these cases, PHR was able to document that there was no imminent danger posed to the IDF in the context of the shooting." It also found "a repetitive pattern of high velocity gunshot wounds to the leg, particularly to the thigh. These wounds cause extreme injury. . . . The majority of victims . . . will have permanent disability in the affected leg. . . . [M]any of those injured in this manner were at most throwing stones." PHR concludes: "The numerous head and eye injuries, the high proportion of thigh wounds and fatal head wounds, and the fact that similar patterns of such shootings occurred over a period of weeks demonstrate two disturbing patterns: 1) IDF soldiers are not firing only in life-threatening situations and 2) they are firing at heads and thighs to injure and kill, not to avoid loss of life and injury."[14] In a March 2002 study, B'Tselem reported the testimony of Major General Mickey Levi, inventor of the device for shooting rubber bullets, that these bullets "should not be categorized as non-lethal." It goes on to cite testimonies from IDF soldiers that "many soldiers alter rubber bullets to make them more lethal."[15] An October 2002 Amnesty International study found that the IDF "regularly" used rubber bullets against child demonstrators "at distances considerably closer than the minimum permitted range, . . . and the pattern of injury indicates that IDF practice has not been to aim at the legs of demonstrators, as the majority of injuries suffered by children from rubber-coated bullets are to the upper body and head." Amnesty concludes: "[T]he large number of children killed and injured by the IDF throughout the Occupied Territories in the past two years and the fact that most children killed or injured were hit in the head or upper body shows that in their use of firearms against Palestinian children, the IDF have consistently breached international standards regulating the use of force and firearms."[16]

14. Physicians for Human Rights, *Evaluation of the Use of Force in Israel, Gaza and the West Bank: Medical and Forensic Investigation* (Boston, 3 November 2000), pp. 2, 17–18.

15. B'Tselem, *Trigger Happy: Unjustified Shooting and Violation of the Open-Fire Regulations during the al-Aqsa Intifada* (Jerusalem, 2002), pp. 19–20. On rubber bullets, see also B'Tselem, *The Use of Firearms* (Jerusalem, 1990), pp. 15–16.

16. Amnesty International, *Killing the Future: Children in the Line of Fire* (London, 2002), p. 13.

================= AVOIDING CIVILIAN CASUALTIES =================

To demonstrate Israel's "commitment to proportionality and to avoid-ing unnecessary civilian casualties," Dershowitz cites on page 146 of *The Case for Israel* the "Israeli attack directed against Salah Shehadeh, a leading Hamas commander who was responsible for hundreds of ter-rorist bombings." Dershowitz goes on to state:

> On several [prior] occasions, the army passed up opportunities to attack him "because he was with his wife or children. Each time Shehadeh's life was spared, he directed more suicide bombings against Israel." In other words, Israel was prepared to risk the lives of its own civilians in order to spare the lives of Palestinian civilians, including the wife of a major terrorist.

The internal quote, from a *Boston Globe* article, is the self-serving testimony of an Israeli officer. Dershowitz also forgets to mention what happened during the "attack directed against Salah Shehadeh," which the author of the *Globe* article placed in the lead paragraph: "an Israel Air Force F-16 dropped a one-ton bomb on Salah Shehadeh's Gaza City apartment building," killing, alongside Shehadeh, "another 14 Palestin-ian civilians, nine of them children."[17] (Scores were injured and many homes destroyed.) Air Force Commander Major General Dan Halutz said on Israeli army radio regarding Shehadeh's assassination: "[W]e fired knowing his wife would be near him."[18] Amnesty International deplored the attack as "disproportionate" and "utterly unacceptable." Although an IDF inquiry subsequently determined that the means of attack had been "inappropriate," Major General Halutz told the pilots who dropped the one-ton bomb, "Guys, sleep well tonight. By the way, I sleep well at night, too," while Prime Minister Sharon hailed the bombing as "a great success."[19] The same attack on Shehadeh receives a different treatment in an interview Dershowitz gave to Salon.com:

17. David B. Green, "Fighting by the Book," *Boston Globe* (20 April 2003).
18. Amnesty International, *Israel Must End Its Policy of Assassinations* (London: July 2003), p. 5.
19. Amnesty International, "Killing Palestinian civilians will not bring security or peace" (press release, 23 July 2002); Aryeh Dayan, "One day in five, the IDF attempts assassination," *Haaretz* (21 May 2003) (air force commander); "Israel, the Occupied West Bank and Gaza Strip, and Palestinian Authority Territories," *Human Rights Watch World Report 2003* (New York) (IDF inquiry, Sharon). Asked how a pilot felt releasing a one-ton bomb over a residential neighborhood, Halutz replied: "I feel a slight ping in the aircraft, the result of releasing the bomb. It passes a second later, and that's it. That's what I feel."

"I was very much against sending that bomb to kill the terrorist in Gaza, which resulted in 14 innocent people being killed. It should never have been done." Referring presumably to Sharon's statement hailing the "great success," Dershowitz goes on to laud the "Israeli government, which condemned the activity."[20]

TERRORIST ABORTION

On page 131 of *The Case for Israel*, Dershowitz writes about female suicide bombers:

> Some of these women have been recruited by the use of emotional and cultural blackmail. For example, terrorist operatives deliberately seduced Andalib Suleiman, a twenty-one-year-old woman from Bethlehem. When she became pregnant, she was told that the only way to avoid the shame was to die a martyr's death. She then agreed to blow herself up in a Jerusalem shopping market, killing six civilians, including two workers from China. A similar example is Ayat al-Ahras [*sic*], an eighteen-year-old woman from Dehaisi [*sic*], who blew herself up in a supermarket, killing two civilians, after having been seduced and made pregnant. This method of terrorist abortion is a despicable example of creating new life in order to generate death. There are other examples of young women being raped in order to turn them into shamed women whose only means of restoring family honor is martyrdom. In one case, the family learned of the attempt by Tanzim operatives to blackmail their daughter and smuggled her out of Bethlehem. She is now living in hiding.

What is Dershowitz's evidence for the practice of "terrorist abortion"? His single source is an official Israeli government website: "Israeli Security Forces, 'Blackmailing Young Women into Suicide Terrorism,' Israeli Ministry of Foreign Affairs Report, February 12, 2002" (p. 252n30). The posted item is based on a confidential "Israeli Military Intelligence Report," which is based on "[r]eliable Palestinian sources"—none of which are identified or independently corroborated.

A recent book by Barbara Victor, *Army of Roses*, examines the "inside world of Palestinian women suicide bombers." She reports that "hundreds" of Palestinian women "beg to be suicide bombers" and that "[i]n Bethlehem alone there are two hundred girls willing and ready to sacrifice themselves for Palestine." It is unclear why "terrorist

---

20. Suzy Hansen, "Why Terrorism Works" (interview with Alan Dershowitz), Salon .com (12 September 2002).

operatives" must rape Palestinian women, given the number of them already volunteering for suicide missions. Victor views a Palestinian woman's decision to become a suicide bomber as "a misguided and pitiful attempt at liberation," and the men who recruit them as "reprehensible." She relies heavily on information provided by Israeli officials, military personnel, and "experts" on terrorism. She repeats many of Israel's discredited assertions such as that the Sabra and Shatila refugee camps in September 1982 "sheltered between two and three thousand terrorists among the civilian population," and she deplores Yasser Arafat as "perhaps the most immoral" of leaders. Yet, although she devotes nearly thirty pages specifically to Andalib Suleiman from Bethlehem and Ayat al-Akhras from Dheisheh camp, and although clearly partisan to Israel, nowhere does Victor allege that Suleiman, al-Akhras, or any other female Palestinian was sexually seduced or raped into becoming a suicide bomber.[21] Joshua Hammer, *Newsweek*'s Jerusalem correspondent and author of *A Season in Bethlehem*, similarly examined the al-Akhras case in detail. He demonstrates that al-Akhras perpetrated an entirely voluntary act, and sought out her dispatcher rather than being recruited. Hammer makes no mention of seduction or pregnancy, or indeed any romantic involvement or sexual relations, as precipitating factors in her decision.[22]

DIABOLICAL PLOTS

On page 127 of *The Case for Israel*, Dershowitz writes:

> Terrorists try everything possible to maximize deaths, even sometimes reportedly *soaking the nails they use in their antipersonnel bombs in rat poison to prevent coagulation of blood*. Recently, Israeli doctors expressed concern that the blood of some of the suicide bombers, which splatters all over the scene and is touched by medical personnel, as well as their bones, which penetrate the bodies of the victims, might contain hepatitis or the AIDS virus, *raising the fear that terrorist leaders could be turning suicide bombers into biological warfare carriers* either by injecting them or selecting carriers as suicide bombers. The first such case was documented in the July 2002 issue of the *Israel Medical Association Journal*. (italics added)

21. Barbara Victor, *Army of Roses* (Emmaus, Penn., 2003), pp. 30–31, 78, 195, 234, 272; for Suleiman, see pp. 192, 248–51; for al-Akhras, see pp. 200–209, 218–30, 250.
22. Joshua Hammer, *A Season in Bethlehem* (New York, 2003), pp. 151–66.

On page 193 of *The Case for Israel,* Dershowitz writes:

[T]here is still no moral equivalence between *exploding an antipersonnel bomb made of nails soaked in rat poison* whose sole purpose is to maximize civilian deaths and injuries, on the one hand, and targeting terrorists under circumstances in which it is likely that some innocent civilians may die, on the other hand. (italics added)

What is Dershowitz's evidence for the diabolical plots? Dershowitz cites three sources: "Karen Birchard, 'Hep B case makes suicide bombers an infection risk,' *Medical Post,* MacLean Hunter Ltd., September 10, 2002"; "Michael Ledeen, 'Hebrew U Survivor: An Interview with Eliad Moreh,' *National Review* online, August 6, 2002"; "'Hepatitis Spread Via Suicide Bombers,' *The Straits Times* (Singapore), July 26, 2002" (p. 251nn16, 19, 20). Yet these articles report only that, based on the case of one suicide bomber apparently infected with hepatitis B, Israeli doctors speculate that the blood and bones of other suicide bombers might be infected with this and other diseases. Not one of the cited references mentions fears that the suicide bombers were being deliberately injected by their dispatchers or even that the bombers or their dispatchers were aware that they were carriers of infectious diseases. Not one of the cited references mentions anything about anti-personnel weapons being soaked in rat poison. A journalist investigating the factual basis for the "rat poison" claim, which occasionally crops up in the U.S. media, discovered an "absence of any forensic proof." It is "the sort of tale that newsroom cynics call 'too good to check,'" he concluded. "We so want to believe that the Palestinians are stinking up their bombs with rat poison that we won't even ask for evidence."[23] Even the right-wing *Jerusalem Post* cites the director-general of an Israeli hospital to the effect that it's "ridiculous to suggest" that a suicide bomber infected with hepatitis B "was selected for his mission specifically because he was a carrier": "Hepatitis B is endemic in the Middle East, and more likely in people from lower socio-economic groups. So it is not surprising that the virus was found."[24] The most exhaustive study to date of Palestinian suicide bombers is Human Rights Watch, *Erased in a Moment: Suicide Bombing Attacks against Israeli Civilians.* It makes no mention of any of these allegations. On the other hand, Amnesty International did call on Israel to investigate the use by Israeli settlers of "toxic chemicals" for the purpose of "poisoning" Palestinian fields.[25]

23. Jack Shafer, "The d-Con Bomb," *Slate* (11 July 2002), http://slate.msn.com/?id=2067819.
24. Judy Siegel, "Hepatitis in suicide bomber 'no threat,'" *Jerusalem Post* (8 June 2001).
25. Human Rights Watch, *Erased in a Moment: Suicide Bombing Attacks against Israeli Civilians* (New York, 2002). Amnesty International, "Israeli authorities must put an immediate end to settler violence" (press release, 25 April 2005).

RESPONSIBILITY

Dershowitz maintains that "[t]he fault for all civilian casualties in the Israeli-Palestinian conflict lies exclusively with the Palestinian terrorists, who deliberately create a situation in which civilians will be killed."[26] The following sections titled "Human Shields," "Endangering Kindergartens," "All Their Fault," and "Blood Libel" examine his attempts to prove this. The section titled "Culture of Death" looks at the broader issue of responsibility for child deaths. The sections titled "Supporting Nonviolence" and "Terrorist Diehard" examine Dershowitz's support of those opposing terrorism.

HUMAN SHIELDS

To demonstrate the culpability of Palestinians for their civilian deaths, Dershowitz writes on page 120 of *The Case for Israel* that they

> use women (including pregnant women) and children as human shields.[27]

Human shields refers to the conscription of civilians for military operations. Dershowitz cites no source for the claim that Palestinians use human shields. Human rights organizations have documented "instances in which armed Palestinians endangered civilians by firing on IDF soldiers from locations that exposed civilians to IDF return fire" (Human Rights Watch). None of these organizations, however, have accused armed Palestinians of forcibly recruiting civilians for life-endangering operations. On the other hand, although human rights reports do extensively document *Israel's* use of Palestinian human shields, Dershowitz omits explicit mention of this. Rather, on page 150 of *The Case for Israel* he writes:

> [T]he army devised a tactic called the neighbor procedure, pursuant to which they first demanded the surrender of the terrorist over a loudspeaker. If that produced no results, they sent a Palestinian neighbor to the house bearing a message to the terrorist asking him to surrender. . . . In the summer of 2002, the procedure resulted in the first casualty of a Palestinian man . . . who was shot and killed by a terrorist who mistook him for an Israeli soldier. . . . As a result of this tragedy . . . , several Israeli rights organizations brought a lawsuit seeking to have the Supreme Court enjoin any further use of the neighbor procedure. . . . The Supreme Court of Israel

---

26. "Q&A with Alan Dershowitz," *Jerusalem Post* (online edition) (20 October 2004).

27. He makes similar claims on pp. 128 and 168.

not only heard the case but issued the injunction prohibiting the IDF from using this procedure in the future.

Human rights organizations paint a different picture. An April 2002 Human Rights Watch report found that "the IDF is systematically coercing Palestinian civilians"—including minors—"to assist military operations." For example, "friends, neighbors, and relatives of 'wanted' Palestinians were taken at gunpoint to knock on doors, open strange packages, and search houses in which the IDF suspected armed Palestinians were present. Some families found their houses taken over and used as military positions by the IDF during an operation while they themselves were ordered to remain inside."[28] A November 2002 report by B'Tselem found that, beyond these practices, Palestinians were ordered to "walk in front of soldiers to shield them from gunfire, while the soldiers hold a gun behind their backs and sometimes fire over their shoulders." It also reported that "the soldiers in the field did not initiate this practice; rather, the use of human shields is an integral part of the orders they receive."[29] In May 2002, human rights organizations petitioned the Israel Supreme Court to prohibit use of human shields. The state committed itself to cease use of human shields as "living shields" against gunfire or attacks, but reserved the right to order Palestinians to direct other Palestinians to leave their house—that is, the "neighbor procedure." Deeming this distinction "incomprehensible," B'Tselem wrote: "In each instance, soldiers jeopardize the lives of innocent civilians to protect themselves; thus, these cases are equally forbidden." In August 2002 a Palestinian conscripted by the IDF for the neighbor procedure was killed approaching the house of a Hamas activist. The Supreme Court then issued a temporary restraining order against use of human shields and the neighbor procedure. To gain the Supreme Court's approval, the state barely recast the neighbor procedure in December 2002 as "operational directive—prior warning." "Despite the cosmetic changes in the procedure," B'Tselem observed, "it remained illegal and immoral." In January 2003 the Supreme Court prohibited use of human shields but allowed "the state to implement the new procedure." In reality, the IDF still conscripted Palestinians in life-endanger-

28. Human Rights Watch, *In a Dark Hour: The Use of Civilians during IDF Arrest Operations* (New York, 2002), p. 2. The prior HRW quote ("armed Palestinians endangered civilians") comes from p. 3 of this report.
29. B'Tselem, *Human Shield: Use of Palestinian Civilians as Human Shields in Violation of High Court of Justice Order* (Jerusalem, November 2002), pp. 2, 19.

ing military operations.[30] In March 2004, B'Tselem reported, "IDF Continues Using Civilians as Human Shields to Make Arrests."[31]

ENDANGERING KINDERGARTENS

To demonstrate Palestinian culpability for civilian deaths, Dershowitz writes on, respectively, pages 120, 132, 168, and 225 of *The Case for Israel,* that Palestinians:

locate . . . bomb-making factories alongside kindergartens

place their bomb-making factories adjacent to kindergartens and elementary schools

place their bomb-making factories adjacent to schools

plac[e] their bomb factories next to kindergartens

The only source Dershowitz cites for this repeated claim reads: "Statements made by Slaim Haga, a senior Hamas operative, and Ahmed Moughrabi, a Tanzim operative, May 27, 2002" (p. 252n33). No other information is provided. Entering the key terms in Google brings up the Israeli Ministry of Foreign Affairs website.[32] The information posted on this site comes from "Israeli security sources." The statements of Haga and Moughrabi about locating "explosives" factories near schools were allegedly "confessed during questioning by the ISA [Israel Security Agency]." Assuming, for argument's sake, that they did actually confess, readers should consult Chapter 6, on torture, to learn how Israeli security extracts confessions.

ALL THEIR FAULT

To demonstrate the full culpability of Palestinians for the deaths of their children, Dershowitz states on pages 131–32 of *The Case for Israel:*

The more that Palestinian leaders break the taboo against using youths as terrorists, the more youths will be injured and killed. Such deliberate

---

30. B'Tselem, "Human Shields," www.btselem.org/english/Human_shield/index.asp.
31. *B'Tselem Email Update* (29 March 2004). For the eyewitness account of an Israeli rabbi who claimed "that police tied a 12-year-old Palestinian boy to the bonnet of a jeep to deter stone-throwing protesters in a village north-west of Jerusalem," see Nuala Haughey, "Israelis used boy (12) as 'human shield,'" *Irish Times* (24 April 2004).
32. "Participation of Children and Teenagers in Terrorist Activity during the 'Al-Aqsa' Intifada" (January 2003), www.mfa.gov.il/mfa/go.asp?MFAHon100.

misuse of children is an extreme form of child abuse, and it is entirely the fault of the abusers, not those who legitimately defend themselves against fire bombers and suicide bombers who happen to be youths.

[T]he fault lies entirely with those who have decided to use children as carriers of deadly explosives. . . . The only way to end the killing of youths and women by Israeli soldiers and police is for the Palestinians to stop using them as terrorists.

Human rights organizations have condemned ("abomination," "war crime") the recruitment of children by Palestinian armed groups.[33] This practice has also come under sharp criticism from Palestinian civil society.[34] No human rights organization maintains, however, that this wrongful recruitment exonerates Israel of its treatment of Palestinian children. A 2001 Amnesty International report found: "Many children were apparently killed by poorly targeted lethal fire; others . . . appear to have been deliberately targeted. In many of the locations where children were killed there was no imminent danger to life nor reasonable expectation of future danger. . . . Children throwing stones are not military objectives for lethal attack by the Israeli forces. The killing and wounding of children [have] revealed a reckless disregard for life by Israeli soldiers"; "In every case investigated by Amnesty International, the killing of a child appeared to have been an unlawful killing"; "According to official Israeli spokespersons, Palestinian gunmen hide behind children. . . . Investigations by Amnesty International have failed to find any specific instance where Palestinian gunmen have used a demonstration as a protective shield and shot at Israelis from among or behind the demonstrators."[35] A 2002 Amnesty International report similarly concluded: "The overwhelming majority of Palestinian children have been killed in the Occupied Territories when members of the Israeli Defense Forces (IDF) responded to demonstrations and stone-throwing incidents with excessive and disproportionate use of force, and as a result of the IDF's reckless shooting, shelling and aerial bom-

33. Amnesty International, "Children must not be used by armed groups" (24 March 2004) ("abomination"); B'Tselem, "Using Children in Combat—A War Crime" (press release, 16 March 2004); Human Rights Watch, "Child Soldier Use 2003," www.hrw .org/reports/2004/childsoldiers0104/9.htm.

34. Human Rights Watch, *Erased in a Moment*, section titled "Recruitment and Use of Children," www.hrw.org/reports/2002/isrl-pa/ISRAELPA1002-05.htm#P939_238764; Atef Saad, "Palestinian Backlash over Child Bombers," *Reuters* (26 March 2004).

35. Amnesty International, *Broken Lives*, pp. 20–23. For slightly discrepant findings on the presence of Palestinian gunmen among demonstrators, see Human Rights Watch, *Center of the Storm: A Case Study of Human Rights Abuses in Hebron District* (New York, April 2001), p. 27.

bardments of residential areas"; "Most of these children were killed when there was no exchange of fire and in circumstances in which the lives of the soldiers were not at risk"; "No judicial investigation into any of the cases of killings of Palestinian children by the IDF in the Occupied Territories is known to have been carried out."[36]

On a related matter, a 2001 study by B'Tselem on the "torture of Palestinian minors" found:

> Israeli security forces, some of them masked and some with their faces blackened, arrested them at their homes late at night. . . . After arriving at the police station, policemen used severe torture when interrogating the detainees and attempted to compel them to admit to committing the offenses of which they were suspected or to provide information about others. The testimonies reveal that a number of interrogation methods were commonly used. These included, in part, severe beatings, splashing cold water on detainees (the events occurred during the winter), putting the detainee's head in the toilet bowl, threats, and curses.

The study also highlighted the complicity of Israeli medical personnel in this torture of Palestinian minors:

> Most of the detainees were taken for a medical check-up immediately upon their arrival at the . . . police station. . . . [T]he physician performed a superficial examination, based in some cases on a quick glance, after which the physician signed a form confirming that they were healthy. At times, the detainees were handcuffed and blindfolded during the medical check-up. Some detainees were taken to the physician after being tortured during interrogation, were treated, and were returned for further interrogation.

B'Tselem concluded that the "shocking" examples of torture of Palestinian minors documented in its report were "not isolated cases or uncommon conduct by certain police officers, but methods of torture adopted at the police station and used against dozens of detainees, with many police officers at the station cooperating and aware of what was taking place. . . . Despite the authorities' repeated promises, and despite the comments of senior officials condemning police violence, the authorities have made no serious effort to address the root of the problem. Similarly, they have made no attempt to prosecute the violent police officers."[37] According to the 2002 *Human Rights Watch World Report,*

36. Amnesty International, *Killing the Future,* pp. 1–2, 16.
37. B'Tselem, *Torture of Palestinian Minors in the Gush Etzion Police Station* (Jerusalem, 2001), pp. 2, 23. On the complicity of Israeli medical personnel in torture, see esp. Neve Gordon and Ruchama Marton (eds.), *Torture: Human Rights, Medical Ethics*

"over three hundred Palestinian minors arrested since October 2000 . . . were reported to have been doused with freezing water, beaten, deprived of sleep, and had their heads covered with sacks during interrogation."[38]

—————————————————— BLOOD LIBEL ——————————————————

To demonstrate that allegations against Israel are motivated by malice, Dershowitz writes on page 153 of *The Case for Israel:*

> [I]gnorance alone cannot explain the alleged "reporting" of a "journalist" like Chris Hedges, who claimed to have personally observed Israeli soldiers "entice children like mice into a trap and murder them for sport."

Dershowitz goes on to compare this charge to a blood libel.[39]

Confirmation of a crucial aspect of Hedges's claim comes from an unlikely source. In its study *Trigger Happy: Unjustified Shooting and Violation of the Open-Fire Regulations during the al-Aqsa Intifada,* B'Tselem reports this testimony of an Israeli soldier:

> Soldiers would enter in jeeps to areas where friction was common. Their objective was to provoke Palestinians to throw stones and petrol bombs. When Palestinians approached, soldiers who had taken up positions at pre-planned positions would shoot at them. The stated goal of this procedure was to move the demonstrations further away. In fact, however, the soldier said: "It is a kind of sport, to 'remove' as many petrol-bomb throwers as possible. It is an obsessive search. It's called 'strive to make contact.' What bothers me is, if the jeeps had not entered, there would not have been any disturbances of the peace."[40]

Dershowitz makes no pretense of giving evidence that Hedges wasn't telling the truth.

———————————

and the Case of Israel (London, 1995), and Amnesty International, *Combating Torture: A Manual for Action* (London, 2003), section 2.2.

38. "Israel, the Occupied West Bank and Gaza Strip, and Palestinian Authority Territories" in *Human Rights Watch World Report 2002* (New York).

39. Hedges, former Middle East bureau chief for the *New York Times,* has received a Pulitzer prize as well as the Amnesty International Global Award for Human Rights Journalism. The quote Dershowitz cites comes from Chris Hedges, "A Gaza Diary," *Harper's* (October 2001). It is repeated in Chris Hedges, *War Is a Force that Gives Us Meaning* (New York, 2002), p. 94, where the full quote reads: "I had seen children shot in other conflicts I have covered—death squads gunned them down in El Salvador and Guatemala, mothers with infants were lined up and massacred in Algeria, and Serb snipers put children in their sights and watched them crumple onto the pavement in Sarajevo—but I had never watched soldiers entice children like mice into a trap and murder them for sport."

40. B'Tselem, *Trigger Happy,* p. 17.

GIDEON LEVY, "KILLING CHILDREN IS NO LONGER A BIG DEAL"
Haaretz (17 October 2004)

More than 30 Palestinian children were killed in the first two weeks of Operation Days of Penitence in the Gaza Strip. It's no wonder that many people term such wholesale killing of children "terror." Whereas in the overall count of all the victims of the intifada the ratio is three Palestinians killed for every Israeli killed, when it comes to children the ratio is 5:1. According to B'Tselem, the human rights organization, even before the current operation in Gaza, 557 Palestinian minors (below the age of 18) were killed, compared to 110 Israeli minors.

Palestinian human rights groups speak of even higher numbers: 598 Palestinian children killed (up to age 17), according to the Palestinian Human Rights Monitoring Group, and 828 killed (up to age 18) according to the Red Crescent. Take note of the ages, too. According to B'Tselem, whose data are updated until about a month ago, 42 of the children who have been killed were 10; 20 were seven; and eight were two years old when they died. The youngest victims are 13 newborn infants who died at checkpoints during birth.

With horrific statistics like this, the question of who is a terrorist should have long since become very burdensome for every Israeli. Yet it is not on the public agenda. Child killers are always the Palestinians, the soldiers always only defend us and themselves, and the hell with the statistics.

The plain fact, which must be stated clearly, is that the blood of hundreds of Palestinian children is on our hands. No tortuous explanation by the IDF Spokesman's Office or by the military correspondents about the dangers posed to soldiers by the children, and no dubious excuse by the public relations people in the Foreign Ministry about how the Palestinians are making use of children will change that fact. An army that kills so many children is an army with no restraints, an army that has lost its moral code.

As MK Ahmed Tibi (Hadash) said, in a particularly emotional speech in the Knesset, it is no longer possible to claim that all these children were killed by mistake. An army doesn't make more than 500 day-to-day mistakes of identity. No, this is not a mistake but the disastrous result of a policy driven mainly by an appallingly light trigger finger and by the dehumanization of the Palestinians. Shooting at everything that moves, including children, has become normative behavior. Even the momentary mini-furor that erupted over the "confirming the killing" of a 13-year-old girl, Iman Alhamas, did not revolve around the true question.* The scandal should have been generated by the very act of the killing itself, not only by what followed.

Iman was not the only one. Mohammed Aaraj was eating a sandwich in front of his house, the last house before the cemetery of the Balata refugee camp, in Nablus, when a soldier shot him to death at fairly close range. He was six at the time of his death. Kristen Saada was in her parents' car, on the way home from a family visit, when soldiers sprayed the car with bullets. She was 12 at the time of her death. The brothers Jamil and Ahmed Abu Aziz were riding their bicycles in full daylight, on their way to buy sweets, when they sustained a direct hit from a shell fired by an Israeli tank crew. Jamil was 13, Ahmed six, at the time of their deaths.

Muatez Amudi and Subah Subah were killed by a soldier who was standing in the village square in Burkin and fired every which way in the wake of stone-throwing. Radir Mohammed from Khan Yunis refugee camp was in a school classroom when soldiers shot her to death. She was 12 when she died. All of them were innocent of wrongdoing and were killed by soldiers acting in our name.

At least in some of these cases it was clear to the soldiers that they were shooting at children, but that didn't stop them. Palestinian children have no refuge: mortal danger lurks for them in their homes, in their schools and on their streets. Not one of the hundreds of children who have been killed deserved to die, and the responsibility for their killing cannot remain anonymous. Thus the message is conveyed to the soldiers: it's no tragedy to kill children and none of you is guilty.

Death is, of course, the most acute danger that confronts a Palestinian child, but it is not the only one. According to data of the Palestinian Ministry of Education, 3,409 schoolchildren have been wounded in the intifada, some of them crippled for life. The childhood of tens of thousands of Palestinian youngsters is being lived from one trauma to the next, from horror to horror. Their homes are demolished, their parents are humiliated in front of their eyes, soldiers storm into their homes brutally in the middle of the night, tanks open fire on their classrooms. And they don't have a psychological service. Have you ever heard of a Palestinian child who is a "victim of anxiety"?

The public indifference that accompanies this pageant of unrelieved suffering makes all Israelis accomplices to a crime. Even parents, who understand what anxiety for a child's fate means, turn away and don't want to hear about the anxiety harbored by the parent on the other side of the fence. Who would have believed that Israeli soldiers would kill hundreds of children and that the majority of Israelis would remain silent? Even the Palestinian children have become part of the dehumanization campaign: killing hundreds of them is no longer a big deal.

[*On 5 October 2004 an Israeli captain, "confirming the killing" of Iman Alhamas, a thirteen-year-old Palestinian schoolgirl, fired two bullets at point blank range into her head while she was lying on the ground already injured, and then, after starting to walk away, turned back to riddle her body with at least twenty more bullets, including seven to her head.—NGF]

CULTURE OF DEATH

To demonstrate Palestinian responsibility for the killings of their children, Dershowitz writes on page 130 of *The Case for Israel:*

> The University of Chicago philosopher Jean Bethke Elshtain, in her book *Just War Against Terror,* compares Islamic terrorist leaders who claim that "Islamic young people are in love with death" to Nazi leaders who sent "5,000 children between the ages of 8 and 17" to near certain death in the last days of the siege of Berlin.

He goes on to quote Elshtain, with approval, to the effect that "[a] willingness to sacrifice children is one sign of a culture of death."

1. Shortly after *Kristallnacht,* David Ben-Gurion, leader of the Zionist movement, stated: "If I knew that it was possible to save all the children in Germany by transporting them to England, but only half of them by transporting them to Palestine, I would choose the second—because we face not only the reckoning of those children, but the historical reckoning of the Jewish people." And at war's end in 1945, Ben-Gurion and the Zionist leadership blocked plans to transfer thousands of child Holocaust survivors in frail health from wretched camps for displaced persons to safe havens elsewhere in Europe, for fear that such resettlement "might weaken the struggle for free immigration of Jewish refugees to Palestine."[41]

2. To arouse international sympathy for its cause, the Zionist movement sought in 1947 to gain entry into Palestine for the boat *Exodus* despite British opposition. It was crammed with survivors of the Nazi holocaust, half of whom were children, mostly orphans. "The saga of the *Exodus* is strewn with the eyes of these orphans," writes the biographer of the ship's captain. These orphans "are the real story of the *Exodus.*"[42] The saga was later immortalized in Leon Uris's best seller *Exodus,*

41. Tom Segev, *The Seventh Million: The Israelis and the Holocaust* (New York, 1993), p. 28. Yosef Grodzinsky, *In the Shadow of the Holocaust* (Monroe, Maine, 2004), pp. 80–99 ("might weaken" at p. 97 is Grodzinsky's paraphrase of Ben-Gurion).
42. For background, see Christopher Sykes, *Crossroads to Israel, 1917–1948* (Bloomington, Ind., 1973), pp. 320–23; Yoram Kaniuk, *Commander of the* Exodus (New York, 1999), p. 107.

which became a canonical text of American Zionism.[43] What *cultural values* did Uris—and American Jewry—celebrate in his semifictionalized account? Uris tells the story of how Jewish orphans were placed on a boat "ready to fall apart." The engine room was loaded with dynamite, the Zionists threatening to "blow ourselves up" if the British fired on the ship. "If the Zionists are so sincere," the British wondered, "why are they endangering the lives of three hundred innocent children?" To which the Zionist hero of Uris's novel, Ari Ben Canaan, retorted: "I am astounded at Whitehall's crocodile tears over our victimizing of children. . . . If Whitehall is so concerned about the welfare of these children, then I challenge them to throw open the gates of Caraolos [where Jewish refugees were being held]. It is nothing more or less than a concentration camp. People are kept behind barbed wire at machine-gun point with insufficient food, water and medical care." (Like Gaza?) Next, Ari Ben Canaan put the orphans on board the *Exodus* on a hunger strike: "Anyone who passes out will be placed on deck for the British to look at. . . . Do you think I like starving a bunch of orphans? Give me something else to fight with. Give me something to shoot at those tanks and those destroyers." (A not unfamiliar lament.) After depicting scenes of the starving children, Uris has Ari Ben Canaan issue the final challenge that "ten volunteers a day" among the Jewish orphans "will commit suicide on the bridge of the ship in full view of the British garrison."[44]

3.   Driven by Zionist conviction, Jewish families have, as a matter of choice, entered a war zone in the Occupied Territories. The Israeli government actively encourages the movement of Jewish families into this conflict zone for the express purpose of strengthening the Zionist claim over it. To achieve their political objectives, the Jewish settlers and government knowingly and deliberately endanger the lives of hundreds of thousands of Jewish children.

"A willingness to sacrifice children is one sign of a culture of death."

---

43. Paul Breines, *Tough Jews* (New York, 1990), pp. 54–56. According to Dershowitz, *Exodus* was also the "all-time *samizdat* best seller among Soviet Jews" (*The Best Defense* [New York, 1982], p. 245).
44. Leon Uris, *Exodus* (New York, 1959), pp. 167–86.

========================= SUPPORTING NONVIOLENCE =========================

In *Why Terrorism Works,* Alan Dershowitz laments that Palestinians "never tried civil disobedience or other nonviolent means" and speculates that "had the Palestinians resorted instead to nonviolent civil disobedience tactics . . . , they would have achieved statehood sooner."[45] Dershowitz's commentary in *The Case for Israel* on the International Solidarity Movement (ISM), a Palestinian-led organization founded in 2001,[46] illustrates the degree to which he supports such nonviolent tactics. On pages 170–71, he writes that the ISM is a

> radical pro-Palestinian group of zealots . . . who are one-sided supporters of Palestinian terrorism. . . . They serve as human shields, working closely with Palestinian terrorist groups. . . . They do not support peace. Instead, these zealots advocate the victory of Palestinian terrorism over Israeli self-defense. . . . The media should stop referring to these people as peace activists and should call them what they are: active supporters and facilitators of Palestinian terrorism.

Here's how an article in Israel's most influential newspaper, *Haaretz,* describes this same organization:

> The ISM is an international pacifist movement that draws its inspiration from a quote by Albert Einstein: "The world is a dangerous place to live; not because of the people who are evil, but because of the people who don't do anything about it." Since the start of the intifada, hundreds of the[se] foreigners, mostly students, have taken a rigorous course in nonviolent theory and practice and then been placed in Palestinian towns and villages, where they report on events at checkpoints, villages under curfew and house demolitions, help move humanitarian aid into besieged areas, and accompany ailing Palestinians to hospitals.

Another *Haaretz* article giving a firsthand account of a training session describes ISM as "a coalition of organizations and individuals who use nonviolent direct action as a means for helping to end the Israeli occupation of the Palestinian territories, and assist the Palestinians in their daily lives." It notes further that each ISM volunteer had to make a commitment "in writing to nonviolent verbal and physical action" and that lectures emphasized that "physical and verbal violence . . . are

---

45. Alan M. Dershowitz, *Why Terrorism Works* (New Haven, 2002), pp. 90, 234n10.
46. For background on, and ongoing activities of, the International Solidarity Movement, see its website, www.palsolidarity.org, and Josie Sandercock et al. (eds.), *Peace under Fire: Israel/Palestine and the International Solidarity Movement* (New York, 2004).

absolutely forbidden where the ISM is operating." Dershowitz quotes from this article but omits mention of these observations (pp. 170, 254n2).[47] On the other hand, he repeats fabricated and trumped-up charges from right-wing Israeli media that ISM is financed by and harbors Palestinian terrorists. According to ISM, some 20 percent of its volunteers are Jewish.[48]

Rachel Corrie, a twenty-three-year-old ISM volunteer from Olympia, Washington, was killed while protecting a Palestinian home from being bulldozed. According to Dershowitz, she **"threw herself in front of the bulldozer"** (p. 170). Several people personally witnessed Corrie's death. Here's the eyewitness account of Tom Dale, an ISM volunteer currently enrolled at Oxford University:

> I was 10 meters away when it happened two days ago, and this is the way it went.
>
> We'd been monitoring and occasionally obstructing the two bulldozers for about two hours when one of them turned toward a house we knew to be threatened with demolition. Rachel knelt down in its way. She was 10–20 meters in front of the bulldozer, clearly visible, the only object for many meters, directly in its view. They were in radio contact with a tank that had a profile view of the situation. There is no way she could not have been seen by them in their elevated cabin. They knew where she was, there is no doubt. The bulldozer drove toward Rachel slowly, gathering earth in its scoop as it went. She knelt there, she did not move. The bulldozer reached her and she began to stand up, climbing onto the mound of earth. She appeared to be looking into the cockpit. The bulldozer continued to push Rachel, so she slipped down the mound of earth, turning as she went. Her face showed she was panicking and it was clear she was in danger of being overwhelmed.
>
> All the activists were screaming at the bulldozer to stop and gesturing to the crew about Rachel's presence. We were in clear view as Rachel had been, they continued. They pushed Rachel, first beneath the scoop, then beneath the blade, then continued till her body was beneath the cockpit. They waited over her for a few seconds, before reversing. They reversed

---

47. "American peace activist killed by army bulldozer in Rafah," *Haaretz* (17 March 2003); Orly Halpern, "How to be a political activist in a few (easy?) lessons," *Haaretz* (20 December 2002).

48. For ISM's detailed rebuttal of the allegation that it harbors terrorists, see "Does ISM protect terrorists?" www.palsolidarity.org, and Sandercock et al., *Peace under Fire*, pp. 261–62, 269–71. Dershowitz quotes from an article in the right-wing *Jerusalem Post* that ISM receives funds from the Palestinian Authority and Hamas (Joel Leyden, "Initial IDF Report: Shot Palestinian Activist May Have Fired First," 12 April 2003) (pp. 171, 254n3). The *Post* bases this claim, which ISM flatly denies, solely on an unidentified "senior security government source."

with the blade pressed down, so it scraped over her body a second time. Every second I believed they would stop but they never did.[49]

Dershowitz's account apparently comes from an initial Israeli army claim that Corrie ran in front of the bulldozer. The IDF has changed its story several times, however, subsequently alleging, for example, that "Corrie was not run over by an engineering vehicle but rather was struck by a hard object, most probably a slab of concrete."[50] As in Stalin's day, it's not easy for apparatchiks to keep up with the party line.

TERRORIST DIEHARD

Shortly after Professor Edward Said's death from cancer, Dershowitz wrote an obituary in an American Jewish Congress periodical entitled "Edward Said: The Palestinian Meir Kahane." Among other things, he claimed that Said was both theoretician and practitioner of terrorism:

> Said was not only a believer in violence and bloodshed, he was himself a practitioner of violence. On one occasion, he and his son threw rocks at Israelis along the Lebanese border. . . . He refused to condemn far more lethal acts of violence directed against innocent Israeli civilians. . . .
>
> Said refused to condemn terrorism and himself demonstrated symbolic support for terrorists.[51]

While celebrating Israel's eviction from Lebanon after more than two decades of brutal occupation, Said threw one stone toward the Israeli-Lebanese border. Leaving aside this horrific act, is it true that Said advocated terrorism? In *The Politics of Dispossession*, he recalled: "[I]n the late seventies I was extremely critical of such phrases as 'armed struggle,' all the rage in Beirut; and when my book *The Question of Palestine* was published in 1980, I was savagely attacked by both Fatah and the Popular Front for talking about the need for a recognition of Israel and accepting a two-state solution, an idea of

49. See "Four eyewitness accounts of Rachel's murder," www.rachelcorrie.org/ statements.htm, and Sandercock et al., *Peace under Fire*, pp. 236–37.

50. Conal Urquhart, "Israeli report clears troops over US death," *Guardian* (14 April 2003); John Sweeney, "Silenced witnesses," *Independent* (Great Britain) (30 October 2003).

51. Alan M. Dershowitz, "Edward Said: The Palestinian Meir Kahane," *Congress Monthly* (September–October 2003).

which I was one of the pioneers. I was unequivocal in my denunciations of terrorist adventurism and immoral violence, although, of course, I did not spare Israeli violence either."[52] In his writing and public interventions, Said explicitly deplored terrorist attacks directed against Israeli civilians as "morally unacceptable"[53] and was emphatic that "I'm against terror—random, horrid."[54]

MEDICAL TREATMENT

Dershowitz maintains that Palestinians bear significant responsibility for deaths arising from lack of access to medical care. On page 125 of *The Case for Israel,* he reports:

> The Palestinian Authority has decided no longer to transfer wounded Palestinians to Israeli hospitals. . . . Israel's health minister "has several times offered to treat all Palestinians wounded in the current Intifada at Israeli hospitals and at Israel's expense." The minister noted that "Palestinian medical facilities are unable to treat many of the wounded adequately." The Palestinians rejected the offer, according to the health minister, "because they prefer that we don't know the truth about the number of their wounded." Whatever the reasons, the reality is that significantly fewer Palestinians would have died of their injuries if their leaders had been willing to have them treated by Israel's excellent first responders rather than by often incompetent Palestinian doctors and inadequate Palestinian hospitals.

The only source Dershowitz cites for these rather large claims is an uncorroborated statement by Israel's minister of health to the *Jerusalem Post.*[55] No Palestinian official, human rights worker, or nongovernmental organization (NGO) in the health field—Palestinian or Israeli—

---

52. Edward W. Said, *The Politics of Dispossession: The Struggle for Palestinian Self-Determination, 1969–1994* (New York, 1994), p. xxv; see also pp. xxiii, 149–50, 349.
53. Edward W. Said, *The End of the Peace Process: Oslo and After* (New York, 2001), p. 45.
54. Gauri Viswanathan, *Power, Politics and Culture: Interviews with Edward Said* (New York, 2002), p. 289.
55. Dershowitz cites two articles by Judy Siegel in the *Jerusalem Post,* "Israel has offered to treat all Palestinian wounded" (22 May 2001) and "Palestinians refuse medical cooperation" (18 April 2002), but the only evidence supporting his textual claim comes from a statement by Minister of Health Nissim Dahan to Siegel in the first article. Indeed, the second article, quoting an IDF officer, seems to contradict the claim that the Palestinian Authority no longer allows injured Palestinians to go to Israel for medical treatment: "[G]reat efforts are being made to ensure that patients who cannot be treated in the territories are quickly taken to Israeli hospitals, even though there is no guarantee of payment. There have been dozens of such cases."

contacted by this writer was aware either of a Palestinian Authority decision not to send any of its wounded to Israel or of an Israeli offer to handle all these Palestinian patients free of charge. Rather the contrary: it was said that the PA does transfer some patients to Israeli hospitals for treatment, while the chief deterrent to transferring more of them is the exorbitant cost, for which Israel almost always demands payment (or deducts it from money due to the PA from the Israeli side).[56]

On the other hand, Dershowitz omits any mention of the extensive body of human rights research assessing the impact of Israeli policy on health care in the Occupied Territories. Consider Dershowitz's dismissal of "incompetent Palestinian doctors." In its detailed study *A Legacy of Injustice*, Physicians for Human Rights–Israel (PHR-Israel) reports that the post-1967 Israeli administration in the Occupied Territories "did not develop a plan for training a future cadre of Palestinian medical professionals, and confined itself to providing short courses and partial specialist training. In some cases, personnel who participated in courses abroad were obliged to cut short their studies and return to the region, due to the threat that otherwise they would lose their residency status [in the Occupied Territories]. Others had no possibility of traveling abroad for professional studies, since the Israeli security services vetoed their departure from the Occupied Territories." The obstacles proved most daunting in Gaza, where arbitrary Israeli restrictions "prevented Palestinians from studying medicine." PHR-Israel concludes that "[i]t takes a remarkable measure of cynicism" to blame Palestinians for the state of medical education in the Occupied Territories.[57]

56. Interview with Dr. Mustapha Barghouthi from the Union of Palestinian Medical Relief Committees (conducted by Michael Tarazi on 13 October 2003); letter faxed from Palestinian Authority minister of health Dr. Munzer Sharif (30 October 2003); email correspondence from B'Tselem executive Jessica Montell (13 October 2003); email correspondence from Shabtei Gold of Physicians for Human Rights–Israel, noting that "free hospitalization . . . is rare and publicized heavily" and, given that Israel has "actively negated the right to health, . . . simply insignificant . . . a drop in the ocean of occupation related problems." And again: "It is as if one burns a whole house and then throws a bucket of water boasting that he helps" (10 October 2003). Regarding Israel's allowing seven sick Palestinian children to travel to Italy for medical treatment, B'Tselem observed: "In light of the great harm to medical services in the West Bank, it seems that the flight crew transporting the children abroad is nothing more than a public relations stunt" (*Harm to Medical Personnel: The Delay, Abuse and Humiliation of Medical Personnel by the Israeli Security Forces* [Jerusalem, December 2003], p. 23).

57. Physicians for Human Rights–Israel, *A Legacy of Injustice: A Critique of Israeli Approaches to the Right to Health of Palestinians in the Occupied Territories* (Tel Aviv, November 2002), pp. 22, 67.

Although "the entire period of Israeli occupation has been characterized by severe restrictions on the Palestinian health system, and by
Israeli interference in Palestinian efforts to manage an independent
health policy,"[58] a dramatic deterioration ensued in the course of the
second intifada. The massive assault on Palestinian health care climaxed during Operation Defensive Shield (March–April 2002), when
Israel "reached an unprecedented low in terms of disrespect for human
life and gross violation of medical neutrality . . . leading to the almost
total paralysis of medical services" in the Occupied Territories.
Throughout this crisis in Palestinian health care, Israel's medical establishment "reacted with silence at best and collaboration at worst."[59]
Table 4.2 samples the impact of Israeli policy on Palestinian health care
during the second intifada. The section titled "Terrorist Ambulances"
illustrates Dershowitz's attempt to prove Israel's solicitude for Palestinian health care despite Palestinian provocation.

TABLE 4.2 IMPACT OF ISRAELI POLICY ON
HEALTH CARE IN THE OCCUPIED TERRITORIES

1. Attacks on ambulances

Physicians for Human Rights, *Evaluation of the Use of Force in Israel, Gaza and the West Bank* (November 2000)	"Between October 1 and October 23, 2000, PHR-Israel reported that 17 Palestinian ambulances were 'utterly destroyed' by the IDF. During the week from October 19 to October 23 alone, PHR-Israel reported that an additional 26 ambulances were damaged by gun fire" (p. 14).[a]
Physicians for Human Rights–Israel, *Medicine under Attack: Critical Damage Inflicted on Medical Services in the Occupied Territories* (April 2002)	"On March 4, 2002, a Red Crescent ambulance carrying three crew members and a physician set out for Jenin refugee camp with the goal of evacuating injured persons. The departure of the ambulance was coordinated with the Red Cross and the Israeli Civil Administration. Despite the coordination, the security forces opened fire on the ambulance, which exploded. Dr. Khalil Suleiman was trapped in the ambulance and burned to death. The other occupants of the vehicle

(continued)

58. Ibid., p. 57.
59. Physicians for Human Rights–Israel, *Medicine under Attack: Critical Damage
Inflicted on Medical Services in the Occupied Territories* (April 2002), n.p.; for the Israeli
medical establishment's shameful reaction, see also Physicians for Human Rights–Israel,
Legacy of Injustice, pp. 74–75.

TABLE 4.2 *(continued)*

were able to jump out, thus saving their lives. All three sustained serious burns. . . . A few days later . . . security forces opened fire on an . . . ambulance in the Tulkarm area. . . . [T]he driver . . . was killed and two crew members were injured. At the same time, a Red Crescent ambulance also came under fire; the driver . . . was killed and two crew members were injured. In both cases, the departure of the ambulances had been coordinated in advance" (n.p.).

2. Attacks on medical personnel

Physicians for Human Rights–Israel, *A Legacy of Injustice: A Critique of Israeli Approaches to the Right to Health of Palestinians in the Occupied Territories* (November 2002)

"March 30, 2002: Five members of a Palestine Red Crescent Society ambulance crew were arrested by the IDF . . . while on their way to evacuate a woman in labor. . . . Three of the crew members were seen by a Red Cross representative on March 30, handcuffed and blindfolded. . . . April 2, 2002: Three Palestine Red Crescent Society ambulances departed to evacuate sick and injured persons. . . . The ambulances were stopped by Israeli tanks at 9 A.M. The crews . . . were ordered to leave the ambulances and crawl in the rain toward the tanks. . . . At 7:30 P.M. the crew was released. Four members of the crew required medical attention" (pp. 61–62).

"On April 4, 2002, . . . Israeli security forces entered the Red Crescent maternity hospital in El-Bireh. . . . The soldiers gathered together all the workers and patients in the hospital, including women who had given birth and new-born babies aged between 3 and 10 hours. The soldiers subsequently . . . searched the hospital rooms. When unable to open doors, the soldiers broke them down with large metal bars. . . . At a later stage, all those present in the hospital were concentrated in the entrance area . . . and a process of humiliation began. Some of the soldiers photographed themselves with the group, while they laughed among themselves. About seven of those present . . . were asked to stand to one side. Their eyes were bound and their hands tied behind their backs. . . . [Two were released.] The remaining Palestinians were taken to an armored troop carrier" (p. 63)[b]

(continued)

TABLE 4.2 *(continued)*

B'Tselem, *Harm to Medical Personnel: The Delay, Abuse and Humiliation of Medical Personnel by the Israeli Security Forces* (December 2003)	"Over the past twelve months, ambulance crews have reported . . . at least 28 cases in which soldiers and border police officers humiliated and beat medical personnel. . . . During the course of the al-Aqsa Intifada, there has been an increase in the number of cases in which soldiers and border police officers have humiliated and beat Palestinians. Despite the many reports, defense officials have continued to treat these cases as 'exceptional' and the perpetrators as 'rotten apples,' and have failed to seriously address the phenomenon. Violence against medical teams has received the same lack of attention" (p. 14).

3. Attacks on medical facilities

Physicians for Human Rights–Israel, *Medicine under Attack: Critical Damage Inflicted on Medical Services in the Occupied Territories* (April 2002)	"[H]ospitals have become the targets of various forms of attack. . . . Tanks have been deployed alongside a large number of medical institutions. . . . Sick persons are denied free access to these medical centers and the departure of ambulances is prevented. . . . On the night of April 3–4, [2002,] the government hospital in Jenin was shelled and surrounded by tanks. The supply of oxygen, water and electricity has been disrupted and the north-facing windows shattered. At 9:30 P.M. on April 4, . . . the staff and patients were crowded on the internal staircase of the hospital, sheltering from the continuous shelling and firing" (n.p.).

4. Blocking and hindering access to medical care

Physicians for Human Rights–Israel, *A Legacy of Injustice* (November 2002)	"The establishment of soil ramps or concrete blocks physically prevents sick people . . . from reaching . . . medical centers. . . . Unstaffed roadblocks—whether in the form of large concrete blocks, mounds of earth, or destroyed sections of road—have now been erected at numerous locations throughout the West Bank. . . . The very design of many roadblocks (physical obstacles, or the stationing of soldiers at a great distance from the residents who arrive at a checkpoint) prevents any possibility for selective passage or for discussion between the patient and the soldier blocking his or her progress" (pp. 49–52).

(continued)

TABLE 4.2 *(continued)*

Physicians for Human Rights–Israel, *A Legacy of Injustice* (continued)	"Every ambulance that leaves to collect a patient, however urgent the case, now requires prior coordination. Every patient requires a transit permit, as does every physician. In order to get the permit, the sick patient must go to the DCO [District Coordinating Office]. He or she will have to walk there, because only Israelis are allowed to travel along the road. On arrival, patients must wait at the gate, hoping that the soldier on guard will let them enter the office. If the permit is not ready, the whole story will be repeated the next day. In many cases, the permit will arrive after the scheduled date for the examination or operation, so that the patient will have to start from scratch" (p. 57).
B'Tselem, *Harm to Medical Personnel* (December 2003)	"The sweeping restrictions on Palestinian movement within the West Bank have severely impaired access to medical treatment. . . . In the West Bank, Palestinian ambulance teams never know if they will be able to reach the patient's home. The teams' difficulty arises from the hundreds of physical roadblocks that the IDF has placed throughout the West Bank and from the delays they face at checkpoints. . . . [I]n many instances, soldiers delay ambulances even in cases of 'urgent medical emergencies.' . . . In some cases, the IDF . . . completely prohibits the passage for ambulances" (pp. 5, 7, 10).[c]

[a]In December 2003 B'Tselem reported that "since the beginning of the current Intifada (September 2000), soldiers have damaged 118 ambulances, 28 of which had to be taken out of service" (*Harm to Medical Personnel*, p. 14).

[b]For medical personnel "shot while evacuating injured persons" already as far back as 1996, see p. 41 of this report.

[c]For a "partial list of Palestinians who needed medical treatment and died after being delayed because of the restrictions on movement," see B'Tselem, *Death of Palestinians following Delay in Obtaining Medical Treatment because of Restrictions on Movement during the al-Aqsa Intifada*, www.btselem.org/English/Freeedom_of_Movement/Al_Aqsa_Death_after_ . . . .

B'TSELEM, *OPERATION DEFENSIVE SHIELD:*
SOLDIERS' TESTIMONIES, PALESTINIAN TESTIMONIES
(Jerusalem, September 2002), p. 23

On Friday, April 5, 2002, Tahani ʿAli ʿAsad Fatouh, a pharmacist from
Al Msakan Ash Shaʾabiya in the Nablus District began having labor
pains. Her husband, Dr. Ghassan ʿAli Nashat Shaʾar, called an ambulance to take his seven months pregnant wife to the hospital. Due to the
curfew imposed on the area, the ambulance could not reach the house
and Dr. Shaʾar had to deliver the baby with the help of his neighbor, Dr.
Sulfeh. The delivery went smoothly. During the delivery, the ambulance
crew tried to reach the couple's home, as the newborn would have to be
placed in an incubator. All attempts failed. Some 30 minutes after the
birth, the baby's health began to deteriorate. Dr. Shaʾar managed to
resuscitate his son twice. On the third attempt, the baby died. Tahani
Fatouh had become pregnant after four years of fertility treatments.
The hospital is only two kilometers away from the couple's home.

=================================== TERRORIST AMBULANCES ===================================

To demonstrate Israel's commitment to safeguarding Palestinian access
to medical care despite Palestinian provocation, Dershowitz writes on
page 184 of *The Case for Israel* that the Israel Supreme Court

> has prohibited the Israeli military from attacking ambulances, despite its
> recognition that ambulances are often used to transport explosives and
> suicide bombers.[60]

To document the claim about the Supreme Court, Dershowitz cites,
apart from an Israel Supreme Court justice's uplifting speech at a
United Jewish Communities convention in Philadelphia, this court decision from April 2002: "*Physicians for Human Rights v. Commander of
I.D.F. Forces in the West Bank,* HCJ 2936, 2002" (p. 254n8).

Referring to this very same Supreme Court decision, Physicians for
Human Rights–Israel reports:

> PHR-Israel petitioned the High Court in an effort to force the security forces
> to respect basic conventions and refrain from attacking ambulances. . . .

60. Dershowitz repeats these claims in "Stop terrorists' vehicle of choice," *New York
Daily News* (29 February 2004).

The petition was prepared in the context of the paralysis of the ambulance system, Israeli mortar attacks on Palestinian hospitals in the West Bank, the prevention of access to hospitals by patients and wounded persons. . . . Despite the long list of attacks specified in the petition—against the fabric of civilian life, medical services and human life—the Israeli High Court of Justice accepted the State's position that the IDF soldiers acted in accordance with humanitarian principles, as well as its claim that, given the fighting in the Territories, it was impossible to examine the specific cases noted in the petition. Accordingly, the Court ruling confined itself to a generalized comment by the High Court regarding the IDF's commitment to humanitarian law.[61]

To document that Palestinian **"ambulances are often used to transport explosives and suicide bombers"** and that after the April 2002 court decision **"Palestinian terrorists continued to use ambulances"** (p. 184), Dershowitz cites only the uncorroborated allegation of an Israeli "senior security official."[62] A November 2002 Physicians for Human Rights–Israel study concluded: "Israel has provided evidence of such abuse in one single case."[63] Even this one single instance lacks certainty. Referring to that same "one, widely publicized occasion when, on 27 March 2002, a suicide belt was found on an ambulance," Amnesty International wrote:

> There are several suspicious circumstances about it. The ambulance passed through four checkpoints on the way to Jerusalem without being searched (which is abnormal) and then was delayed for more than an hour before being searched to allow TV cameras to arrive (which suggests that the IDF had, at the least, prior knowledge of something hidden there).[64]

Apart from the alleged March 2002 incident, the only documented misuses of an ambulance were committed *by Israel*. For example, "soldiers were crammed into a bullet-proof ambulance in order to get as quickly as possible to the house" of a wanted Palestinian; "IDF soldiers in Nablus forced several ambulance drivers to stop, get out of their ambulances, and stand between the soldiers and stone throwers"; "soldiers took control of an ambulance and used it to block entry to the

61. Physicians for Human Rights–Israel, *Legacy of Injustice*, pp. 61–63; see also pp. 73–74. For the text of the court decision, see "Red Cross and Red Crescent: Decision of the Supreme Court Sitting as a High Court of Justice (April 8, 2002)," www.israel-mfa .gov.il/mfa/go.asp?MFAHOlkgO.
62. Greg Myre, "The Mideast Turmoil: Security," *New York Times* (21 May 2003).
63. Physicians for Human Rights, *Legacy of Injustice*, p. 60.
64. Amnesty International, *Shielded from Scrutiny*, p. 35n12.

hospital in Tulkarm." B'Tselem comments on these incidents and Israeli allegations:

> The IDF's use of ambulances for military purposes is especially disturbing in light of the repeated claims made by the IDF that Palestinians use ambulances to transport weapons and explosives. . . . It should be noted that, with the exception of one case, and despite repeated requests by Physicians for Human Rights and the International Red Cross, the IDF has not presented any evidence to support this contention, not even in response to petitions filed in the Supreme Court.

And again: "Official [Israeli] sources repeatedly state the claim that Palestinians use ambulances to transport weapons and explosives without providing proof of this claim."[65] Finally, it bears emphasizing that (1) Israel already targeted Palestinian ambulances long before the alleged March 2002 incident and "deliberately damaged ambulances" long after the April 2002 Supreme Court decision; and (2) even if the March 2002 incident did happen, it "cannot justify deliberate attacks on an entire network of ambulances performing their medical function and enjoying legal protection" (PHR-Israel).[66]

65. Physicians for Human Rights–Israel, *Legacy of Injustice*, p. 61 ("crammed into"); B'Tselem, *Harm to Medical Personnel*, pp. 20–21, 23–24.

66. For earlier attacks on Palestinian ambulances, see Physicians for Human Rights, *Evaluation of the Use of Force*, pp. 13–14, where PHR also notes: "The Israeli army claims that the ambulances are not being used properly, but the PHR team received no documentation of an ambulance being used for purposes other than transporting the wounded"; for recent attacks, see B'Tselem, *Harm to Medical Personnel*, pp. 14–19. Physicians for Human Rights–Israel, *Legacy of Injustice*, p. 60.

5

Three in the Back of the Head

"**WHILE ASSASSINATIONS** only became official and declared [Israeli] policy during the Al Aqsa Intifada," human rights organizations report, "the assassination of Palestinian activists and those suspected of organizing and carrying out attacks against Israelis is not new." Initiated in the 1970s, liquidation of "wanted," masked, and stone-throwing Palestinians was widely practiced from early on in the first intifada (1987-1993), when Deputy Chief of Staff Ehud Barak organized special undercover assassination squads. It "intensified" in 1992, when Yitzhak Rabin, on becoming prime minister, sanctioned destruction of Palestinian property to capture or kill "wanted" Palestinians, "rendering homeless hundreds of Palestinians who have been accused of no wrongdoing." More than 120 Palestinians were liquidated during these operations or executed after capture. A 1992 Palestine Human Rights Information Center investigation found that "there was no serious attempt to arrest" the victims, while only a handful of these suspects carried weapons or were involved in resistance activities at the time of the shooting. "The majority were performing normal activities in the course of their daily lives." A 1992 B'Tselem (Israeli Information Center for Human Rights in the Occupied Territories) study similarly found that, for a "large percentage" of the victims of the "liquidation squads," it was "possible to apprehend the suspects without killing them" and that, although "the percentage of persons killed who were armed when they clashed with undercover units has risen in recent months, . . . [s]till fifty percent of those killed are unarmed."

In a major 1993 study, Human Rights Watch concluded: "The undercover units operate according to a distinct, officially denied set of rules. . . . These rules effectively give the undercover forces a license to shoot to kill 'wanted' and masked suspects in many situations where the use of lethal force is unjustified. . . . Despite official claims that undercover units concentrate their efforts on the pursuit of 'hard-core,' 'wanted' activists who have blood on their hands, these units are also commonly used to ambush masked activists when they are engaged in non-life-threatening activities such as manning a roadblock or ordering shopkeepers to observe strikes. In these types of operations as well, the undercover units have license to kill." The study found that less than half of those killed were "wanted" Palestinians, while the rest were masked youths, stone throwers, and so on "who were neither armed nor posing any imminent threat to the security agents or anyone else."[1]

The current, openly acknowledged policy of political liquidations was initiated by Prime Minister Ehud Barak after the outbreak of the second intifada and intensified after Ariel Sharon took office in 2001. From November 2000 through mid-2003, the Israeli army and security services assassinated more than one hundred Palestinians and "killed scores and injured hundreds of other Palestinian men, women and children bystanders." There were reportedly "no less than 175 liquidation attempts" or "one attempt every five days." "Israel is the only democratic country," B'Tselem observed in a 2001 position paper, "which regards such measures as a legitimate course of action."[2] Dershowitz has defended this policy mainly against its *Israeli* critics. In chapter 25

---

1. Public Committee Against Torture in Israel (PCATI) and LAW—The Palestinian Society for the Protection of Human Rights, *The Assassination Policy of the State of Israel* (May 2002), p. 7 ("not new"); Palestine Human Rights Information Center, *Targeting to Kill: Israel's Undercover Units* (Jerusalem, 1992), p. 4 (Barak), 22 (conclusions); B'Tselem (Israeli Information Center for Human Rights in the Occupied Territories), *Activity of the Undercover Units in the Occupied Territories* (Jerusalem, May 1992), pp. 8 ("large percentage"; cf. 20–21), 75 ("fifty percent"). Human Rights Watch, *A License to Kill: Israeli Operations against "Wanted" and Masked Palestinians* (New York, 1993), pp. 1 (number and profile of victims), 4 ("intensified," "rendering"), 10 (executions while in custody), 20 ("set of rules"). The armed wing of the Zionist movement was already committing political liquidations in Palestine as far back as the 1920s.

2. Amnesty International, *Israel Must End Its Policy of Assassinations* (London, July 2003), p. 1 ("scores"). (B'Tselem's website, *Assassinations—Extra-Judicial Executions*, lists 110 targeted killings and 71 bystanders [including 23 infants or minors] killed through June 2003 [www.btselem.org/english/statistics/fatalities_lists/extra_judicial_eng

of *The Case for Israel* he juxtaposes B'Tselem's malign "accusations" against the "reality" of political liquidations. After a group of reserve pilots in the Israeli air force declared in a public letter their refusal to participate any longer in "illegal and immoral" political liquidations, Dershowitz, who "objected to the pilots' letter," headed for Israel "to support the IAF pilots and to persuade them as to the legality and morality of the targeted killing operations," and "to meet with the commanders of the IAF and to discuss with them ways of dealing with the pilots' letter." Defending the liquidations policy in a German news-paper, Dershowitz explained that "[i]t strengthens civil liberties, not those of the Israelis, but those of the Palestinians" and that critics who oppose the policy—presumably including B'Tselem and the "refusenik" pilots—did so because they "love dead Jews."[3]

The claim that Israel's liquidations policy "strengthens" Palestinian civil liberties is of a piece with much of Dershowitz's argumentation. "The killing of Sheikh Yassin was a moral and lawful instance of pre-emptive self-defense," Dershowitz avers, explaining that Yassin "was a combatant under any reasonable definition of that term, and combat-ants . . . are appropriate military targets during an ongoing war of the kind Hamas has declared against Israel."[4] It's hard to make out how a political liquidation can be justified at one and the same time as "pre-emptive self-defense"—in which case it took place *prior to* outbreak of armed hostilities—and on the grounds that the target was a "combat-ant" in an "ongoing war"—in which case the rationale of preemptive self-defense is altogether irrelevant. In *The Case for Israel*, Dershowitz separates these arguments, justifying liquidations on each ground:

> *It is legitimate to target Palestinians for liquidation because they are com-batants, not civilians.* "Under international law and the laws of war, it is

---

.asp].) Aryeh Dayan, "One day in five, the IDF attempts assassination," *Haaretz* (21 May 2003) ("every five days"); B'Tselem, *Position Paper: Israel's Assassination Policy: Extra-judicial Executions* (Jerusalem, February 2001), p. 14.

3. Lily Galili, "Reserve Pilots to Refuse Liquidations," *Haaretz* (19 September 2003); Amos Harel and Lily Galili, "Air Force to Oust Refusenik Pilots," *Haaretz* (25 September 2003). (For the reserve pilots' public statement, "A Letter from Israeli Pilots Who Refuse to Serve," see www.xs4all.nl/~pieth/PilotsLetter.pdf.) Itamar Eichner and Tova Tzimuki, "Dershowitz Wants to Obtain 'Acquittal' for Israel," *Yediot Ahronot* (18 November 2003) ("support the IAF"); Alan M. Dershowitz, "Alle lieben tote Juden . . . ," *Die Welt* (15 June 2002).

4. Alan Dershowitz, "Critics of Sheikh Yassin Killing Reveal Own Moral Blindness," *Forward* (26 March 2004). Elsewhere in the article he similarly writes that "terrorist leaders" like Yassin "should be regarded as combatants and thus appropriate targets for preemption."

entirely legal to target and kill an enemy combatant who has not surrendered. Palestinian terrorists—whether they are the suicide bombers themselves, those who recruit them, those in charge of the operation, or commanders of terrorist groups—are undoubtedly enemy combatants." (pp. 174–75)

It is legitimate to liquidate Palestinians if they can't be captured, if they pose an imminent danger, and if bystanders aren't injured. "I believe that targeted assassination should only be used as a last recourse when there is no opportunity to arrest or apprehend the murderer (although this is not required by the law of war if the murderer is a combatant), when the terrorist is involved in ongoing murderous activities, and when the assassination can be done without undue risk to innocent bystanders." (p. 175)[5]

Under international law, combatants are members of "the armed forces of a Party to the conflict as well as members of militias or volunteer corps forming part of such armed forces," or members of "other militias and . . . other volunteer corps" that are "commanded by a person responsible for his subordinates," have "a fixed distinctive sign recognizable at a distance," "carry arms openly," and "conduct their operations in accordance with the laws and customs of war."[6] The consensus among human rights organizations is that Palestinian targets of Israel's liquidation policy do not fit this description.[7] Accordingly, they benefit from the legal protection of civilians under occupation, who "cannot be killed at any time other than while they are firing upon or otherwise posing an immediate threat to Israeli troops or civilians. Because they are not combatants, the fact that they participated in an armed attack at an earlier point cannot justify targeting them for death later on." The targeting of civilians for assassination constitutes a form of extrajudicial execution—that is, "an unlawful and deliberate killing carried out by order of a government . . . to eliminate specific individuals as an alternative to arresting them and bringing them to justice."[8] Israel's targeting of Palestinians amounts to such extrajudicial execution: the target is (a) denied the right to defend himself in a court of law, although

5. See also Alan M. Dershowitz, Why Terrorism Works (New Haven, 2002), pp. 120, 184.

6. Geneva Convention Relative to the Treatment of Prisoners of War, Article 4.

7. Amnesty International, State Assassinations and Other Unlawful Killings (London, 2001), p. 20; PCATI and LAW, Assassination Policy, pp. 69–70. The latter study further notes that "Israel does not recognize members of Palestinian organizations who directly take part in hostilities as combatants. . . . If the State of Israel prefers to view them as 'combatants,' then it must treat them as prisoners of war rather than try them within its domestic criminal legal system."

8. Amnesty International, State Assassinations, pp. 1, 19–20; see also PCATI and LAW, Assassination Policy, p. 7.

(b) posing no imminent threat to life, and although (c) apprehending him for trial is an option.

(a) "The decision to assassinate," B'Tselem reports, "is made in back rooms with no judicial process to examine the intelligence information on which it is based. The target of assassination is not given a chance to present evidence in his defense or to refute the allegations against him." On a similar note, the Public Committee Against Torture in Israel (PCATI) and the Palestinian Society for the Protection of Human Rights (LAW) observe: "[T]o date, the Israeli military has not made public any evidence to substantiate the allegations against those assassinated. After every assassination, the Israeli military only takes great care to publicly level accusations of involvement in terror attacks against those assassinated, which appear in the media to garner public support for its assassination policy. However, evidence to prove the accusations is never presented. There is therefore no possibility of estimating how many of those assassinated were indeed involved in violent actions as the Israeli authorities claim and how many were assassinated as innocent victims of a draconian system that is more expected from a dark dictatorship rather than a democracy of the 21st Century."[9]

(b) Recalling the specific circumstances of Israel's liquidations, PCATI and LAW observe: "[A] pilot who flies his helicopter above a Palestinian city and launches a missile into the apartment occupied at the moment by a suspect, a sniper who fires through his rifle view-finder at a person sitting on his porch, a unit that places explosives in someone's car—all these are cases of intended murder and there is no element of self-defense. The suspect is not posing an immediate threat to human life."[10] On page 175 of *The Case for Israel*, Dershowitz maintains that, "[u]nder any reasonable standard, Israeli policy with regard to targeted assassinations of 'ticking-bomb terrorists' does not deserve the kind of condemnation it is receiving." Yet, on the one hand, the guidelines of Israel's liquidation policy allow for

---

9. B'Tselem, *Position Paper: Israel's Assassination Policy,* p. 8; PCATI and LAW, *Assassination Policy,* p. 61.
10. PCATI and LAW, *Assassination Policy,* p. 60 (cf. pp. 8, 67).

the army "to act against known terrorists even if they are not
on the verge of committing a major attack"; and, on the other,
"the Israeli army has not offered evidence that the Palestinians
whom it has assassinated were about to, or on their way to,
carry out attacks. Those who have been assassinated were
in areas of the Occupied Territories removed from potential
Israeli targets (such as settlements, settlers' roads or army
positions)."[11]

(c) "The Israeli army has proved that it can and does exercise full
and effective control over the Occupied Territories, including
the areas which fall under the Palestinian Authority jurisdiction," Amnesty International observed in the summer of 2003.
"In the past two years the Israeli army and security services
have arrested tens of thousands of Palestinians whom they
accuse of having perpetrated, participated in or planned attacks
against Israeli soldiers or civilians. Such arrests continue daily
throughout the Occupied Territories. Those arrested have been
apprehended individually or in groups, in their homes or other
private houses, in universities or student dormitories, at their
work place or at checkpoints, when moving around openly or
while in hiding. . . . Palestinians who were alleged to have been
on their way to carry out suicide bombings or other attacks
have been arrested by the Israeli army and security forces in the
West Bank and Gaza Strip, inside Israel, at checkpoints and
as they were attempting to cross the borders in other areas to
avoid checkpoints." Given this ability to nab Palestinians at will,
Amnesty concludes, "Israel's claims that it only resorts to assassinations in response to an immediate security threat which
cannot be otherwise dealt with, are not credible and . . . such
practices cannot be justified." PCATI and LAW likewise conclude that "the many cases in which the Israeli military abducted
wanted Palestinians . . . show that the Israeli military is able,
when it so decides, to capture wanted persons. Therefore assas-
sinating them is clearly not the only possible act available."[12]

11. Ibid., p. 6 ("major attack"); Amnesty International, *Israel Must End*, p. 2 ("not offered").
12. Amnesty International, *Israel Must End*, pp. 3–4 (cf. Amnesty International, *State Assassinations*, p. 5); PCATI and LAW, *Assassination Policy*, p. 73 (cf. p. 8).

In addition, numerous bystanders have been indiscriminately killed and injured in the course of liquidations. "Israeli government and military officials have repeatedly stated that all care is taken not to cause harm to other Palestinians when they carry out such assassinations," Amnesty observes. "The facts, however, indicate otherwise. Scores of men, women and children bystanders have been killed and hundreds have been injured in the course of assassinations or attempted assassinations of Palestinians by the Israeli army. . . . Claims that efforts are made not to harm bystanders are inconsistent with the practice of carrying out attacks on busy roads and densely populated areas." Likewise, PCATI and LAW conclude: "In many cases the Israeli military harmed civilians who were by no means targets for assassination. This harming of innocent civilians is a clearer proof of the reckless and excessive use of force that certainly is not proportional to the danger posed, if at all, by the person targeted for assassination."[13]

Under the Israeli Penal Code, the assassination of wanted Palestinians by the state is a "premeditated act of murder," while under international law it constitutes a "war crime." Dershowitz himself stated that "targeted assassination should only be used" in instances where "there is no opportunity to arrest or apprehend the murderer," "the terrorist is involved in ongoing murderous activities," and "the assassination can be done without undue risk to innocent bystanders." Even by his own standard, Israel's policy of political liquidations cannot be justified. "Of all the types of human rights violations of the right to life by official representatives of a state, the policy of assassination is the most grave," PCATI and LAW conclude. "It is not negligent shooting, entering into a situation in which there is no choice but shoot to kill, or an incident that began with a legal goal and went awry. It is a pre-planned mission, the goal of which is from the outset a human rights violation, and carrying it out is therefore a heinous crime both legally and ethically." By engaging in such a policy, "Israel joins an infamous group of states that grossly violates basic moral and humane norms that the international community considers binding."[14]

Putting to one side the moral and legal questions, it remains to consider the political impact of these liquidations. "The claim that this is

13. Amnesty, *Israel Must End*, pp. 4–6; PCATI and LAW, *Assassination Policy*, p. 60.
14. PCATI and LAW, *Assassination Policy*, pp. 8–9 ("murder," "war crime"), 60 ("most grave"), 76 ("infamous").

AMNESTY INTERNATIONAL, *STATE ASSASSINATIONS AND OTHER UNLAWFUL KILLINGS*
(London, February 2001), pp. 10–11

DR THABET THABET, *FATAH*, KILLED 31 DECEMBER 2000 IN TULKAREM

Thabet Thabet, aged 49, had been a *Fatah* activist. Detained or put under town arrest in the past by the Israeli security forces, he was released in 1991 on the eve of the peace talks which started in Madrid. He was named as a PLO representative for the Madrid talks and was said to have promoted peace before and after the Oslo Agreement, developing many friendships with members of the Israeli peace movement. According to his wife, Dr Thabet was criticized by some Palestinians for being a strong supporter for the normalization of relations with Israel. Dr Thabet Thabet had worked as a dentist for UNRWA [United Nations Relief and Works Agency] and been Head of the Palestinian Dentists' Association before the setting up of the Palestinian Authority; then he worked as a director in the Ministry of Health in Tulkarem and taught public health at the Tulkarem branch of al-Quds Open University. He was also Secretary General of *Fatah* in the district. On 16 November 2000, during helicopter attacks on *Fatah* targets, which according to official Israeli statements were carried out in response to increased violence and drive-by shootings near Ofra settlement earlier in the week, Dr Thabet's office in the *Fatah* headquarters was destroyed by a missile.

. . . His wife, Dr Siham Thabet, also a dentist, said:

> I left home five minutes before the shooting. I called out to him to ask if he would travel to the clinic with me. He asked me to wait till he was ready. But since I had a patient waiting, I decided to leave at once. I heard the shooting. I didn't think it was from home. When I got to the clinic a friend asked me where it came from. I called home, and found no one. Then I called my neighbour; she said my husband was wounded. Till then, I never believed it was him; he was a man of peace.

Soon after his wife left, at 9.45 am, Dr Thabet Thabet had got into his green Peugeot. . . . There was a burst of gunfire; seven bullets smashed through the rear window of the car. The maid, who saw the shooting from the kitchen window, ran down and saw Thabet Thabet dead in his car and his body mangled—"there was no flesh left on his arm," she said.

According to his wife, Dr Thabet Thabet could have been arrested by the Israeli authorities if suspected of any offence without difficulty since he regularly drove to Nablus and each Friday he attended a mosque in Far'un in [an Israeli-controlled area].

Basing her case on the prohibition under Israeli law of execution without trial, Dr Siham Thabet petitioned the Israeli Supreme Court on the killing of Dr Thabet Thabet. The Supreme Court accepted the petition and required Ehud Barak, who combined the posts of Prime Minister and Defence Minister, to explain the government's policy by 31 January 2001. A document was submitted to the Court by Major-General Giora Eiland, Head of the IDF Operations Branch, stating that Dr Thabet Thabet "was indeed a physician, but his role as commander of a Tanzim cell, who instructed his people where to carry out attacks... removes him from the civilian category." Prime Minister Ehud Barak also submitted a letter stating that: "International law allows a strike against someone identified with certainty as being prepared to commit an attack against Israeli targets. . . . This pertains to a war situation in general and to the right of self-defence specifically." During his plea to the Supreme Court on 12 February, State prosecutor Shay Nitzan included an opinion by Attorney General Elyakim Rubenstein:

> The laws of combat, which are part of international law, permit injuring, during a period of warlike operations, someone who has been positively identified as a person who is working to carry out fatal attacks against Israeli targets. These people are enemies who are fighting against Israel, with all that implies, while committing fatal terror attacks and intending to commit additional attacks—all without any countermeasures by the Palestinian Authority.

The hearing before the Supreme Court is continuing.*

*Human Rights Watch reports: "Thabet had worked closely with Israeli peace activists for more than a decade, and had been credited with arranging the safe return of some twenty Israeli soldiers who apparently blundered into Palestinian-controlled Tulkarem on October 20, 2000. Israeli officials have alleged that Thabet was involved in planning attacks on Israelis, but have not made public any evidence to substantiate this allegation" ("Letter to Ehud Barak: Halt 'Liquidations'" [29 January 2001]). See also Public Committee Against Torture in Israel and LAW—The Palestinian Society for the Protection of Human Rights, *The Assassination Policy of the State of Israel* (May 2002), pp. 23–25.

an effective policy is debatable," B'Tselem observes. "Those who profess the effectiveness of the method have not provided one shred of evidence in support of their claim that the policy has contributed to security in any way." High-ranking Israeli security officials similarly assert that liquidations haven't enhanced Israel's security; rather the contrary. Former General Security Service chief Ami Ayalon suggested that "isolated suicide bombers may increase in number to dozens or hundreds" if the liquidations policy continued.[15]

The evidence strongly suggests that *the main, anticipated, and intended effect of political liquidations has been to stimulate terrorist attacks.* "Whoever gave a green light to this act of liquidation knew full well that he is thereby shattering in one blow the gentleman's agreement between Hamas and the Palestinian Authority," Israeli journalist Alex Fishman wrote in *Yediot Ahronot* after the November 2001 assassination of a Hamas leader. "Under that agreement, Hamas was to avoid in the near future suicide bombings inside the Green Line." "After the destruction of the houses in Rafah and Jerusalem, the Palestinians continued to act with restraint," Shulamit Aloni of Israel's Meretz party wrote in *Yediot Ahronot* in January 2002. "Sharon and his army minister, apparently fearing that they would have to return to the negotiating table, decided to do something and they liquidated Raed Karmi [a local militia leader]. They knew that there would be a response, and that we would pay the price in the blood of citizens." In July 2002 militant Palestinian organizations, including Hamas, reached a preliminary accord to suspend all attacks inside Israel, perhaps paving the way for a return to the negotiating table. Just ninety minutes before it was to be announced, however, Israeli leaders—fully apprised of the imminent declaration—ordered an F-16 to drop a one-ton bomb on a densely populated civilian neighborhood in Gaza, killing, alongside a Hamas leader, fourteen Palestinian civilians, nine of them children, and injuring 140. (See section titled "Avoiding Civilian Casualties" in Chapter 4 of this book.) Predictably, the declaration was scrapped and Palestinian attacks resumed with a vengeance. "What is the wisdom here?" a Meretz party leader wondered. "At the very moment that it appeared that we were on the very brink of a chance for reaching something of a cease-fire, or diplomatic activity, we always go back to this experience—just when there is a period of calm, we liquidate."[16] "[T]he history of Palestinian terrorism clearly shows that terrorism increases

15. B'Tselem, *Position Paper: Israel's Assassination Policy*, p. 14; "Ayalon: Israeli killings create more suicide bombers," *Jerusalem Post* (online edition) (18 December 2001); see also Amos Harel, "Security brass: Targeted killings don't work; no military solution to terror," *Haaretz* (19 December 2001).

16. Alex Fishman, "A dangerous liquidation," *Yediot Ahronot* (25 November 2001); Shulamit Aloni, "You can continue with the liquidations," *Yediot Ahronot* (18 January 2002); Bradley Burston, "Background: Shehada 'hit' sends shockwaves back to Israel," *Haaretz* (25 July 2002) (Meretz leader); Akiva Eldar, "How to cease from a cease-

whenever Israel offers peace," Dershowitz declares on page 178 of *The Case for Israel*. "Terrorism has been used as a deliberate tactic to derail any movement toward peace." Not for the first time he inverts reality.

---

fire," *Haaretz* (25 July 2002); Gideon Samet, "It's a horror story, period," *Haaretz* (26 July 2002); Akiva Eldar, "If there's smoke, there's no cease-fire," *Haaretz* (30 July 2002); "Letter for an American editor," *Haaretz* (30 July 2002) (text of planned public statement). For further discussion and references, see Norman G. Finkelstein, *Image and Reality of the Israel-Palestine Conflict*, 2nd ed. (New York, 2003), pp. xxii–xxiii, xxvi–xxvii.

6

Israel's Abu Ghraib

HUMAN RIGHTS ORGANIZATIONS have extensively documented Israel's systematic torture of Palestinian detainees.[1] "From 1967," Amnesty International reports, "the Israeli security services have routinely tortured Palestinian political suspects in the Occupied Territories."[2] Although allegations of torture circulated early in the occupation, they reached a much wider audience after the *London Sunday Times* published a detailed and unusually careful exposé in 1977. Its five-month-long inquiry concluded that "Israeli interrogators routinely ill-treat and often torture Arab prisoners" and had done so "throughout the 10 years of the Israeli occupation." The methods of torture it itemized included these: "Prisoners are often hooded or blindfolded or hung by their wrists for long periods. Many are sexually assaulted. Others are given electric shocks. At least one detention centre has (or had) a specially

---

1. For this and the following paragraph, see especially B'Tselem (Israeli Information Center for Human Rights in the Occupied Territories), *The Interrogation of Palestinians during the Intifada: Ill-treatment, "Moderate Physical Pressure" or Torture?* (Jerusalem, March 1991), pp. 27–32, and Amnesty International, *Report and Recommendations of an Amnesty International Mission to the Government of the State of Israel 3–7 June 1979, Including the Government's Response and Amnesty International Comments* (London, September 1980), pp. 5–13.

2. See section titled "Occasional Abuses" in this chapter.

constructed 'cupboard,' about two feet square and five feet high, with concrete spikes set in the floor." The *Times* subsequently published Israel's reply to these charges as well as its own devastating point-by-point rejoinder.[3]

After publication of the *Times* study, numerous governmental and nongovernmental agencies—including the United States Department of State, the Swiss League of Human Rights, the International League of Human Rights, the International Association of Catholic Jurists, the U.S.-based National Lawyers Guild, and Amnesty International—as well as the international (including Israeli and American) press reported Israel's ill-treatment and torture of Palestinian detainees. During Menachem Begin's term of office (1977–1983), there was some decline in ill-treatment and torture compared with previous years after the prime minister, apparently reacting to the *Times* story, imposed restraints on its use by Israeli interrogators. In 1984—shortly after Begin resigned—human rights organizations reported an escalation of ill-treatment and torture. In its influential study *Torture in the Eighties*, Amnesty International stated that it "has continued to receive reports of ill-treatment" in Israeli prisons: "The frequency and consistency of these reports indicate that some Palestinians from the Occupied Territories arrested for security reasons . . . have been hooded, handcuffed and forced to stand without moving for many hours at a time for several days, and have been exposed while naked to cold showers or cold air ventilators for long periods of time. Detainees have also been deprived of food, sleep, and toilet and medical facilities, and have been subjected to abuse, insults and threats against themselves and the female members of their families." It also pointed to "detailed reports of individual prisoners being beaten, sometimes severely, during interrogation in the Occupied Territories." In one such case, a Palestinian detainee alleged that, "while hooded, handcuffed and sometimes stripped naked, he was, over a period of two weeks, beaten all over the body, including the

---

3. "Israel Tortures Arab Prisoners: Special Investigation by INSIGHT," *Sunday Times* (19 June 1977); "Torture: Israel Replies," *Sunday Times* (3 July 1977); "Torture: A Flawed Defence," in *Sunday Times* (10 July 1977). For analysis of the *Times*'s allegations, Israel's reply, and the *Times*'s rejoinder, see Amnesty International, *Report and Recommendations*, pp. 9–11, which found: "In sum then, the Israeli response to the *Sunday Times* allegations addressed only six of the named 22 cases. Even in these cases, their response was circumstantial and did little to weaken the specific allegations themselves." Amnesty's broader conclusion on Israel's treatment of Palestinian detainees "reaffirms its view stated on several occasions since 1970 that there is sufficient *prima facie* evidence of ill-treatment of security suspects in the Occupied Territories by interrogators and detaining officials to warrant the establishment of a public inquiry into this matter" (p. 43).

genitals, with clubs and fists. His head was also repeatedly hit and banged against the wall causing injury and necessitating medical treatment."[4] An al-Haq study issued that same year reported interrogation techniques similar to those cited by Amnesty International as well as the sexual humiliations and other personal degradations documented in the *Sunday Times* inquiry.[5]

With the onset of the first intifada in December 1987, human rights reports alleging Israeli torture of Palestinian detainees proliferated. In annual reports covering 1988 and 1989 respectively, al-Haq produced a detailed analysis of Israeli torture practices, while Amnesty International stated that "[t]housands of Palestinians were beaten while in the hands of Israeli forces or were tortured or ill-treated in detention centres," citing, for example, "beatings on various parts of the body, hooding, prolonged standing, sleep deprivation and confinement in coffin-sized cells."[6] In Israel accounts of torture appeared in the press and human rights organizations like the Public Committee Against Torture sprang up to expose these practices. A groundbreaking study published in March 1991 by B'Tselem (Israeli Information Center for Human Rights in the Occupied Territories) found that "forms of ill-treatment that fit accepted definitions of torture are carried out in a widespread and routine way by agents of the Shin Bet [General Security Service]" and that "nearly 50% of interrogations end up with no charges being pressed, or any other steps taken against the detainee."[7] Soon thereafter, major human rights organizations published studies reaching identical conclusions.[8]

· · · ·

4. Amnesty International, *Torture in the Eighties* (London, 1984), pp. 233–34.

5. International Commission of Jurists and Law in the Service of Man (al-Haq), *Torture and Intimidation in the West Bank: The Case of Al-Fara'a Prison* (Ramallah, 1984).

6. Al-Haq, *Punishing a Nation: Human Rights Violations during the Palestinian Uprising, December 1987–December 1988* (Ramallah, December 1988), pp. 341–45; 351–57; al-Haq, *A Nation under Siege: Annual Report on Human Rights in the Occupied Palestinian Territories, 1989* (Ramallah, 1990), pp. 173–79; "Israel and the Occupied Territories," in *Amnesty International Report 1990* (London).

7. B'Tselem, *Interrogation*, pp. 6, 23. See also B'Tselem, *The Interrogation of Palestinians during the Intifada: Follow-up to March 1991 B'Tselem Report* (Jerusalem, March 1992), which reports that, despite the "immediate and extensive attention" given its original findings, "the picture is much the same as we revealed a year ago" (pp. 11, 43). For Israeli media and human rights organization coverage of torture during the intifada, see also Norman G. Finkelstein, *The Rise and Fall of Palestine: A Personal Account of the Intifada Years* (Minneapolis, 1996), pp. 48–49.

8. See section titled "Occasional Abuses" in this chapter.

B'TSELEM, *THE INTERROGATION OF PALESTINIANS DURING THE INTIFADA: ILL-TREATMENT, "MODERATE PHYSICAL PRESSURE" OR TORTURE?* (Jerusalem, 1991), pp. 43–59

TECHNIQUES OF INTERROGATION

THE "CLOSET" AND THE "REFRIGERATOR"

During interrogation, suspects are placed in solitary confinement in the "Tzinok" (isolation cell) . . . and in two other much smaller cells:

Closet. This is a very small cell, in some prisons 1 x 1 meters, in others a smaller size, very dark and almost completely closed. The air comes in through a small crack in the door or in the ceiling. Detainees are held in closets for long hours, sometimes tied and hooded. Some closets have a built-in stone step, and the detainees can only sit there. In other closets it is impossible to sit or lie down, and the detainees have no choice but to stand.

Refrigerator. This is a cell the size of a closet. It is also dark, and it has extremely low temperatures. We have heard no reports of refrigerators being used in the West Bank, but every single interviewee who had been held in Gaza Central Prison reported that he had been confined in refrigerator cells. The standard Gaza method alternates beatings with periods in the refrigerator.

TYING UP ("AL-SHABAH")

Being tied is the most frequent occurrence reported by all the interviewees. They were all, without exception, tied up for long hours before or between interrogations. The standard form of reception to the prison is to be tied up for many hours without water or food, sometimes outside, in any weather. This is a way to initially "prepare" the detainee. The particular technique known as "al-Shabah" is standard in every interrogation center. Soldiers, police or prison staff tie the detainees' hands behind and over the head. In most centers, the bound hands are also tied to pipes or bars embedded in the wall. The hands are usually fixed so high that the individual finds it very difficult to stand on his legs, which are also bound. In addition, the detainee is usually blindfolded or hooded. "Al-Shabah" lasts for 5–6 hours between interrogation sessions, or for 12 hours during the night.

THE "BANANA" TIE

Most interviewees reported that they were tied during the course of the investigation when their interrogators were roughing them up. An especially brutal method is the "banana" tie, which is the accepted form of tying up in the Gaza Strip as well as in most centers in the West Bank.

There are two methods which are called the banana tie. One consists of binding the suspect's legs to the legs of a chair without a backrest, and then tying his hands to the back legs of the chair. The second is binding the detainee's hands to his legs so that his body is bent backward. Thus, the tied up body looks like a banana and is exposed and vulnerable to the blows of the interrogators.

BEATINGS

Out of all the forty-one interviewees, only one (a journalist), was not beaten. All others were beaten routinely in the course of the interrogation. The interrogators beat with their fists, sticks, shoes and with any other instruments at hand such as an electric water heater or a tree branch. In Dahariya [detention center], a metal bar in the shape of a screw and covered with a plastic material was used to beat three of our interviewees. In the Shati Detention Centers (Gaza), they used a stick made of plastic material, thirty to forty centimeters long.

The interrogators beat the suspects on the face, the chest, the testicles, the stomach, in fact on all parts of the body. In the course of the beatings, the detainees' heads are sometimes smashed against the wall or the floor and they are kicked in their legs.

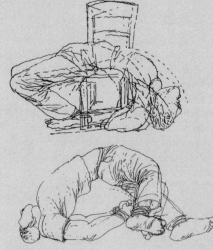

Figure 3. The "closet." Illustration by David Gerstein from B'Tselem, *The Interrogation of Palestinians during the Intifada: Ill-treatment, "Moderate Physical Pressure" or Torture?* (Jerusalem, 1991).

Figure 4. The "banana" tie. Illustration by David Gerstein from B'Tselem, *Interrogation of Palestinians during the Intifada.*

Alan Dershowitz personally intervened in the debate on Israeli ill-
treatment and torture of Palestinian detainees on at least two separate
occasions during this period. Before examining them, however, it is
worth recalling one of Dershowitz's earliest interventions on a Palestinian human rights issue, which foreshadows what comes later. In these
three instances—two of them judicial hearings—Dershowitz directly
sought to deny the human rights of those most in need of them. The
interventions illustrate both his long history of misrepresenting Israel's
human rights record and his abuse of an academic pedigree and civil
libertarian reputation for squalid ends.

The Case of Fouzi El-Asmar. Fouzi El-Asmar, a Palestinian citizen of
Israel, a poet as well as a writer critical of Israeli treatment of
Palestinians, was put under administrative detention in 1969. He
was released fifteen months later after a public campaign waged
in Israel (by, among others, Uri Avnery, editor of the popular
Israeli magazine *Ha-Olam ha-Zeh*, alongside a prominent right-
wing Israeli politician and the Israeli League for Human and Civil
Rights) and abroad (by, among others, Amnesty International,
which initiated a letter-writing campaign on his behalf). Upon
release from administrative detention, El-Asmar was confined to
the town of Lydda for another year. He was subsequently invited
to lecture in the United States, where he elected to remain, although
retaining his Israeli passport.[9] While still in administrative detention, El-Asmar received a visit from Alan Dershowitz. Dershowitz
afterwards wrote a long article stating that, based on the evidence
shown him by Israeli intelligence, which had alleged that El-
Asmar was in charge of an assassination squad, "I am personally
convinced . . . that Fawzi al-Asmar is the leader of a terrorist
group." Dershowitz's article was first published in *Commentary*
magazine, after which a significantly revised version came out in
the *Israel Yearbook on Human Rights*, in a collection of essays
edited by American "democratic socialists," and as a pamphlet
distributed wherever El-Asmar spoke in the United States.[10] After

9. For details, see Fouzi El-Asmar, *To Be an Arab in Israel* (Beirut, 1978), esp. chap. 6.
10. "Terrorism and Preventive Detention: The Case of Israel," *Commentary* (December 1970), pp. 67–78; "Preventive Detention of Citizens during a National Emergency—
A Comparison between Israel and the United States," in *Israel Yearbook on Human
Rights* (Tel Aviv, 1971), pp. 295–321; "Civil Liberties in Israel: The Problem of Preventive Detention," in Irving Howe and Carl Gershman (eds.), *Israel, the Arabs and the Middle East* (New York, 1972), pp. 266–99.

the article's appearance, *Commentary* published rebuttals from El-Asmar and two Israeli Jews.[11]

For example, Dershowitz initially claimed that El-Asmar's father "had been in trouble with the authorities even before the Six-Day War, having made illegal contact with an Arab government." In his reply El-Asmar stated: "All the facts repeated by Mr. Dershowitz about my father are outright lies. The best proof is the fact that for thirty years, many of them under the Israeli government, my father was a civil servant. Had he ever been found guilty of 'having made illegal contact with an Arab government,' he would have been thrown out of his post immediately." In the revised version of his article, this claim of Dershowitz vanished. Likewise, in the original article, Dershowitz named "Felicia Langer, a Jewish communist," as El-Asmar's lawyer. In Langer's reply as well as El-Asmar's, it was emphatically noted that she was *not* his lawyer. This claim was also quietly dropped from the revised version. All the versions of Dershowitz's article contained the assurance that, "[i]n every instance where I could, I myself checked the details with independent sources." Yet not only did he fail to check Israeli intelligence charges with El-Asmar's lawyer but, although claiming to independently assess and corroborate his guilt, Dershowitz *didn't even know who El-Asmar's lawyer was*. Challenged to explain why El-Asmar was released from administrative detention if he was a terrorist leader, Dershowitz went on to say: "[I]t is part of the Israeli policy in administrating their detention law to free everyone—regardless of how dangerous—after a reasonable time." Truly it is an extraordinary country that frees terrorist leaders plotting assassinations; and truly it's an extraordinary civil liberties lawyer who puts such faith in the words of a state intelligence agency. Once El-Asmar resettled abroad (which Israeli security had "encouraged" during his confinement), he was allowed to travel around Israel and the Occupied Territories without hindrance, and favorable mention of his name occasionally turned up in the Israeli press. A lengthy 1991 profile in *Haaretz* newspaper recalled that El-Asmar had been released from administrative detention after "having been falsely accused of being a member of the Popular Front for the Liberation of Palestine" and that "the allegations [against him] were

11. "Preventive Detention in Israel" (Letters), *Commentary* (June 1971).

never proven, and he was never brought to trial"; and, after citing Dershowitz's characterization of El-Asmar as a "terrorist leader," it ironically observed that "Israeli fears of El-Asmar have apparently dwindled considerably. When he infrequently arrives in Israel for a visit, the security men no longer even put him through the routine interrogation, to which almost every Arab returning to Israel is subject."[12] Meanwhile, as Israelis ridiculed the allegations against El-Asmar, Dershowitz continued to insist that "Fouzi El-Asmar . . . served time in an Israeli detention center as a suspected terrorist organizer after a captured Jordanian terrorist fingered him as 'very active in the field of sabotage and terrorism.'"[13]

The Case of Sami Esmail. In December 1977 Israeli authorities arrested a Palestinian American named Sami Esmail at Tel Aviv airport. He was en route to the West Bank to visit his dying father. Charged with being a terrorist, Esmail was convicted after signing a confession that, he alleged, was coerced. He claimed to have been stripped naked and humiliated, deprived of sleep, placed in solitary confinement in a tiny cell, forced to stand in place holding a chair over his head for many hours, and subjected to verbal threats ("You are going to die a slow death. . . . You are going to rot in this cell. . . . We are going to arrest your family") as well as physical assaults (punching, kicking, slapping, hair pulling). Only after being driven suicidal from exhaustion and fear, Esmail said, did he provide the self-incriminating statement. His lawyer was Felicia Langer, a well-known Israeli advocate of Palestinian detainees. Dershowitz and Monroe Freedman, another civil liberties lawyer highly regarded for his "original and influential scholarship in the field of lawyers' ethics," wrote a lengthy op-ed piece for the *New York Times* in June 1978 on the Esmail case.[14] In his 1991 autobiography, *Chutzpah,* Dershowitz presents this account of their joint intervention:

> In 1978, another law professor and I traveled to Israel at the behest of a group of human rights lawyers to look into allegations of torture

12. Yoav Karni, "Israel Lies between Washington and Riyadh," *Haaretz* (19 April 1991).
13. Alan Dershowitz, *Contrary to Popular Opinion* (New York, 1992), p. 389.
14. Monroe H. Freedman and Alan M. Dershowitz, "Israeli Torture, They Said," *New York Times* (2 June 1978). The quote on Freedman comes from the citation of the American Bar Association's highest award for professionalism that he received (posted on the Hofstra University School of Law faculty website, www.hofstra.edu).

being raised by supporters of an Arab American named Sami Esmail, who was being tried in Israel for receiving terrorist training in Libya by the Popular Front for the Liberation of Palestine. We spoke to Mr. Esmail, his lawyers, and the Israeli authorities. We carefully investigated each of the allegations and came to the conclusion that the evidence contradicted most of them. Rather than being held incommunicado, as he had claimed, Esmail had been visited by his brother and several American consular officials both before and after he confessed to his crimes. There was no evidence of sleep deprivation or physical torture.[15]

Although in this, as in almost any other, case regarding interrogation procedures, it's impossible to prove definitively the allegations of a detainee, on specific key points, the Dershowitz-Freedman account in the *Times* (as well as the rendering in *Chutzpah*) is demonstrably false. This became clear during a 1989 extradition hearing of another alleged Palestinian terrorist where Dershowitz and Freedman were called as expert witnesses (more on which presently).[16]

1. *Was Esmail held incommunicado?* In the 1978 *Times* op-ed piece and in his 1991 autobiography, Dershowitz flatly asserted that Esmail had never been held incommunicado. Yet, under cross-examination at the 1989 extradition hearing, Dershowitz explicitly acknowledged that "there certainly was a period of time that Sami Esmail was held certainly outside the ability to see his lawyer, yes," and that his being held incommunicado was a "fairly serious matter."[17] Likewise, Freedman conceded under cross-examination that Esmail had been held incommunicado during a "critical period of time" and that there was "no question" that he (Freedman) "would be pretty upset" if one of his own clients were similarly treated.[18]

2. *Did Langer argue that the confession was coerced?* In the *Times* op-ed as well as initially in testimony at the 1989 extradition hearing, Dershowitz and Freedman maintained that defense attorney Felicia Langer made no "arguments or claims" that Esmail's confession was involuntarily extracted and "no allegations that the confession, as a whole, in its general part, shouldn't be believed or admitted."[19] Yet, under cross-examination at the extradition hearing, Dershowitz, confronted with unimpeachable evidence directly contradicting him, was

15. Alan Dershowitz, *Chutzpah* (New York, 1991), pp. 236–37.
16. United States District Court, Eastern District of New York, Trial Transcripts, *Mahmoud Abet Atta a/k/a Mahmoud el-Abed Ahmad v. Wigen, et al.* The version of the transcript used here was generously provided by June Lowe, case manager for Judge Jack Weinstein, who presided. It is dated 2 August 1989.
17. *Ahmad v. Wigen*, pp. 450–51.
18. Ibid., pp. 501–3.
19. Ibid., pp. 384–85.

forced to acknowledge that Langer *did* argue the confession was coerced by Israeli interrogators, who resorted to, among other things, "beatings."[20] Likewise, Freedman conceded under cross-examination at the extradition hearing that Langer "did not abandon allegations of mistreatment."[21] Indeed, the claim that Langer never argued that Esmail's confession was coerced is, on its face, absurd. In Israeli legal procedure, the defense attorney is entitled to demand a "trial within a trial," or "little trial," to contest the evidentiary value of a confession on the grounds that it was involuntary. It is a matter of record that Langer requested a "little trial" and that it was conducted. The court held against the defendant, but Langer still must have *argued* the confession was coerced, else there would have been no point to the "little trial." Although critical of Langer's political partisanship (she was a Communist), Dershowitz has spoken very favorably of her professionalism. He described her as "an exceptionally able lawyer," "a very devoted lawyer with an excellent reputation and very committed to her legal principles. She tries her cases very, very well, according to the book"; "In the courtroom she does not argue a case like a political lawyer. She's very, very much by the books, by the cases. She's very familiar with the cases."[22] Langer does not speak very highly of Dershowitz (and Freedman), however, referring rather to the "big lie" and "disgusting lie" that she never claimed Esmail's confession was coerced. Indeed, prior to her plea in the little trial, she filed a complaint about Esmail's ill-treatment before another Israeli judge and submitted a copy of it to the U.S. embassy. After listing in a letter to this writer other distortions by Dershowitz, Langer ended: "I think that he does not know about what he speaks."[23]

Dershowitz and Freedman used the opportunity of the *Times* op-ed not only to misrepresent crucial aspects of the Esmail case but also to discredit generally charges that Israel ill-treated and tortured Palestinian detainees. "Allegations of systematic torture" and "allegations of systematic violations of human rights by

20. Ibid., p. 404.
21. Ibid., p. 507.
22. Ibid., pp. 382–86.
23. Personal correspondence dated 13 March 2004. While Dershowitz and Freedman, by their own (albeit reluctant) admission, engaged in partisan advocacy to discredit Sami Esmail, Langer played a rather different role, which deserves recognition. When asked at the 1989 extradition hearing whether he "considered Felicia Langer to be a reliable and faithful attorney," Esmail replied: "I considered Felicia Langer to be a mother. I'm proud to say that. I've recently had a daughter that I named after Felicia Langer, just to express my gratitude, appreciation for the fact that she saved my life. I consider her a second mother in every meaning of the word" (ibid., pp. 601–2). Langer was the recipient in 1990 of the Alternative Nobel Prize for her human rights work and was named one of the fifty most important women in Israeli society in 1998 by *YOU*, a prominent Israeli women's weekly.

Israel," these self-styled civil libertarians went on to urge, "must be viewed with more than a little skepticism"—even if (or probably because) the *London Sunday Times* had produced copious evidence, which Israeli authorities couldn't refute, that from the occupation's beginning Israeli interrogators "routinely" ill-treated and "often" tortured Arab prisoners. "Israel's justice system," the duo concluded from personal observation, was "one of the most highly civilized and refined in the world." American Communists observing the Soviet purge trials were similarly impressed.

The Case of Mahmoud el-Abed Ahmad. Dershowitz presents this account in *Chutzpah* of his intervention in the Ahmad case:

> The prosecution of Sami Esmail by Israel in 1978 became an issue in an American courtroom in 1989. A Palestinian named Mahmoud Abed Atta was accused by the Israeli government of machine-gunning a civilian bus en route from Tel Aviv to Jerusalem, killing its driver and wounding several passengers. Atta was arrested in the United States and Israel requested his extradition. He resisted on the ground that in Israel he would be tortured and beaten, just as Sami Esmail claimed he had been. Sami Esmail, who had been released by Israel after serving a short prison term, was Atta's star witness. I was called as an expert witness by the U.S. government, which supported Israel's extradition request.[24]

The thrust of Dershowitz's "expert" testimony was on Israel's interrogation methods. It should be borne in mind that he delivered these remarks in 1989—*after* publication of the *London Times*'s 1977 study documenting Israeli ill-treatment and torture of Palestinian detainees; *after* the 1984 reports of, respectively, Amnesty International and al-Haq on Israel's ill-treatment and torture of Palestinian detainees; and *after* the onset in December 1987 of the first intifada, when according to Amnesty, B'Tselem, and other human rights organizations as well as reports in the Israeli press, thousands of Palestinian detainees were being "tortured or ill-treated" by Israel's security service.

These are excerpts from the testimony *sworn to under oath* by Dershowitz:

- "The consensus that I've gathered is that Israeli General Security Services use primarily stratagems for eliciting confessions and that these stratagems rely on the fear and the assumption by the person being interrogated that he might be subjected to physical pressure. . . .

---

24. Dershowitz, *Chutzpah*, pp. 237–38.

[T]he toughest methodology for eliciting statements, both confessions for use in trial but primarily information for use in information gathering to fight against terrorism, is to frighten the person being interrogated into believing that the situation is actually going to be worse than it would become."

- "All of my sources of information have categorically denied that actual torture has been used in the sense of direct use of physical force, direct use of physical pain to elicit the confession, but that threats and fear of torture are used. . . . [T]he actual use of physical torture in the sense of direct pain designed to produce a statement or confession is and has always been prohibited both by Israeli law and by the internal rules of the General Services Administration [*sic*— General Security Service]."

- "I have heard no allegation from any lawyer or professor that I have spoken to which makes an allegation that torture in the sense that I've defined it is used; that is, direct use of producing a physical pain in order to get the statement or confession."

- "[T]he General Services people do engage in occasional pushing and shoving calculated, that is, physical touching, calculated to persuade the interrogatees that there is no sharp barrier involving physical touching, . . . not torture in the sense of produce pain for pain's sake . . . but to maintain a credible belief of the person being interrogated that they are able to and willing to engage in even further physical contact."[25]

In short, the "toughest" methods resorted to by Israeli interrogators, according to Dershowitz's sworn testimony, were "stratagems" coupled with an "occasional pushing and shoving" or "physical touching" that inflicted fear but not pain. After this rendering of Israel's interrogation methods and after claiming that—contrary to the consensus of human rights organizations and other independent investigators—Israeli interrogation methods didn't constitute torture, Dershowitz was asked by the presiding judge whether, in his expert opinion, it would legally constitute not torture but simply "inhumane" treatment if "a person is kept incommunicado for long periods, is humiliated, given cold showers, is lied to about what will happen to him physically, being threatened so he believes that he will be physically assaulted." Dershowitz replied: "I can't say yes to that."[26] In his autobiography Dershowitz gloats that "[t]he judge, relying on my testimony, con-

25. *Ahmad v. Wigen*, pp. 339–45.
26. Ibid., p. 464.

cluded that the evidence presented at the extradition hearing showed it was unlikely that Atta would be tortured," and that "Atta was ordered extradited to Israel for trial."[27] If not the performance, at any rate the boast would likely have caused even a jaded Stalinist hack to blush in shame.

• • • •

"Torture," Alan Dershowitz recently wrote, "is a staple in tyrannical regimes."[28] By his own reckoning, Israel's regime in the Occupied Territories would seem to qualify as a tyranny—except that Dershowitz still denies in *The Case for Israel* that Israel has tortured Palestinian detainees. The sections below titled "Occasional Abuses," "Amnesty Lied," "Torture Lite," "Medical Condition," "Ticking Bomb," "Double Standard," and "No More Torture" illustrate Dershowitz's attempt to refute the documented charges of human rights organizations.

OCCASIONAL ABUSES

In September 1999, Israel's Supreme Court rendered a judgment on the torture of Palestinian detainees.[29] On pages 134–35 of *The Case for Israel,* Dershowitz reports:

> Prior to this decision the Israeli security services did *sometimes* employ physical measures similar to those now being used by U.S. authorities against suspected terrorists. (emphasis added)

27. Dershowitz, *Chutzpah,* p. 239. For the record, presiding judge Jack Weinstein credited Dershowitz's testimony only on the relatively minor matters that, after extradition from the United States, accused Ukrainian war criminal John Demjanjuk was not tortured by Israel and that the Israeli prison system was comparable to most in the Western world. On the other hand, Weinstein, to his credit, dissented from Dershowitz's strictures on torture and Israel's resort to it. Directly contradicting Dershowitz's claim that torture, and even inhumane treatment, mean only the infliction of physical pain, Weinstein stated that "[t]orture and cruel and unusual punishment must be defined for our purposes as including threats and other inhuman psychological harms including trickery designed to cause despair." In addition, contrary to Dershowitz's claim that Israeli interrogation techniques comprise only "stratagems" that inflict fear but not pain, Weinstein directly adduced the U.S. "State Department's own report on human rights conditions in Israel," according to which "[r]eports of beatings of suspects and detainees continue, as do reports of harsh and demeaning treatment of prisoners and detainees." Weinstein allowed for Atta's extradition mainly because Israel, in a special letter to the court, "formally provided assurance that petitioner, if extradited, will not be subject to torture or other inhuman and degrading treatment." See *Ahmad v. Wigen,* 726 F. Supp. 389, 415–18 (1989).
28. Alan Dershowitz, *Why Terrorism Works* (New Haven, 2002), p. 124.
29. See section titled "No More Torture" in this chapter.

He describes these physical measures as **"a modified form of non-lethal torture."** Leaving aside Dershowitz's euphemistic qualification of this torture, human rights organizations reported that Israel's resort to it wasn't occasional but standard practice.

YEAR   AMNESTY INTERNATIONAL ANNUAL REPORT[30]

1991   "Thousands of Palestinians were punitively beaten or otherwise tortured or ill-treated"

1992   "Palestinians under interrogation were systematically tortured or ill-treated"

1993   "Palestinians under interrogation were systematically tortured or ill-treated"

1994   "Palestinians were systematically tortured or ill-treated during interrogation"

1995   "Torture or ill-treatment during interrogation remained systematic"

1996   "Palestinian detainees continued to be systematically tortured or ill-treated during interrogation"

1997   "Torture and ill-treatment of Palestinians during interrogation continued to be systematic and officially sanctioned"

1998   "Torture and ill-treatment of detainees during interrogation continued to be systematic and officially sanctioned"

1999   "Torture and ill-treatment continued to be officially sanctioned and used systematically during interrogation of security detainees"

In *Combating Torture*, Amnesty reported that "[f]rom 1967 the Israeli security services have routinely tortured Palestinian political suspects in the Occupied Territories."[31]

"Israel's two main interrogation agencies in the occupied territories engage in a systematic pattern of ill-treatment and torture—according to internationally recognized definitions of the terms—when trying to extract

30. *Amnesty International Report*s (New York) for 1991–1999. The report for 1991 covers the period January to December 1990, and so on.
31. Amnesty International, *Combating Torture* (London, 2003), section 2.2.

from Palestinian security suspects confessions or information about third parties."

"Nearly all Palestinians undergoing interrogation are put through some combination of the same basic methods. . . . Thus, the number of Palestinians tortured or severely ill-treated while under interrogation during the intifada is in the tens of thousands—a number that becomes especially significant when it is remembered that the universe of adult and adolescent male Palestinians in the West Bank and Gaza Strip is under three-quarters of one million."[32]

B'TSELEM

"GSS [General Security Service] interrogators have tortured thousands, if not tens of thousands, of Palestinians."

"[S]ome eighty-five percent of persons interrogated by the GSS were interrogated by methods constituting torture."[33]

═══════════════ AMNESTY LIED ═══════════════

Referring to the September 1999 Israel Supreme Court decision on torture,[34] Dershowitz writes on page 137 of *The Case for Israel:*

> In light of this courageous decision, it is ironic that in May 1999 the Dutch sections [*sic*] of Amnesty International publicly opposed the awarding of a human rights prize to the author of that, and many other, human rights rulings supporting Palestinian claims on the ground that "the Israel Supreme Court's decisions with regard to human rights . . . have been devastating." Amnesty International specifically claimed that "Israel is the only country in the world to have effectively legalized torture." It should not be surprising that so many human rights advocates have lost faith in Amnesty International's objectivity when it comes to reporting on Israel.

But what was the formal status of torture in Israel *prior to* September 1999, when Amnesty registered its objection? The interrogation methods used by the General Security Service (GSS) on Palestinian

---

32. Human Rights Watch, *Israel's Interrogation of Palestinians from the Occupied Territories* (New York, 1994), pp. x, 4. Throughout the 1990s the annual *Human Rights Watch World Report* similarly concluded that Israeli torture and ill-treatment of Palestinian detainees was systematic.

33. B'Tselem, *Legislation Allowing for the Use of Physical Force and Mental Coercion in Interrogations by the General Security Service*, Position Paper (Jerusalem, January 2000), p. 31.

34. See section titled "No More Torture" in this chapter.

detainees were based on the secret recommendations of a 1987 judicial commission headed by retired Supreme Court justice Moshe Landau.[35] "[T]he Commission," B'Tselem concluded in a groundbreaking study, "ended up legitimating the use of torture."[36] Application of these methods (and subsequently "enhanced" versions of them) was "systematic" and, outside Israel, universally characterized as "torture."[37] The prospective recipient of the human rights prize, President of the Court Aharon Barak, was a leading proponent of the Landau recommendations allowing for torture, maintaining that "the solution offered by the Landau Commission for the problem of GSS interrogations 'is appropriate.'"[38] The Court itself rendered a series of rulings "permitting the GSS to use physical force and a variety of specific means of 'pressure.'... Israel's High Court has supported the government and sanctioned the use of force against detainees."[39] Like Amnesty, B'Tselem concluded that "Israel was the only country in the world where torture was legally sanctioned."[40]

Referring to the September 1999 Supreme Court decision on torture, Dershowitz repeatedly praises Israel for being **"the only country in the world whose judiciary has squarely faced the difficult issue of whether it is ever justified to engage in even a modified form of nonlethal torture"** (p. 134; see also pp. 184, 199). Yet the reason Israel's judiciary was the only one in the world rendering judgment on use of torture was that Israel was the only country in the world that had previously

35. For excerpts from the Landau report and critical commentary, see esp. *Israel Law Review* (Jerusalem), vol. 23, nos. 2–3 (spring–summer 1989). Dershowitz, in his contribution to the issue ("Is It Necessary to Apply 'Physical Pressure' to Terrorists—and to Lie about It?"), takes no position on the Landau commission's recommendation that torture be sanctioned: "I lack the information necessary to reach any definitive assessment of whether the GSS should be allowed to employ physical pressure in the interrogation of some suspected terrorists under some circumstances" (p. 199).

36. B'Tselem, *Interrogation*, p. 31.

37. See section titled "Occasional Abuses" in this chapter.

38. Public Committee Against Torture in Israel, *Flawed Defense: Torture and Ill-Treatment in GSS Interrogations following the Supreme Court Ruling, 6 September 1999–6 September 2001* (Jerusalem, September 2001), p. 9n6.

39. B'Tselem, *Legitimizing Torture: The Israeli High Court of Justice Rulings in the Bilbeisi, Hamdan and Mubarak Cases* (Jerusalem, January 1997), n.p. (see this report for previous quote "enhanced").

40. B'Tselem website under "Torture," www.btselem.org/english/Torture/Toture_by _GSS.asp; see also Eitan Felner, executive director of B'Tselem, in *Le Monde*: "Israel is the only country in the world that has legitimated torture both juridically and rhetorically.... [T]he High Court of Justice has effectively legalized torture by approving its use in individual cases" (11 December 1998).

legalized it. In addition, were it not for pressures exerted by the very human rights monitors that Dershowitz maligns throughout *The Case for Israel*, the Supreme Court would never have faced this issue:

> [A] powerful campaign against torture was mounted. On the national level, it included court cases and petitions to the Israeli High Court of Justice by human rights lawyers. At the international level, the campaign involved the mobilization of international public opinion. At the same time, the practice of torture was coming under increased scrutiny by UN bodies and mechanisms, including the Committee against Torture and the Human Rights Committee. As a result, pressure increased on the High Court of Justice, which until 1998 had largely accepted the pleas of the security services that certain interrogation methods were a "necessity" in their fight against "terrorism."[41]

TORTURE LITE

On pages 137–38 of *The Case for Israel*, Dershowitz writes regarding the **"interrogation tactics"** used by Israel on Palestinian detainees:

> **[T]hey were universally characterized as torture without even noting that they were nonlethal and did not involve the infliction of sustained pain.**

Leaving aside that, on the one hand, "interrogation tactics" that were deliberately lethal would seem to defeat the purpose and, on the other hand, if deliberately lethal they would constitute not simply torture but extrajudicial killing, is it true that these tactics "did not involve the infliction of sustained pain"? In his previous book *Why Terrorism Works*, Dershowitz suggested otherwise: **"Israeli security services were employing what they *euphemistically* called 'moderate physical pressure'"** (emphasis added); **"In Israel, the use of torture to prevent terrorism was not hypothetical; it was very real and recurring."**[42] As a *legal* matter and regardless of Dershowitz's personal opinion, however, it is undisputed that Israel's interrogation tactics have constituted torture. Israel accepts the authority of the U.N. Committee Against Torture (composed of ten experts) to interpret the Convention Against Torture. Acknowledging "the terrible dilemma that Israel confronts in dealing with terrorist threats to its security," the committee nonetheless concluded in May 1997, in a judgment Dershowitz himself cites (p. 138), that its "methods of interrogation . . . constitute torture as defined in

41. Amnesty International, *Combating Torture*, section 2.2.
42. Dershowitz, *Why Terrorism Works*, pp. 139–40.

Figure 5. Humiliation during interrogation. Public Committee Against Torture in Israel, *Back to a Routine of Torture: Torture and Ill-treatment of Palestinian Detainees during Arrest, Detention and Interrogation, September 2001–April 2003* (Jerusalem, April 2003), p. 51.

Figure 6. "Shabeh," a standard torture technique. Public Committee Against Torture in Israel, *Back to a Routine of Torture*, p. 55.

article 1 of the Convention."[43] In his annual report that same year to the Commission on Human Rights, U.N. Special Rapporteur on Torture Nigel Rodley, a leading expert in the field, likewise concluded that Israel's interrogation tactics "can only be described as torture." Although if deployed separately these tactics "may not provoke severe pain or suffering," Rodley found, "[t]ogether—and they are frequently used in combination—they may be expected to induce precisely such pain or suffering, especially if applied on a protracted basis of, say, several hours. In fact, they are sometimes apparently applied for days or even weeks on end."[44] B'Tselem observes that "Israel has not been able to convince even one international official or body that these methods do not constitute torture or ill-treatment." Indeed, it cites a 1998 poll finding that fully 76 percent of Israelis believe these methods constitute torture.[45] Finally, an Israel Supreme Court landmark decision on torture, which Dershowitz praises, concluded that the interrogation tactics used on Palestinian detainees "give rise to pain and suffering."[46]

MEDICAL CONDITION

To demonstrate that Israeli **"interrogation tactics"** were **"nonlethal and did not involve the infliction of sustained pain,"** Dershowitz appends this tally on page 252 of *The Case for Israel:*

> One person died following shaking, but an independent investigation attributed his death to an unknown preexisting medical condition. See *Public Committee Against Torture,* HCJ (Israeli Supreme Court) 5100/94.

Yet human rights organizations report multiple deaths of Palestinian detainees during Israeli interrogation. For example, the entry for "Israel and the Occupied Territories" in *Amnesty International Report 1993* states: "Palestinians under interrogation were systematically tortured or ill-treated. Four died in circumstances related to their treatment under interrogation." The Public Committee Against Torture in Israel reports that "approximately 20 Palestinian detainees died under suspi-

43. "Summary record of the public part of the 297th meeting: Israel. 04/09/97" (CAT/C/SR.297/Add.1).
44. "Report of the Special Rapporteur, Mr. Nigel S. Rodley, submitted pursuant to Commission on Human Rights resolution 1995/37 B" (E/CN.4/1997/7).
45. B'Tselem, *Legislation Allowing for the Use of Physical Force,* pp. 25, 54.
46. *Public Committee Against Torture v. Israel* (HCJ 5100/94), p. 27.

cious circumstances while in interrogation and detention during the first Intifada."[47]

In April 1995 Palestinian detainee Abd al-Samad Harizat died after falling into a coma during Israeli interrogation. Israeli authorities originally sought to pin blame for Harizat's death on a prior medical condition, Amnesty International reports, "[b]ut it so happened that Abd al-Samad Harizat was in good health at the time of his sudden death." Dr. H. Kugel and Dr. B. Levi from the Institute for Forensic Medicine in Tel Aviv conducted the official autopsy, while Dr. D. Pounder, a professor of forensic pathology at Dundee University in Scotland, observed the autopsy on behalf of the family. Pounder attributed Harizat's death to a brain hemorrhage caused by "sudden jarring movements of the head"—that is, "violent shaking." Likewise, the autopsy report of the Israeli forensic pathologists concluded that Harizat died from "brain damage due to rotational acceleration of the head." Likewise, the report of the Department of Investigations of Police found that Harizat "lost consciousness" after interrogators "shook him roughly" multiple times. Likewise, an "expert opinion" on the official autopsy report by Dr. Y. Hiss, director of the Institute of Forensic Medicine, attributed Harizat's death to "lethal damage to the brain . . . caused by shaking."[48] Likewise, the Israeli Ministry of Justice stated that Harizat died "as a result of a rapid twisting of the head."[49] The Supreme Court decision cited by Dershowitz (HCJ 5100/94) states that "[a]ll agree" that Harizat "expired after being shaken."[50] The Court decision makes no

47. Orah Maggen, Information Coordinator, Public Committee Against Torture in Israel (1 December 2003, personal communication). See also B'Tselem, *Interrogation*, pp. 32–36.

48. Amnesty International, *Death by Shaking: The Case of Abd al-Samad Harizat* (October 1995) (autopsy reports). The interrogator who tortured Harizat to death was never criminally indicted and, "after a not-too-long suspension, [he] resumed interrogating—and probably also torturing—Palestinian detainees" (Public Committee Against Torture in Israel, *Flawed Defense*, p. 19). Prime Minister Yitzhak Rabin acknowledged in 1995 that "shaking" had been used against eight thousand Palestinian detainees, while a former Israeli attorney general stated that "the use of the interrogation method called shaking is a routinely-used method of interrogation" (B'Tselem, *Legislation Allowing for the Use of Physical Force*, pp. 31–32).

49. "Report Issued on Circumstances Surrounding Death of Detainee (Communicated by Justice Ministry Spokeswoman)" (Jerusalem, 7 June 1995), www.israel-mfa .gov.il/mfa/go.asp?MFAHOa4eO.

50. *Public Committee Against Torture v. Israel* (HCJ 5100/94), p. 9. This Supreme Court decision refers back to HCJ 4054/95, a prior court decision bearing on the Harizat case.

mention of an "independent investigation" attributing Harizat's death to "an unknown preexisting medical condition." Indeed, no record of this independent investigation exists.

TICKING BOMB

On page 139 of *The Case for Israel*, Dershowitz states that the purpose of Israel's interrogation tactics against Palestinian detainees was to **"elicit lifesaving information."**[51] Yet in his earlier book *Why Terrorism Works*, Dershowitz suggested that this "ticking bomb" scenario was merely a pretext for methodical abuse of Palestinian detainees: "[T]he extraordinarily rare situation of the hypothetical ticking bomb terrorist was serving as a moral, intellectual, and legal justification for a pervasive *system* of coercive interrogation, which, though not the paradigm of torture, certainly bordered on it" (pp. 140–41; emphasis in original).[52]

"'[S]pecial' methods of interrogation," Professor David Kretzmer of the Hebrew University reports in a major scholarly study, "had become almost standard practice in interrogation of Palestinians, and were certainly not limited to the classic 'ticking-bomb' situation."[53] Although the Israeli government "often argues . . . frightening claims of 'the ticking bomb' type to justify violent interrogations by the GSS [General Security Service]," B'Tselem extensively documents, "[m]ost of these cases . . . were totally unsubstantiated." The GSS claims to deprive Palestinian detainees of sleep for prolonged periods due to the "ticking bomb," it further notes, yet "[t]he lethal bomb ticks away during the week, ceases, miraculously, on the weekend, and begins to tick again when the interrogators return from their day of rest."[54] "In practice, not only was torture not limited to 'persons who planted ticking bombs,'" B'Tselem reported in another study, but

> it was not even limited to persons suspected of membership in terrorist organizations, or to persons suspected of criminal offenses. The GSS regularly tortured political activists of Islamic movements, students suspected of being pro-Islamic, religious sages, sheiks and religious leaders, and persons active in Islamic charitable organizations, the brothers and other relatives of persons listed as "wanted" (in an attempt to obtain information about

51. Dershowitz implies this claim on pp. 134, 135, and 199.
52. Dershowitz, *Why Terrorism Works*, pp. 140–41.
53. David Kretzmer, *The Occupation of Justice* (Albany, 2002), pp. 141–42. The quote refers to the period prior to a September 1999 Israel Supreme Court decision on torture.
54. B'Tselem, *Routine Torture: Interrogation Methods of the General Security Service* (Jerusalem, 1998), pp. 16, 29 (see pp. 30–31 for multiple examples of Palestinians

them), and Palestinians in professions liable to be involved in preparing explosives—an almost infinite list. In a number of cases, wives of detainees were arrested during their husbands' detention, and the interrogators even ill-treated them to further pressure their husbands. Also, GSS agents used torture to recruit collaborators.

Finally, B'Tselem emphasizes that those claiming the necessity of torture in a "ticking bomb" scenario "have not provided a shred of evidence that physical force is the only or the most effective means to prevent attacks."[55]

DOUBLE STANDARD

Regarding Israel's interrogation tactics, Dershowitz writes on, respectively, pages 135 and 186 of *The Case for Israel:*

> England employed tactics similar to those used by Israel—uncomfortable positions, loud music, hoods, and so forth—when interrogating suspected terrorists in Northern Ireland. But only Israel has been so repeatedly and viciously condemned for a practice that their current law does not even permit.

> Israel has been in greater compliance with the rule of law than any other country facing comparable dangers.

Leaving aside what Israel's "current law" permits,[56] B'Tselem, in a January 2000 report, systematically compared Israel's record on torture in the Occupied Territories with Great Britain's record in Northern Ireland. Its findings merit extensive quotation:

> The early 1970s was the most violent period Northern Ireland had experienced in recent history: from 1971 to March 1975, more than 1,100 persons were killed and 11,500 wounded. During 1971 and 1972 alone, 1,130 planted bombs exploded, and an armed group, the IRA, was responsible for these attacks. During a short period in 1971, British security forces in Northern Ireland used coercive interrogation methods against fourteen IRA suspects. These methods, known as the "five techniques," were the subject of the action in *Ireland v. United Kingdom* [before the European Court of Human Rights (ECHR)]. . . .
> [T]he GSS [Israel's General Security Service] used methods comparable to those used by the British in 1971, i.e., sleep deprivation, infliction of

tortured on grounds of a "ticking bomb" scenario yet subsequently released without being indicted or administratively detained).

55. B'Tselem, *Legislation Allowing for the Use of Physical Force*, pp. 32, 48.
56. See section titled "No More Torture" in this chapter.

physical suffering, and sensory isolation. But the GSS used them for much longer periods, so the resulting pain and suffering were substantially greater. In addition, the GSS used direct violence. . . . Thus, . . . in practice, the GSS methods were substantially more severe than those used by the British in 1971. . . .

Furthermore, already in March 1972, before the ECHR had given its decision prohibiting use of the "five techniques," the British government, in the midst of a wave of terrorist attacks, stated that it would no longer use these interrogation methods. . . .

Thus, Israel in 1999 continued to rely on interrogation methods used in Great Britain in 1971, twenty-eight years ago, for an extremely short period against only fourteen persons, which ceased immediately afterwards and became absolutely prohibited. In the meantime, European and international legislation and case law have increasingly strengthened the prohibition on torture and ill-treatment. . . .

Terrorist acts in England and Northern Ireland did not cease in the 1970s. Despite this, protection of prisoner rights in particular has steadily improved. . . . As a result, the number of complaints of torture and ill-treatment fell sharply.

"The normative difference between Israel and other democratic countries is reflected in the scope of the use of torture in interrogations," B'Tselem concludes. "While Israel uses it routinely and against thousands of interrogees, in other liberal democracies, torture is exceptional and rare."[57]

NO MORE TORTURE

Regarding a 6 September 1999 Israeli court decision, Dershowitz writes on page 206 of *The Case for Israel:*

> [T]he Israeli Supreme Court outlawed the use of all physical pressure in eliciting information from potential terrorists. Israel is the only country in the Middle East to have abolished any kind of torture, in fact as well as in law.[58]

Yet, just one year before in his book *Why Terrorism Works,* Dershowitz, referring to the same court decision, himself acknowledged

57. B'Tselem, *Legislation Allowing for the Use of Physical Force,* pp. 43–46.
58. Dershowitz repeats versions of this same claim on pp. 134 ("officially outlawed all forms of physical pressure," "absolutely prohibited"), 135 ("current law does not even permit," "prohibiting the use of physical pressures"), 138 ("has now outlawed them"), 184 ("prohibited their use"), 199 ("such pressure is now illegal"), 206 ("stopped doing").

that it did not absolutely prohibit torture: "[T]he Supreme Court left open the possibility that a member of the security service who honestly believed that rough interrogation was the only means available to save lives in imminent danger could raise this defense."[59] In *Flawed Defense*, the Public Committee Against Torture in Israel reports this as well as other lacunae in the court decision:

> The Court avoided adopting the position of international law that rejects torture in any situation, and left intact the applicability of the "necessity defense," for torturers during a "ticking bomb" situation, thereby creating an opening both for the existence of torture in practice, and lending legal and ethical legitimacy to this deplorable crime. The Court allowed, under limited conditions, sleep deprivation and prolonged tying of detainees, creating cracks into which the GSS [General Security Service] hastily squeezed through to find ostensibly legal methods of torture and ill-treatment. The result is that protection for Palestinian detainees from torture and ill-treatment is still lacking.[60]

Although "the use of torture declined or stopped in the days immediately after the 6 September High Court ruling,"[61] the Public Committee Against Torture found, in a subsequent major study, *Back to a Routine of Torture*, that the GSS—with active complicity of the Supreme Court—resumed systematic torture of Palestinian detainees: "The achievements of the HCJ [High Court of Justice] ruling of 1999, which was to have put an end to large-scale torture and ill-treatment, . . . have worn thin, among other reasons, as a result of the HCJ's reluctance to enforce international standards which prohibit torture and ill-treatment under any circumstances. . . . [T]he HCJ, the State Prosecutor's Office, and the Attorney General have, regarding this matter, transformed themselves from guardians and protectors of the law into sentries at the gates of the GSS torture chambers." And again: "The achievements of the HCJ ruling of 1999 have been ground to dust." Estimating that "[e]ach month, hundreds of Palestinians have been subjected to one degree or another of torture or other cruel, inhuman or degrading treatment," it concludes that torture techniques are applied in a "methodical and routine" fashion and that "GSS agents who interrogate Palestinian detainees torture them, degrade them, and otherwise ill-treat them routinely." The number of detainees "against whom no

---

59. Dershowitz, *Why Terrorism Works*, pp. 251–52n26.
60. Public Committee Against Torture in Israel, *Flawed Defense*, p. 14.
61. *Human Rights Watch World Report 2000* (New York).

method of ill-treatment whatsoever was used is negligible."[62] In its 2003 publication *Combating Torture,* Amnesty International likewise concluded that "many of the methods used in the past had been revived, and the torture of Palestinians held by the GSS was once again widespread."[63]

. . . .

Apart from systematic torture of Palestinian detainees, human rights organizations have documented the routine brutalization of Palestinians generally. "During the first weeks of the intifada," Amnesty International reported in a 2001 study, "more than a thousand people, including Palestinians from the Occupied Territories, Jewish and Palestinian citizens of Israel, were arrested by the Israeli authorities, many of them children. Police brutality, amounting to torture or other cruel, inhuman or degrading treatment, accompanied the arrests and was used indiscriminately against demonstrators."[64] A 2001 study by B'Tselem entitled *Standard Routine: Beatings and Abuse of Palestinians by Israeli Security Forces during the Al-Aqsa Intifada* found that, although "the phenomenon itself has existed for many years," there was a "significant increase in the number of beatings and abuse" of Palestinians. The study continues: "In most cases, the abuse is given in a 'small dose,' such as a slap, a kick, an insult, a senseless delay at checkpoints, or humiliating treatment. Over the years, these acts have become an integral part of the daily life of Palestinians in the Occupied Territories. At times, though, the violence is severe." It documents, for example, the case of "an infant of three, whose hand was broken by border policemen." Indeed, border police "all the time" not only assaulted Palestinians but "even took pictures of their acts"; "many join the Border Police to 'beat up Arabs.'" Not a single complaint filed by Palestinians protesting this pervasive abuse was acted on by Israeli officials ("all the investigation files were closed with no action taken"), and "[b]oth the army and the Border Police have yet to make it unequivocally clear to security forces serving in the Occupied Territories that it is absolutely

62. Public Committee Against Torture in Israel, *Back to a Routine of Torture: Torture and Ill-treatment of Palestinian Detainees during Arrest, Detention and Interrogation, September 2001–April 2003* (Jerusalem, April 2003), pp. 9–14, 21, 89. For the Supreme Court's complicity, see esp. chap. 4 ("Rubber Stamps for the GSS: The High Court of Justice, the Attorney General, and the State Prosecutor's Office").

63. Amnesty International, *Combating Torture,* section 2.2.

64. Amnesty International, *Broken Lives—A Year of Intifada* (London, 2001), p. 50.

forbidden to abuse and beat Palestinians." "If a message is sent to security forces," B'Tselem concluded, "it is that . . . the lives and dignity of Palestinians are meaningless and that security forces can continue, pursuant to the function they serve, to abuse, humiliate, and beat Palestinians with whom they come into contact."[65]

65. B'Tselem, *Standard Routine: Beatings and Abuse of Palestinians by Israeli Security Forces during the Al-Aqsa Intifada* (Jerusalem, 2001), pp. 2–3, 5, 21–22, 36 (quotations regarding border police come from testimony of those police as reported in *Haaretz*). For further documentation, see B'Tselem, *In Broad Daylight: Abuse of Palestinians by IDF Soldiers on 23 July 2001* (Jerusalem).

7

Return of the Vandals

SINCE THE START of the new intifada in September 2000, "Israel has implemented a policy of mass demolition of Palestinian houses in the Occupied Territories," B'Tselem (Israeli Information Center for Human Rights in the Occupied Territories) reports. "In that period, Israel has destroyed some 4170 Palestinian homes."[1] The egregious policy of house demolitions reaches back to the beginnings of Israel's occupation after June 1967. It's been variously justified as a form of punishment, an administrative measure, and a military/security measure. Each of these will be examined in turn.

HOUSE DEMOLITIONS AS PUNISHMENT

House demolition as a form of punishment is inflicted on suspected Palestinian security offenders. According to B'Tselem, it is used against Palestinians "suspected of any kind of violent activity against Israelis regardless of its consequences, from suicide-bombings that left many casualties to failed attempts to harm soldiers," as well as "against

1. B'Tselem (Israeli Information Center for Human Rights in the Occupied Territories), *Through No Fault of Their Own: Punitive House Demolitions during the al-Aqsa Intifada* (Jerusalem, November 2004), p. 4.

Palestinians who initiate, plan, or assist in carrying out such attacks."
The Israeli government itself acknowledges that "in forty percent of the
attacks for which the suspect's house was demolished, no Israeli was
killed." Contrariwise, "[t]he measure has never been used against
Israeli civilians who committed acts similar to those for which Palestinian houses are demolished."[2] Some 1,400 homes were demolished
(or sealed) during the first two decades of the Israeli occupation
(1967–1987), while about 700 homes were demolished (or sealed) during the first intifada (1988–1992) as punishment. Since the beginning of
the new intifada through October 2004, Israel has completely demolished more than 600 homes (sheltering nearly four thousand persons)
as punishment.[3] "The implications of this for the individual families,"
Amnesty International observes, "are immense: virtually all houses are
built by and for a particular family and (partly because of lack of other
opportunities for investment) the house is a larger proportion of a family's wealth than in countries not living under occupation. Additional to
the value of the house is the value (emotional and financial) of furnish-
ings and possessions: when the troops arrive (which may be several
years after the order) the family is often too outraged and terrified to
rescue possessions in the period given by the soldiers (not more than one
hour) to evacuate the house. An additional loss is the land itself: the land
on which the house has been built may be subject to confiscation."[4]
Middle East Watch has reported that, apart from Israel, the only other
country in the world that "punished the families of suspected offenders
by demolishing their homes" was Iraq under Saddam Hussein.[5]

2. Ibid., pp. 6 ("never been used"), 15 ("regardless," "initiate," "forty percent").
Regarding the discriminatory use of this punitive measure, B'Tselem recalls that "the
home of Baruch Goldstein, who committed the attack in the Tomb of the Patriarchs in
1994, in which twenty-nine Palestinians were killed, was not demolished, nor was the
home of Shahar Dvir Zeliger, who was convicted of membership in a terrorist organization that intended to carry out attacks against Arabs, and between 2001 and 2003 carried
out shooting attacks and laid explosives intended to harm Palestinians" (p. 6n7; on this
point, see also Amnesty International, *Under the Rubble: House Demolition and
Destruction of Land and Property* [London, May 2004], p. 9).
3. David Kretzmer, *The Occupation of Justice: The Supreme Court of Israel and the
Occupied Territories* (Albany, 2002), p. 145; B'Tselem, *House Demolitions—Statistics,*
www.btselem.org/english/House_Demolitions/Statistics.asp; B'Tselem, *Through No Fault
of Their Own*, pp. 4–7.
4. Amnesty International, *Demolition and Dispossession: The Destruction of Palestinian Homes* (London, December 1999), p. 15 (cf. B'Tselem, *Through No Fault of Their
Own*, pp. 20–24).
5. *Human Rights Watch World Report 1992* (New York). The United States has apparently resorted to this tactic on occasion since its occupation of Iraq; see Kenneth Roth,
"Letter to Defense Secretary Donald Rumsfeld" (Human Rights Watch, 12 January 2004).

"The destruction of a suspect's home is an administrative process carried out without trial, and without the need to prove the guilt of the suspect before any judicial body," B'Tselem notes. "In the majority of cases, the sanction is carried out prior to conviction. In other words, this form of punishment is carried out primarily against individuals who are only suspected offenders." In cases where the suspect is dead, "the demolition sometimes takes place before an autopsy is performed and the individual's identity is verified."[6] Before the new intifada the Israeli army typically issued a demolition order, the Palestinian occupants being given forty-eight hours to appeal the military commander's order and, if the appeal was denied, to petition the High Court of Justice against the demolition. Currently, however, "the rule is that the IDF [Israeli Defense Force] does not give prior warning. Exceptions to this rule are almost non-existent." A High Court decision affirmed that the Israeli army was not obliged to issue a prior demolition order, the Court subsequently stating that "[r]esidents of the region, who fear that their houses will be damaged because of the acts of their terrorist relatives that resulted in the loss of life, may direct their requests to the respondent [i.e., IDF commander]. In this context, they can provide the respondent with information that in the opinion of the family should affect his decision. . . . In acts that are planned sufficiently in advance, the respondent will not demolish a house before considering this information." B'Tselem caustically observed:

> In making this ruling, the High Court gave the military commander not only the power to decide if and when to punish innocent persons, but also the absolute power to determine if they are to be given an opportunity to be heard. The High Court thus eliminated judicial review and placed the fate of the potential victims in the hands of the military commander. . . . The High Court's decision, which exempts the state authority from its duty to give notification before demolishing a house, while imposing on the individual the obligation of laying out his objections to the expected harm he will suffer, makes the injury automatic, and makes it seem that it is the individual who seeks to alter the existing situation, and not the army. Placing the responsibility on the family is especially astonishing in that the family members do not always know the offenses attributed to their relative. The state's position creates the absurd situation in which Palestinians are required, in effect, to present their house to the IDF as a candidate for demolition.[7]

6. B'Tselem, *House Demolition and Sealing as a Form of Punishment in the West Bank and Gaza Strip, Follow-up Report* (Jerusalem, November 1990), p. 4 ("administrative process"); B'Tselem, *Through No Fault of Their Own*, p. 14 ("autopsy").
    7. B'Tselem, *Through No Fault of Their Own*, pp. 16 ("almost non-existent"), 39–42 ("Residents of the region" and "In making this ruling" at p. 42); for the Israeli army's jus-

The consensus among human rights organizations and academic specialists is that house demolition as a form of punishment is illegal under international humanitarian law (the Hague Regulations and Geneva Convention), which proscribes the destruction of property as a punitive measure, and collective punishment generally.[8] Former president of the Israel Supreme Court Shimon Agranat called the demolition of homes an "inhuman" punishment.[9] Nonetheless, Dershowitz justifies the demolition of Palestinian homes on several grounds:

1. *House demolition is a "benign" punishment.*

   In *The Case for Israel*, Dershowitz maintains that "Israel's policy of demolishing the homes of terrorists or those who harbor them is a soft form of collective punishment directed against the property of those who are deemed somewhat complicit" (p. 170; see also Alan Dershowitz, *Why Terrorism Works* [New Haven, 2002], p. 176). The "major problem with the destruction of houses," he explains, is not the suffering inflicted on innocents—to the contrary, it is "among the most moral and calibrated responses"—but "that it plays poorly on television . . . the inevitable picture of the crying woman bemoaning the loss of her home creates sympathy" (pp. 171; *Why Terrorism Works*, p. 179). Already in the early years of Israel's occupation he was similarly defending this "soft" punitive measure. At a 1971 Tel Aviv symposium, Dershowitz maintained that, although a "technical violation of some Convention," house demolition was nonetheless "realistically" an

---

tification for not providing prior warning and B'Tselem's refutation, see pp. 17, 43; for the High Court's rationale in its original decision affirming no prior warning and B'Tselem's refutation, see pp. 41–42.

8. For discussion of the relevant international law, see Yoram Dinstein, "The Israel Supreme Court and the Law of Belligerent Occupation: Demolitions and Sealing Off of Houses," in *Israel Yearbook on Human Rights* (Tel Aviv, 1999), pp. 292–95; Kretzmer, *Occupation*, pp. 146–48; Amnesty International, *Under the Rubble*, pp. 44–46; B'Tselem, *The Legal Basis for Demolition and Sealing of Houses*, www.btselem.org/english/House_Demolitions/Statistics.asp; B'Tselem, *Through No Fault of Their Own*, pp. 25–41.

9. B'Tselem, *House Demolition and Sealing as a Form of Punishment*, p. 5; B'Tselem, *Through No Fault of Their Own*, p. 47. On the altogether separate question of the punishment's efficacy as a deterrent, B'Tselem reports that it is open to dispute, citing the opinion of a "senior defense establishment official" that "in most cases" it doesn't work, as well as an internal IDF report that "there is no proof of the deterrent effect of house demolitions" and "the number of attacks . . . rose a few months after the policy began to be implemented" (ibid., pp. 46–47).

acceptable option: as a mere "monetary punishment," it was less onerous than, say, detention of the accused.[10] This argument has been roundly ridiculed by Israeli legal scholars. Professor Yoram Dinstein, Israel's leading specialist in international law and a person generally cautious in his judgments, opined that Dershowitz's argument "verges on the bizarre":

> When the framers of an international treaty negotiate its strictures, they have an opportunity to contemplate competing interests and values. Once the text is consolidated, a Contracting Party must abide by it to the letter. . . . If every Occupying Power were given leave to determine unilaterally that it can absolve itself of an unwelcome duty—by sacrificing a right that it prefers not to exercise— this would "wreak havoc" in international humanitarian law. The danger inherent in the Dershowitz approach is underscored by his own assessment that "detention is a much more serious violation than economic punishment—specifically, the destroying of houses." Many victims of the pair of sanctions would beg to differ.

Moreover, Israel typically inflicts house demolition not in lieu of but *in addition to* detention.[11] Finally, Dershowitz's scale of punishments in *The Case for Israel* merits notice on another count. Whereas the demolition of a Palestinian family's home ranks as a "soft" or "benign" (p. 168) economic punishment, he is rather less indulgent of any sanctions applied to Israel, which constitute "economic capital punishment" (p. 209).

2. *Collective responsibility and collective punishment are misnomers.*

The primary victim of a house demolition is not the alleged perpetrator of the act of violence that precipitated the punishment (who either faces a long prison sentence, has escaped apprehension, or is already dead), but rather the family of the alleged perpetrator and in many cases others who happen to live in the building.[12] Accordingly, the consensus among human

---

10. "Symposium on Human Rights (Tel Aviv, July 1971)," in *Israel Yearbook on Human Rights* (Tel Aviv, 1971), pp. 376–77.
11. Dinstein, "Demolitions," pp. 302–3. A scholar generally falling within the Israeli mainstream consensus, Dinstein supports, e.g., Israel's policy of political liquidations (Anthony Dworkin, "Defence or murder?" *Guardian* [30 March 2004]). For another dismissal of Dershowitz, see Kretzmer, *Occupation*, pp. 147, 233n9.
12. According to B'Tselem, "thirty-two percent of the suspected offenders were in detention at the time of demolition, twenty-one percent were 'wanted,' and forty-seven

rights organizations is that house demolitions constitute "a flagrant form of collective punishment, a violation of a fundamental principle of international law" (Amnesty International); a
"gross violation of the proscription on collective punishment, a
draconian measure against relatives who bore no responsibility
for the suspects' acts and were not charged with any offense"
(B'Tselem); "a clear form of collective punishment since people
who are not accused of any offence are punished" (al-Haq
[Law in the Service of Man]); and so on.[13] Although the Israel
Supreme Court has sought to deny that house demolitions constitute collective punishment, respected Israeli legal scholars
dismiss its arguments ("a rather feeble attempt").[14]

In *Why Terrorism Works*, Dershowitz deplores resort to
collective punishment as "the most immoral" tactic for fighting
terrorism, one typical of "tyrannical regimes." He specifically
cites as a heinous example of collective punishment that "Hitler
destroyed the entire Czech village of Lidice" after a senior Nazi
officer was assassinated. "Directly punishing the innocent raises
the most pointed moral objections, but it is also most effective,"
Dershowitz concludes. "Notwithstanding the effectiveness of
this extreme form of collective punishment, we are morally constrained—and legally prohibited—from imposing it" (pp. 29,
117–19). Yet, although the consensus among human rights
organizations and scholars is that house demolitions constitute
collective punishment and although Dershowitz deplores collective punishment, he nonetheless defends Israel's resort to
this punitive measure. He adduces two sorts of argument:

---

percent were dead." In addition, B'Tselem reports that "some of the demolitions involved
houses that were rented by the suspect," in which case "the main victims (at least in material terms) were the property owners, who had no involvement whatsoever with the relevant acts of the suspect." Finally, the IDF has on occasion deliberately "demolished
houses adjacent to the suspect's house. . . . This practice is common when the occupants
are members of the suspect's extended family." Of the roughly six hundred homes Israel
has demolished as punishment since the start of the new intifada, nearly half did not
belong to the suspect's nuclear family, but rather "were next to the house in which the
suspect lived" (B'Tselem, *Through No Fault of Their Own*, pp. 9–13).

13. Amnesty International, *Under the Rubble*, p. 11; B'Tselem, "Demolition and
Sealing of Houses as Punishment," www.btselem.org/english/House_Demolitions/index
.asp; al-Haq (Law in the Service of Man), *Punishing a Nation: Human Rights Violations
during the Palestinian Uprising, December 1987–1988* (December 1988), p. 225.

14. Kretzmer, *Occupation*, p. 149; see also Dinstein, "Demolitions," p. 296.

a. *Punishment is often collective punishment.*

Dershowitz maintains that innocents suffer in many punitive acts. Thus, "[t]he atomic bombings of Hiroshima and Nagasaki killed thousands of innocent Japanese for the crimes of their leaders" (*The Case for Israel,* p. 167; see also *Why Terrorism Works,* p. 172). Putting aside that the *best* case Dershowitz can make for Israel's demolition policy is to compare it with Hiroshima and Nagasaki, Israel's Supreme Court adduced a similar argument that punitive measures often hurt innocents: the "sanction of demolition is no different from the punishment of imprisonment which is imposed on the head of a family, a father to small children, who will remain without a supporter and breadwinner." Calling the analogy between collective suffering caused by the arrest of a head of household, on the one hand, and a house demolition, on the other, "unconvincing," Professor Kretzmer elucidated the elementary distinction: "[T]he *direct aim* of imprisonment is to deny freedom of movement to the perpetrator of an offense; suffering caused to others may be an inevitable consequence of the imprisonment, but it is not its aim. If the effect of the culprit's imprisonment on his family could be neutralized, the aim of the punishment would not be frustrated. On the other hand, when a person has already been apprehended and is no longer living in a house (and is in fact liable to life imprisonment), and especially when he has been killed, the *immediate aim* of demolishing the house is not to deny rights or freedoms of that person but to cause suffering to his family" (emphases in original).[15] In fact, Dershowitz is perfectly aware of this distinction between a punitive measure that unintentionally harms innocents and one the *main or only purpose of which* is to harm innocents. "There is a real difference, of course," he wrote in *Why Terrorism Works* (pp. 118–19), "between punishing criminals directly, with the realization that some innocents will also be hurt, and specifically targeting the innocent to deter or punish the guilty." Yet he justifies house demolition although the "express goal" of this punishment— to quote B'Tselem—is "to deter and make people aware that violent acts have an injurious effect not only on the perpetrator, but on his family as well."[16]

b. *Responsibility is often collective responsibility.*

Arguing against the "bright line separating civilians from combatants," Dershowitz maintains in *The Case for Israel* that there exists a "continuum" of responsibility. Those who morally abet a criminal act bear "some moral complicity" in it and accord-

---

15. Kretzmer, *Occupation,* pp. 149–50; see also Dinstein, "Demolitions," pp. 298–99.
16. B'Tselem, *Legal Basis.*

ingly are liable to punitive sanctions. He adduces Nazi Germany
as an illustration: "[I]t was right for the entire German people
to suffer for what their elected leader had unleashed on the
world. . . . [T]he vast majority of Germans should have been held
accountable for their complicity with evil. . . . That is part of
what it means to be a nation or a people. Those who start wars
and lose them often bring suffering to their people. That is rough
justice" (pp. 168–71; *Why Terrorism Works*, p. 173). A "mini-
mal appropriate" punishment for the "collective responsibility of
the German people," including those who supported Hitler "pas-
sively so as to live the good life," he elsewhere counsels, "should
have been a generation of poverty."[17] For argument's sake, let us
put to one side the extreme version of Dershowitz's contention,
which he proclaimed at a 2003 symposium in Israel: "[E]very-
body in the nation takes accountability for the actions of its leaders. To be part of a nation, to be part of a group is to be in part
accountable."[18] Instead, let's consider the "milder" claim that if
a criminal state policy enjoys widespread civilian support, the
entire "nation or people" should be punished. Presumably, collective accountability also increases along a second continuum: a
"nation or a people" in an open and free society, having greater
access to information and space to dissent, bear greater accountability for criminal acts of state than those living in a totalitarian
society. To judge by Dershowitz's principle and its logical corollary, shouldn't the American people (including Dershowitz) have
suffered massive sanctions, given that the "vast majority" supported for the longest time and in a notably free society the evil
unleashed by the U.S. government on Vietnam, to cite one of a
long list of countries devastated by American policy? To be sure,
it's rather easier to apply moral principles to others than to one-
self. In the case of Israel, Dershowitz justifies the resort to sanctions such as house demolitions on the ground that, judging by
poll data, Palestinians overwhelmingly "supported continuing
terrorist attacks" and, accordingly, are "themselves complicit" in
these attacks (pp. 168–69; *Why Terrorism Works*, pp. 174–75).
Indeed, he advocates not only individual house demolitions but
also "the destruction of a small village which has been used as
a base for terrorist operations" after each Palestinian attack.
"The response will be automatic." Such massive destruction, he
concludes, will further the "noble causes" of reducing terrorism
and promoting peace.[19] Israel categorizes attacks on its military

17. Alan M. Dershowitz, *Chutzpah* (Boston, 1991), p. 137.
18. Alan Dershowitz, "Defending against Terrorism within the Rule of Law," www
.herzliyaconference.org.
19. Alan M. Dershowitz, "New response to Palestinian terrorism," *Jerusalem Post* (11
March 2002); see also *Why Terrorism Works* (New Haven, 2002), pp. 176–78. Although

personnel as terrorism; the Czech people undoubtedly supported
the assassination of the Nazi officer. It is hard to make out any
difference between the policy Dershowitz advocates and the
Nazi destruction of Lidice, for which he expresses abhorrence—
except that Jews, not Germans, would be implementing it. Furthermore, consider the case if Dershowitz's criterion of collective
responsibility were applied to Israelis: (i) When Israel attacked
Lebanon in June 1982 in order to "safeguard the occupation of
the West Bank" (Yehoshafat Harkabi's phrase), the popularity
ratings of Defense Minister Ariel Sharon and Prime Minister
Begin soared, while more than 80 percent of Israelis held the
invasion to be fully justified. When Israel's battering of Beirut
in August 1982 reached new heights of savagery, more than half
of Israelis still supported the Begin-Sharon government, while
more than 80 percent still supported the invasion—which in
the end, left up to twenty thousand Lebanese and Palestinians,
almost all civilians, dead, and which the U.N. General Assembly
condemned by a vote of 143 to 2 (United States and Israel) for
inflicting "severe damage on civilian Palestinians, including
heavy losses of human lives, intolerable sufferings and massive
material destruction."[20] Only when the costs of the Lebanon

---

chapter 24 of *The Case for Israel,* which defends the morality of house demolitions,
reproduces almost verbatim the comparable section in *Why Terrorism Works* (pp.
172–81), Dershowitz discreetly omits this passage on the automatic destruction of villages, perhaps because open advocacy of wholesale terrorism might not help the case for
Israel. Incidentally, the duplication of argument in *Why Terrorism Works* reflects the fact
that Dershowitz's current preoccupation with terrorism springs less from the topic per se
or the threat terrorism poses to the United States than its utility for exculpating Israel:
Why Terrorism Works might just as well be titled *Why Israel Is Justified in Trampling on
Human Rights in Its War against Terrorism.* The heart of *Why Terrorism Works* is twenty
pages of correlation tables that, according to Dershowitz, demonstrate why Palestinians
have come to believe terrorism pays. For example, in the left-hand column titled "Palestinian terrorist acts," he lists "September 4, 1997—Three explosions, one after another,
kill at least four Israelis and three suicide bombers in Jerusalem's main outdoor shopping
mall," while for the corresponding "Benefits to Palestinian cause" in the right hand column he lists, "March 22, 2000—Pope John Paul visits Arafat in Bethlehem" (pp. 77–78).
The correlation is so obvious—a terrorist attack in 1997, the pope's visit in 2000—it
would be a wonder if Palestinians didn't notice.
    20. Yehoshafat Harkabi, *Israel's Fateful Hour* (New York, 1986), p. 101. Harkabi
writes that "[c]alling the Lebanon War 'The War for the Peace of Galilee' is more than a
misnomer. It would have been more honest to call it 'The War to Safeguard the Occupation of the West Bank'"; see also Meron Benvenisti, *Intimate Enemies* (Berkeley, 1995), p.
79; Major-General Avraham Tamir, *A Soldier in Search of Peace* (New York, 1988), pp.
93, 116, 117, 122; and Shimon Shamir, "Israeli Views of Egypt and the Peace Process," in
William Quandt (ed.), *The Middle East* (Washington, D.C., 1988), p. 207. Avner Yaniv,
Dilemmas of Security (New York, 1987), pp. 127–28 (polls); Noam Chomsky, *Fateful
Triangle* (Boston, 1983), pp. 221 (casualty figures), 253–54 (polls); Robert Fisk, *Pity the
Nation* (New York, 1990), pp. 257, 418–19 (casualty figures); U.N.G.A. Resolution
37/134, *Assistance to the Palestinian People* (17 December 1982).

aggression proved too onerous—initially, from the worldwide outcry against the Sabra-Shatila massacres and, later, from the escalating military casualties—did Israelis turn against it. (ii) When Israel's violent repression of the first intifada reached new heights of brutality in 1989, more than half of all Israelis supported the deployment of yet "stronger measures" to quell the largely nonviolent civil revolt (only one in four supported any lessening of the repression), while "an overwhelming 72 percent . . . saw no contradiction between the army's handling of the uprising and 'the nation's democratic values.'"[21] (iii) Operation Defensive Shield (March–April 2002), although wreaking devastation on Palestinian society and culminating in the commission by Israeli forces of "serious violations" of humanitarian law and "war crimes" in Jenin and Nablus, was supported by fully 90 percent of Israelis.[22] Beyond the emotional support that Israelis have lent to crimes of state, it bears emphasis that Israel relies on a citizen army to implement policy: the collective responsibility of the Israeli people accordingly runs much deeper than "moral complicity."[23] Finally, Israel couldn't commit such crimes without unconditional political and economic support from the United States, and it's the likes of Dershowitz who, through shameless apologetics and brazen distortions, crucially facilitate this unconditional support. What if Dershowitz's home were subject to the "benign form of collective accountability" (p. 168) he urges for Palestinians?

ADMINISTRATIVE DEMOLITION OF "ILLEGAL" PALESTINIAN HOMES

To demonstrate that Israel isn't a "racist state," Dershowitz cites a 2000 Supreme Court decision—itself ambiguous in content and consequence—upholding access of Israeli Arabs to state-owned land in Israel.[24] Dershowitz omits mention, however, of the massive demolition of Palestinian homes in the Occupied Territories due to discriminatory access to building permits. In a 1997 study entitled *Demolishing Peace: Israel's Policy of Mass Demolition of Palestinian Houses in the West Bank*, B'Tselem reported that "over the past dozens of years, Israel has

21. Joel Brinkley, "Majority in Israel Oppose P.L.O. Talks Now, Poll Shows," *New York Times* (2 April 1989). For Israel's egregious human rights record during the first intifada, see Norman G. Finkelstein, *The Rise and Fall of Palestine: A Personal Account of the Intifada Years* (Minneapolis, 1996), chap. 3.

22. Jessica Montell, "Operation Defensive Shield: The propaganda war and the reality" *Tikkun* (July–August 2002); for Israeli crimes during Operation Defensive Shield, see section titled "No Evidence" in Chapter 4.

23. For discussion, see Finkelstein, *Rise and Fall*, chap. 4.

24. See section titled "Equality" in Chapter 9.

created a situation in the West Bank in which thousands of Palestinians are unable to obtain a permit to build on their land. Consequently they are compelled to build without a permit." The impetus behind this "illegal" Palestinian construction is not political but narrowly personal: "Their act is not intended as a political statement or as opposition to Israeli control in the area, but rather to meet a need for housing for themselves and their families that Israel's policy does not allow them to realize." Contrariwise, although Israel pretends that the decision to demolish Palestinian homes is based strictly on planning considerations, the reality is different: "Palestinian homes are demolished in the context of a declared policy of strengthening and expanding Israeli settlements in the West Bank, and of creating permanent facts"—for example, in order to clear areas for Jewish-only bypass roads or to remove Palestinians from areas adjacent to (illegal) Jewish-only settlements. The "planning" decision to demolish homes is also used as a reprisal and collective punishment after Palestinian attacks. If there's any doubt about the discriminatory nature of these demolitions, Israel's treatment of illegal Jewish construction in the Occupied Territories dispels it: "Israeli settlers built thousands of housing units, public facilities, and industrial structures without permits. . . . The authorities take a forgiving attitude toward building without a permit in the settlements, and have refrained—except for one case, as far as we know—from demolishing houses built without a permit. Instead, the authorities approve retroactively plans validating such construction." B'Tselem concludes that these discriminatory "planning" demolitions of Palestinian homes violate key provisions of international covenants to which Israel is a party and, accordingly, are illegal.[25]

A 1999 Amnesty International study entitled *Demolition and Dispossession: The Destruction of Palestinian Homes* similarly reported on the devastating impact of Israel's demolition of "illegal" Palestinian homes in the Occupied Territories: "[T]housands of Palestinian homes have been demolished. Some had been built and inhabited for years; they are furnished, occupied often by more than one family with many children, who are often given only 15 minutes to gather their possessions and leave. A squad of workers may throw the furniture into the street; or the furniture may be still in the house when the family sees the bulldozers move in. Other houses are still uninhabited but have been

25. B'Tselem, *Demolishing Peace: Israel's Policy of Mass Demolition of Palestinian Houses in the West Bank* (Jerusalem, December 1997), pp. 2, 26–27, 30, 34–36, 39.

built as the fruit of months of work and the expenditure, sometimes, of all the family's savings." The study conservatively estimated that from 1987 to 1999 fully 2,400 homes had been demolished and 14,500 Palestinians (of whom 6,000 were children) rendered homeless. The Oslo "peace process" didn't slow the rate of demolitions, which "remained at the same high level." Amnesty likewise concluded that, although Israel claims Palestinian homes were demolished based on planning considerations, its policy has in fact been discriminatory— "Palestinians are targeted for no other reasons than that they are Palestinians"—the purpose being to maximize the area available for Jewish settlers: "Virtually no opportunity has been given for legitimate development to take place. The result has been the demolition of houses which, without the possibility of building with a permit, Palestinians have had to build without a permit. The objective has apparently been to confine Palestinian development to existing urban areas in order to preserve maximum opportunity for land confiscation and Jewish settlement." Similarly, in East Jerusalem the purpose of house demolitions has been "to transform the ethnic character of the annexed area from Arab to Jewish." "The main policy (indeed, the only policy) on Palestinian development has been to restrict it—and thereby to minimise the Palestinian population." From 1987 to 1999, 284 Palestinian homes were demolished in East Jerusalem, and by 1999 "well over one third of the Palestinian population of East Jerusalem live[d] under threat of having their house demolished." Not only has Israel demolished "illegal" Palestinian homes while denying Palestinians any option to build legally, but *Palestinians must themselves pay the costs of the house demolition plus often a substantial fine* ("which may be 100,000 shekels [$23,600] or more"). And like B'Tselem, Amnesty International concluded that, "[i]n its demolition of houses and use of land confiscation and planning laws targeted against the Palestinian population, Israel has breached international humanitarian and human rights treaties," indeed, is guilty of "grave breaches" of the Geneva Convention.[26] A November 2004 B'Tselem study found that between 2001 and 2004 Israel had demolished nearly one thousand "illegal" Palestinian homes in the West Bank and East Jerusalem.[27]

26. Amnesty International, *Demolition and Dispossession: The Destruction of Palestinian Homes* (London, December 1999), pp. 1, 2, 11, 14, 17, 19, 20–21, 23, 24–25. See also Amnesty International, *Under the Rubble*, part 5 ("Demolitions of unlicensed houses: discriminatory planning and building policies and enforcement measures").
27. B'Tselem, *Through No Fault of Their Own*, p. 4.

AMNESTY INTERNATIONAL, *DEMOLITION AND DISPOSSESSION: THE DESTRUCTION OF PALESTINIAN HOMES*
(London, December 1999), p. 3

CASE STUDY: THE JABER FAMILY HOMES

The Jaber family have farmed their own land, near Hebron, at least since Ottoman times. But, with land near a bypass road and the expanding settlement of Giv'at Harsina, to own land is no protection. Thirteen houses have demolition orders in the area. On 19 August 1998 the home of Atta Jaber, who had no license to build, was bulldozed by the Israeli Defence Force (IDF). The following day he decided to rebuild it, but one month later, on 16 September, the house was again destroyed. Five months later it was the turn of the home of Atta Jaber's brother, Fayez Jaber, 22—a house which contained only two rooms to house 12 members of the family. At 7 AM on 4 February 1999 officials from the Civil Administration and the Higher Planning Council arrived unannounced with a large number of soldiers and demolished his house. The soldiers used force, beating Fadi Jaber, 18. In May they came again and demolished three water cisterns, collecting water off the hills in the winter to be used in the summer. The Civil Administration said the cisterns were using water from the Hebron water supply; there was no sign of any pipes—rather there were a number of little channels running into the cisterns from above in the traditional manner. At the same time the house of Atta's brother, Isma'il, has a demolition order against it and both Isma'il and Qa'id Jaber have been ordered not to plant on their land.

MILITARY/SECURITY DEMOLITIONS AND PROPERTY DESTRUCTION

In addition to demolishing Palestinian homes as punishment and for violating "planning" restrictions, Israel also resorts to massive destruction of Palestinian property on military/security grounds. In a February 2002 study entitled *Policy of Destruction: House Demolitions and Destruction of Agricultural Land in the Gaza Strip*, B'Tselem reported that since the beginning of the new intifada (September 2000), Israel had demolished some six hundred homes, leaving more than five thousand Palestinians homeless; uprooted thousands of trees; and destroyed thousands of acres of land in the Gaza Strip: "Israel caused this damage to people although it did not contend that they themselves were involved in attacks, or attempted attacks, against Israeli civilians or security forces." The house demolitions "generally take place in the middle of the night without any warning being given to the residents. . . . [I]n many instances, these residents had to flee from their homes after they were awakened by the noise of tanks and bulldozers that were already at their doorstep." "The army also did not give warning of its intention to destroy fields and uproot orchards. Such warning would, at least, have enabled the Palestinians to remove the irrigation pipes and other objects from the fields." Although limited destruction of property can be justified under international law on grounds of "military necessity," B'Tselem observed, the "extreme magnitude" of the destruction and its manner of implementation "clearly and unequivocally indicate that . . . the injury to the civilian population was excessive." For example: "The IDF forces destroyed entire residential neighborhoods, claiming that, under some of the houses, tunnels had been dug through which weapons were being smuggled. In other cases, the army destroyed dozens of houses on the grounds that Palestinians were firing from the area at IDF soldiers." "In some of the cases, the IDF's destruction of property took place immediately after Palestinians attacked Israeli civilians or security forces, though at times in locations other than where the Palestinian attack occurred. This phenomenon raises the concern that the objective of these acts was to punish the Palestinians for the attack and to deter others from committing similar acts. . . . A policy that harms thousands of innocent people and whose consequences are so horrendous and long lasting constitutes collective punishment." Noting that the International Committee of the Red Cross, delegations from the U.N. Human Rights Commission, and even the U.S.-based Mitchell Commission "harshly criticized Israel's extensive destruction in the Gaza Strip," B'Tselem concluded that this policy "flagrantly violates international humanitarian law." Finally, it bears notice that, although obliged under international law to pay compensation for such illegal destruction, Israel has refused to do so.[28]

A May 2004 Amnesty International study entitled *Under the Rubble: House Demolition and Destruction of Land and Property* also focuses on recent Israeli devastation in the Occupied Territories, mostly justified on military/security grounds:

28. B'Tselem, *Policy of Destruction: House Demolitions and Destruction of Agricultural Land in the Gaza Strip* (Jerusalem, February 2002), pp. 2, 6, 8, 10, 24, 28–29, 32, 35–36.

In the past three and a half years the scale of the destruction carried out by the Israeli army in the Occupied Territories has reached an unprecedented level. The victims are often amongst the poorest and most disadvantaged. . . . Most of the houses demolished . . . were the homes of refugee families, who were expelled by Israeli forces or who fled in the war that followed the creation of Israel in 1948. . . . More than 3,000 homes, hundreds of public buildings and private commercial properties, and vast areas of agricultural land have been destroyed. . . . Tens of thousands of men, women and children have been forcibly evicted from their homes and made homeless or have lost their source of livelihood. Thousands of other houses and properties have been damaged, many beyond repair. In addition, tens of thousands of other homes are under threat of demolition, their occupants living in fear of forced eviction and homelessness. . . . Thousands of families have had their homes and possessions destroyed under the blades of the Israeli army's US-made Caterpillar bulldozers. In the wake of the demolitions, men, women and children return to the ruins of their homes searching for whatever can be salvaged from under the rubble.

Regarding the economic impact of destroying Palestinian agricultural land, Amnesty further notes: "Hundreds of thousands of olive, citrus, almond, date and other trees have been uprooted. . . . The trees and orchards uprooted . . . constituted a source, and in many cases the only source, of livelihood for hundreds of thousands of people. . . . Many had invested their savings to develop and improve their family farms with costly greenhouses and irrigation networks, only to see them destroyed by Israeli army bulldozers, often before they could harvest their crops."

The report dates the current round of massive indiscriminate destruction from Operation Defensive Shield (March–April 2002), when Israel invaded the West Bank: "In every refugee camp and town they raided, Israeli soldiers left a trail of destruction." The climax of Defensive Shield was Israel's leveling of large swaths of Jenin refugee camp, leaving four thousand Palestinians homeless. Although Israel claimed that the destruction took place in the course of combat, "the evidence, including aerial photographs of the refugee camp, indicates that when the Israeli army carried out much of the bulldozing of houses the armed clashes between Israeli soldiers and Palestinian gunmen had already stopped and Palestinian gunmen had already been arrested or had surrendered." The most extensive destruction in recent years, however, has been in Gaza: between October 2000 and October 2003, more than 2,150 homes were destroyed and more than 16,000 damaged, and more than 10 percent of the agricultural land was destroyed. In the case of Rafah camp, bordering Egypt, where the largest number of homes have been leveled, "the destruction . . . has been progressive, targeting row after row of houses—contrary to claims by the Israeli authorities that only houses used by Palestinians to shoot at Israeli soldiers patrolling the border and houses used as cover for tunnels used for smuggling weapons from Egypt were destroyed." Indeed, generally, "Amnesty International delegates, international humanitarian and human rights workers, journalists and others have repeatedly witnessed Israeli soldiers destroying and damaging houses, land and other properties at times when there were no disturbances or confrontations with Palestinians." In this context Amnesty pointedly recalls that, despite repeated requests from the international community, Israel has "consistently and vigorously opposed the presence of international human rights monitors" who "could play an important role to establish the veracity of the claims made by each side concerning the actions of the other side." Amnesty also found spurious Israeli pretenses that the homes the Israeli army demolished were "abandoned" or "unpopulated": "The sight of pots of cooked food, half-full bottles of soft drinks or shampoo, pieces of newspapers from the previous day, smashed fridges and television sets, clothes, children's toys and schoolbooks lying amongst the rubble stood in stark contrast with Israeli army claims." Like B'Tselem, Amnesty concludes that Israel's "extensive destruction of homes and properties throughout the West Bank and Gaza . . . is not justified by military necessity." "Some of these acts of destruction amount to grave breaches of the Fourth Geneva Convention and are war crimes."[29]

Finally, in October 2004 Human Rights Watch (HRW) released a major study entitled *Razing Rafah: Mass Home Demolitions in the Gaza Strip*. It found that since the beginning of the new intifada, "the Israeli military has demolished over 2,500 Palestinian houses in the occupied Gaza Strip," mostly in the densely populated refugee camp of Rafah bordering Egypt, and that "[s]ixteen thousand people—more than ten percent of Rafah's population—have lost their homes, most of them refugees, many of whom were dispossessed for a second, or third time." "The pattern of destruction," it continued, "strongly suggests that Israeli forces demolished homes wholesale, regardless of whether

29. Amnesty International, *Under the Rubble*, pp. 1, 7, 12, 14, 16, 17, 24, 46; see also Amnesty International, "Wanton destruction constitutes a war crime" (press release, 13 October 2003).

they posed a specific threat." During a "major military campaign" in
May 2004 the IDF

> razed entire rows of houses along the buffer zone and destroyed extensively
> deep inside Rafah. Armored Caterpillar D9 bulldozers plowed through
> houses and shops, indiscriminately ripped up roads, destroyed water and
> sewage systems, and turned agricultural fields into barren patches of earth.
> Fifty-nine Palestinians were reportedly killed in Rafah during a series of
> incursions from May 12–24, including eleven people under age eighteen
> and eighteen armed men. In total these incursions left 254 houses destroyed
> and nearly 3,800 people homeless; another forty-four houses were razed in
> the Rafah area during the same month in smaller operations.

Disputing Israeli claims that this massive destruction was inflicted due
to military necessity, HRW found that "armed Palestinian resistance
. . . was light, limited and quickly overwhelmed within the initial hours
of each incursion." During one attack, the IDF destroyed, in a "time-
consuming and deliberate act" lacking any military justification, a zoo
in Rafah: "The zoo was one of the few recreational areas in an over-
crowded camp whose residents have been denied access to the sea by
Israeli settlements for the past four years. Thousands of animals,
including jaguars, crocodiles, wolves, snakes and birds escaped from
the zoo or were killed during its demolition." Meanwhile, a plan
approved by the Israeli government in May 2004 would "result in
destroying approximately 30 percent of the central camp" and "the displacement of tens of thousands of Palestinian civilians, already living in
one of the most densely populated areas on earth."

Israel's "main stated reason" for its continual onslaughts against
Rafah is that a vast network of tunnels connects weapons' smugglers
operating on the Egyptian side of the border with homes in Rafah.
HRW found, however, that Israel was "exaggerating" the extent of this
underground network and that it had destroyed homes containing
"inoperative tunnels," tunnel shafts that could have been "effectively
sealed with poured concrete," and "tunnel shafts that had already been
sealed" by the Palestinian Authority. Moreover, a "number of less
destructive alternatives exist for the effective detection and destruction
of smuggling tunnels." For example: "No demolitions of structures
were employed to close tunnels on the U.S.-Mexico border, even though
some of the houses used were also densely clustered within meters
of the border." Until just recently, the IDF bulldozed Palestinian
homes covering tunnel entrance shafts without even bothering to close

the tunnels themselves. This "use of puzzlingly ineffective methods for two years," HRW observes, "contrast[s] sharply with the stated gravity of this longstanding threat." The real purpose behind Israel's massive destruction of homes, according to HRW, is not to enhance the IDF's security but rather to clear the border areas in order to "facilitate long-term control over the Gaza Strip," even after implementation of its "disengagement" plan. Palestinians "have nowhere to turn in Israel for legal protection against unlawful demolitions and forced evictions," HRW concludes. Israel hasn't conducted "any investigations into cases of unlawful or improper house demolitions"; the "Israeli Supreme Court has consistently sanctioned IDF policies that violate international law, including house demolitions"; and "under Israeli law, compensation is ruled out in cases of 'combat activity,' which . . . includes virtually every IDF action" in the Occupied Territories. Among its recommendations HRW calls on international donor governments to "press Israel to either pay reparations to victims or to compensate donors directly for any funds spent on repairing unlawful destruction," and it calls on the United States to "[r]estrict Israel's use of Caterpillar D9 armored bulldozers, Apache and Cobra helicopter gunships, and other U.S.-origin weapons systems that are used in the commission of systematic violations of international human rights and humanitarian law" and to "[i]nform the Government of Israel that continued U.S. military assistance requires that the government take clear and measurable steps to halt its security forces' serious and systematic violations of international human rights and humanitarian law in the West Bank and Gaza Strip." The Caterpillar D9 is the "main IDF tool to demolish homes, structures, and agricultural areas in Gaza and the West Bank." In a separate recommendation, HRW called directly on Caterpillar Inc. to "[s]uspend sales of D9 bulldozers, parts or maintenance services to the IDF" so long as Israel is in breach of international humanitarian law. "Otherwise, Caterpillar will remain complicit in the international humanitarian law violations that occurred because of excessive and unwarranted demolitions by the Israeli government while using the company's bulldozers."[30] A November 2004 B'Tselem study found that

30. Human Rights Watch, *Razing Rafah: Mass Home Demolitions in the Gaza Strip* (New York, October 2004), pp. 2, 3, 4–6, 9–10, 15, 18–19, 20, 41–54, 63, 68–69, 94–97, 113–15; see also Human Rights Watch, "Israel: End Unlawful Use of Force against Civilians in Gaza: Israeli Government Should Repudiate Plans for Mass House Demolition" (20 May 2004).

since the start of the new intifada, more than 2,500 Palestinian homes, sheltering nearly twenty-four thousand Palestinians, had been demolished "in the course of the IDF's 'clearing operations.'"[31]

The following section illustrates how Dershowitz seeks to prove Arab distortion of Israel's demolition policy.

EMPTY HOUSES

On pages 171 and 219 of *The Case for Israel*, Alan Dershowitz writes:

[I]n some Muslim countries [television] viewers are led to believe that the houses are destroyed with people still in them!

[M]any Palestinians, Arabs, and Muslims throughout the world . . . are shown pictures of houses being destroyed without being told that they were emptied of residents prior to the bulldozers arriving.

In its study of Israel's April 2002 siege of Jenin, Human Rights Watch reported that, "[a]lthough warnings were issued on multiple occasions by the IDF, many civilians only learned of the risk as bulldozers began to crush their houses. Jamal Fayid, a thirty-seven-year-old paralyzed man, was killed when the IDF bulldozed his home on top of him, refusing to allow his relatives the time to remove him from the home. Sixty-five-year-old Muhammad Abu Saba'a had to plead with an IDF bulldozer operator to stop demolishing his home while his family remained inside; when he returned to his half-demolished home, he was shot dead by an Israeli soldier."[32] Likewise, Amnesty International reported in its study of the April 2002 siege in Jenin that "[h]ouses were destroyed, sometimes without ensuring that the residents had left" and "six [people] had been crushed by houses," while in Nablus "the IDF demolished several houses by D-9 bulldozers, on at least two occasions while their occupants were alive. They made no attempt to check or to rescue them."[33] Likewise, in its study of the April siege, B'Tselem reported, "Many residents of the [Jenin] camp were given no notice

---

31. B'Tselem, *Through No Fault of Their Own*, p. 4.

32. Human Rights Watch, *Jenin: IDF Military Operations* (New York, May 2002), section 2, p. 2.

33. Amnesty International, *Shielded from Scrutiny: IDF Violations in Jenin and Nablus* (London, November 2002), pp. 7, 10, 12; see also Amnesty International, *Killing the Future: Children in the Line of Fire* (London, September 2002), p. 7, and Amnesty International, "Demolition of houses is an act of collective punishment" (14 January 2002).

B'TSELEM, *OPERATION DEFENSIVE SHIELD:*
SOLDIERS' TESTIMONIES, PALESTINIAN TESTIMONIES
(Jerusalem, September 2002), p. 15

TESTIMONY OF FATHIYA SULIMAN, AGED 70
The day that the bulldozers came and started to demolish the houses
in our neighborhood, we ran out after dark. There were seven of us:
my husband, my daughter-in-law, my daughter, and my three sons. One
of my sons, Jamal, 38, is deaf and a paraplegic. We fled to my brother-
in-law's house. When the bulldozer approached our house, which is
next to my brother-in-law's, we asked the soldiers to let us get Jamal
out. The soldiers refused. Other women, a male neighbor who spoke
Hebrew, and I continued to beg them. At first, they told us that the
commanding officer was sleeping. Then a soldier agreed that we could
get him out. But, he said, only the women were allowed to take him
out. We went into the house, but the operator of the bulldozer wouldn't
wait even one minute so that we could take Jamal out of the house.
The soldiers who said we could go into the house called out to the soldier who was operating the bulldozer to stop for a moment, but he
refused. We rushed in while the bulldozer was already eating away at
the house. Amal, my daughter, some women neighbors, and I found
Jamal in the house under the rubble. The house began to collapse, and
we ran for our lives. The house was completely destroyed with Jamal
underneath.

JENIN REFUGEE CAMP, APRIL 6, 2002

before their houses were demolished. In cases where they were given
notice, it was too late. They could not leave their houses because of the
intense gunfire outside. People were buried alive under the ruins. Some
were rescued; others were not." The report also stated that when camp
residents sought to rescue those buried beneath the rubble, "IDF soldiers shot at the rescuers and drove, accompanied by a tank, in their
direction. The rescuers fled"; that "[t]he IDF refused to allow foreign
rescue workers to enter the camp and assist in extricating the victims
buried under the rubble"; that one driver of a bulldozer publicly
boasted, "I didn't give anybody a chance. I didn't wait. I didn't strike
once and wait for them to leave. I would smash the house really hard so

AMNESTY INTERNATIONAL, *KILLING THE FUTURE: CHILDREN IN THE LINE OF FIRE*
(London, October 2002), p. 7

CHILDREN KILLED AS A RESULT OF THE DEMOLITION OF HOUSES

In Jenin, Nablus and other places the IDF bulldozed a number of houses while residents, including children, were still inside. On other occasions the IDF used explosives to blow up houses without evacuating the surrounding houses, which were also destroyed or damaged in the process. In some cases civilians, including children, were killed or buried alive under rubble of the demolished house. In the cases researched by Amnesty International, no warnings were apparently given for the safe evacuation of civilians before houses were demolished.

Three children, Abdallah, Azam and Anas al-Shuʾbi, aged four, seven and nine years, their pregnant mother and four other relatives died under the rubble of their house which was demolished by the IDF on 6 April 2002 in the Qasbah (Old City) of Nablus during a period of strict curfew imposed by the IDF. Two survivors were eventually pulled from under the rubble, nearly one week after the house was demolished. Neighbours of the family interviewed by Amnesty International stated that the IDF had given no warning before beginning to destroy the house with bulldozers, and that they had been fired upon by the IDF when they defied the curfew in an attempt to search for survivors under the rubble of the destroyed house.

Mahmud Umar al-Shuʾbi, the children's cousin, told Amnesty International that on the afternoon of 12 April the curfew was lifted for two hours and he went to look for his father and sister. When he arrived at the family house, he found that it had been demolished. Mahmud said that he started to dig with the help of his neighbours, hoping to find his relatives alive under the rubble. Because it started to rain, the mud made the process more difficult. He carried on digging after the curfew was reimposed and was fired upon several times; late that night, the rescuers came across a small opening on the ground floor of where the house once stood. In the small space that remained, they found his 68-year-old uncle, Abdallah, and his 67-year-old wife, Shamsa, who had managed to survive. They carried on digging throughout the night and at 1.30 AM, found the bodies of the rest of the family, who had died huddled in a circle, in one small room: his father Umar, his sister Fatima, his cousins Samir and his 7-month pregnant wife, Nabila, and their three children: Abdallah, Azam and Anas, as well as another cousin Abir. Afterwards neighbours told Mahmud that they could hear the screams of the family above the noise of the bulldozer but had not been able to help and that the bulldozer had actually collapsed down on top of the house, which was built on a slope.

that it would collapse as quickly as possible."[34] In a February 2002 report on house demolitions in Gaza, B'Tselem reported, "The demolitions generally take place in the middle of the night without any warning being given to the residents. . . . [I]n many instances, these residents had to flee from their homes after they were awakened by the noise of tanks and bulldozers that were already at their doorstep." An October 2002 Human Rights Watch press release from Gaza reported one case (in a "very disturbing pattern") of a "two-year-old boy [who] was killed after being buried under the rubble of his home . . . when IDF soldiers demolished a neighboring house . . . [S]urrounding residents were unable to leave their houses and no warning was given before the explosion."[35]

34. B'Tselem, *Operation Defensive Shield: Soldiers' Testimonies, Palestinian Testimonies* (Jerusalem, September 2002), pp. 12–14.

35. B'Tselem, *Policy of Destruction,* p. 8; Human Rights Watch, "Gaza: IDF House Demolition Injures Refugees" (press release, 24 October 2002).

8

Blight unto the Nations

IN *THE CASE FOR ISRAEL,* Alan Dershowitz maintains that Palestinians accrued tangible benefits from the Israeli occupation. "[T]he Israeli occupation, unlike any of the other current occupations," he writes, "has brought considerable dividends to the Palestinians, including significant improvements in longevity, health care, and education. It has also brought about a reduction in infant mortality" (p. 161). Let us leave to one side that Dershowitz never specifies to what other "current" occupations he's comparing the Israeli one (arguably, there aren't any) and that, historically, many other peoples, perhaps most, under foreign occupation accrued some benefits. It is correct that, especially in the early years of the occupation and by standard indices, Palestinians enjoyed a measure of prosperity. However, the overarching framework of this prosperity merits close scrutiny. But first it warrants recalling that Palestinians during the British Mandate period also arguably accrued significant benefits from Jewish settlement. The authoritative 1937 British Royal Commission (Peel) Report, after careful sifting of the claims and counterclaims, concluded: "[B]roadly speaking, the Arabs have shared to a considerable degree in the material benefits which Jewish immigration has brought to Palestine."[1] Yet

1. *Palestine Royal Commission Report* (London, 1937), pp. 125–30 (cf. p. 241).

these benefits vanished, as it were, overnight when the Zionist movement ethnically cleansed Palestine in 1948. It would be one thing if the
ethnic cleansing were circumstantial—that is, unanticipated and unde-
sired. But the growing consensus among historians is that the putting
of the Palestinian Arabs to flight was premeditated, indeed, deeply
entrenched in the Zionist goal of creating an overwhelmingly Jewish
state in a territory overwhelmingly non-Jewish.[2] From this perspective,
it's a moot point whether or not Palestinians during the Mandate benefited from Jewish settlement: prosperity was an ephemeral moment in
their eventual, planned dispossession. The same basic principle applies
to the initial years of Palestinian prosperity in the West Bank and Gaza.
As individual Palestinians briefly experienced relative prosperity, crucial resources and huge swaths of their territorial base were being alienated while their indigenous economy was being methodically and pre-
meditatedly destroyed, now standing on the verge of total collapse.

In an important study, Sara Roy, a Harvard-trained political economist and currently senior research scholar at Harvard's Center for Middle Eastern Studies, argues that the distortions of the Palestinian economy under Israeli occupation go beyond those typical of colonized
and otherwise externally dominated territories.[3] This is because Israel's
fundamental aim hasn't been to exploit but rather to dispossess the
Palestinians, clearing as much of the Occupied Territories as is feasible
to make way for exclusively Jewish settlement. The vagaries of the
Palestinian economy, including "a decade of rapid economic growth"
and "marked improvements in the standard of living," must be seen,
according to Roy, in the context of its "de-development"—that is,
Israel's systematic expropriation of crucial Palestinian resources for
Jewish settlement, on the one hand, and the dispossession and dena-
tionalization of the Palestinians, on the other. If, as Dershowitz claims,
"the Israeli occupation [is] unlike any of the other current occupations," it's for reasons rather different than those he cites. "Israel's ideological and political goals have proven more exploitative than those of
other settler regimes," Roy contends, "because they rob the native population of its most important economic resources—land, water, and
labor—as well as the internal capacity and potential for developing

2. For mainstream Zionism's support for "transferring" the Arabs out of Palestine,
see Norman G. Finkelstein, *Image and Reality of the Israel-Palestine Conflict,* 2nd ed.
(New York, 2003), p. xii and sources cited.
    3. Sara Roy, *The Gaza Strip: The Political Economy of De-Development* (Washing-
ton, D.C., 1995).

those resources."[4] In the case of the Gaza Strip, the focus of Roy's study, Israel's discriminatory policy restricting Palestinian access to water "has had a particularly devastating effect on agriculture, the primary consumer of water and the traditional focus of economic activity, as well as on domestic consumption." Annual per capita water consumption hovers around 2,240 cubic meters for Jewish settlers as against 140 cubic meters for Gaza's Palestinians, a ratio of 16:1. Likewise, Israel has illegally confiscated more than 50 percent of Gaza Strip land and allocated 25 percent of Gaza land for Jewish settlers who, according to the Israeli Central Bureau of Statistics, number 7,500, representing 0.5 percent of the Strip's total population of 1.3 million. "The increasing absorption of land by the state and the installation of Jewish civilian settlements," Roy reports, "have had a considerable effect on Gaza's development"—for example, the loss of agricultural lands and the economic and social ills attendant on massive overcrowding. In one of the world's most densely populated areas, each Jewish settler has been allotted fully eighty-five times more land than a Palestinian.[5]

Similar discriminatory policies have been implemented throughout the Occupied Territories. Two water systems supply Israel and the Occupied Territories: the Mountain Aquifer and the Jordan Basin. Israel receives 79 percent of the Mountain Aquifer water and the Palestinians 21 percent, while Palestinians have no access at all to the Jordan Basin, Israel utilizing 100 percent of its water. "Palestinians have not

---

4. Ibid., pp. 3–5. For the distinctiveness of Israel's economic policy in the Occupied Territories, see esp. chap. 5, where, e.g., Roy writes:

The study of the Gaza Strip describes a peculiar set of conditions—new forms and mechanisms of underdevelopment—not commonly seen in other third world settings and that cannot be explained by existing development theories. Underlying Gaza's peculiar form of underdevelopment is an Israeli policy that prioritizes the political-national realm over the economic. This has been expressed in Israel's desire to acquire land rather than exploit the economic potential of the people living on it. Israel's ideological goal of creating a strong Jewish state has always superseded any need or desire to generate profit through economic exploitation of the Palestinian population, although that has occurred. Israel has physically removed segments of the Palestinian population from the land and dispossessed others of their resources and power. Indeed, in the history of modern Palestine, Israel is the first occupying regime that has deliberately and forcibly dispossessed Palestinians of their land, water, and labor. (p. 128)

For Israel's calculated policy of allowing for the individual prosperity of Palestinians while simultaneously dismantling their indigenous economy, see esp. chap. 6 of Roy's study.

5. Ibid., pp. 165–67, 175–81. The cited figures for Gaza's settler population come from this study.

realized their rights to their portion of the shared resources," B'Tselem (Israeli Information Center for Human Rights in the Occupied Territories) reports, "and division of those resources has gradually become discriminatory and unfair." Annual per capita water consumption of Israelis for domestic, urban, and industrial use is 128 cubic meters as against 26 cubic meters for Palestinians in the West Bank, a ratio of 5:1. As a case in point of Israeli policy, B'Tselem cites this example: "Several cities in the West Bank are compelled to implement rotation plans, particularly during the summer, to distribute the little water available. Under these plans, residents in a particular area of the city receive water for a number of hours. The flow to their homes is then shut off, and water is supplied to other areas until their turn comes again. . . . The rotation plans are necessary because of the increase in demand for water during the hot season. However, while demand increases both among Palestinians and Israeli settlers, [Israel's] response is discriminatory. It increases supply to the settlers, but does not increase, or even decreases, the quantity of water supplied to these Palestinian cities."[6] Another B'Tselem study found that "the reliance of the Jordan Valley settlements on agriculture . . . denies Palestinian residents the opportunity to enjoy a large proportion of the water resources in the region." Water consumption of the fewer than five thousand Jewish settlers in the Jordan Valley is equivalent to 75 percent of the water consumption for domestic and urban uses of the entire two million Palestinian residents of the West Bank.[7] In an authoritative study of Israel's settlement policy in the West Bank, B'Tselem found that Israel has illegally confiscated nearly half of the West Bank (excluding East Jerusalem) and allocated more than 40 percent of West Bank land for 200,000 illegal Jewish settlers representing less than 10 percent of the total West Bank population. The Jewish settlements "prevent the maintenance of meaningful territorial contiguity between the Palestinian communities" and "the possibility of establishing an independent and

6. B'Tselem (Israeli Information Center for Human Rights in the Occupied Territories), *Thirsty for a Solution: The Water Crisis in the Occupied Territories and Its Resolution in the Final-Status Agreement* (Jerusalem, July 2000), pp. 3–4, 8 ("discriminatory and unfair"), 38, 43–44 ("rotation plans"). The data for the West Bank and Gaza are not strictly comparable; e.g., the ratio of Jewish to Palestinian water consumption in Gaza includes its use in the crucial agricultural sector, while for the West Bank it includes only domestic, urban, and industrial use; and the ratio for Gaza juxtaposes water consumption of Jewish settlers against Palestinians, while for the West Bank it juxtaposes Israelis generally against Palestinians.

7. B'Tselem, *Land Grab: Israel's Settlement Policy in the West Bank* (Jerusalem, May 2002), p. 81.

viable Palestinian state"; "drastically restrict the possibilities available to Palestinians for economic development in general, and for agriculture in particular"; "restrict the possibilities for urban development of the Palestinian communities, and in some cases prevent such possibilities almost completely." B'Tselem's conclusion merits special notice: "Israel has created in the Occupied Territories a regime of separation based on discrimination, applying two separate systems of law in the same area and basing the rights of individuals on their nationality. This regime is the only one of its kind in the world, and is reminiscent of distasteful regimes from the past, such as the apartheid regime in South Africa."[8] Dershowitz proclaims that the "analogy" between Israel and South African apartheid is "demonstrably false" (p. 204), yet he makes no argument to refute B'Tselem's conclusion. Likewise, he asserts that "there is no intellectually or morally defensible case for singling out Israel for divestiture" (p. 198). Yet, if singling out South Africa for divestment was defensible, it would seem equally defensible to single out Israel's occupation, which uniquely resembles the apartheid regime.

In a study of prospects for the Palestinian economy published before the outbreak of the new intifada, George Abed, director of the Middle Eastern Department at the International Monetary Fund, found that "the Palestinian economy faces the future severely handicapped by the legacy of a 27-year occupation followed by four years of a severely constraining 'interim arrangement,' during which time real income per capita declined by nearly 25 percent."

> There is no doubt that the occupation . . . has had its corrosive impact on human and physical capital, on the resource base, on external economic relations, and on all other aspects of life. . . . [S]ome of the advantages the West Bank (and to a lesser extent the Gaza Strip) possessed on the eve of the occupation—a productive agricultural sector with no water constraint, thriving trade with the eastern part of Jordan and other Arab countries, a strong tourism sector, an adequate infrastructure, an excellent basic educational system (for the period), a growing professional and entrepreneurial class—have been dissipated during 27 years of economic repression and isolation, so that the economic situation . . . now is worse than it was

8. Ibid., pp. 12 (200,000), 31 (nearly half), 94 ("prevent the maintenance"), 95 (more than 40 percent), 104 (conclusion). Other key findings of the report include the facts that, during the Oslo "peace process" years, the Jewish settler population in the West Bank nearly doubled, the total settler population in the West Bank including East Jerusalem increased from 247,000 to 375,000, not even one Jewish settlement was evacuated, and the sharpest increase in housing start-ups occurred in 2000 under the Barak government (pp. 4, 12). In 2003 the Israeli Central Bureau of Statistics put the number of Jewish settlers in the West Bank (excluding East Jerusalem) at 220,000.

in 1967 when measured relative to the advances made by other states in the region.[9]

Moreover, the decades-long occupation constituted no fiscal burden on the Israeli treasury. "On the contrary, Palestinians contribute large sums to Israeli public expenditure"—what Meron Benvenisti, a leading Israeli authority on the Occupied Territories, dubbed an "occupation tax." This net surplus extracted from the Palestinians, Benvenisti continued, "refutes Israeli claims that the low level of public expenditure and investment [in the Occupied Territories] derives from budgetary limitations. If net fiscal transfers had been invested in the area, rather than added to Israeli public expenditure, it would have been possible to improve local services significantly, and in particular, to develop local economic infrastructure."[10]

Since the outbreak of the new intifada the Occupied Territories have verged, according to a United Nations study, on a "humanitarian catastrophe."[11] An in-depth World Bank report presented these grim statistics: GDP (gross domestic product) and GNI (gross national income) per capita shrunk respectively by 40 and 45 percent between 1999 and 2002. Unemployment hovers around 40 percent, while 60 percent of the population is living under the poverty line of US$2.10 per day. Food consumption has fallen by 25 percent since 1998, and "the prevalence of acute malnutrition recently observed in Gaza, 13.3 percent, constitutes an emergency with serious long-term implications for Palestinian health and development." A total collapse of Palestinian society has been averted only due to emergency budget subsidies from donor countries (mostly the Arab League and, less so, the European Union), as well as the resourcefulness and mutual support of Palestinians themselves. Regarding the latter, the normally unsentimental World Bank observes: "Palestinian society has displayed great cohesion and resilience. Despite violence, economic hardship and the daily frustrations of living under

---

9. George Abed, "Beyond Oslo: A Viable Future for the Palestinian Economy," in Sara Roy (ed.), *The Economics of Middle East Peace: A Reassessment,* Research in Middle East Economics, Vol. 3, Middle East Economic Association (Stamford, Conn., 1999), pp. 46–47.

10. Meron Benvenisti, *1986 Report—Demographic, Economic, Legal, Social and Political Developments in the West Bank* (Boulder, Colo., 1987), pp. 18–19; Arie Arnon et al., *The Palestinian Economy—Between Imposed Integration and Voluntary Separation* (New York, 1997), pp. 30–34; Roy, *Gaza Strip,* p. 195.

11. U.N. Commission on Human Rights, *The Right to Food: Report by the Special Rapporteur, Jean Ziegler; Addendum, Mission to the Occupied Palestinian Territories* (31 October 2003) (E/CN.4/2004/10/Add.2).

curfew and closure, lending and sharing are widespread and families for the most part remain functional. Even with a dearth of formal safety nets, outright destitution is still limited—those who have income generally share it with those who do not. The West Bank and Gaza have absorbed levels of unemployment that would have torn the social fabric in many other societies." It goes on to deem this achievement "quite remarkable." Given the repeated attacks on the United Nations Relief and Works Agency (UNRWA)—which is the second-largest provider of social services in the Occupied Territories after the Palestinian Authority and is responsible for delivering health, schooling, and humanitarian assistance to refugees (half the total population and over 70 percent of Gazans)—it also merits quoting the World Bank's observation that "UNRWA's emergency programs . . . continue to be held in high regard by the population."[12]

The "proximate cause of the Palestinian economic crisis," according to the World Bank, is "closure"—that is, the restrictions Israel has imposed on the movement of Palestinian goods and people across borders and within the Occupied Territories—and "[t]he sine qua non of economic stabilization is a significant easing of the current regime of internal closures and curfews, and the granting of easy access to external markets."[13] An Amnesty International study assessing the impact of Israel's closure and curfew policies on Palestinians reported that its "impact on their right to work and to an adequate standard of living, education and healthcare has been devastating." Among its findings were these: "Some villages have been completely sealed off and urban areas are frequently placed under 24-hour curfew, during which no one is allowed to leave the house, often for prolonged periods"; "Trips of a few kilometers, where they are possible, take hours, following lengthy detours to avoid the areas surrounding Israeli settlements and settlers' roads"; "By the year 2000 most of the 1.3 million Palestinians living in

12. World Bank, *Twenty-Seven Months—Intifada, Closures and Palestinian Economic Crisis: An Assessment* (Jerusalem, May 2003), pp. xi–xiv ("Palestinian society" at xiii), 8 ("acute malnutrition"; cf. 36–37), 9, 21, 24–25, 31, 33–34 ("remarkable"), 48 (UNRWA), 52–53, 57. According to this study, by December 2002 Israeli military operations had inflicted nearly a billion dollars in "[r]aw physical damage," while "if account is taken of the additional wear and tear on equipment and infrastructure, total damage climbs to about US$1.7 billion." From a sectoral perspective, "the damage inflicted on public infrastructure is the greatest" (roads and sidewalks, water and wastewater networks, electricity stations and street lighting, solid waste collection trucks and bins, etc.), and "most of this infrastructure has been financed by donors" (pp. xi, 17–19).

13. Ibid., p. xii, xvii, 82.

Gaza had never left the Gaza Strip, an area totalling a mere 348 square kilometers"; "[T]he main roads of the West Bank are for Israeli cars, clearly identifiable by yellow number plates, and military vehicles. Palestinian vehicles, distinguishable by their green license plates, are prohibited. In recent years, Amnesty International delegates have rarely seen a green-plated car on main roads, apart from a few shared taxis. Palestinians have often been in carts pulled by donkeys or mules, a rare sight three years ago"; "After the Israeli army retook control of the six main West Bank towns . . . in March–April 2002, 24-hour curfews were enforced for days and in some cases weeks. Civilians were confined to their homes and movement outside was prohibited. . . . Bethlehem was under curfew for 40 consecutive days. . . . Nablus . . . remained under 24-hour curfew for five months after 21 June 2002, apart from one month when it was under a night curfew only"; "Palestinian vehicles and passengers [in Gaza] have been stuck between . . . checkpoints for hours, unable even to get out of their cars for fear of being shot"; "Closures and curfews are controlled by military force. Members of the Israeli security forces have frequently resorted to lethal force to enforce restrictions, killing or injuring scores of Palestinians who were unarmed and presented no threat. Soldiers opened fire on Palestinians bypassing checkpoints, crossing trenches, removing barriers and breaking curfews."[14]

While strongly affirming that "Israeli authorities have not only a right but a duty to take necessary measures to protect Israelis," Amnesty goes on to point out that "the increasingly sweeping and stringent restrictions imposed indiscriminately on all Palestinians have not put a stop to the attacks." On the contrary, "attacks intensified as restrictions on the movements of Palestinians increased, calling into question the effectiveness of indiscriminate restrictions that treat every Palestinian as a security threat and punish entire communities for the crimes committed by a few people." In addition, it notes the frequent arbitrariness of internal closures: "The fact that soldiers enjoy broad, individual discretion to permit or prevent Palestinians' movement undermines the Israeli authorities' contention that the internal closure is a rational system of control, based strictly on security needs." Indeed,

14. Amnesty International, *Surviving under Siege: The Impact of Movement Restrictions on the Right to Work* (London, September 2003), pp. 2 ("sealed off," "kilometers"), 11 (Gazans), 12 ("main roads"), 16 ("curfews"), 17 ("stuck between checkpoints"), 19 ("frequently resorted"), 25 ("impact on").

Amnesty questions altogether the legitimacy of internal closure, insofar as its relationship to Israeli security is highly dubious:

> It is important to differentiate between restrictions on Palestinian movement from the Occupied Territories into Israel, and movement restrictions within the Occupied Territories. Movement restrictions may be necessary to prevent attackers entering Israel and carrying out suicide bombings and other attacks. . . . However, it cannot be said that preventing or restricting the movement of Palestinians between Ramallah and Nablus is necessary to prevent attackers from entering Israel to carry out an attack in Jerusalem or Tel Aviv. Yet closures and curfews are often justified on these grounds and are routinely imposed or tightened following Palestinian attacks inside Israel. Like the bombardments of PA [Palestinian Authority] buildings which usually follow Palestinian suicide bombings or other attacks, closures and curfews often appear to be intended more as punishment or retaliation for attacks by Palestinians (both inside Israel and against Israeli settlers or soldiers in the Occupied Territories) as well as to show the Israeli public that the army is taking action. This is particularly obvious in the Gaza Strip, where Palestinians have rarely succeeded in crossing the surrounding electric fence into Israel. None of those who have carried out attacks inside Israel in recent years are known to have come from the Gaza Strip. Yet, in the wake of every major Palestinian attack inside Israel, the Israeli army usually attacks PA installations in Gaza, such as the airport, the seaport or police stations, most of which have been bombed several times.[15]

Apart from preventing attacks on Israel proper, the main Israeli justification for closure is protecting illegal Jewish settlers. "Even though only a very small percentage of Palestinians have been engaged in attacks against Israeli settlers or soldiers, every Palestinian is regarded as a potential attacker," Amnesty observes, and consequently, "the Israeli army has increasingly confined more than three million Palestinians to some form of house, village or town arrest." Moreover, the imposition of these mass arrests, according to Amnesty, is "fundamentally discriminatory": "They are imposed on the Palestinian population alone, and not on Israeli settlers, and are often imposed on Palestinians for the benefit of Israeli settlers. Even on occasions when Israeli settlers have initiated confrontations, attacking Palestinians or destroying their property, the Israeli army invariably imposed closures, curfews or other restrictions on the Palestinians, including by declaring a closed military area and excluding them from it." Finally, Amnesty notes that the set-

15. Ibid., pp. 15 ("soldiers enjoy"), 24–25 ("not only a right," "important to differentiate").

AMNESTY INTERNATIONAL, *SURVIVING UNDER SIEGE: THE IMPACT OF MOVEMENT RESTRICTIONS ON THE RIGHT TO WORK*
(London, September 2003), p. 21

A widespread punishment regularly meted out by soldiers at check-points is holding Palestinians on the spot for hours, with no shelter from sun or the rain, and in some cases placing men in metal cages. On Monday, 14 July 2003, the Israeli women group Machsom Watch (Checkpoint Watch) were alerted at 10.00 AM that Nasser Abu Joudeh from al-Arroub refugee camp was being held inside a metal cage (base area of 1.2 square meters) at the Gush Etzion checkpoint (between Hebron and Bethlehem) since 6 AM, and that some 30 others were also held at the same checkpoint since 5.30 AM. After Machsom Watch con-tacted the Israeli Civil Administration, the detainee was eventually released from the cage at approximately 12.00 noon and the others were allowed to leave at 1.30 PM, that is, after up to seven hours in the sun and heat. The previous week two other Palestinians had also been held in the cage together at the same checkpoint, one for four hours and the other (aged 17) for seven hours.

tlers constitute the main obstacle to restoring a semblance of normalcy in the Occupied Territories: "Most of the restrictions on movement placed on Palestinians . . . are imposed to prevent the Palestinian popu-lation from coming into contact with the Israeli settlers."[16]

Israel's resort to "widespread and prolonged closures, curfews and other restrictions on movement currently imposed cannot be justified on security grounds," Amnesty concludes. "The sweeping restrictions on the movement of Palestinians are disproportionate and discrimina-tory—they are imposed on all Palestinians *because* they are Palestini-ans, and not on Israeli settlers who live illegally in the Occupied Ter-ritories. . . . They have a severe negative impact on the lives of millions of Palestinians who have not committed any offence" (emphasis in original).[17]

Besides claiming improved quality of life in the West Bank and Gaza, Dershowitz points to this benefit of the Israeli occupation in *The Case*

16. Ibid., pp. 35–36 ("small percentage," "discriminatory"), 38 ("contact").
17. Ibid., pp. 5 ("widespread and prolonged"), 7 ("sweeping restrictions").

for Israel: "Ironically, being occupied by Israelis as distinguished from Jordanians and Egyptians also promoted Palestinian nationalism" (p. 161). It is equally true that anti-Semitism promoted Jewish nationalism. Does it mitigate the evil of Nazism that it won world Jewry over to Zionism and facilitated the creation of a Jewish state? It seems not to have occurred to Dershowitz that perhaps the reason Israel's occupation, as compared to those of Jordan and Egypt, uniquely stimulated Palestinian nationalism is that it has been uniquely oppressive.

• • • •

In December 2003 the U.N. General Assembly called upon the International Court of Justice (ICJ or World Court) to render an "advisory opinion" on the "legal consequences" arising from Israel's construction of a wall cutting deeply into the West Bank. Alan Dershowitz, who was "advising [Israeli] officials on confronting the court," denounced the World Court, claiming that it would conduct an "'Alice in Wonderland' legal proceeding" and that "it would be insulting to kangaroos to call it a kangaroo court." Maintaining that a verdict against Israel was "a foregone conclusion," he went on to liken the ICJ to "racist" courts in the American South during the Jim Crow era, which "could do justice in a lawsuit brought by a white against a white, but did horrible racist injustices in cases involving whites against blacks"; the ICJ could accordingly "do a wonderful job in a border dispute between Sweden and Norway, but when it comes to anything having to do with the Middle East it has zero credibility, and nobody should take seriously any conclusion it reaches with regards to Israel." Dershowitz provides no evidence or argument for any of these claims about the World Court, even if they do complement his pronouncement quoted in Part I of this book that Israel is not bound by international law. In addition, Dershowitz justifies Israel's construction of the wall as its "last alternative to combating terrorism."[18] What is the merit of this argument?

18. Ori Nir, "Israel Fears Isolation, Sanctions over Fence," *Forward* (9 January 2004) ("advising," "kangaroo court," "blacks," "Sweden," "foregone"); Andrew C. Esensten, "Dershowitz Advises Israel on Wall Dispute," *Harvard Crimson* (24 February 2004) ("Alice in Wonderland," "last alternative," "kangaroo court"); Alan Dershowitz, "The case against picking on Israel," *The Australian* (8 May 2004) ("racist"). For background on the World Court's deliberations, see esp. Andreas Mueller, "Crippled Justice: Limping towards the Wall," *News from Within* (March–April 2004).

In April 2002 the Israeli cabinet publicly announced that "fences and other physical obstacles" would be constructed to "improve and reinforce the readiness and operational capability in coping with terrorism," and in June 2002 it approved the first phase of the project. Consisting of concrete walls, ditches, trenches, roads, razor wire, and electronic fences, stretching for fully 680 kilometers and averaging sixty meters in width, the portion of the wall approved by the Israeli government as of October 2003 will have "severe humanitarian consequences" for more than 680,000 Palestinians living in the West Bank (30 percent of its population). Only 11 percent of the wall runs along Israel's internationally recognized boundary (the "Green Line"), the remainder of it cutting off some 15 percent of the West Bank, including some of its richest land and water resources, as well as 274,000 Palestinians, who will live either in closed areas between the wall and the Green Line or in enclaves totally surrounded by the wall. More than 10,000 of these Palestinians must already apply for green-colored permits, valid for up to six months, to continue residing in their homes. "These permits," a U.N. report concludes, "have turned a 'right' of Palestinians to live in their own homes into a privilege." Another 400,000 Palestinians living to the east of the wall will need to cross it in order to reach their farms, jobs, and social services, while yet another 200,000 to 300,000 Palestinians living in East Jerusalem will be cut off from the West Bank. The plan for the wall calls for several gates and crossings to enable passage of people and goods, although the modalities of such passage have yet to be formalized. "Whatever the crossing arrangements will be, it is clear that hundreds of thousands of Palestinians will be dependent on Israel's security system when they want to cross the barrier from either side," observes B'Tselem, while past experience "raises the fear that the crossing points along the barrier will be closed for prolonged periods and the passage of Palestinians may be completely prohibited." "Even if the barrier does not create total isolation," B'Tselem concludes, "it will clearly reduce the ability of many residents to work and earn sufficient income to ensure a minimum standard of living," and it "is liable to force additional thousands of Palestinian families into poverty." Some six hundred shops and enterprises have reportedly closed in the town of Qalqilya alone due to the wall's construction. Huge swaths of Palestinian land on which the wall is to be erected have already been subject to a "disguised expropriation of property," and much more Palestinian land west of the wall is likely to be confiscated in the future. Even crediting Israel's argument that it was for the purpose of fighting terrorism, such expropriation, according to human rights organizations, is illegal under international law. "While land owners are entitled to demand compensation, the vast majority have not done so (on the urging of the Palestinian Authority)," a University of Oxford study further notes, "so as not to legitimise the Israeli seizure. In any case, the amount of compensation offered has been well below the real value of the land"—in Qalqilya, for example, only 10 percent of the actual value. "After taking control," B'Tselem reports, "the contractors level the land by uprooting the crops, including field crops, greenhouses, and, primarily, olive trees." An estimated 100,000 trees have been uprooted in the course of the wall's construction. With official sanction, uprooted Palestinian olive trees have been subsequently sold by the Israeli contractors for profit *to themselves* in Israel.[19]

Like Dershowitz, the Israeli government has maintained that construction of the wall was undertaken only after all other options for "curbing the wave of terror" had been exhausted. Human rights organizations dispute this, however. The Israeli government has itself acknowledged that most Palestinian suicide bombers entering Israel passed through inadequately supervised checkpoints. Security at these

---

19. U.N. Office for the Coordination of Humanitarian Affairs, *New Wall Projections* (New York, 9 November 2003) ("severe humanitarian," "privilege"); B'Tselem, *Behind the Barrier: Human Rights Violations as a Result of Israel's Separation Barrier, Position Paper* (Jerusalem, 2003), pp. 13–14 ("crossing arrangements"), 15–17 ("reduce the ability"), 19–20 ("disguised expropriation," "uprooting" and theft of olive trees); *Report of the Special Rapporteur of the Commission on Human Rights, John Dugard, on the situation of human rights in the Palestinian territories occupied by Israel since 1967, submitted in accordance with Commission resolution 1993/2A* (E/CN.4/2004/6) (New York, 8 September 2003) (shops closed); *Anti-Apartheid Wall Campaign Fact Sheet: The Wall's "First Phase"* (www.stopthewall.org) (number of uprooted trees). For detailed analysis of the barrier's economic impact on Palestinians, see esp. *The Impact of Israel's Separation Barrier on Affected West Bank Communities: A Follow-up Report to the Humanitarian and Emergency Policy Group (HEPG) and the Local Aid Coordination Committee (LACC)* (31 July 2003). For discussion of current "irregular and unpredictable" closures of the barrier's gates by Israeli soldiers, and Israelis' arbitrariness in granting a "permanent resident permit" to Palestinians, see Amnesty International, *The Place of the Fence/Wall in International Law* (London, February 2004), pp. 9–10, and Oxford Public Interest Lawyers (OXPIL) for the Association for Civil Rights in Israel (ACRI), *Legal Consequences of Israel's Construction of a Separation Barrier in the Occupied Territories* (University of Oxford, February 2004), pp. 35–36, 40. For expropriation of Palestinian land for the barrier, and its prohibition under international law even on grounds of military necessity, see B'Tselem, *Behind the Barrier*, pp. 37–38; Amnesty International, *The Place of the Fence/Wall*, pp. 10–11; and OXPIL for ACRI, *Legal Consequences of Israel's Construction*, pp. 21–23 ("compensation"), 38–40. All figures cited in the above text for Palestinians affected by the separation barrier should be treated as orders of magnitude; for comparison of the varying estimates, see ibid., p. 6.

checkpoints could have been beefed up, while Israeli troops could have been deployed along the "open areas" between the checkpoints. In addition, if its concern was curbing terrorist attacks on Israel proper, the government could simply have erected the wall along the Green Line, which would have been legally unobjectionable. As Amnesty notes, "it is not unlawful for Israel to establish fences or other structures on its own territory to control access to its territory." Finally, the Oxford study observes that "[i]f the Barrier is meant to prevent suicide bombings, it is unclear why Israel is apparently unconcerned about the hundreds of thousands of Palestinians who will end up on the Israel side of the Barrier . . . unless it is ultimately planning to remove them" —more on which presently.[20]

The real motive behind construction of the wall appears to be securing for Israel its settlements in the West Bank. Winding around scores of Jewish settlements that house more than 320,000 settlers (80 percent of the total), the wall will not just serve to protect them but, crucially, will enable their annexation, along with adjoining land and water resources, to Israel. Uncontroversially, the settlements are illegal—indeed, they constitute "war crimes"—under international law. Even Dershowitz exerts no effort in *The Case for Israel* to justify them. Erecting a wall that inflicts massive injury on Palestinians in order to protect illegal settlements would mean compounding one injustice with another. "The Israeli government cannot use security concerns for Israelis living in illegal settlements," Human Rights Watch observes, "to justify further encroachments into occupied territory." In fact, however, these Jewish settlements could be protected without erecting a wall; for example, by surrounding them with electrified fences, as will be done with those falling outside the wall. The "underlying reason" for the wall, B'Tselem suggests, is "not to provide maximum protection of the settlers" but rather "to establish facts on the ground that would perpetuate the existence of settlements and facilitate their future annexation into Israel." Likewise, Human Rights Watch concludes that "[t]he existing and planned route of the barrier appears to be designed chiefly to incorporate and make contiguous with Israel illegal civilian settlements." The de facto new boundary created by the

20. B'Tselem, *Behind the Barrier*, pp. 28–31; Amnesty International, *The Place of the Fence/Wall*, pp. 4 ("not unlawful"), 14n15; OXPIL for ACRI, *Legal Consequences of Israel's Construction*, pp. 17–18 ("apparently unconcerned").

wall will, if a planned extension along the Jordan Valley wins approval, ultimately incorporate about half the West Bank. The indigenous Palestinian population, including those currently residing between the wall and Israel but who will be forced by intolerable living conditions to relocate on the Palestinian side of it ("voluntary transfer"), will be trapped in a fragmented territory resembling the South African Bantustans and comprising some 10 percent of historic Palestine. Human Rights Watch has urged the U.S. government to "deduct the cost of the West Bank separation barrier from U.S. loan guarantees" for Israel.[21]

Contrary to Dershowitz's claim, the wall is not Israel's "last alternative to combating terrorism," nor, for that matter, is it designed to fight terrorism. The facts are clear, as is the consensus among human rights groups about them: the real purpose of the wall is to decide, *preemptively, unilaterally, and definitively,* the future of the Jewish settlements. Dershowitz correctly anticipated that, were the International Court of Justice to accept the case, a verdict against Israel would be "a foregone conclusion"—not because the ICJ is a kangaroo court, however, but because the injustice against Palestinians is so transparent, if not to Dershowitz, at any rate even to a kangaroo. In July 2004 the World Court handed down its advisory opinion "Legal Consequences of the Construction of a Wall in the Occupied Palestinian Territory" (General List No. 131). By a vote of fourteen to one (United States), it concluded that "[t]he construction of the wall being built by Israel, the occupying Power, in the Occupied Palestinian Territory, including in and around East Jerusalem, and its associated régime, are contrary to international law"; that "Israel is under an obligation to terminate its breaches of international law; it is under an obligation to cease forthwith the works

21. Amnesty International, *The Place of the Fence/Wall,* p. 6 ("war crimes"); Human Rights Watch (HRW), "Letter to President Bush on Israel Loan Guarantees and Separation Barrier" (New York, 30 September 2003) ("further encroachments"); B'Tselem, *Behind the Barrier,* pp. 32–33 ("underlying reason"); HRW, *Israel's "Separation Barrier" in the Occupied West Bank: Human Rights and International Humanitarian Law Consequences, A Human Rights Watch Briefing Paper* (New York, February 2004), p. 4 ("make contiguous"); HRW, "Israel: West Bank Barrier Endangers Basic Rights: U.S. Should Deduct Costs from Loan Guarantees" (press release, 1 October 2003) ("deduct"). For removal of Palestinians currently residing on the Israeli side of the barrier, the separation barrier in the Jordan Valley, and the reduction of the Palestinian land area to half the West Bank, see esp. Amnon Barzilai, "The fence: A path to voluntary transfer," *Haaretz* (18 February 2004). For comparison with the Bantustans, see Finkelstein, *Image and Reality,* p. xxvii and chap. 7.

of construction of the wall being built in the Occupied Palestinian Territory, including in and around East Jerusalem, to dismantle forthwith the structure therein situated"; that "Israel is under an obligation to make reparation for all damage caused by the construction of the wall in the Occupied Palestinian Territory, including in and around East Jerusalem"; that "[t]he United Nations, and especially the General Assembly and the Security Council, should consider what further action is required to bring to an end the illegal situation resulting from the construction of the wall and the associated régime." By a vote of thirteen to two (United States, Netherlands), it also found that "[a]ll states are under an obligation not to recognize the illegal situation resulting from the construction of the wall and not to render aid or assistance in maintaining the situation created by such construction; all States parties to the Fourth Geneva Convention relative to the Protection of Civilian Persons in Time of War of 12 August 1949 have in addition the obligation, while respecting the United Nations Charter and international law, to ensure compliance by Israel with international humanitarian law as embodied in that Convention." Apart from these findings of the Court, the decision was noteworthy in other respects as well: on a semantic point, it upheld usage of the term *wall* to designate the structure Israel is building (para. 67); it repeatedly cited the preambular paragraph of U.N. Security Council Resolution 242, which emphasizes "the inadmissibility of the acquisition of territory by war," as well as a 1970 U.N. General Assembly resolution emphasizing that "[n]o territorial acquisition resulting from the threat or use of force shall be recognized as legal," denoting this principle a "corollary" of the U.N. Charter and as such "customary international law" and a "customary rule" (paras. 74, 87, 117); it upheld the applicability of the Fourth Geneva Convention to the Occupied Territories (para. 101); it found that "the Israeli settlements in the Occupied Palestinian Territory (including East Jerusalem) have been established in breach of international law" (para. 120). On all these counts, the World Court's findings represent a sweeping repudiation of the official Israeli position. Even the dissenting statement of the U.S. representative on the Court crucially conceded that the Fourth Geneva Convention applied to the Occupied Territories and that the existence of Israeli settlements in the West Bank "violates" the convention ("Declaration of Judge Buergenthal"). On the latter point it bears notice that, against the consensus of legal opinion and in a category virtually all his own, Dershowitz upholds the "legal rights" of the Jewish settlers to "live anywhere in the West Bank and in Gaza."[22]

22. "Q&A with Alan Dershowitz," *Jerusalem Post* (online edition) (20 October 2004). In the face of international outrage and, apparently, wanting to preserve some credibility as well as take the sting out of the impending World Court decision, Israel's High Court rendered a mildly dissenting opinion on the wall in late June 2004, *Beit Sourik Village Council v. The Government of Israel* (HCJ 2056/04). It called on the Israeli government to slightly reroute the wall's path in order to mitigate humanitarian damage. However, against all the evidence and conclusions of human rights organizations, it upheld the government's claim that the wall "is motivated by security concerns" on the grounds that this is what the government asserted and "we have no reason not to believe [its] sincerity," and also upheld the legality of constructing the wall deep inside occupied land (paras. 28–32, 44–45). Although still uncertain, the new route will probably reduce the area of the West Bank affected by some 2.5 percent (from 12.7 to 10.1 percent). See United Nations Office for the Coordination of Humanitarian Affairs, "Preliminary Analysis of the Humanitarian Implications of February 2005 Barrier Projections" (East Jerusalem, February 2004).

9

High Court Takes the Low Road

ALAN DERSHOWITZ has always lavished unstinting praise on Israel's Supreme (or High) Court.[1] During the first intifada, he typically declared: "Israel's supreme court has responded magnificently to the occasional overreactions of the Israeli army and security officials. That court, which is among the best in the world, has repeatedly ruled in favor of Arab claimants who have been treated unfairly."[2] In *Why Terrorism Works*, published after the outbreak of the second intifada, Dershowitz similarly asserted: "Despite significant restrictions on the rights of Palestinians, . . . [t]hey know that the Supreme Court of Israel stands as an independent bastion of liberty, even when the military or the government seeks restrictions."[3] The exemplary performance of the Supreme Court figures as a central theme of *The Case for Israel*: "Its Supreme Court is among the best in the world, and it has repeatedly overruled the army and the government and made them operate under the rule of law"; "The Israeli Supreme Court [is] by all accounts one of

---

1. *Supreme Court* and *High Court* refer to the same judicial body, one or the other title used depending on the judicial function it is serving. For simplicity's sake, "Supreme Court" will be used throughout this text.
2. Alan Dershowitz, "Israel Is Still a True Democracy" (February 1988), in *Contrary to Popular Opinion* (New York, 1992), pp. 343–44 (see also p. 362).
3. Alan Dershowitz, *Why Terrorism Works* (New Haven, 2002), pp. 127–28.

the finest in the world. . . . Although obviously sensitive to the need for security, the Israeli Supreme Court has repeatedly enjoined the Israeli government and its military from undertaking actions in violation of the highest standards of the rule of law" (p. 183); and so forth. Dershowitz dedicates *The Case for Israel* to Aharon Barak, the current president of Israel's Supreme Court, "whose judicial decisions make a better case for Israel and for the rule of law than any book could possibly do."

Yet those knowledgeable on this subject reach diametrically opposed conclusions. "What renders Israel's abuses unique throughout the world," the executive director of B'Tselem (Israeli Information Center for Human Rights in the Occupied Territories) observes, "is the relentless efforts to justify what cannot be justified."[4] Israel's Supreme Court has served as the main judicial instrument for this justifying of the unjustifiable. The most exhaustive study to date of Israel Supreme Court decisions regarding the Palestinians is David Kretzmer's *The Occupation of Justice: The Supreme Court of Israel and the Occupied Territories*. The central findings of Kretzmer, a distinguished professor of law at the Hebrew University of Jerusalem, merit extensive quotation:

> [T]he Court has interfered infrequently in decisions of the military. . . . [I]n almost all of its judgments relating to the Occupied Territories, especially those dealing with questions of principle, the Court has decided in favor of the authorities, often on the basis of dubious legal arguments. It is indeed true that in a few cases the Court has decided against the authorities. However, these "landmark cases" serve only to enhance the legitimizing function of the Court by reinforcing the "image of the court as an impartial body which boldly challenge[s] the government in pursuit of justice."

> [W]hile the Court has frequently mentioned the duty of the commander to balance security factors with other considerations, it has almost invariably refused to enter the balancing issue itself, and has bowed to the discretion of the military commander. The duty to balance has more often been part of the Court's rhetoric than of its actual decision-making.

> The Court has not seen itself as a body that should question the legality under international law of policies or actions of the authorities, or should interpret the law in a rights-minded fashion. On the contrary it has accepted and legitimized policies and actions the legality of which is highly dubious and has interpreted the law in favor of the authorities.

> In its decisions relating to the Occupied Territories, the Court has rationalized virtually all controversial actions of the Israeli authorities, especially

---

4. B'Tselem (Israeli Information Center for Human Rights in the Occupied Territories), "Israel's Contempt for Fundamental Legal Principles" (press release, 15 July 1998).

those most problematic under principles of international humanitarian law. . . . The jurisprudence of these decisions is blatantly government-minded.[5]

In his analysis of specific decisions, Kretzmer typically describes the reasoning of the Court as "highly questionable," "highly problematic," "sophistry," and so on.[6]

Table 9.1 reports the findings of human rights organizations and scholars on the legality of key Supreme Court decisions regarding the Occupied Territories. Table 9.2 samples other court decisions regarding the Occupied Territories.

The sections below titled "Vote of Confidence," "Required Reading," "Bargaining Chips," and "Equality" examine Dershowitz's attempts to prove that the Israel Supreme Court defends Palestinian rights, while the last, "Frightening Order," uses Dershowitz's standard to judge Israel's legal system in the Occupied Territories.

VOTE OF CONFIDENCE

To demonstrate the Israel Supreme Court's defense of Palestinian rights, Alan Dershowitz quotes a Palestinian human rights activist on page 184 of *The Case for Israel:*

> **Even Raji Sourani, the director of the Palestinian Center for Human Rights in Gaza and a strident critic of Israel, says that he remains "constantly amazed by the high standards of the legal systems [*sic*]."**

Cited from the *New York Times,* the passage reads in full: "Despite his many frustrations with the Israeli courts, Mr. Sourani says he remains 'constantly amazed by the high standards of the legal system.' 'On many issues,' he said, 'when the courts are dealing with *purely Israeli questions,* like gay rights, I admire their rulings. *But when it comes to the Palestinians, these same people seem to be totally schizophrenic'*" (emphases added).[7]

5. David Kretzmer, *The Occupation of Justice: The Supreme Court of Israel and the Occupied Territories* (Albany, 2002), pp. 2–3 ("image of the court" cited from article in Israeli law journal), 61, 163, 187–88.
   6. Ibid., pp. 81, 138, 152.
   7. Greg Myre, "Trial of Palestinian Leader Focuses Attention on Israeli Courts," *New York Times* (5 May 2003).

TABLE 9.1 LEGALITY OF KEY SUPREME COURT DECISIONS REGARDING THE OCCUPIED TERRITORIES

Settlements	"[T]he Court's jurisprudence on settlements and related issues rests on a dubious assumption of legality. . . . [T]he Court provided legitimization for government actions that are highly questionable." —Professor Kretzmer[a]
Deportations	"Article 49 [of the Fourth Geneva Convention] . . . was designed to ensure that . . . *any* deportation of protected persons from occupied territories would be unlawful. . . . [E]very deportation of protected persons from occupied territories is interdicted, regardless of the individual or collective nature of the act or its motive." "The policy of the Israeli military command of the West Bank and the Gaza Strip to resort to deportations . . . has obtained the seal of approval of the Supreme Court, notwithstanding Article 49 of the Geneva Convention." —Yoram Dinstein, Professor and President, Tel Aviv University[b]
Administrative Detention	"Israel's use of administrative detention in the Occupied Territories . . . is . . . illegal under international law." "It is likely that the Court's unmitigated support for administrative detention serves as a disincentive for Palestinians to turn to the High Court." —B'Tselem (Israeli Information Center for Human Rights in the Occupied Territories). (President of the Court Aharon Barak wrote among the most egregious administrative detention decisions.)[c]
House Demolitions	"The inescapable conclusion . . . is that the jurisprudence constante of the Israel Supreme Court on the important topic of demolitions and sealing off of buildings in the occupied territories is singularly unsatisfactory. There can be little doubt that the application of Section 119(1) of the Defense (Emergency) Regulations [the basis in Israeli law for demolitions and sealings] is in breach of international humanitarian law." —Professor Dinstein. (President of the Court Aharon Barak wrote among the most egregious house demolition decisions.)[d]

[a]David Kretzmer, *The Occupation of Justice: The Supreme Court of Israel and the Occupied Territories* (Albany, 2002), p. 99 (see pp. 75–99 for analysis of relevant Court decisions); see also B'Tselem (Israeli Information Center for Human Rights in the Occupied Territories), *Land Grab: Israel's Settlement Policy in the Occupied Territories* (Jerusalem, 2002), pp. 32–35, 104–5 (see pp. 20–29 for discussion of relevant international law).

[b]Yoram Dinstein, "The Israel Supreme Court and the Law of Belligerent Occupation: Deportations," in *Israel Yearbook on Human Rights* (Tel Aviv, 1993), pp. 14–15 (emphasis in original), 26. (Dinstein is Israel's leading authority on international law.) See also Kretzmer, *Occupation*, pp. 45–55, 165–86. For the official Israeli government position on deportations and related issues, see Meir Shamgar, "The Observance of International Law in the Administered Territories," in *Israel Yearbook on Human Rights* (Tel Aviv, 1971), pp. 262–77. For excerpts of key Supreme Court decisions upholding deportation, see *Kawasme v. Minister of Defense* (HC 698/80), in *Israel Yearbook on Human Rights* (Tel Aviv, 1981), pp. 349–54; *Abd el Afu v. Commander of IDF Forces in the West Bank* (HC 785/87, 845/87, 27/88), in *Israel Yearbook on Human Rights* (1993), pp. 277–86.

[c]B'Tselem, *Prisoners of Peace: Administrative Detention during the Oslo Process* (Jerusalem, 1997), pp. 50, 36 (for Barak's decisions, see pp. 15–17); see also Kretzmer, *Occupation*, pp. 129–35, for analysis of relevant Court decisions.

[d]Yoram Dinstein, "The Israel Supreme Court and the Law of Belligerent Occupation: Demolitions and Sealing Off of Houses," in *Israel Yearbook on Human Rights* (Tel Aviv, 1999), p. 304; see also Kretzmer, *Occupation*, pp. 145–63 (Barak decisions at 154, 160). For the court's approval of the demolition of Palestinians homes, the owners of which were discriminatorily denied building permits, see Amnesty International, *Demolition and Dispossession: The Destruction of Palestinian Homes* (London, December 1999), p. 14, and B'Tselem, *Demolishing Peace: Israel's Policy of Mass Demolition of Palestinian Houses in the West Bank* (Jerusalem, 1997), pp. 34–38 (Barak decisions at pp. 36–38); for the court's rejection of "all petitions submitted thus far" against "IDF combat operations that damaged Palestinian private property" in the Gaza Strip, see B'Tselem, *Policy of Destruction: House Demolitions and Destruction of Agricultural Land in the Gaza Strip* (Jerusalem, February 2002), p. 41; for a "decision by the Israeli High Court of Justice that will allow demolition, without the right to judicial review, of homes belonging to families of people who are believed to have carried out attacks against Israelis," see Amnesty International, "High Court decision gives green light for collective punishment" (press release, 6 August 2002); for a court ruling that "allows the IDF to continue its mass house demolitions" in Gaza and "gives the IDF full discretion as to when to allow a court hearing prior to demolition," see B'Tselem, "The Rule of Law Ends at the Border" (press release, 16 May 2004), as well as B'Tselem, *Through No Fault of Their Own: Punitive House Demolitions during the al-Aqsa Intifada* (Jerusalem, November 2004), pp. 39–45; for the court having "failed to protect Palestinians in the Occupied Territories from arbitrary destruction of their homes and property and from forced evictions, leaving open the door for Israeli demolitions for almost *any* ostensible military purpose," see Amnesty International, *Under the Rubble: House Demolition and Destruction of Land and Property* (London, May 2004), p. 25 (emphasis in original); for the court having "consistently legitimized house demolitions while developing a limited and deeply flawed jurisprudence regarding the right of owners to be heard in advance of demolitions," and criticism of the court because it "invariably defers to the IDF's invocation of 'military necessity.' Even when faced with expert opinions on the military necessity or efficacy of proposed actions, the Court as a rule sides with the IDF without assessing the merits of competing arguments," see Human Rights Watch, *Razing Rafah: Mass Home Demolitions in the Gaza Strip* (New York, October 2004), pp. 127–30. For excerpts from Supreme Court decisions upholding house demolitions and sealings, see *Sakhwil v. Commander of the Judea and Samaria Region* (HC 434/79), in *Israel Yearbook on Human Rights* (Tel Aviv, 1980), pp. 345–46; *Khamri v. Commander of the Judea and Samaria Region* (HC 361/82) in *Israel Yearbook on Human Rights* (Tel Aviv, 1987), p. 314; *Dagalis v. Military Commander of the Judea and Samaria Region* (HC 698/85) in *Israel Yearbook on Human Rights* (1987), pp. 315–16; *Jab'r v. IDF O.C. Central Command and Minister of Defense* (HC 897/86) in *Israel Yearbook on Human Rights* (Tel Aviv, 1988), pp. 252–53; *Alfasfus v. Minister of Defense* (HC 779/88) in *Israel Yearbook on Human Rights* (1993); *Bakhari v. Commander of IDF Forces in the Judea and Samaria Region* (HC 610/89) in *Israel Yearbook on Human Rights* (1993), p. 325; *The Association for Civil Rights in Israel v. Commander of the Southern District* (HC 4112/90) in *Israel Yearbook on Human Rights* (1993), pp. 333–36; *Hagba v. Commander of the IDF Forces in the Judea and Samaria Region* (HC 574/90) in *Israel Yearbook on Human Rights* (1993), pp. 336–37; *Samar v. Commander of IDF Forces in the Gaza Strip* (HC 658/89) in *Israel Yearbook on Human Rights* (1995), pp. 324–25; *Alamrin v. Commander of the IDF Forces in the Gaza Strip* (HC 2722/92) in *Israel Yearbook on Human Rights* (1995), pp. 337–40; *Nazal v. Commander of IDF Forces in the Judea and Samaria Region* (HC 6026/94) in *Israel Yearbook on Human Rights* (1999), pp. 264–71; *Ganimat v. Commanding Officer of the Central District* (HC 2006/97) in *Israel Yearbook on Human Rights* (Tel Aviv, 2000), pp. 333–35.

TABLE 9.2 OTHER SUPREME COURT DECISIONS
REGARDING THE OCCUPIED TERRITORIES

Residency and Family Unification	"The Court accepted the legitimacy of the policy according to which marriage of a resident to a nonresident was not a good enough reason for allowing the nonresident to live permanently in the area."[a]
Political Liquidations	"The Israeli High Court has dismissed two petitions regarding state assassinations on the grounds that 'the court does not usually render rulings on security matters.'" "In so doing the Israeli High Court adopted the position of the state."[b]
Access to Medical Care	"PHR [Physicians for Human Rights]–Israel and the Palestine Red Crescent Society jointly petitioned the High Court, arguing that Israel is violating its undertaking to enable the passage of sick persons through the roadblocks that dissect the Occupied Territories. . . . The High Court rejected the petition. . . . [T]he Court refused to accept an affidavit from the Palestine Red Crescent Society detailing *121 cases* reflecting the delay or prevention of passage of patients or medical personnel at the checkpoints. The Court also refused to issue an order requiring the state to observe the procedures to which it had committed itself. The High Court also accepted the State's claim that . . . there were no villages or regions in the West Bank and Gaza Strip to which access was completely blocked by physical roadblocks. . . . This argument [that no areas were inaccessible] has been repeatedly disproved."[c]

[a]David Kretzmer, *The Occupation of Justice: The Supreme Court of Israel and the Occupied Territories* (Albany, 2002), p. 106.

[b]Public Committee Against Torture in Israel and LAW—The Palestinian Society for the Protection of Human Rights and the Environment, *The Assassination Policy of the State of Israel, November 2000–January 2002* (May 2002), pp. 6, 25.

[c]Physicians for Human Rights–Israel, *A Legacy of Injustice: A Critique of Israeli Approaches to the Right to Health of Palestinians in the Occupied Territories* (Tel Aviv, November 2002), pp. 47–50 (emphasis in original). See also Physicians for Human Rights–Israel, *Blocked—A Visit to the Villages of Salem, Deir al Hatab and Azmut* (Tel Aviv, February 2003), for detailed accounts of blockaded villages, concluding: "As we left the villages behind us, we felt that we were moving not only from one region to another, but from one era to another. As the iron gate swung shut, we were aware that we had been transient visitors to the largest prison administered by the State of Israel—a prison in which millions of Palestinian civilians are held: the prison of the Occupied Territories. Neither a High Court petition nor a formal procedure drafted by well-intentioned officers can change this reality" (n.p.).

============================ REQUIRED READING ============================

To illustrate the Israel Supreme Court's protection of "**the rights of Palestinians,**" Alan Dershowitz writes on pages 184–86 of *The Case for Israel:*

> On September 3, 2002, the court decided a case in which the Israeli military ordered the expulsion of the sister and brother of a terrorist who had organized several suicide bombings. They were expelled from the West Bank for a period of two years and moved to the Gaza Strip on the basis of a finding that the sister had sewn explosive belts and the brother served as a "look out when his brother and members of his group moved two explosive charges from one place to another." The court ruled that the expulsion order, which constituted a temporary "assignment of residence" within the occupied territories rather than a transfer out of the territories, was valid only if "the person himself [who is being expelled] presents a real danger."

Dershowitz goes on to recommend this decision as "**required reading for those who claim that Israel does not comply with the rule of law.**"

The decision, *Ajuri v. IDF Commander,* was written by President of the Court Aharon Barak. The original conviction of the defendants, Intissar Muhammed Ahmed Ajuri and Ahmed Ali Ajuri, was based on "privileged material" and "testimonies of members of the General Security Service." Barak nonetheless affirms it: "We asked counsel for the State why the petitioner is not indicted in a criminal trial. The answer was that there is no admissible evidence against her that can be presented in a criminal trial, for the evidence against her is privileged and cannot be presented in a criminal trial. We regard this as a satisfactory answer."[8] Thus, Dershowitz judges exemplary the court's decision to uphold forcible transfer on the basis of secret evidence. According to Amnesty International, however, it violated fundamental provisions of international law:

> [The] ruling effectively allows for a grave violation of one of the most basic principles of international human rights law—notably the right of any accused to a fair trial and to challenge any evidence used against them. . . . [The] ruling also allows for a grave breach of international humanitarian law. According to the Fourth Geneva Convention, Palestinians living in the territories which have been under Israeli military occupation since 1967 are protected persons. The unlawful forcible transfer of protected persons constitutes a war crime. . . . Under the Rome Statute such violations may also constitute crimes against humanity. . . . In its decision today the High Court

8. *Ajuri v. IDF Commander* (HCJ 7015/02), pp. 26–27. Ahmed Ajuri was convicted on the same basis (p. 29).

of Justice ruled that forcible transfer to the Gaza Strip can only be used for people who have been personally involved in serious crimes and cannot be used as a deterrent. However, Amnesty International believes that such unlawful forcible transfer of relatives of people allegedly responsible for attacks against Israelis is being used by the Israeli government and army as a form of collective punishment. Such [a] measure is forbidden by Article 33 of the Fourth Geneva Convention.[9]

Amnesty subsequently reported that the Ajuris "remain in the Gaza Strip, where they have no family, no home and no means of subsistence other than charity."[10]

<hr>
BARGAINING CHIPS
<hr>

To demonstrate that the Israel Supreme Court is **"by all accounts one of the finest in the world,"** Alan Dershowitz cites this decision on page 185 of *The Case for Israel:*

> The Israeli Supreme Court has prohibited Israel from holding prisoners as "bargaining chips" for the exchange of prisoners illegally being held by its enemies.

It is correct that the Supreme Court prohibited hostage taking in an April 2000 decision. Dershowitz omits mention, however, of the precedent and consequence of this decision. It came only after the Supreme Court first *legalized* hostage taking. Twenty-one Lebanese nationals had been imprisoned in Israel, Human Rights Watch (HRW) reported in a comprehensive 1997 study, "for up to ten years, some . . . in secret locations, denied even the guarantees of due process and humane treatment required by the laws of war." Several had reportedly been tortured during interrogation in south Lebanon "with electric shocks" administered by Lebanese mercenaries "in the presence of Israelis who gave orders." They were being held as "hostages," according to HRW, in order to secure the release of Israeli POWs and MIAs from the Lebanon war.[11] In a November 1997 ruling "unprecedented in the

9. Amnesty International, "Forcible transfers of Palestinians to Gaza constitutes a War Crime" (press release, 3 September 2002).
10. Amnesty International, "Fear of forcible transfer" (urgent action, 15 October 2003).
11. Human Rights Watch, *Without Status or Protection: Lebanese Detainees in Israel* (New York, October 1997). In March 2000 Israeli courts agreed to hear the petition of one of the Lebanese detainees charging torture and rape while in Israeli custody. For Israeli funding, control, and supervision of the notorious prison facility Khiam in south Lebanon, where scores of Lebanese were held hostage for up to fifteen years and "torture

world" (Amnesty International),[12] the Israel Supreme Court authorized the use of these Lebanese detainees as "bargaining chips." President of the Court Aharon Barak held that "a detention is legal if it is designed to promote State security, even if the danger to State security does not emanate from the detainees themselves," and that "detention of the appellants for the purpose of release of the captured and missing soldiers is a vital interest of the State."[13] The Court's ruling "is contemptible and explicitly legitimizes hostage-taking," Amnesty declared. "These are real people, not objects to be used as political pawns."[14] Deploring the decision, B'Tselem observed that Israel "has granted legitimacy to one of the trademarks of terrorist groups around the world."[15] In his April 2000 reversal, Barak himself acknowledged that "there is probably no State in the Western world that permits an administrative detention of someone who does not himself pose any danger to State security," and that "holding persons as 'bargaining cards' actually means holding them as 'hostages.'" It bears notice that among the grounds Barak adduced for his reversal was the strictly pragmatic one that "there is no probability or even a reasonable possibility that the

---

is endemic," see Amnesty International, *The Khiam Detainees: Torture and Ill-treatment* (London, May 1992); Aviv Lavie, "Khiam Prison in the Security Zone: A Nazi-type Concentration Camp," *Ha'ir* and *Kol Hair* (17 January 1997); Amnesty International, *Israel's Forgotten Hostages: Lebanese Detainees in Israel and Khiam Detention Centre* (London, July 1997); Amnesty International, "Fear of torture and ill-treatment" (legal concern, 18 April 2000); Amnesty International, "Amnesty International welcomes Khiam releases, calls for respect for human rights standards" (press release, 23 May 2000), Amnesty International, "'Where is the door?' Letter from an Amnesty International delegation visiting Khiam detention centre in South Lebanon" (press release, 30 May 2000); and Human Rights Watch, "Israel's Withdrawal from South Lebanon: The Human Rights Dimensions" (press release, May 2000) ("endemic"). Amnesty reported regarding Khiam: "a systematic pattern of torture, including the use of electric shocks and beatings with electric cables, often after being soaked with water"; "detainees testified to the direct involvement in interrogation and torture of Israeli personnel"; "eleven detainees have died, . . . some of them after torture, others because of lack of medical treatment"; "the head of the Israeli army's Operations Division admitted . . . that members of Israel's internal security service . . . 'hold meetings several times annually with [Lebanese] interrogators at Khiam prison' . . . [and] that the salaries of the interrogators at Khiam . . . were paid by the Israeli army" (*Israel's Forgotten Hostages*, pp. 8, 10; "Fear of torture and ill-treatment").

12. Amnesty International, "Supreme Court to rule on torture and the holding of hostages" (25 May 1999), and Amnesty International, "Israeli Government should release all Lebanese hostages" (press release, 12 April 2000).

13. *Plonim v. Minister of Defense* (A.D.A. 10/94) in *Israel Yearbook on Human Rights* (Tel Aviv, 2000), pp. 337–38; cf. Human Rights Watch, *Human Rights Watch Submission to the Human Rights Committee* (New York, 13 July 1998) (quoting Barak).

14. Amnesty International, "Israeli Supreme Court endorses hostage-taking" (press release, 6 March 1998).

15. B'Tselem, "Israel's Contempt for Fundamental Legal Principles."

continued detention of the petitioners would lead to the release of the captured and missing soldiers."[16] Even after the 2000 decision, two of the Lebanese detainees "continued to be held incommunicado in a secret place of detention as hostages" (Amnesty International).[17] In 2000 the Israeli Cabinet approved draft legislation, *Imprisonment of Combatants Not Entitled to Prisoner of War Status Law*, "to legalize hostage-taking" (HRW).[18] In 2001 an Israeli court "renewed both men's detention orders . . . after the state contended that their release endangered national security."[19] In 2002 the Israeli Knesset approved the Imprisonment of Combatants law.[20] In January 2004, the two Lebanese hostages were freed in a prisoner swap with Hezbollah.

EQUALITY

To demonstrate that Israel is not a **"racist state,"** Alan Dershowitz writes on page 157 of *The Case for Israel:*

> A decision by the Israel Supreme Court in 2002 [*sic*] ruled that the government may not allocate land based on religion or ethnicity and may not prevent Arab citizens from living wherever they choose.

In March 2000 the Supreme Court ruled that in principle the state couldn't directly or indirectly allocate land to its citizens "on the basis of religion or nationality," although it also allowed that under unspecified "special circumstances," discrimination might be permissible. The decision itself applied only to state-owned land and not land owned by the Jewish National Fund, whose holdings are considerable. Apart from these last caveats, let us also put to one side that when Dershowitz

16. *Plonim v. Minister of Defense* (Cr. F.H. 7048/97) in *Israel Yearbook on Human Rights* (Tel Aviv, 2000), pp. 343, 345 (all Barak quotes are paraphrases by *Israel Yearbook*).
17. "Israel and the Occupied Territories," in *Amnesty International Report 2001* (London); see also Human Rights Watch, "Israel's Withdrawal from South Lebanon: The Human Rights Dimensions" (May 2000). For the release of the other Lebanese hostages, see B'Tselem, "Lebanese Hostages Held in Israel," www.btselem.org.
18. "Israel, the Occupied West Bank, Gaza Strip, and Palestinian Authority Territories" in *Human Rights Watch World Report 2001* (New York) ("legalize"); Amnesty International, "Detention as hostages" (press release, 22 June 2000); and Human Rights Watch, "Background Briefing: Israel's Proposed 'Imprisonment of Combatants Not Entitled to Prisoner of War Status Law'" (June 2000), www.hrw.org/backgrounder/mena/isro622-back.htm.
19. "Israel, the Occupied West Bank, Gaza Strip, and Palestinian Authority Territories," in *Human Rights Watch World Report 2002* (New York).
20. "Israel, the Occupied West Bank, Gaza Strip, and Palestinian Authority Territories," in *Human Rights Watch World Report 2003* (New York).

had been defending Israel's sterling democracy prior to 2000, it had been, by his own admission now, discriminating against its Arab citizens. In the case at hand, the Court held that "the State of Israel must consider the petitioners' request [an Arab couple named Ka'adan] to acquire land for themselves in the settlement of Katzir for the purpose of building their home" and "must determine with deliberate speed whether to allow the petitioners to make a home within the communal settlement."[21] In April 2001 "the High Court rejected another petition filed by ACRI [Association for Civil Rights in Israel] against ILA [Israel Lands Administration], the Jewish Agency, and the settlement of Katzir for contempt of court. ACRI claimed these bodies had not carried out the High Court's precedent-setting Ka'adan ruling. . . . The respondents argued that they retained the right to interview the Ka'adan family before reaching a decision. They were instructed to do so by the court within sixty days. In November 2001, the Katzir admissions board rejected the Arab couple's application" (Human Rights Watch).[22] In May 2004, the Israel Lands Administration informed the Ka'adan family that they could purchase a plot of land and build a house in Katzir, but *Haaretz* reported in June 2005 that ten years after they petitioned the court and five years after the court decided in their favor, the Ka'adan family is "still not living there."[23] Meanwhile, on another front, in July 2002 "[t]he government decided . . . to support a bill . . . that would enable state land to be apportioned for Jewish use only," annulling (if passed) the Court's already circumscribed decision.[24]

FRIGHTENING ORDER

On pages 214–17 of *Why Terrorism Works,* Alan Dershowitz warns of the dangers of a **"frightening order"** issued by the Bush administration:

> A long-term resident of the United States who President Bush believes may have aided a terrorist can now be tried in secret by a military commission.

---

21. Israel Ministry of Foreign Affairs, "High Court: Decision on Katzir" (8 March 2000); for analysis of the decision, see "Israel, the Occupied West Bank and Gaza Strip, and Palestinian Authority Territories," in *Human Rights Watch World Report 2001.*
22. "Israel, the Occupied West Bank and Gaza Strip, and Palestinian Authority Territories," in *Human Rights Watch World Report 2002.*
23. Yuval Yoaz and David Ratner, "ILA to allow Israeli Arab family [to] build in Jewish town," *Haaretz* (10 May 2004). "Showing a sour face to the Arabs" (editorial), *Haaretz* (16 June 2005).
24. Aluf Benn and Moshe Reinfeld, "Government backs bill to allot state land only to Jews," *Haaretz* (8 July 2002).

... Noncitizens suspected of membership in al-Qaeda, or of harboring an "aim to cause injury or adverse effects on the United States," can be rounded up and "detained at an appropriate location" for an indefinite time without access to the courts. . . . Nor will the suspect have an adequate opportunity to defend himself, since the ordinary rules of evidence will not be followed. The military commission will be allowed to base its decision on any evidence that would "have probative value to a reasonable person." Translated from the legalese, this means that hearsay, coerced confessions, and the fruits of illegal searches can be considered, and that cross-examinations will not always be allowed. It also means that the prosecution need not even disclose the sources of its hearsay if such disclosure would reveal a "state secret"—a broad term that is nowhere specifically defined.

On pages 242–43 of *Why Terrorism Works*, he likewise deplores laws instituted by the Nazis right after seizing power that **"did not include any provision guaranteeing an arrested person a quick hearing, access to legal counsel, or redress for false arrest. Those arrested often found their detention extended indefinitely without legal proceedings of any kind."**

A 1991 Amnesty International study entitled *The Military Justice System in the Occupied Territories: Detention, Interrogation and Trial Procedures* reported these findings regarding the "[t]ens of thousands of Palestinian civilians" tried before military courts in the Occupied Territories since 1967:

[D]etainees are held in prolonged incommunicado detention. They are normally not brought before a judge for 18 days. They may be prevented any meaningful contact with their lawyers and relatives well after that, in any case until interrogation is over, which is often 20 or 30 days after arrest. . . . Confessions obtained under interrogation during this period of incommunicado detention are often the primary evidence against defendants appearing before the military courts. Many defendants claim that these confessions are false and have been obtained by the use during arrest and interrogation of torture or other forms of cruel, inhuman or degrading treatment or punishment. The lack of safeguards in the system to protect against torture and ill-treatment, as well as the evidence accumulated over the years, lends credibility to these claims.

Regarding the offenses tried before military courts, Amnesty observed that "in sweeping terms" one military order "criminalizes and makes punishable by up to 10 years' imprisonment almost every form of political expression in the Occupied Territories, including non-violent forms of political activity," such as "raising the Palestinian flag, wearing its colours or making the 'V' sign."[25]

25. Amnesty International, *The Military Justice System in the Occupied Territories: Detention, Interrogation and Trial Procedures* (London, July 1991), pp. 5–7, 20–21.

In lieu of military trials, Israel has also resorted to administrative detention—that is, imprisonment without charge or trial. Under international law, it can be imposed only when an individual poses an imminent danger that can't be otherwise averted. A 1992 B'Tselem study entitled *Detained without Trial: Administrative Detention in the Occupied Territories since the Beginning of the Intifada* reported these findings regarding "over 14,000 administrative detention orders [that] have been issued to Palestinians since the beginning of the Intifada":

> [A] great number of detainees are placed in administrative detention after their interrogators fail to elicit a confession, or as a form of collective punishment, or simply because it is simpler to detain them without charge than to bring them to trial. . . . [A]ll appeals by Palestinian detainees take place at least one month after their arrest, while most are heard even later. The overwhelming majority of the evidence on which the detention is based is considered confidential. The appellant and his lawyer are not shown this evidence, and receive only summary information that is not substantial enough to be contested. . . . Many detainees do not know on what grounds they were detained. . . . Among the administrative detainees are many Palestinian journalists, trade unionists, physicians, merchants, laborers and students. . . . Palestinian leaders who openly support the peace talks with Israel and dialogue to promote Palestinian-Israeli understanding also number among the administrative detainees. In recent years, a Jewish-Palestinian dialogue group has been meeting in Beit Sahur. Almost all of the Palestinian members of this group have been held in administrative detention.[26]

As of 1991 each administrative detention order was for up to six months, renewable for successive six-month periods. A subsequent B'Tselem study, *Prisoners of Peace: Administrative Detention during the Oslo Process* (1997), found that Israel "continues to employ administrative detention on a large scale"; that the period for each detention order was extended to up to one year, renewable for six-month periods; that "length of detentions has increased dramatically" (eleven detainees having been held for over three consecutive years); that administrative detention was imposed on those engaging in "non-violent political activity and the expression of political opinions," as well as on minors as young as fifteen years of age; and that either before or during their administrative detention, "individuals may be subjected to . . . interrogation methods which constitute torture or other ill-treatment."[27] In

---

26. B'Tselem, *Detained without Trial: Administrative Detention in the Occupied Territories since the Beginning of the Intifada* (Jerusalem, 1992), pp. 1–33 passim.

27. B'Tselem, *Prisoners of Peace: Administrative Detention during the Oslo Process* (Jerusalem, 1997), pp. 1–51 passim.

1998 Human Rights Watch called on Israel to "[i]mmediately end the practice of arbitrary or prolonged administrative detention, and revise its laws to ensure that all detainees are guaranteed at minimum the right to prompt and effective judicial review of the lawfulness and conditions of their detention; the right to receive an explanation of one's rights upon arrest in one's own language or soon thereafter and to be informed of the specific, detailed, and personalized reasons for the deprivation of liberty; the right of immediate access to family, legal counsel, and a medical officer."[28] B'Tselem reports that as of March 2003 Israel held "more than one thousand Palestinians in administrative detention."[29]

It seems that the "frightening order" Dershowitz warns of in the United States was implemented long ago in the Occupied Territories.

28. Human Rights Watch, *Israel's Record of Occupation: Violations of Civil and Political Rights* (New York, 1998), pp. 2–3.

29. B'Tselem, "Administrative Detention," www.btselem.org/English/Administrative _Detention/index.asp.

Conclusion

The next task facing the legal profession is to make it easier
for the ordinary citizen to tell the difference between the honest lawyer and the shyster.

Alan M. Dershowitz, *Letters to a Young Lawyer*

A WIDE AND DIVERSE array of human rights organizations—Palestinian as
well as Israeli, United Nations–affiliated as well as independent groups
with a global mandate—have closely monitored Israeli conduct in the
Occupied Territories. Both their conclusions regarding application of
international law and their factual determinations on major as well
as minor details are remarkably consistent. In many respects, Israel's
record, as distilled from thousands of pages of human rights reports, is
quite singular. "What renders Israel's abuses unique throughout the
world," B'Tselem observes, "is the relentless efforts to justify what cannot be justified." The Israel Supreme Court has "rationalized virtually
all controversial actions of the Israeli authorities" (Hebrew University
professor David Kretzmer). For example, in a 1997 ruling "unprecedented in the world" (Amnesty International), the Supreme Court legalized hostage taking. As of November 2003 well over two thousand
Palestinians had been killed in the current intifada, overwhelmingly
civilians. "When so many civilians have been killed and wounded,
the lack of intent makes no difference," B'Tselem concludes. "Israel
remains responsible." Indeed, *New York Times* reporter Chris Hedges
has observed regarding his stint in Gaza, "I had seen children shot
in other conflicts I have covered . . . but I had never watched soldiers

entice children like mice into a trap and murder them for sport." Israel was "the only country in the world," according to B'Tselem, "where torture was legally sanctioned." Since the beginning of the occupation in 1967, Israel has "routinely tortured Palestinian political suspects" (Amnesty International). Due to this "systematic pattern," Human Rights Watch estimated in 1994, "the number of Palestinians tortured or severely ill-treated"—often without even a pretense that these detainees were guilty of any wrongdoing—"is in the tens of thousands." Torture briefly declined after a 1999 Israel Supreme Court decision but, according to the Public Committee Against Torture in Israel, has since been reinstituted in a "methodical and routine" fashion. According to Human Rights Watch, apart from Iraq under Saddam Hussein, Israel has been the only country in the world resorting to house demolitions as a form of punishment. In addition to such punitive demolitions, illegal under international law, of more than two thousand Palestinian homes, Israel has also been condemned for demolishing thousands more Palestinian homes on spurious "administrative" and "security" grounds. Israel is "the only democratic country" that regards political liquidations as a "legitimate course of action" (B'Tselem), placing it "among an infamous group of states that grossly violates basic moral and humane norms that the international community considers binding" (Public Committee Against Torture in Israel and the Palestinian Society for the Protection of Human Rights). Israel presents no evidence supporting its charges against those targeted for assassination. The targets typically don't pose any imminent danger and, alternatively, could have been apprehended, while numerous bystanders have been indiscriminately killed and injured. Israel's economic policies in the Occupied Territories have "proven more exploitative than those of other settler regimes" (Harvard research scholar Sara Roy), resulting in the massive illegal expropriation of Palestinian land and vital water resources. Mainly on account of Israel's closure policy, the West Bank and Gaza currently verge on a "humanitarian catastrophe" (U.N. Commission on Human Rights). Finally, Israel's "regime of separation" in the Occupied Territories "is the only one of its kind in the world," according to B'Tselem, "and is reminiscent of distasteful regimes from the past, such as the Apartheid regime in South Africa."

Yet, against this copiously documented record of egregious human rights violations, Alan Dershowitz contends, and purports to have proven, that Israel's human rights record in the Occupied Territories is "generally superb." The chasm separating these respective accounts of

Israel's record cannot be bridged. Either mainstream human rights organizations and independent experts have engaged in a vast anti-Semitic conspiracy to defame Israel, or Dershowitz has egregiously misrepresented the factual record. No third possibility exists.

Beyond his presentation of Israel's human rights record, Dershowitz has taken significant personal initiatives that merit notice. His early legal defense of Israeli house demolitions was deemed by Israel's leading authority on international law as "verg[ing] on the bizarre." He is on record as supporting collective punishment, including the "automatic destruction" of a Palestinian village after each Palestinian attack. Repeatedly disregarding and distorting evidence, Dershowitz publicly claimed in 1970 that a Palestinian under administrative detention was a terrorist leader; in 1979 that a Palestinian detainee had not been held incommunicado and that his lawyer did not maintain he had been tortured; and in 1989, in sworn testimony, that the most extreme tactic of Israeli interrogators was an occasional "physical touching." He currently advocates the application of "excruciating" torture on suspected terrorists such as a "needle being shoved under the fingernails." When Israeli air force pilots issued a public statement deploring the immorality of political liquidations, Dershowitz publicly aligned himself with the Israeli government in denouncing these courageous dissenters. When young members of the International Solidarity Movement nonviolently protesting Israeli human rights violations were injured and killed by Israeli soldiers, he denounced them as "supporters of Palestinian terrorism." Dershowitz has called for a reversal of the last century's progress in international humanitarian and human rights law, dismissing ethnic cleansing, for example, as a "fifth-rate issue" akin to "massive urban renewal." And, at a conference in Israel attended by Prime Minister Sharon, he declared that Israel was not at all bound by international law.

Dershowitz is also a senior professor of law at Harvard University, where he has taught legal ethics, and is widely acclaimed in the United States as a leading civil libertarian. There is illuminating precedent for Dershowitz's defense of civil liberties at home and apologetics for their egregious violation abroad. Communist party members often proved the most steadfast defenders of civil liberties in the United States. Elizabeth Gurley Flynn was a founding member of the American Civil Liberties Union and, simultaneously, a leading member of the American Communist party during its years of blind support for Stalin's Russia. Likewise, Communists and sympathizers filled the ranks of the National Emergency Civil Liberties Committee, the National

Lawyers Guild, and other organizations defending basic human rights. To reconcile their avowed commitment to civil liberties with slavish support for the Soviet Union, Communists used to maintain both that the Soviet system was the most democratic in the world (witness the 1936 Soviet constitution) and, with little regard for consistency, that in the face of the "threats to its survival—both external and internal threats" (to borrow Dershowitz's phrase), the Soviet Union couldn't allow itself the luxury of "bourgeois rights," which primarily served its enemies. Substitute "luxury of human rights" for "luxury of bourgeois rights," and you get Dershowitz on Israel. When the United States joined ranks with the Soviet Union in the "war against fascism," the Communist party abandoned its prior commitment to civil liberties at home, supporting government suppression of political dissenters. When the United States joined ranks with Israel in the "war against terrorism," Dershowitz began advocating draconian domestic legislation like the "torture warrant." Yet no analogy is perfect. However corrupted, the ideals of Communists were real, as were the sacrifices they made for these ideals. The likes of Dershowitz are opportunists and their purported defense of Israel in the face of overwhelming opposition is all theater.

· · · ·

A recurrent theme of Alan Dershowitz's writing is that, just like everyone else, those in high positions of authority should be held accountable for their malfeasance. "I feel a special responsibility," he professes in *The Best Defense*, "to expose the cheat elite form of corruption." He cites as one egregious example "judges [who] have made false claims about what they have read, distorted records, and engaged in other deceptions."[1] In *The Vanishing American Jew*, he excoriates the lectures of "Afrocentric" demagogues like City University of New York professor Leonard Jeffries: "It is not scholarship. It is not even propaganda. It is educational malpractice. The primary victims are not those who are the targets of Jeffries's attacks. . . . The real victims are the students whom Jeffries defrauds of their time and tuition on a daily basis" in the classroom.[2] In *The Case for Israel*, Dershowitz decries as a

---

1. Alan M. Dershowitz, *The Best Defense* (New York, 1983), pp. xx–xxi. The matter of Dershowitz's "false claims" about what he has read is explored in Appendix I, while his distortions of records and "other deceptions" are further documented in Appendices II and III.
2. Alan M. Dershowitz, *The Vanishing American Jew* (New York, 1997), p. 129.

"particularly nasty form of educational malpractice" those who "set out quite deliberately to misinform, miseducate, and misdirect their own students" (p. 207), and calls for the sacking of professors like an obscure French Holocaust "revisionist" who publishes spurious scholarship: "There was no extensive historical research. Instead, there was the fraudulent manufacturing of false antihistory. It was the kind of deception for which professors are rightly fired—not because their views are controversial but because they are violating the most basic canons of historical scholarship" (p. 213).[3] Shouldn't those at Harvard Law School also be held to this standard?

In *The Holocaust Industry*, this writer documented that American Jewish elites didn't become enamored of Israel until after the June 1967 war, when it became politically and personally expedient to be a Zionist.[4] Likewise, they didn't discover the Nazi holocaust until after the June war, when it proved useful for deflecting criticism of Israel. Alan Dershowitz perfectly fits this profile. He reports that it was only in 1967 that "I first began to make the case for Israel on university campuses, in the media, and in my writings" (p. vii)—that is, when it required roughly as much pluck as for his counterpart at Moscow University to make the case for Cuba. He also informs readers that the Nazi holocaust didn't figure at all in his life growing up: "I do not remember any discussion—not a single one—either in class, in the schoolyard, or even at home, about the Holocaust"; "The Holocaust was not part of my personal memory. . . . It was never mentioned in yeshiva, in Jewish camp, in discussions among my friends, or even at the synagogue."[5] And again: "My friends from Brooklyn and I, who never discussed the Holocaust when we were growing up, talk about it all the time now."[6] No doubt they do, since, in contrast to the 1950s, it's now politically convenient to invoke the Nazi holocaust.[7] Dershowitz's convenient love affair with Israel and anguish over the Holocaust points to the ugliest truth about his wretched book. Throughout the past year this writer has stated in public lectures that *The Case for Israel* is replete with egregious falsehoods. Yet the biggest fraud is the

3. Compare Alan M. Dershowitz, *Chutzpah* (Boston, 1991), p. 175, for the same injunction.

4. Norman G. Finkelstein, *The Holocaust Industry: Reflections on the Exploitation of Jewish Suffering*, 2nd ed. (New York, 2003), chap. 1.

5. Dershowitz, *Best Defense*, p. 10; Dershowitz, *Chutzpah*, p. 49 (cf. p. 207).

6. Dershowitz, *Chutzpah*, p. 180.

7. For the taboo on discussing the Nazi holocaust in the 1950s, see Finkelstein, *Holocaust Industry*, pp. 13–16.

title itself. Dershowitz hasn't written a case for Israel. How could anyone genuinely concerned about the Israeli people counsel policies certain to sow seeds of hatred abroad and moral corruption within? What he has in fact written is the case for the destruction of Israel. Letting others—Palestinians as well as Jews—pay the price while he plays the "tough Jew": isn't this what Dershowitz's chutzpah really comes down to?

APPENDICES

It is the job of the defense attorney—especially when
representing the guilty—to prevent, by all lawful
means, the "whole truth" from coming out.

Alan M. Dershowitz, *The Best Defense*

Of Crimes and Misdemeanors

Today I write nearly every day and publish a book almost
every year. . . . My test for publication is certainly not
perfection.

> Alan M. Dershowitz, *Letters to a Young Lawyer*

NEXT TO ALAN DERSHOWITZ'S egregious falsification of Israel's human
rights record and the real suffering such falsification causes, Dershowitz's academic derelictions seem small beer. Yet he has written a
book that purports to be an academic study, and its success is largely
owing to Dershowitz's academic pedigree. His violations of elementary
academic standards accordingly warrant exposure. In addition, they
illustrate the complete absence of quality control when it comes to discourse on the Israel-Palestine conflict. Dershowitz can appropriate
from a hoax with impunity due to an environment that tolerates such
derelictions so long as the conclusions are politically correct.

Some twenty years ago one Joan Peters published *From Time Immemorial: The Origins of the Arab-Jewish Conflict over Palestine.*[1] Although
a national best seller and critically acclaimed upon publication, the book
was soon shown to be a hoax. Baruch Kimmerling (of the Hebrew
University) and Joel S. Migdal, in their authoritative study, *Palestinians: The Making of a People,* observe that Peters's book is "based
on materials out of context, and on distorted evidence." Citing this
writer's own conclusion that the book is "the most spectacular fraud

---

1. New York, 1984.

ever published on the Arab-Israeli conflict," they report that "[s]imilar evaluations were expressed by notable historians" in Israel and Europe.[2] Returning to *The Case for Israel*, we find that the work relies heavily on either a single scholarly study by historian Benny Morris or "pro"-Israel websites and publications. The notable exceptions are chapters 1 and 2, which cite an impressive array of primary materials from nineteenth-century Palestine, such as British consular reports. How did Dershowitz chance upon these recondite sources? Table AI.1 juxtaposes the documentation in chapters 1 and 2 of *The Case for Israel*[3] against the documentation in Peters's *From Time Immemorial*. Fully twenty-two of the fifty-two quotations and endnotes in chapters 1 and 2 of *The Case for Israel* match almost exactly—*including, in long quotes, the placement of ellipses*—those in *From Time Immemorial*.

When evidence of his apparently unacknowledged lifting of Peters's research became public,[4] Dershowitz vehemently denied any wrongdoing. He alleged both that this didn't constitute plagiarism and that it was proper to cite the primary sources rather than Peters on the ground that he independently consulted the primary sources. Leaving aside the highly dubious contention that another author's research can be claimed as one's own merely by virtue of checking that author's sources, did Dershowitz in fact check the originals before citing them? Consider a couple of examples from Table AI.1:

· Young to Viscount Canning, January 13, 1842 (Row 7)

Quoting a statement depicting the miserable fate of Jews in mid-nineteenth-century Jerusalem, Peters cites a British consular letter from "W. T. Young to Viscount Canning." Dershowitz cites the same statement as Peters, reporting that Young "attributed the plight of the Jew in Jerusalem" to pervasive anti-Semitism. It

2. Kimmerling and Migdal, *Palestinians: The Making of a People* (Cambridge, 1994), pp. xvi–xvii, 321n5. For background on the Peters affair, see Edward Said and Christopher Hitchens (eds.), *Blaming the Victims: Spurious Scholarship and the Palestinian Question* (New York, 2001), chap. 1; for extensive documentation of the fraud and recent developments including the book's republication, see Norman G. Finkelstein, *Image and Reality of the Israel-Palestine Conflict*, 2nd ed. (New York, 2003), p. xxxii and chap. 2.

3. All citations are from the first printing of *The Case for Israel* (Hoboken, N.J., 2003).

4. The charges were first leveled on 24 September 2003 on Amy Goodman's nationally syndicated radio program *Democracy Now!* during a debate between this writer and Dershowitz. The charges were first written up two days later by Alexander Cockburn on

turns out, however, that the statement did not come from Young but, as is unmistakably clear to anyone who actually consulted the original, from an enclosed memorandum written by an "A. Benisch," which Young was forwarding to Canning.

· Mark Twain, *The Innocents Abroad* (Row 8)

In his public defense Dershowitz was especially emphatic that he independently found the passages quoted from Twain (*Crimson*, 30 September 2003; *The Nation*, 27 October 2003). These passages are cited by Dershowitz from pages 349, 366, 375, and 441–42 of a 1996 edition of Twain's book. The same passages are cited by Peters from pages 349, 366, 375, and 441–42 of an 1881 edition of Twain's book. But the quoted passages do not appear on the pages of the 1996 edition cited by Dershowitz. Anyone who actually consulted the 1996 edition would have known this. In addition, Dershowitz cites two paragraphs from Twain as continuous text, just as Peters cites them as continuous text, but in Twain's book the two paragraphs are separated by eighty-seven pages. It would have been impossible for anyone who actually checked the original source to make this error. (Exhibit A, pp. 244–45, below.)

Scrutiny of the advance uncorrected proofs of *The Case for Israel*,[5] a copy of which was obtained by this writer from a correspondent, dispels any lingering doubts that Dershowitz lifted from Peters. (Exhibit B, p. 246, below.) Many of the footnotes in these proofs either are not yet filled in or are in provisional form, and instructions are left

---

his Counterpunch.org website ("Alan Dershowitz, Plagiarist"). For subsequent discussion, see Lauren A. E. Schuker, "Dershowitz Accused of Plagiarism," *Harvard Crimson* (29 September 2003); Alan Dershowitz, "Plagiarism Accusations Political, Unfounded" (letter), *Harvard Crimson* (30 September 2003); Lauren A. E. Schuker, "Dershowitz Defends Book," *Harvard Crimson* (2 October 2003); Alan Dershowitz, "Professor Dershowitz 'Rests His Case,'" *Harvard Crimson* (3 October 2003); Norman G. Finkelstein, "Finkelstein Proclaims 'The Glove *Does* Fit,'" *Harvard Crimson* (3 October 2003); Alex Beam, "Another Middle East Conflict," *Boston Globe* (2 October 2003); Eric Marx, "Dershowitz Rebuts Critics' Plagiarism Charges," *Forward* (3 October 2003); Adina Levine, "Dershowitz Denies Plagiarism Charges," *Harvard Law Record* (9 October 2003); Alexander Cockburn, "Alan Dershowitz, Plagiarist," *The Nation* (13 October 2003); Alan Dershowitz and Alexander Cockburn, "Letters Exchange," *The Nation* (27 October 2003 and 15 December 2003). Many of these items are posted on www.NormanFinkelstein.com ("The Dershowitz Hoax").

5. Proofs are the advance copy of a text made for examination or correction.

TABLE AI.1. PROFESSOR DERSHOWITZ'S RESEARCH

Row Number	Dershowitz	Peters
1	*In the sixteenth century, according to British reports, "as many as 15,000 Jews" lived in Safad, which was "a center of rabbinical learning." (p. 17)* SOURCE CITED: *Palestine Royal Commission Report*, pp. 11–12.	Safed at that time, according to the British investigation by Lord Peel's committee, "contained as many as 15,000 Jews in the 16th century," and was "a centre of Rabbinical learning." (p. 178) SOURCE CITED: *Palestine Royal Commission Report*, pp. 11–12.
2	*[A]ccording to the British consul in Jerusalem, the Muslims of Jerusalem "scarcely exceed[ed] one quarter of the whole population." (p. 17)* SOURCE CITED: James Finn to Earl of Clarendon, January 1, 1858.	In 1858 Consul Finn reported the "Mohammedans of Jerusalem" were "scarcely exceeding one-quarter of the whole population." (p. 197) SOURCE CITED: James Finn to Earl of Clarendon, January 1, 1858.
3	*By the middle of the nineteenth century [. . .] Jews also constituted a significant presence, often a plurality or majority, in Safad, Tiberias, and several other cities and towns. (p. 17)* SOURCE CITED: James Finn to Viscount Palmerston, November 7, 1851.	Meanwhile, the Jewish population had been growing. They were the majority in Safed and Tiberias by 1851. (p. 199) SOURCE CITED: James Finn to Viscount Palmerston, November 7, 1851.

4

In 1834, Jewish homes in Jerusalem "were sacked and their women violated." (p. 18)

SOURCE CITED: Jacob de Haas, *History of Palestine* (New York, 1934), p. 393.

[I]n 1834, [...] "Forty thousand fellahin rushed on Jerusalem [...]. The Jews were the worst sufferers, their homes were sacked and their women violated." (p. 183)

SOURCE CITED: Jacob de Haas, *History of Palestine* (New York, 1934), p. 393.

5

The British consul, William Young, in a report to the British Foreign Office [...] painted a vivid and chilling picture of the life of the Jews of Jerusalem in 1839: "I think it my duty to inform you that there has been a Proclamation issued this week by the Governor in the Jewish quarter—that no Jew is to be permitted to pray in his own house under pain of being severely punished— such as want to pray are to go into the Synagogue.... There has also been a punishment inflicted on a Jew and Jewess—most revolting to human nature which I think it is my duty to relate. In the early part of this week, a House was entered in the Jewish Quarter, and a robbery was committed—the House was in quarantine—and the guardian was a Jew—he denied having any knowledge of the thief or the circumstances. In order to compel him to confess, he was laid down and beaten, and afterwards imprisoned. The following day he was again brought before the Governor, when he still declared his innocence. He was then burned

In May 1839, for instance, the complaints registered with the British Foreign Office by Consul Young in Jerusalem were appalling. In one day, in one report: "I think it my duty to inform you that there has been a Proclamation issued this week by the Governor in the Jewish quarter— that no Jew is to be permitted to pray in his own house under pain of being severely punished—such as want to pray are to go into the Synagogue ... There has also been a punishment inflicted on a Jew and Jewess—most revolt-ing to human nature which I think it my duty to relate— In the early part of this week, a House was entered in the Jewish Quarter, and a robbery was committed—the House was in quarantine—and the guardian was a Jew— he denied having any knowledge of the thief or the circumstances. In order to compel him to confess, he was laid down and beaten, and afterwards imprisoned. The following day he was again brought before the Governor, when he still declared his innocence. He was then burned with a hot iron over

Row Number	Dershowitz	Peters
5 (continued)	*with a hot iron over his face, and various parts of the body—and beaten on the lower parts of his body to the extent that the flesh hung in pieces from him. The following day the poor creature died. He was a young Jew of Salonica about 28 years of age—who had been here but a very short time, he had only the week before been applying to enter my service. A young man—a Jew—having a French passport was also suspected—he fled—his character was known to be an indifferent one—his mother, an aged woman, was taken under suspicion of concealing her son—She was tied up and beaten in the most brutal way. . . . I must say I am sorry and am surprised that the Governor could have acted so savage a part—for certainly what I have seen of him, I should have thought him superior to such wanton inhumanity—but it was a Jew—without friends or protection—it serves well to show, that it is not without reason that the poor Jew, even in the nineteenth century, lives from day to day in terror of his life."* (p. 18)	his face, and in various parts of the body—and beaten on the lower parts of his body to that extent that the flesh hung in pieces from him. The following day the poor creature died. He was a young Jew of Salonica about 28 years of age—who had been here but a very short time, he had only the week before been applying to enter my service. A young man—a Jew—having a French passport was also suspected—he fled—his character was known to be an indifferent one—his mother an aged woman was taken under the suspicion of concealing her son—She was tied up and beaten in the most brutal way. . . . I must say I am sorry and am surprised that the Governor could have acted so savage a part—for certainly what I have seen of him, I should have thought him superior to such wanton inhumanity—but it was a Jew—without friends or protection—it serves well to show, that it is not without reason that the poor Jew, even in the nineteenth century, lives from day to day in terror of his life." (pp. 184–85)
	SOURCE CITED: Wm. T. Young to Colonel Patrick Campbell, May 25, 1839.	SOURCE CITED: Wm. T. Young to Colonel Patrick Campbell, May 25, 1839.

6

Nor could the Jew seek redress, as the report observed: "Like the miserable dog without an owner he is kicked by one because he crosses his path, and cuffed by another because he cries out—to seek redress he is afraid, lest it bring worse upon him; he thinks it better to endure than to live in the expectation of his complaint being revenged upon him." (p. 20)

SOURCE CITED: Wm. T. Young to Viscount Palmerston, May 25, 1839.

[T]he life for Jews described in 1839 by British Consul Young: "[. . .] Like the miserable dog without an owner he is kicked by one because he crosses his path, and cuffed by another because he cries out—to seek redress he is afraid, lest it bring worse upon him; he thinks it better to endure than to live in the expectation of his complaint being revenged upon him." (p. 187)

SOURCE CITED: Wm. T. Young to Viscount Palmerston, May 25, 1839.

7

Several years later, the same consul attributed the plight of the Jew in Jerusalem to "the blind hatred and ignorant prejudice of a fanatical populace," coupled with an inability of the poverty-stricken Jewish community to defend itself either politically or physically. (p. 20)

SOURCE CITED: Wm. T. Young to Viscount Canning, January 13, 1842.

In Palestine, [it] was reported: "It is a fact that the Jewish Subjects [. . .] do not enjoy the privileges granted to them. . . . This Evil may in general be traced [. . .]: I. To the absence of an adequate protection whereby they are more exposed to cruel and tyrannical treatment. II. To the blind hatred and ignorant prejudices of a fanatical populace [. . .]. IV. To the starving state of numerous Jewish population." (p. 188)

SOURCE CITED: W. T. Young to Viscount Canning, January 13, 1842.

Row Number	Dershowitz	Peters
8	*Mark Twain, who visited Palestine in 1867, offered this description: "Stirring scenes . . . occur in the valley [Jezreel] no more. There is not a solitary village throughout its whole extent—not for thirty miles in either direction. There are two or three small clusters of Bedouin tents, but not a single permanent habitation. One may ride ten miles hereabouts and not see ten human beings. . . . Come to Galilee for that . . . these unpeopled deserts, these rusty mounds of barrenness, that never, never, never do shake the glare from their harsh outlines, and fade and faint into vague perspective; that melancholy ruin of Capernaum: this stupid village of Tiberias, slumbering under its six funereal palms. . . . We never saw a human being on the whole route. Nazareth is forlorn. . . . Jericho the accursed lies in a moldering ruin today, even as Joshua's miracle left it more than three thousand years ago; Bethlehem and Bethany, in their poverty and their humiliation, have nothing about them now to remind one that they once knew the high honor of the Savior's presence, the hallowed spot where the shepherds watched their flocks by night, and where*	Mark Twain [. . .] visited the Holy Land in 1867. In one location after another, Twain registered gloom at his findings[:] "Stirring scenes . . . occur in the valley [Jezreel] no more. There is not a solitary village throughout its whole extent—not for thirty miles in either direction. There are two or three small clusters of Bedouin tents, but not a single permanent habitation. One may ride ten miles hereabouts and not see ten human beings. [. . .] Come to Galilee for that . . . these unpeopled deserts, these rusty mounds of barrenness, that never, never, never do shake the glare from their harsh outlines, and fade and faint into vague perspective; that melancholy ruin of Capernaum: this stupid village of Tiberias, slumbering under its six funereal palms. . . . We reached Tabor safely. . . . We never saw a human being on the whole route. Nazareth is forlorn. . . . Jericho the accursed lies a moldering ruin today, even as Joshua's miracle left it more than three thousand years ago; Bethlehem and Bethany, in their poverty and their humiliation, have nothing about them now to remind one that they once knew the high honor of the Savior's presence; the hal-

the angels sang, 'Peace on earth, good will to men,' is untenanted by any living creature. . . . Bethsaida and Chorzin have vanished from the earth, and the 'desert places' round about them, where thousands of men once listened to the Savior's voice and ate the miraculous bread, sleep in the bush of a solitude that is inhabited only by birds of prey and skulking foxes." (pp. 23–24)

SOURCE CITED: Mark Twain, *The Innocents Abroad* (New York, 1996), pp. 349, 366, 375, 441–42.

lowed spot where the shepherds watched their flocks by night, and where the angels sang, 'Peace on earth, good will to men,' is untenanted by any living creature. . . . Bethsaida and Chorzin have vanished from the earth, and the 'desert places' round about them, where thousands of men once listened to the Savior's voice and ate the miraculous bread, sleep in the hush of a solitude that is inhabited only by birds of prey and skulking foxes." (pp. 159–60)

SOURCE CITED: Mark Twain, *The Innocents Abroad* (London, 1881), pp. 349, 366, 375, 441–42.

9

A Christian historian has reported that several villages throughout Palestine "are populated wholly by settlers from other portions of the Turkish Empire within the nineteenth century. There are villages of Bosnians, Druzes, Circassians and Egyptians." (p. 26)

SOURCE CITED: James Parkes, *Whose Land?* p. 212.

"In some cases villages [in Palestine] are populated wholly by settlers from other portions of the Turkish Empire within the nineteenth century. There are villages of Bosnians, Druzes, Circassians and Egyptians," one historian has reported. (p. 156)

SOURCE CITED: James Parkes, *Whose Land?* p. 212.

Row Number	Dershowitz	Peters
10	*The 1911 edition of Encyclopaedia Britannica described the population of Palestine as comprising widely differing "ethnological" groups speaking "no less than fifty languages." It was daunting therefore to "write concisely" about "the ethnology of Palestine," especially following the influx of population from Egypt "which still persists in the villages." In addition to Arabs and Jews, the other ethnic groups in Palestine at the end of the nineteenth and the beginning of the twentieth century included Kurds, German Templars, Persians, Sudanese, Algerians, Samaritans, Tatars, Georgians, and many people of mixed ethnicities.* (p. 26) SOURCE CITED: No volume or page number cited.	Another source, the *Encyclopaedia Britannica*, 1911 edition [. . .], finds the "population" of Palestine composed of so "widely differing" a group of "inhabitants"—whose "ethnological affinities" create "early in the 20th century a list of no less than fifty languages"—that "it is therefore no easy task to write concisely . . . on the ethnology of Palestine." In addition to the "Assyrian, Persian and Roman" elements of ancient times, "the short-lived Egyptian government introduced into the population an element from that country which still persists in the villages." . . . "There are [. . .] Persians [. . .] Kurds . . . German 'Templar' colonies [. . .] a large Algerian element [. . .] Sudanese [. . .] the Samaritan sect." (pp. 156–57) SOURCE CITED: *Encyclopaedia Britannica*, 11th ed., vol. XX, p. 604.
11	*An 1857 communiqué from the British consul in Jerusalem reported that "the country is in a considerable degree empty of inhabitants and therefore its greatest need is that of a body of population."* (p. 26) SOURCE CITED: James Finn to the Earl of Clarendon, September 15, 1857.	The British Consul in Palestine reported in 1857 that "The country is in a considerable degree empty of inhabitants and therefore its greatest need is that of a body of population." (p. 159) SOURCE CITED: James Finn to the Earl of Clarendon, September 15, 1857.

12	*It also noted that although the Arabs tended to leave and not return, the Jewish population was more stable: "[W]e have Jews who have traveled to the United States and Australia," and "instead of remaining there, do return hither." (p. 26)*	Finn wrote further that "[. . .] we have here Jews, who have been to the United States, but have returned to their Holy Land—Jews of Jerusalem do go to Australia and instead of remaining there, do return hither." (p. 485n127)
	SOURCE CITED: James Finn to the Earl of Clarendon, September 15, 1857.	SOURCE CITED: James Finn to the Earl of Clarendon, September 15, 1857.
13	*Four years later, it was reported that "depopulation is even now advancing." (p. 26)*	In the 1860s, it was reported that "depopulation is even now advancing." (p. 159)
	SOURCE CITED: J. B. Forsyth, A Few Months in the East (Quebec, 1861), p. 188.	SOURCE CITED: J. B. Forsyth, A Few Months in the East (Quebec, 1861), p. 188.
14	*And four years after that, it was noted that in certain parts of the country "land is going out of cultivation and whole villages are rapidly disappearing . . . and the stationary population extirpated." (p. 26)*	H. B. Tristram noted in his journal that "The north and south [of the Sharon plain] land is going out of cultivation and whole villages are rapidly disappearing [. . .] and the stationary population extirpated." (p. 159)
	SOURCE CITED: H. B. Tristram, The Land of Israel: A Journal of Travels in Palestine (London, 1865), p. 490.	SOURCE CITED: H. B. Tristram, The Land of Israel: A Journal of Travels in Palestine (London, 1865), p. 490.

Row Number	Dershowitz	Peters
15	*Other historians, demographers, and travelers described the Arab population as "decreasing," and the land as "thinly populated," "unoccupied," "uninhabited," and "almost abandoned now." (pp. 26–27)* SOURCES CITED: Samuel Bartlett, *From Egypt to Palestine* (New York, 1879), p. 409. Cited in Fred Gottheil, "The population of Palestine, Circa 1875," Middle Eastern Studies, vol. 15, no. 3, October 1979. Edward Wilson, *In Scripture Lands* (New York, 1890) p. 316. Cited in Gottheil. W. Allen, *The Dead Sea: A New Route to India* (London, 1855), p. 113. Cited in Gottheil. William Thomson, *The Land and the Book* (New York, 1871), p. 466. Cited in Gottheil.	Report followed depressing report, as the economist-historian Professor Fred Gottheil pointed out: [. . .]"almost abandoned now"; "unoccupied"; "uninhabited"; "thinly populated." (p. 160) SOURCES CITED: S. C. Bartlett, *From Egypt to Palestine* (New York, 1879), p. 410. Cited in Fred Gottheil, "The Population of Palestine, Circa 1875," Middle Eastern Studies, vol. 15, no. 3, October 1979. W. Allen, *The Dead Sea: A New Route to India* (London, 1855), p. 113. Cited in ibid. W. M. Thomson, *The Land and the Book* (New York, 1862), p. 466. Cited in ibid. E. L. Wilson, *In Scripture Lands* (New York, n.d.), p. 316. Cited in ibid.
16	*The Plain of Sharon [. . .] was described by Reverend Samuel Manning in 1874 as "a land without inhabitants" that "might support an immense population." (p. 27)* SOURCE CITED: Reverend Samuel Manning, *Those Holy Fields* (London, 1874), pp. 14–17.	Many writers, such as the Reverend Samuel Manning, mourned the atrophy of the coastal plain, the Sharon Plain [. . .]: "This fertile plain, which might support an immense population, is [. . .] 'the land [. . .] without inhabitants.'" (p. 160) SOURCE CITED: Reverend Samuel Manning, *Those Holy Fields* (London, 1874), pp. 14–17.

17

J. L. Burkhardt [sic] reported that as early as in the second decade of the nineteenth century, "Few individuals . . . die in the same village in which they were born. Families are continually moving from one place to another . . . they fly to some other place, where they have heard that their brethren are better treated." (p. 27)

SOURCE CITED: John Lewis Burckhardt, *Travels in Syria and the Holy Land* (New York, 1983), p. 299.

John Lewis Burckhardt graphically described the migratory patterns he found in the early 1800s: "[. . .] Few individuals . . . die in the same village in which they were born. Families are continually moving from one place to another [. . .] in a few years [. . .] they fly to some other place, where they have heard that their brethren are better treated." (p. 163)

SOURCE CITED: John Lewis Burckhardt, *Travels in Syria and the Holy Land* (London, 1882), p. 299.

18

A study of the Jewish settlement of Risbon L'Tzion, first established in 1882, showed that the 40 Jewish families that settled there had attracted "more than 400 Arab families," many of which were Bedouin and Egyptian. These families moved into areas around the Jewish settlement and formed a new Arab village on the site of "a forsaken ruin." The report observed a similar pattern with regard to other settlements and villages. (p. 27)

SOURCE CITED: A. Druyanow, *Ketavim Letoldot Hibbat Ziyyon Ve-Yishshuv Erez Yisra'el* (Writings on history of Hibbat Ziyyon and the settlement of the land of Israel) (Odessa, Tel Aviv, 1919, 1925, 1932), vol. 3, pp. 66–67.

[I]n the Jewish settlement Rishon l'Tsion (founded in 1882), by the year 1889 the "forty Jewish families" settled there had attracted "more than four hundred Arab families," most of them "Bedouin and Egyptian." They had come to "surround the moshava" (settlement) in a "now-thriving village" that, before the founding of Rishon l'Tsion, had been Sarafand—"a forsaken ruin." The report from Rishon pointed out that many other Arab villages had sprouted in the same fashion. (p. 252)

SOURCE CITED: A. Druyanow, *Ketavim letoldot bibbat ziyyon ve-yishshuv erez yisra'el* (Odessa, Tel Aviv, 1919, 1925, 1932), vol. 3, pp. 66–67.

Row Number	Dershowitz	Peters
19	*According to one historian, "at least 25% of [the Muslims who lived in all of Palestine in 1882] were newcomers or descendants of those who arrived after [the Egyptian conquest of 1831]." (p. 28)* SOURCE CITED: Ernst Frankenstein, *Justice for my People* (London, 1943), p. 127.	One historian deduced that of 141,000 settled Muslims living in all of Palestine (all areas) in 1882, "at least 25% of those 141,000 . . . were newcomers or descendants of those who arrived after 1831 (Egyptian conquest)." (pp. 196–97) SOURCE CITED: Ernst Frankenstein, *Justice for my People* (London, 1943), p. 127.
20	*A British official reported in 1937 that "the growth in [the numbers of Arab fellahin] had been largely due to the health services combating malaria, reducing infant death rates, improving water supply and sanitation." (p. 28)* SOURCE CITED: *Report by His Britannic Majesty's Government to the Council of the League of Nations on the Administration of Palestine and Trans-Jordan for the Year 1937*, Colonial No. 146, pp. 223–24.	An official 1937 report found that "The growth in their numbers [Arab *fellahin*-peasants] has been largely due to the health services, combating malaria, reducing the infant deathrate, improving water supply and sanitation." (pp. 223–24) SOURCE CITED: *Report by His Britannic Majesty's Government to the Council of the League of Nations on the Administration of Palestine and Trans-Jordan for the Year 1937*, Colonial No. 146, pp. 223–24.

for Dershowitz's research assistants on how to complete the text. Consider these examples from Table AI.1:

- The footnote for the Twain quotes (Row 8) in the proofs reads:

  The Creation of Yesterday, pp. 159–60.

  "The Creation of Yesterday" is a section heading of *From Time Immemorial*, and the Twain quotes appear on the cited pages of that book. So much for Dershowitz having independently found them.

- The footnote for the cluster of testimonies regarding Palestine's population (Row 15) in the proofs reads:

  Holly Beth: cite sources on pp. 160, 485, 486, fns 141–145.

  Holly Beth Billington was one of Dershowitz's research assistants, credited on the acknowledgments page. Turning to these pages in *From Time Immemorial*, we find the quotes and sources cited in *The Case for Israel*. (Exhibit C, p. 247, below.)

- The footnote for the Zionist settlement (Row 18) in the proofs reads:

  A. Druyanow [**cite p. 527**]

  The boldface is in the proofs. (Exhibit D, p. 248, below.) Turning to page 527 of *From Time Immemorial*, we find the Druyanow citation.

Notice, finally, the wording in these examples. It doesn't say "check sources on . . ."; rather, it says "cite sources on. . . ." Moreover, neither Joan Peters nor *From Time Immemorial* is even named: Dershowitz's assistants already knew exactly where to go.

Beyond denying that he plagiarized *From Time Immemorial*, Dershowitz defended his reliance on Peters on the grounds that *The Case for Israel* explicitly rejects her demographic conclusions. But does it? The central argument of *From Time Immemorial* was that Palestine was virtually empty on the eve of Zionist colonization. After Zionists "made the desert bloom" in the areas of Palestine they colonized, Arabs from other parts of Palestine and from neighboring Arab states settled in these areas to exploit new economic opportunities. It was these recent Arab arrivals, according to Peters, who left what became Israel during the 1948 war. The "Arab refugees" from that war, Peters concludes, weren't really refugees because they had only just settled there. As already

The Palestine to which the European Jews of the First Aliyah immigrated was vastly underpopulated, and the land onto which the Jews moved was, in fact, bought primarily from absentee landlords and real estate speculators.

In addition to Palestine being an appropriate place for Jewish refugees because of its close connection to their history and ideology, it was also seen as appropriate because of the demographics of the land to which they were moving, or, in their word, *returning*.

Mark Twain, who visited Palestine in 1867, offered this description:

> Stirring scenes . . . occur in the valley [Jezreel] no more. There is not a solitary village throughout its whole extent—not for thirty miles in either direction. There are two or three small clusters of Bedouin tents, but not a single permanent habitation. One may ride ten miles hereabouts and not see ten human beings. . . . Come to Galilee for that . . . these unpeopled deserts, these rusty mounds of barrenness, that never, never, never do shake the glare from their harsh outlines, and fade and faint into vague perspective; that melancholy ruin of Capernaum: this stupid village of Tiberias, slumbering under its six funereal palms. . . . We reached Tabor safely. . . . We never saw a human being on the whole route.
>
> Nazareth is forlorn. . . . Jericho the accursed lies in a moldering ruin today, even as Joshua's miracle left it more than three thousand years

a

> Come to Galilee for that . . . these unpeopled deserts, these rusty mounds of barrenness, that never, never, never do shake the glare from their harsh outlines, and fade and faint into vague perspective; that melancholy ruin of Capernaum: this stupid village of Tiberias, slumbering under its six funereal palms. . . . We reached Tabor safely. . . . We never saw a human being on the whole route.[133]
>
> *Nazareth is forlorn. . . . Jericho the accursed lies a moldering ruin today, even as Joshua's miracle left it more than three thousand years ago;* Bethlehem and Bethany, in their poverty and their humiliation, have nothing about them now to remind one that they once knew the high honor of the Savior's presence; the hallowed spot where the shepherds watched their flocks by night, and where the angels sang, "Peace on earth, good will to men," *is untenanted by any living creature.* . . . Bethsaida and Chorzin have vanished from the earth, and the "desert places" round about them, where thousands of men once listened to the Savior's voice and ate the miraculous bread, sleep in the hush of a *solitude that is inhabited only by birds of prey and skulking foxes.* *[134]

"Palestine sits in sackcloth and ashes. . . . desolate and unlovely . . . ," Twain

b

Exhibit A. Dershowitz quotes paragraphs from Twain as continuous text (a, *top*) just as Peters quotes them as continuous text (b, *above*). But in Twain's book (1996 edition)—which Dershowitz claims to have independently consulted—they are separated by eighty-seven pages (c, *opposite page*). Notice also that in Dershowitz, just as in Peters, the last sentence of the first paragraph reads, "We never saw a human being on the whole route." The actual sentence in Twain continues, "We never saw a human being on the whole route, much less lawless hordes of Bedouins."

found Saladin Lord of Palestine, the Christian chivalry strewn in heaps upon the field, and the King of Jerusalem, the Grand Master of the Templars, and Raynauld of Chatillon, captives in the Sultan's tent. Saladin treated two of the prisoners with princely courtesy, and ordered refreshments to be set before them. When the King handed an iced Sherbet to Chatillon, the Sultan said, "It is thou that givest it to him, not I." He remembered his oath, and slaughtered the hapless Knight of Chatillon with his own hand.

It was hard to realize that this silent plain had once resounded with martial music and trembled to the tramp of armed men. It was hard to people this solitude with rushing columns of cavalry, and stir its torpid pulses with the shouts of victors, the shrieks of the wounded, and the flash of banner and steel above the surging billows of war. A desolation is here that not even imagination can grace with the pomp of life and action.

We reached Tabor safely, and considerably in advance of that old iron-clad swindle of a guard. We never saw a human being on the whole route, much less lawless hordes of Bedouins. Tabor stands solitary and alone, a giant sentinel above the Plain of Esdraelon. It rises some fourteen hundred feet above the surrounding level, a green, wooden cone, symmetrical and full of grace—a prominent landmark, and one that is exceedingly pleasant to eyes surfeited with the repulsive monotony of desert Syria. We climbed the steep path to its summit, through breezy glades of thorn and oak. The view presented from its highest peak was almost beautiful. Below, was the broad, level plain of Esdraelon, checkered with fields like a chess-board, and full as smooth and level, seemingly; dotted about its borders with white, compact villages, and faintly penciled, far and near, with the curving lines of roads and trails. When it is robed in the fresh verdure of spring, it must form a charming picture, even by itself. Skirting its southern border rises "Little Hermon," over whose summit a glimpse of Gilboa is caught. Nain, famous for the raising of the widow's son, and Endor, as famous for the performances

hing desolation that surrounds them like much to see the fringes of the nd Shechem, Esdraelon, Ajalon and ut even then these spots would seem vide intervals in the waste of a limit-

loth and ashes. Over it broods the withered its fields and fettered its en- nd Gomorrah reared their domes and towers, that solemn sea now floods the plain, in whose bitter waters no living thing exists—over whose waveless surface the blistering air hangs motionless and dead—about whose borders nothing grows but weeds, and scattering tufts of cane, and that treacherous fruit that promises refreshment to parching lips, but turns to ashes at the touch. Nazareth is forlorn; about that ford of Jordan where the hosts of Israel entered the Promised Land with songs of rejoicing, one finds only a squalid camp of fantastic Bedouins of the desert; Jericho the accursed, lies a moldering ruin, to-day, even as Joshua's miracle left it more than three thousand years ago; Bethlehem and Bethany, in their poverty and their humiliation, have nothing about them now to remind one that they once knew the high honor of the Saviour's presence; the hallowed spot where the shepherds watched their flocks by night, and where the angels sang Peace on earth, good will to men, is untenanted by any living

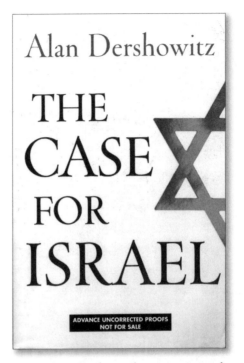

Exhibit B. Cover from advance page proofs
for Alan Dershowitz's *The Case for Israel*.

mentioned, the scholarly consensus is that her demographic findings
were sheer fraud: Palestine was "underpopulated" only by "modern
standards . . . where rapid population growth is endemic"; there is no
evidence of any significant Arab internal migration in Palestine due to
Zionist enterprise; there is no evidence of any significant Arab immigration into Palestine during the Ottoman or British Mandate period.
Peters managed to "prove" her thesis only by mangling documents and
falsifying numbers.[6] Returning to *The Case for Israel*, Dershowitz writes
that Palestine was "vastly underpopulated" when the Zionist settlers
came (p. 23), while in a publicity interview for the book, he flatly stated

6. Justin McCarthy, *The Population of Palestine* (New York, 1990) ("underpopulated" and "modern standards" at p. 16). McCarthy deems Peters's book "demographically worthless" (pp. 40–41n20). His study is generally considered the most authoritative; for other major studies directly contradicting Peters's demographic claims, see
sources cited in Finkelstein, *Image and Reality*, pp. 214 n2 and 235–36n26. On the other
hand, Dershowitz assesses *From Time Immemorial* as containing "some overstatement"
(*Boston Globe*) but still a "serious piece of scholarship" (*Democracy Now!*).

port city of Jaffa, from whence Jonah began his fateful journey, had become, by the middle of the 18ᵗʰ century, a town populated by Turks, Arabs, Greeks, Armenians and others. A Christian historian has reported that several villages throughout Palestine "are populated wholly by settlers from other portions of the Turkish Empire within the nineteenth century. There are villages of Bosnians, Druzes, Circaesian and Egyptians."[14] The 1911 edition of the Encyclopedia Britannica described the population of Palestine as comprising widely differing "ethnological" groups, speaking "no less than fifty languages." It was daunting therefore to "write concisely" about "the ethnology of Palestine", especially following the influx of population from Egypt "which still persists in the villages." Among the other ethnic groups in Palestine at the end of the 19ᵗʰ and beginning of the 20ᵗʰ century – in addition to Arabs and Jews—were Kurds, German Templars, Persians, Sudanese, Algerians, Samaritans, Tatars, Motanilas, Georgians, and many people of mixed ethnicities.

Prior to the arrival of the European Jews at the beginning of the 1880's, the number of Arabs, particularly in the part of Palestine that was to be partitioned into a Jewish state, was small and shrinking. An 1857 communiqué from the British Consul in Jerusalem reported that "the country is in a considerable degree empty of inhabitants and therefore its greatest need is that of a body of population."[15] It also noted that although the Arabs tend to leave and not return, the Jewish population was more stable: "[W]e have Jews who have traveled to the United States and Australia" and "instead of remaining there, do return hither."[16] Four years later, it was reported that "depopulation is even now advancing,"[17] And four years after that, it was noted that in certain parts of the country "land is going out of cultivation and whole villages are rapidly disappearing...and the stationary population extirpated."[18]

Other historians, demographers and travelers described the Arab population as "decreasing,"[19] and the land as "thinly populated,"[20] "unoccupied,"[21], "uninhabited"[22], and "almost abandoned now." The Plain of

---

[14] Parks, Whose Land?, p. 212
[15] James Finn to the Earl of Clarendon, September 15, 1857, quoted in A. H. Hyamson ed, The British Consulate in Jerusalem (London 1939-41, Vol UNREADABLE
[16] Id at _____
[17] J.B. Forsyth, A Few Months in the East (Quebec, 1861), p. 188.
[18] H.B. Tristram, The Land of Israel: A Journal of Travels in Palestine (London 1865), p. 490.
[19] Holly Beth: cite sources on pp. 160, 485, 486, fns 141-145
[20] ???
[21] ???
[22] ???

Exhibit C. "Holly Beth: cite sources on pp. . . . ."

Muslim-Arab population. It is noteworthy, that the area that was portioned for a Jewish state that now contains several million people, was then populated by a total of fewer than 200,000 people, a significant number of whom may already have been Jewish, near the very beginning of the first Aliya.[31]

Some of these Muslims—the numbers are uncertain—had been attracted to the new areas of Jewish settlement by the jobs made available by Jewish immigration and cultivation of land. A study of the Jewish settlement of Rishon L'Tzion, first established in 1882, showed that the 40 Jewish families that settled there had attracted "more than 400 Arab families," many of which were Bedouin and Egyptian. These families moved into areas around the Jewish settlement and formed a new Arab village on the site of "a forsaken ruin."[32] The report observed a similar pattern with regard to other settlements and villages. This magnet phenomenon preceded the Turkish census of 1893, and suggests that before the first Aliya began, the Muslim-Arab population of what eventually became the Jewish area under the partition was even smaller than the 56,000 recorded by that census.

Although it is impossible to reconstruct with any confidence the precise number of Arab-Muslim-Palestinians who had lived for generations in what eventually became the Jewish area under the partition, the number is far below that claimed by Palestinian polemicists. The maximum possible number is well under 100,000. The likely figure of Muslim-Palestinians with deep roots and long-term connections to the area—those who claim to descend from people who have lived there since time immemorial—is considerably less than that. According to one historian "at least 25% of [the Muslims who lived in all of Palestine in 1882] were newcomers or descendants of those who arrived after" the Egyptian conquest of 1831.[33] In addition to the Egyptian influx, there was a considerable immigration of Turks, Greeks and Algerians. Moreover, many of the Palestinian Muslims who were attracted to Western Palestine between 1882 and 1893 came from Eastern Palestine (the West and East Banks of the Jordan). Combining these figures leads to a likely conclusion that no more than 50,000 Palestinian Muslims (and probably fewer) had deep roots in the area of Jewish settlement. Some of these remained in the area even after Israel became a state

---

[31] Jean Peters, in her book FROM TIME IMMEMORIAL, argues that the Jews actually constituted a majority of the population in that by the end of the 19th century, because Arab population figures were inflated. Peters at p. 251, and Jewish figures were deflated because only Ottoman subjects were counted in the official census.
[32] A. Druyanow [cite p. 527]
[33] Ernest Frankenstein, JUSTICE FOR MY PEOPLE (London, 1943) p. 127.

Exhibit D. "A. Druyanow [cite p. 527]"

that "[a]lmost nobody lived there."[7] So where did all those Arabs in the areas settled by Jews come from? According to Dershowitz, "many of the Palestinian Muslims who were attracted to western Palestine between 1882 and 1893 came from eastern Palestine (the West and East Banks of the Jordan)," and "[t]he number of Muslims who lived in the Jewish areas grew dramatically after the Jewish settlements blossomed" (p. 28). From these findings he reaches the "inescapable" conclusions, "beyond reasonable dispute," that "[a]mong the few [Palestinian refugees] who actually left more than half a century ago and who are still alive, many lived in Israel for only a few years"; that "an Arab was counted as a refugee if he moved just a few miles from one part of Palestine to another—even if he *returned* to the village in which he had previously lived and in which his family still lived"; that "the number of Palestinians with deep roots in the areas of Jewish settlement—although impossible to estimate with confidence—constitutes a tiny fraction of the more than a million Palestinian Arabs who now live in Israel"; and that "the myth of displacement by the European Jewish refugees of a large, stable, long-term Muslim population that had lived in that part of Palestine for centuries is demonstrably false" (pp. 28, 86, 239; Dershowitz's emphasis). Does this sound like someone who "fundamentally disagree[s]" (*Forward*, 3 October 2003) with Peters's fraudulent demographics?

To prove the claim that those calling themselves Palestinian refugees had only recently settled in Palestine, Dershowitz provides this sensational piece of evidence:

> The United Nations, recognizing that many of the refugees had not lived for long in the villages they left, made a remarkable decision to change the definition of refugee—*only* for purposes of defining who is an *Arab* refugee *from Israel*—to include any Arab who had lived in Israel for *two years* before leaving. (p. 86; Dershowitz's emphases)

Yet the only source Dershowitz cites for this allegation, which he keeps repeating (pp. 5, 87, 239), fails to support, or even imply, the claim that many refugees from the 1948 war had only recently settled in Palestine.[8] In fact, the import of the U.N. definition is exactly the reverse of what Dershowitz alleges. The definition reads: "A Palestinian refugee is a person whose normal residence was Palestine for a minimum of two

7. MSNBC, "The Abrams Report" (Transcript #093000cb.464) (30 September 2003).
8. His citation is to Ruth Lapidoth, "Legal Aspects of the Palestinian Refugee Question" (1 September 2002), www.jcpa.org/jl/vp485.htm.

years preceding the conflict in 1948." Contrary to Dershowitz's insin-
uation, the purpose of this definition was to put a *limit* on who quali-
fied as a Palestinian refugee, *excluding seasonal workers from neighboring Arab states*.[9] That Dershowitz should get things upside down
won't, at this point, come as much of a surprise. What's more interest-
ing is the real, unacknowledged source of his big find. Turning to *From
Time Immemorial*, we read this revelation of Peters:

> [W]hile I was examining United Nations data from 1948 onward, a seem-
> ingly casual alteration of the definition of what constitutes an Arab
> "refugee" from Israel caught my attention. . . . In the case of the *Arab*
> refugees, . . . the definition had been broadened to include as "refugees"
> any persons who had been in "Palestine" for only *two years* before Israel's
> statehood in 1948. (p. 4; Peters's emphases)

But, of course, Dershowitz did "not in any way rely" (p. 246n31) on
Peters for his demographic argument. Dershowitz asserts that his detrac-
tors have failed to come up with a single example in which he directly
cites from another source without attribution. Yet is this not an incontrovertible example that he has not only done so, but—not less impor-
tantly—in the process has presented demonstrably false statements from
a discredited book?

Finally, in a genuine tour de force, he even manages to outfalsify
Peters. For instance, to document that "[e]ven many Arab intellectuals
acknowledge the mythical nature" of an indigenous Palestinian Arab
population, Dershowitz cites this statement of "Palestinian leader
Musa Alami" from Peters: "The people are in great need of a 'myth' to
fill their consciousness and imagination" (p. 28). Not even Peters pretends, however, that Alami meant in this statement that Palestinians
had fabricated their place of origin (compare Peters, pp. 13–14). Dershowitz just made it up. Amid these falsifications from—*and of*—
Peters, he deplores the "mendacious rewriting of . . . the demographic
history of the Arabs of Palestine" to deny Jewish rights there, and
admonishes those who "play games with the demographics in order to
support . . . agenda-driven conclusions" (pp. 7, 68).

To defend himself against the allegation that he lifted from Peters,
Dershowitz resorted to other means as well. He claimed that "[t]he
experts I consulted—real experts, with vast experience and no ideological ax to grind—know of no case in which a student or faculty member
was ever disciplined for doing what I did" (*The Nation*, 15 December

9. Information from United Nations Relief and Works Agency (UNRWA) Liaison
Office, New York.

2003). The one and only expert he named, however, is James Freedman, former president of Dartmouth College and of the American Academy of Arts and Sciences. No doubt his are impressive credentials, although Freedman might have made a more compelling independent witness if he weren't—as the *Boston Globe* reports—one of Dershowitz's closest confidants ("'Dershy,' as Freedman calls his old friend Alan Dershowitz"); if he weren't an apologist for Israel, even lobbying Brandeis University (where he is a trustee) to grant Ariel Sharon an honorary degree (for his humanitarian work?); and if he didn't mangle *The Chicago Manual of Style*'s meaning when citing it in Dershowitz's defense.[10]

Faced with some of the derelictions in *The Case for Israel*, one doesn't know whether to laugh or cry. The book was published in August 2003. Footnote citations date from as late as June 2003, which means that work on the manuscript continued until shortly before publication. By Dershowitz's own admission, *The Case for Israel* is not a scholarly tome replete with minutiae, but rather a work of "advocacy" organized into thirty-two very short, simple chapters. In September 2003—just one month after the book's publication—this writer debated Dershowitz on Amy Goodman's nationally syndicated program *Democracy Now!* The debate was in two parts, only one of which has been broadcast.

In the first part, Dershowitz's misattribution of the locution *turnspeak* came up. This is a verbatim transcription of the segment:

Finkelstein: In Joan Peters's book *From Time Immemorial* she coins a phrase. The phrase is *turnspeak*.[11] And she says

Dershowitz: and she borrows it from

Finkelstein: no

Dershowitz: she borrows it

Finkelstein: sir

Dershowitz: from, from, um, who is it?

Finkelstein: sir, I'm sorry

Dershowitz: oh, she attributes it and borrows it

10. Patrick Healy, "To Him, Leading Is Academic: Ailing Ex–Dartmouth Chief Wants College Presidents to Speak Up," *Boston Globe* (24 January 2003) ("Dershy" and honorary degree); *Harvard Crimson* (29 September 2003) (Freedman citing *Chicago Manual*); *The Nation* (27 October 2003) (Cockburn demonstrating misuse of *Manual*). To deflect exposure of his plagiarism, Dershowitz subsequently conjured up yet new lies; see www.NormanFinkelstein.com ("Dershowitz Exposed Yet Again—The Critique of Pure Cant").

11. Peters used this term in *From Time Immemorial* to denote the propagandistic inversion of facts (pp. 174, 402).

Finkelstein: sir, I'm sorry

Dershowitz: *from someone else. It's not her phrase.*

Finkelstein: She coins the phrase. You see, you don't know what you're talking about, and that's pretty terrible.

Dershowitz: It's not her phrase.

Finkelstein: She coins a phrase *turnspeak,* and she says that she is using it as a play off of George Orwell, who, as all listeners know, used the phrase *newspeak.*

Dershowitz: Right.

Finkelstein: And she coined her own phrase *turnspeak.* You go to Mr. Dershowitz's book, he got so confused in his massive borrowings from Joan Peters, that on two occasions, I'll cite them for those who have a copy of the book, on page 57, and on page 153 he uses the phrase—quote—George Orwell's *turnspeak.*

Dershowitz: Uh-huh.

Finkelstein: *Turnspeak* is not Orwell, Mr. Dershowitz. You're the Felix Frankfurter chair at Harvard.

Dershowitz: Yes

Finkelstein: You must know that Orwell would never use such a clunky phrase as *turnspeak.*

Dershowitz: I like it. I think it's a helluva phrase.

Finkelstein: Well, maybe you might like it

Dershowitz: I do.

Finkelstein: and evidently Joan Peters liked it, but George Orwell never heard of it.

The point is not simply that *The Case for Israel* confounds Peters with Orwell. Look closely at the phrases of Dershowitz placed in italics. He did not even know to whom the locution *turnspeak* was repeatedly ascribed in *The Case for Israel.* (Exhibit E, opposite.) *He did not even know Orwell.* It couldn't be that he forgot a name from his research, unlikely as that would anyhow be just a month after the book's publication and regarding a name highlighted on more than one occasion in the book. An author might forget a more or less obscure name cited from the source material, but how likely is it that an author would forget a prominent-name error *of his or her own creation?* Someone repeatedly writing in a book "Aristotle's 'Shazaam!'" would almost certainly remember associating *Shazaam!* with Aristotle. How did Dershowitz not remember Orwell? Were this not perplexing enough, in an otherwise minatory letter addressed to New Press when it was considering publication of *Beyond Chutzpah,* Dershowitz conceded:

for the murder of European Jewry, its official leadership was certainly far from blameless in the Holocaust. It actively supported Hitler's final solution as well as Nazi victory over the Americans and their Allies. The grand mufti of Jerusalem was personally responsible for the concentration camp slaughter of thousands of Jews. In one instance, when he learned that the Hungarian government was planning to allow thousands of children to escape from the Nazis, he intervened with Eichmann and demanded they reverse the plan. They did and the children were sent to the death camps.[13] The mufti also supported the Nazis militarily, offering his Arab Legion to fight against the Allies, so as to counteract the Jewish Brigade, which was fighting on the side of the Allies.[14]

In light of the close association between the Palestinian leadership and Nazism throughout the 1930s and 1940s, it is ironic that many pro-Palestinian groups have chosen the swastika as the symbol with which to attack Israel. Just as the Nazis called the Jews *communists* and Stalin called the Jews *fascists,* many Palestinians and their supporters—both on the extreme right and the extreme left—now use the word "Nazi" to characterize Israel, the Jews, and Zionism. The Jews have again been caught between the black and the red, as one scholar put it. They are back in the uncomfortable position once again, as the extreme left and the extreme right both seek to demonize the Jewish state by falsely comparing it to an ideology that practiced genocide against the Jewish people—a genocide widely supported and assisted by Palestinian leaders.

The Palestinian police chief, Ghazi Jabali, has compared Israel's first prime minister, the Socialist David Ben-Gurion, to the evil monster against whom he fought: "There is no difference between Hitler and Ben Gurion."[15] On today's college campuses, you can often hear Israel's prime minister compared to Hitler with the following chant: "Sharon and Hitler—just the same—the only difference is the name." No one ever compares Sharon to, say, Pinochet, or even Stalin. It is always Hitler and Nazism. Signs juxtaposing the Star of David and the swastika are commonplace. These sign-carriers are, of course, deliberately using George Orwell's "turnspeak" by trying to associate the Star of David with the swastika, knowing how deeply offensive the swastika is to Jews.

Some Jewish groups have called me over the years and asked me to try to ban the use of the swastika in attacks on Israel. Since I am opposed to censorship, I have always urged them to use the Palestinian attempt to equate Israel with Nazism as an educational opportunity to remind the world of the widespread Palestinian support for Nazism and of the fact that Nazi war criminals were given asylum in Egypt and helped the Egyptian government in its attacks against Israeli civilian targets. If Palestinian supporters insist on using the swastika, they certainly cannot complain when this symbol is turned against them to remind the world of

ation in 1948, the targeting of 48, 1967, and 1973 wars, and illed thousands of Israeli, Jewized as attempted genocide. Israel's efforts to protect its citizens from these mass murders by attacking Arab military targets can only be labeled as genocide by a bigot willing to engage in Orwellian turnspeak against a people that was truly victimized by the worst form of genocide.

Perhaps nothing more can be expected of Professor Boyle, who has long been a one-sided propagandist for Palestinian terrorism, but more is certainly expected of a Nobel Prize–winning author such as Jose Saramago, who recently characterized Israeli efforts to defend its citizens against terrorism as "a crime comparable to Auschwitz." When Saramago was pressed about "where . . . the gas chambers" are, he responded, "Not here

Exhibit E. ". . . from, from, um, who is it?"

I did, mistakenly believe that the <u>word</u> "turnspeak" had come from Huxley. I confused turnspeak with newspeak. (underscore is Dershowitz's)[12]

From Huxley? Leaving aside that Dershowitz has now managed the trifecta blunder of confusing Peters with Orwell and Orwell with Aldous Huxley,[13] it seems he hasn't a clue of his book's content.

Alan Dershowitz lifted material from a hoax in a book that has become an influential best seller. To date, Dershowitz's employers and colleagues have either remained silent or rallied behind him. A spokesman for Dean Elena Kagan of Harvard Law School reported in December 2004 that former Harvard president Derek Bok, "a scholar of unquestioned integrity," had looked into the charges against Dershowitz and "found that no plagiarism had occurred." The matter was "closed."[14]

Yet what is one to make of the evidence assembled in this appendix? Harvard University's own manual states that "plagiarism is passing off a source's information, ideas, or words as your own by omitting to cite them" (*Writing with Sources: A Guide for Harvard Students*, 1995, Section 3.1). The same source also states that "when quoting or citing a passage you found quoted or cited by another scholar, and you haven't actually read the original source, cite the passage as 'quoted in' or 'cited in' that scholar both to credit that person for finding the quoted passage or cited text, and to protect yurself in case he or she has misquoted or misrepresented" (ibid., Section 2.1). The unambiguous evidence in this appendix shows that Dershowitz directly appropriates a crucial idea from Peters—which he keeps repeating and which is demonstrably false—without referencing her. Equally to the point, Kagan and others who have risen to Dershowitz's defense have without exception done so on the basis of his insistence that he consulted the original texts cited in *The Case for Israel*. Yet not one of them has refuted the overwhelming evidence in this appendix—perhaps unavailable to them—that Dershowitz in fact repeatedly copied information directly from *Time Immemorial*.

12. Letter from Alan Dershowitz to Colin Robinson dated 30 April 2004 and marked "Confidential—Not for Publication." Dershowitz CC'd a copy of this letter to a research assistant of this writer, from which the sentence is quoted.

13. Dershowitz's general level of culture gives pause. For example, the *New York Times Sunday Book Review* ran a critical notice of one of his books by the editor of the now defunct magazine *Lingua Franca*. In a subsequent letter to the *Times*, Dershowitz criticized the newspaper for assigning the review to the "editor of a French magazine" (21 December 2001).

14. Email from Michael Armini, Director of Communications, Harvard Law School, to Norman G. Finkelstein (22 December 2004).

History of the Israel-Palestine Conflict

Defense lawyers often develop what I call DLBS—defense lawyers' blind spot. They refuse to see the evidence of their client's guilt, even when it is staring them in the eye.

Alan M. Dershowitz, *Letters to a Young Lawyer*

A. ROOTS OF CONFLICT, 1880–1947

Topic	The Case for Israel	What the Evidence Actually Shows
1. WHAT WAS ZIONISM'S RELATIONSHIP TO EUROPEAN IMPERIALISM?	*Those who absurdly claim that the Jewish refugees who immigrated to Palestine in the last decades of the nineteenth century were the "tools" of European imperialism must answer the following question: For whom were these socialists and idealists working? . . . They came to Palestine without any of the weapons of imperialism. They brought with them few guns or other means of conquest. Their tools were rakes and hoes. (p. 14; emphasis in original)* SOURCES: None	From its inception under Theodor Herzl and across its political spectrum, Zionism aligned itself with European imperialism. According to historian Yosef Gorny, for example, Zionist leader Chaim Weizmann, who "had the greatest impact on the formulation of Zionist policy" after Herzl, acted "above all, on the assumption that the alliance with Great Britain was the sole external guarantee for the achievement of Zionist goals. . . . Hence Weizmann's untiring efforts to persuade the British Government of the identity of interests between the national goals of the two peoples. In this respect there was a consensus from the first within the Zionist movement, encompassing all sectors." Throughout his tenure Weizmann sought "to persuade the British leaders that a large Jewish community in Palestine would effectively further British imperialist interests in the Middle East and elsewhere," while his successor, socialist-Zionist David Ben-Gurion, likewise shaped policy "in accordance with the interests of the British Empire."[1] And the "tools" of the Zionist settlers included rather more than farm implements. Sociologist Uri Ben-Eliezer reports that among Jewish settlers, the "worker-fighter was . . . the archetypal figure . . . conquer[ing] the land with a popular, militia-like army which would complete the work of settlement," while kibbutzniks aspired to and sanctified the "ideal and perfect fusion between the plow and the rifle."[2]
2. WHAT DID PALESTINIANS WANT?	*(a) Between 1880 and 1967, virtually no Arab or Palestinian spokesperson called for a Palestinian state. Instead they wanted*	From the onset of the British mandate to the present, virtually all Palestinian leaders have called for the creation of an independent Arab state in Palestine. Consider Dershowitz's own reference. In 1936 a British royal commission chaired by Lord William Robert Peel was charged with ascertaining the

the area that the Romans had designated as Palestine to be merged into Syria or Jordan. As Auni Bey Abdul-Hati [sic—Abdelhadi], a prominent Palestinian leader, told the Peel Commission in 1937, "There is no such country.... Palestine is a term the Zionists invented.... Our country was for centuries part of Syria." (p. 7) causes of the Palestine conflict and means for resolving it. Regarding the aspirations of Palestinian Arabs, its final report stated that "[t]he overriding desire of the Arab leaders ... was ... national independence" and that "[i]t was only to be expected that Palestinian Arabs should ... envy and seek to emulate their successful fellow-nationalists in those countries just across their northern and southern borders. For now of all the Arab peoples in the Middle East they were the only people, except the people of Trans-Jordan, who had not attained or were not soon to attain full national freedom: and ... the Government of Trans-Jordan had long been recognized as an 'independent government.'"[3]

(b) The Peel Commission implicitly recognized that it was not so much that the Arabs wanted self-determination as that they did not want the Jews to have self-determination or sovereignty over the land the Jews themselves had cultivated and in which they were a majority. After all, the Palestinians wanted to be part of Syria and be ruled over by a distant monarch. (p. 51)

SOURCES:
(a) None
(b) None

1. Yosef Gorny, *Zionism and the Arabs, 1882–1948: A Study of Ideology* (Oxford, 1987), pp. 108, 207, 260; cf. pp. 114, 227, 234, 255. See also Simha Flapan, *Zionism and the Palestinians* (London, 1979), esp. pp. 19, 20, 22, 25, 28, 32–33, 55, 79, 131, 133, 134, 156, 168.
2. Uri Ben-Eliezer, *The Making of Israeli Militarism* (Bloomington, Ind., 1998), pp. 62, 89.
3. *Palestine Royal Commission Report* (London, 1937), pp. 76, 94.

Topic	The Case for Israel	What the Evidence Actually Shows
3. WHAT WAS THE ROOT CAUSE OF THE PALESTINE CONFLICT?	[The British] *blamed the murders* [of Jews] *on "racial animosity on the part of the Arabs." (p. 43)* SOURCES: *Peel Report*, p. 68.	The British attributed Arab anti-Jewish animus to the Jewish claim over Palestine, which denied Arabs an independent state, and to Arab fear of being subjugated in an eventual Jewish state. The Peel Report affirmatively quoted a prior inquiry headed by Sir Thomas Haycraft that "the root of the trouble . . . was the Arab fear of a steady increase of Jewish immigration," which would ultimately tend to their political and economic subjection." It went on to affirmatively quote a second inquiry headed by Sir Walter Shaw that "[t]here can . . . be no doubt that racial animosity on the part of the Arabs, *consequent upon the disappointment of their political and national aspirations and fear for their economic future*, was the fundamental cause" of hostilities; and it then restated that the Shaw Report "attributed . . . the main cause of the outbreak to Arab antagonism to the National Home, as being on the one hand an obstacle to the attainment of their national independence and as tending, on the other hand, . . . to lead to their economic and political subjection." Dershowitz has lifted the phrase *racial animosity* from the crucial context underlining that the root cause of the conflict was *not racial*. The Peel Commission itself similarly concluded that the "underlying causes" of Arab-Jewish hostilities were, "first, the desire of the Arabs for national independence; secondly, their antagonism to the establishment of the Jewish National Home in Palestine, quickened by their fear of Jewish domination." *Explicitly repudiating the "racial" explanation Dershowitz ascribes to it*, the Peel Report stated: "Nor is the conflict in its essence an interracial conflict, arising from any old instinctive antipathy of Arabs towards Jews. There was little or no friction . . . between Arab and Jew in the rest of the Arab world until the strife in Palestine engendered it. And there has been precisely the same political trouble in Iraq, Syria and Egypt—agitation, rebellion and bloodshed—where there are no 'National Homes.' Quite obviously, then, the problem of Palestine is political. It is, as elsewhere, the problem of insurgent nationalism. The only difference is that in Palestine Arab nationalism is inextricably interwoven with antagonism to

the Jews. And the reasons for that, it is worth repeating, are equally obvious. In the first place, the establishment of the National Home [for Jews] involved at the outset a blank negation of the rights implied in the principle of national self-government. Secondly, it soon proved to be not merely an obstacle to the development of national self-government, but apparently the only serious obstacle. Thirdly, as the Home has grown, the fear has grown with it that, if and when self-government is conceded, it may not be national in the Arab sense, but government by a Jewish majority. That is why it is difficult to be an Arab patriot and not to hate the Jews."[4]

Dershowitz scrupulously omits a central conclusion of Morris and among the most notable of his research findings: the "transfer idea"—including outright expulsion—was "one of the main currents in Zionist ideology from the movement's inception." Morris goes on to say, and copiously document, in *Righteous Victims* that, "[f]or many Zionists, beginning with Herzl, the only realistic solution lay in transfer. From 1880 to 1920, some entertained the prospect of Jews and Arabs coexisting in peace. But increasingly after 1920, and more emphatically after 1929, for the vast majority a denouement of conflict appeared inescapable. Following the outbreak of 1936, no mainstream leader was able to conceive of future coexistence and peace without a clear physical separation between the two peoples—achievable only by way of transfer and expulsion."[5]

4. WHAT DID ZIONISTS INTEND TO DO WITH THE INDIGENOUS POPULATION?	(a) The Second Aliyah, although largely inspired by Zionist ideology, was also an immigration from persecution, and it contemplated cooperation with local Muslims to create better lives for all residents of Palestine. (p. 30) (b) Many, although not all, of the Jewish refugees sought to establish good relations with their Arab neighbors. (p. 30; cf. pp. 39–40, where Dershowitz juxtaposes "The goal of the Arab leadership . . . to transfer the Jews of Palestine out of their historic home and to make all of Palestine empty of

4. Ibid., pp. 51, 68, 70, 131, 363 (emphasis added); cf. pp. 110, 136.
5. Benny Morris, *Righteous Victims: A History of the Zionist-Arab Conflict, 1881–1999* (New York, 1999), p. 139.

Topic	The Case for Israel	What the Evidence Actually Shows
4. WHAT DID ZIONISTS INTEND TO DO WITH THE INDIGENOUS POPULATION? *(continued)*	Jews" against "Jewish leaders" who "were willing to make painful compromises as long as they could have a Jewish homeland in those areas of Palestine in which they were a majority.") SOURCES: (a) None (b) [Benny Morris, *Righteous Victims* (New York: 2001)], pp. 57–59.	

B. THE FIRST ARAB-ISRAELI WAR (1947–1949) AND ITS AFTERMATH

Topic	The Case for Israel	What the Evidence Actually Shows
1. WHY DID THE ZIONISTS WIN THE 1948 WAR?	At great cost in human life . . . the ragtag Israeli army defeated the invading Arab armies and the Palestinian attackers. They won in large part because, as Morris argues, the stakes were much greater for them. They had the "morale-boosting stimulus" of fighting for their "own home and fields. . . ." (p. 76) SOURCES: Morris[, *Righteous Victims*], p. 233 [*sic*—p. 223].	Morris doesn't state that the Zionist army prevailed "in large part" because more was at stake for them. He lists this as a contributory factor. Like all serious historians of the war, Morris regards as decisive Israel's military preponderance: "The Haganah enjoyed superiority in both quality and quantity of manpower, unity of command, and relatively short lines of communication. . . . By and large the Haganah had better trained, more capable commanders." "The truth," Morris observed in another of his studies, "is that the stronger side won. . . . [I]t was superior Jewish firepower, manpower, organization and command and control that determined the outcome of battle."[76]

2. WHAT HAPPENED AT ETZION BLOC AND DEIR YASSIN?

(1) ETZION BLOC

While the Arab armies tried to kill Jewish civilians and did in fact massacre many who tried to escape, the Israeli army allowed Arab civilians to flee to Arab-controlled areas. For example, when the Arab Legion's Sixth Battalion conquered Kfar Etzion, they left no Jewish refugees. The villagers surrendered and walked, hands in the air, into the center of the compound. Morris reports that the Arab soldiers simply "proceeded to mow them down." The soldiers massacred 120 Jews; 21 of them were women. (p. 79)

SOURCES: Morris], *Righteous Victims*], p. 214.

Dershowitz uses this massacre to illustrate the Arab military's genocidal intent. However, he significantly misrepresents what Morris writes in *Righteous Victims*. The thrust of what Morris reports is this: Etzion Bloc—four Jewish settlements north of Hebron—was defended by four hundred men and one hundred women (the children had been evacuated). After Bloc fighters harassed and ambushed Arab traffic along a strategic route, an Arab Legion force backed by hundreds of local villagers attacked the Bloc, which had been under intermittent siege since January, on May 4 and again on May 12. When Legion forces finally broke into the main settlement of Kfar Etzion, "[v]illagers shouting 'Deir Yassin, Deir Yassin' poured through the breach. The remaining defenders laid down their weapons and walked, hands in the air, into the center of the compound. There, according to one of the few survivors, the villagers (and perhaps some legionnaires as well) proceeded to mow them down. In all about 120 defenders, 21 of them women, died that day. Of the 4 survivors, 3 were saved by Arabs. The remaining three kibbutzim held on until the morning of May 14, but their position was hopeless. The Haganah general staff gave them permission to surrender, and all the defenders and settlers, except four more who were murdered by their captors, were trucked off to a Legion prison camp. . . . About 350 of the bloc's defenders ended up in captivity."[7] In another study, *The Road to Jerusalem*, Morris reports the testimony of a Legion officer (quoted in an official Israeli history) regarding Kfar Etzion that "there was no formal organized [Jewish] surrender; that after some defenders had surrendered others continued to fire at the Arabs; that villagers indeed massacred surrendering Jews; that Legionnaires killed a number of villagers and two Legionnaires

6. Ibid., p. 223; Benny Morris, *1948 and After*, rev. and expanded ed. (Oxford, 1994), pp. 14–15.
7. Morris, *Righteous Victims*, p. 214.

Topic	The Case for Israel	What the Evidence Actually Shows
2. WHAT HAPPENED AT ETZION BLOC AND DEIR YASSIN? **(I) ETZION BLOC** (*continued*)		were badly wounded defending three Jewish prisoners who were then taken away by villagers and murdered"; as well as the testimony of a Jewish doctor that "the Legion troops (officers and men) behaved very well" following the surrender of the other Etzion Bloc settlements.[8] Thus, a massacre did in fact occur at Kfar Etzion but, *contrary to Dershowitz's mangling of Morris*, the Jewish victims weren't "civilians" or "villagers" but surrendering combatants; the massacre was committed not by an Arab army but Arab villagers proclaiming revenge for Deir Yassin; and, when combatants from the three other Etzion Bloc settlements surrendered without resistance, they were taken prisoner. In another episode reported by Morris, after the supposedly genocidal Arab Legion took over East Jerusalem, "its ultra-orthodox inhabitants and 300-odd Haganah defenders raised the white flag. The Haganah men went off to a prisoner-of-war camp in Transjordan and the 1,500 inhabitants were shepherded and transferred, under Red Cross supervision, to Jewish West Jerusalem."[9]
(II) DEIR YASSIN	*On April 9, 1948, paramilitary units fought a difficult battle for control of Deir Yassin, an important Arab village on the way to Jerusalem. The battle was fierce, with Etzel and Lechi forces losing more than a quarter of their fighters. The Jewish fighters were pinned down by sniper fire and threw grenades through the windows of many of the houses from which the snipers were firing. Most of the villagers eventually*	"The fighting continued" is how Dershowitz summarizes this passage in Morris: "Deir Yassin is remembered not as a military operation, but rather for the atrocities committed by the IZL and LHI troops during and immediately after the drawn-out battle: Whole families were riddled with bullets and grenade fragments and buried when houses were blown up on top of them; men, women, and children were mowed down as they emerged from houses; individuals were taken aside and shot. At the end of the battle, groups of old men, women and children were trucked through West Jerusalem's streets in a kind of 'victory parade' and then dumped in (Arab) East Jerusalem. According to Jerusalem Shai commander Levy, . . . 'the conquest of the village was carried out with great cruelty. Whole families—women, old people, children—were killed, and there were piles of dead [in various places]. Some of the prisoners moved to places of incarceration,

including women and children, were murdered viciously by their captors.' In a report the following day, he added: 'LHI members tell of the barbaric behavior of the IZL toward the prisoners and the dead. They also relate that the IZL men raped a number of Arab girls and murdered them afterward (we don't know if this is true).' The Shai operative who visited the site hours after the event, Mordechai Gichon, reported . . . : 'Their [i.e., the IZL's?] commander says that the order was: to capture the adult males and to send the women and children to Motza. In the afternoon, . . . the order was changed and became to kill all the prisoners. . . . The adult males were taken to town in trucks and paraded in the city streets, then taken back to the site and killed with rifle and machine-gun fire. Before they were put on the trucks, the IZL and LHI men searched the women, men, and children [and] took from them all the jewelry and stole their money. The behavior toward them was especially barbaric."[10]

fled. An Etzel armored car with a loudspeaker demanded that the remaining villagers lay down their arms and leave their houses. Morris reports that "the truck got stuck in a ditch" and the message was not heard. The fighting continued, and when it was over, 100 to 110 Arabs were dead. (p. 81)

SOURCES:

Morris], Righteous Victims], p. 208.
Ibid., p. 209. [Endnote also states:] Original reports placed the number of dead as high as 254, but this number was, it turned out, an exaggeration.

3. WAS DEIR YASSIN AN ABERRATION?

(a) Deir Yassin stands out in the history of Arab-Jewish conflict in Palestine precisely because it was so unusual and so out of character for the Jews. (p. 82)

(b) Deir Yassin remained an isolated although tragic and inexcusable blemish on Israeli paramilitary actions in defense of its civilian population. (p. 82–83)

In Benny Morris's standard study, The Birth of the Palestinian Refugee Problem, which Dershowitz cites in other contexts, as well as in Morris's 1948 and After, it is reported that "Jewish atrocities" were "far more widespread than the old histories have let on." The Arab death toll in several of the numerous massacres Morris catalogs—Lydda (250 killed), Ad Dawayima (hundreds killed)—exceeded the total at Deir Yassin. A soldier eyewitness of the Ad Dawayima massacre in October 1948 described how Israeli forces, capturing the village "without a fight," initially "killed about 80 to 100 [male] Arabs, women and children. The children they killed by breaking their heads with sticks. There was not a house without dead." The remaining Arabs were then closed off in houses "without food and water," as the vil-

8. Benny Morris, The Road to Jerusalem (New York, 2003), pp. 135–40.
9. Ibid., p. 165.
10. Morris, Righteous Victims, p. 208.

Topic	The Case for Israel	What the Evidence Actually Shows
3. WAS DEIR YASSIN AN ABERRATION? *(continued)*	SOURCES: (a) None. (b) [Endnote states:] There were other episodes involving individuals and paramilitary groups in which claims of massacre were made, but none of the scale and seriousness of Deir Yassin.	lage was systematically razed: "One commander ordered a sapper to put two old women in a certain house . . . and to blow up the house with them. The sapper refused. . . . The commander then ordered his men to put in the old women and the evil deed was done. One soldier boasted that he had raped a woman and then shot her. One woman, with a newborn baby in her arms, was employed to clean the courtyard where the soldiers ate. She worked a day or two. In the end they shot her and her baby." The soldier eyewitness concluded that "cultured officers . . . had turned into base murderers and this not in the heat of battle . . . but out of a system of expulsion and destruction. The less Arabs remained—the better. This principle is the political motor for the expulsions and the atrocities." At a meeting of the leftist Mapam party in November 1948, Israeli atrocities in the Galilee were described as "Nazi acts." A Mapam leader remarked at another party meeting that "I couldn't sleep all night. . . . Jews too have committed Nazi acts." A respected Zionist official observed in his diary: "Where did they come by such a measure of cruelty, like Nazis? They [i.e., the Jewish troops] had learnt from them [the Nazis]. One officer told me that those who had 'excelled' had come from [the Nazi concentration/extermination] camps." In December a Mapam leader declared that "[m]any of us are losing their [human] image." One last observation of Morris merits quoting: "Two of the three major Arab massacres of Jews . . . were revenge attacks triggered by Jewish atrocities against Arabs. On the other hand, Jewish atrocities against Arabs . . . were generally unconnected to or lacked any previous, direct Arab provocation."[11] In a new edition of his study on the Palestinian refugees, Morris reported "20-odd cases of massacre" by Zionist forces during the war, frequent random killings of Palestinians, and "several dozen cases of rape, a crime viewed with particular horror in Arab and Muslim societies."[12]

4. HOW DID PALESTINIANS BECOME REFUGEES?

Morris, who is harshly critical of traditional Israeli history with regard to the refugee issue, summarizes the problem caused by the Palestinian and Pan-Arab attack: "The Palestinian Refugee problem was born of war, not by design. . . . The Arab leadership inside and outside Palestine probably helped precipitate the exodus. . . . No guiding hand or central control is evident." Morris states that "[d]uring the first months, the flight of the middle and upper classes from the towns provoked little Arab interest." (p. 83)

In *Birth*, Morris eschews an overarching explanation of the Arab flight and enters multiple caveats on every conclusion critical of the Zionist side. He is nonetheless clear that Zionist attacks or fear of them were the main impetus behind the flight. Yet the *"summary" offered by Dershowitz manages to elide this central conclusion of Morris, repeatedly stated on the pages from which Dershowitz cites.* For the period up to June 1948, Morris writes, "Jewish attack directly and indirectly triggered most of the Arab exodus," and "from July onwards, there was a growing readiness in the IDF units to expel. . . . Ben-Gurion clearly wanted as few Arabs as possible to remain in the Jewish State. He hoped to see them flee. He said as much to his colleagues and aides in meetings in August, September and October. . . . [W]hile there was no 'expulsion policy,' the July and October offensives were characterised by far more expulsions and, indeed, brutality towards Arab civilians than the first half of the war." Regarding "[w]hat happened in Palestine/Israel over 1947–9" as a whole, Morris writes: "In general, in most cases the final and decisive precipitant to flight was Haganah, IZL, LHI or IDF attack or the inhabitants' fear of such attack."[13]

SOURCES:

Benny Morris, *The Birth of the Palestinian Refugee Problem* (The Birth) (Cambridge: Cambridge University Press, 1988), pp. 286–89.

Ibid., p. 289.

---

11. Benny Morris, *The Birth of the Palestinian Refugee Problem, 1947–1949* (Cambridge, 1987), pp. 205–6, 211, 222–23, 230–33, 350n37; Morris, *1948 and After*, pp. 1, 22, 42, 192.

12. Benny Morris, *The Birth of the Palestinian Refugee Problem Revisited* (Cambridge, 2004), p. 592.

13. Morris, *Birth* (1987), pp. 287, 292–93, 294. Dershowitz reports that, according to Morris, during April–June 1948 "between two and three thousand Arabs fled their homes" (*Case for Israel*, p. 80). The figure Morris actually gives is between two and three *hundred* thousand (*Righteous Victims*, p. 256).

Topic	The Case for Israel	What the Evidence Actually Shows
5. WHY DID PALESTINIANS ATTACK ISRAEL AFTER THE WAR?	(a) Between 1948 and 1967, Palestinian fedayeen sponsored by Egypt and Syria murdered Israeli civilians in hundreds of cross-border raids. (p. 142) (b) Between 1951 and 1955, nearly a thousand Israeli civilians were killed by fedayeen in cross-border attacks. (p. 161) SOURCES: (a) None (b) None	In *Israel's Border Wars*, Benny Morris reports that the main motives behind Palestinians' infiltration of Israel were economic (such as hunger and coveting "lost houses, lands, crops and movable goods") and, less so, social (such as seeing their former homes and relatives). Only the tiniest percentage of the infiltration ("probably less than 10 percent") was "politically motivated or undertaken for terrorist purposes." Those few Palestinian infiltrators arming themselves mainly did so on account of, or to exact revenge for, Israel's murderous policies along its border. Morris reports that Israel turned border areas, including the Arab side of them, into free-fire zones. The "overall attitude" was that "killing, torturing, beating and raping Arab infiltrators was, if not permitted, at least not particularly reprehensible and might well go unpunished." Captured Palestinian infiltrators were routinely murdered, even children shot in the head and elderly Palestinians castrated. The atmosphere in the army "was epitomized in the words of one officer: 'Wherever I can kill an Arab—it is a pleasure.'" In addition, Israel carried out massive "retaliatory strikes" targeting "the attackers' clan, village or district"—notably the Qibya massacre led by Ariel Sharon, which left some seventy Arab civilians dead. Morris tallies as many as 250 Israeli civilians and another 250 Israeli combatants killed between 1949 and 1956—not, as Dershowitz claims, "nearly a thousand Israeli civilians." Morris further states: "A small proportion of Jewish casualties was caused by infiltrators who set out with the intent to kill or injure Jews. Most of the Israeli casualties seem to have resulted from unpremeditated encounters." On the other hand, he reports that as many as *five thousand* Palestinians were killed by Israel during this same period, the "vast majority" being "unarmed 'eco-

nomic' and social infiltrators." From right after the 1948 war until early 1955, Morris further reports, Egypt (as well as Jordan) "consistently opposed"—not, as Dershowitz states, "sponsored"—Palestinian infiltration, often resorting to brutal measures against Palestinian infiltrators "to avoid sparking IDF attacks." Focused on an agenda of domestic reform, Egypt's Nasser initially evinced "little interest in Israel and the Palestine problem." However, from 1954 Israel sought to provoke a violent Egyptian reaction: Israeli leaders such as Ben-Gurion and Dayan "wanted war, and periodically . . . hoped that a given retaliatory strike would embarrass or provoke the Arab state attacked into itself retaliating, giving Israel cause to escalate the shooting until war resulted—a war in which Israel could realize such major strategic objectives as the conquest of the West Bank or Sinai, or the destruction of the Egyptian army." In February 1955 it attacked Gaza, killing forty Egyptian soldiers. Only after these Israeli provocations, especially the Gaza attack, did Egypt begin to sponsor Palestinian raids on Israel.[14]

14. Benny Morris, *Israel's Border Wars, 1949–1956* (Oxford, 1993), pp. 11, 29–30, 35, 46, 47, 49, 51, 53, 67, 85, 90, 97–99, 124ff., 130, 132, 135, 137, 138, 166, 169, 169n178, 171, 176, 178–79, 229–30, 244ff., 271–72, 279, 324–26, 411–13, 415. Dershowitz's account of Palestinian raids from Syria similarly inverts the documentary record; see Norman G. Finkelstein, *Image and Reality of the Israel-Palestine Conflict*, 2nd ed. (New York, 2003), pp. 131–34.

C. JUNE 1967 AND OCTOBER 1973 WARS

Topic	The Case for Israel	What the Evidence Actually Shows
1. WHICH SIDE WAS HELD RESPONSIBLE FOR THE JUNE 1967 WAR?	*Although Israel fired the first shots, virtually everyone recognizes that Egypt, Syria, and Jordan started the war. The illegal Egyptian decision to close the Straits of Tiran by military force was recognized by the international community to be an act of war. (pp. 91–92)* SOURCES: None	Right after the June 1967 war, the United Nations General Assembly convened for an emergency session. Not one government in the world—not even the United States—took the unilateral position that the Arab states alone "started the war." Opinion was divided between the belief, on the one hand, that Israel was the aggressor and, on the other, that all parties to the conflict shared some responsibility or that adjudicating responsibility served no useful purpose. The U.S. ambassador to the U.N. refused to sign on to a Soviet-sponsored resolution condemning Israel, not because it condemned Israel, however, but because it didn't *also* condemn the Arab states: "Israel alone is to be condemned as an aggressor—though surely, in the light of all the events, both recent and long past, that led up to the fighting, it would be neither equitable nor constructive for this Organization to issue a one-sided condemnation."15
2. DID ISRAEL EXHAUST DIPLOMATIC OPTIONS BEFORE ATTACKING?	*After exhausting all diplomatic options and learning that Egypt was preparing an imminent attack and had flown surveillance flights over Israeli territory, the Israeli air force attacked. (p. 92)* SOURCES: [Michael B. Oren, *Six Days of War* (Oxford: 2002)], p. 99.	Toward the end of May, Israel considered sending a letter to the Johnson administration to win its backing for a first strike. According to Oren on the page Dershowitz cites, "Rabin concluded the discussion: 'I want it to be recorded for history that, before acting, we did everything we could to find a diplomatic solution." For Dershowitz this rhetorical flourish of Rabin clinches his point. In fact, Israel had many options—including the restationing of U.N. forces on its side of the border with Egypt, a two-week moratorium proposed by U.N. secretary-general U Thant, and World Court arbitration of the Straits of Tiran question—all of which it peremptorily rejected.16

3. WHY DID ISRAEL ATTACK IN JUNE 1967?	*(a) Egypt was preparing an imminent attack.* (p. 92) *(b) Arab armies were massing along Israel's border poised to strike.* (p. 92) *(c) The only question was whether the Arab armies would be able to strike the first military blow.* (p. 92) SOURCES: (a) None, (b) None, (c) None	Dershowitz provides no scholarly basis for this claim, for the good reason that there isn't any. The consensus is that Egypt almost certainly didn't intend to attack when Israel launched its "preemptive" strike. "[T]he Egyptian buildup in Sinai lacked a clear offensive plan," Avraham Sela of the conservative Shalem Center in Jerusalem typically concludes, "and Nasser's defensive instructions explicitly assumed an Israeli first strike."[17]
4. WHICH SIDE WAS HELD RESPONSIBLE FOR THE OCTOBER 1973 WAR?	*(a) The unprovoked attack on Israel was unjustified and in violation of the U.N. charter.* (p. 100) *(b) No one disputes that the Egyptians and Syrians . . . started the Yom Kippur War.* (p. 101) SOURCES: (a) None, (b) None	Not one country in the world—not even the United States—condemned Egypt for its "unprovoked" and "unjustified" attack or chastised it for having "started" the war. "The Egyptian attack on Israel on Yom Kippur aroused no international revulsion," Abba Eban rued in his memoir. "Not a single government accused Egypt of 'aggression.'" To the contrary, to recover the Israeli-occupied Sinai, Egypt had offered to sign a peace treaty with Israel in February 1971. After Israel rebuffed this peace overture, and after the United Nations and Egypt repeatedly warned Israel that war was inevitable if it rejected a diplomatic settlement, Egypt (along with Syria) finally attacked in October 1973.[18]

15. *Official Records of the General Assembly Fifth Emergency Special Session, Plenary Meetings, Verbatim Records of Meetings 17 June–18 September 1967*, 1,527th Plenary Meeting. Dershowitz's claim that the Egyptian blockade "was recognized by the international community to be an act of war" likewise finds zero support in the documentary record; see Finkelstein, *Image and Reality*, pp. 137–41.
16. Finkelstein, *Image and Reality*, pp. 127–30, 137–41.
17. Avraham Sela, *The Decline of the Arab-Israeli Conflict* (Albany, 1998), p. 91.
18. Abba Eban, *Personal Witness* (New York, 1992), p. 541; Finkelstein, *Image and Reality*, chap. 6.

Topic	The Case for Israel	What the Evidence Actually Shows
5. WERE THE ARABS INTENT ON GENOCIDE IN OCTOBER 1973?	(a) *Again, the Arab goal was to kill as many civilians as possible, despite the fact that deliberately attacking civilian targets is a war crime and a violation of international law. Egypt's initial assault included an attempt to drop bombs on Tel Aviv, which was prevented by Israeli air force interceptors.* (p. 101)	Morris states that, on the first day of the October War, "two [Egyptian] bombers flew low across the Mediterranean and launched two KELT missiles at Tel Aviv. But one missile fell into the sea and the other was shot down by an IAF interceptor. Egypt's aim may have been to deter Israel from 'strategic' bombing by signaling in advance that it, too, had a capacity to hit civilian centers." This is the one and only Egyptian attack on Israel proper throughout the war reported by Morris. Egypt's "goal" wasn't to "kill as many civilians as possible"—a claim for which Dershowitz doesn't supply a jot of evidence—or even to threaten Israel proper, but only to break the diplomatic impasse by establishing a beachhead on the Suez Canal's eastern bank, while Syria aimed to recover the occupied Golan Heights. Morris states this on the
	(b) *Morris has described Sadat's and Assad's motives for attacking Israel: "For both Sadat and Assad, the war promised major gains, beginning with a restoration of Arab pride.... Merely daring to go to war against the invincible IDF would be seen as profoundly courageous; wiping out the shame of 1967, indeed the shame of Arab history since 1948, would bring both regimes rewards in terms of popularity, legitimacy, and longevity, as well as large contributions from the oil kingdoms."* (p. 102)	very same page from which Dershowitz quotes him on "Sadat's and Assad's motives" but omits the crucial paragraph: "In the October war . . . Presidents Anwar Sadat of Egypt and Hafez Assad of Syria sought to regain the territories lost in 1967. Neither aimed to destroy Israel, though during the opening hours of the conflict, its leaders could not be sure of this. . . . Syrian defense minister Tlass later wrote: 'We sought to liberate the conquered Arab lands, while Egypt sought to cross the Canal and remain on [both] its banks . . . out of a desire to push things forward on the international plane' (that is, to get hold of a strip of territory on the east bank of the Canal so as to jolt Israel and the world community into breaking the political deadlock)."[19]

SOURCES:

(a) [Morris, *Righteous Victims*], p. 413.

(b) Morris[, *Righteous Victims*], p. 387.

6. DID ISRAEL RETURN THE SINAI AFTER THE OCTOBER 1973 WAR BECAUSE SADAT FINALLY OFFERED PEACE?

Sadat achieved both of his goals in attacking Israel on Yom Kippur of 1973. In addition to restoring Egyptian honor, he also restored the entire Sinai to Egyptian control. As soon as Sadat courageously indicated a willingness to make peace with Israel in exchange for the Sinai, the Israeli government, then under the control of the hawkish Likud Party and its tough-talking leader, Menachem Begin, uprooted the Jewish settlers in the Sinai and returned it, oil fields and all, to Egypt." (p. 103)

SOURCES: None

In February 1971 Egypt offered Israel full peace in exchange for full Israeli withdrawal from the Sinai. Israel rejected this proposal, prompting Egypt, after another two years of fruitless diplomacy, to attack in October 1973. Egypt performed better than expected in the war, giving rise to foreboding in Israel about its prospects in another war and, concomitantly, causing Israel to reconsider its prior rejection of the Egyptian peace offer. "Exact prediction of the nature of a future war is impossible, but the general trends may be deduced. It will obviously be more difficult than its predecessor, more vicious and bloodier. The civilian rear will be hit, and Israel must assume that she will have immediately to fight on three fronts," veteran Israeli military correspondent Zeev Schiff wrote after the October war. "Israel's military supremacy has been placed in doubt." He concluded that "[i]n the new conditions, the importance of a political settlement obviously increases. Time isn't on Israel's side, and she must make greater efforts to achieve a true peace."[20] This is exactly what Israel proceeded to do, accepting the settlement with Egypt that it rejected in February 1971—not because Egypt finally offered to "make peace," however, but because it proved a credible force to wage war.[21]

19. Morris, *Righteous Victims*, pp. 387, 413. All scholarly studies concur on the Arabs' limited war objectives; see Finkelstein, *Image and Reality*, p. 165 and many sources cited at p. 270n37.

20. Zeev Schiff, *October Earthquake* (Tel Aviv, 1974), pp. 314, 318.

21. Finkelstein, *Image and Reality*, pp. 167–71. On a related point, Dershowitz writes that Israel "is the only country in modern history to have returned disputed territory captured in a defensive war and crucial to its own self-defense in exchange for peace" (*Case for Israel*, p. 2). Leaving aside the dubious claim that its first strike in June 1967 was "defensive," Israel agreed to return the Egyptian Sinai to Egypt and, later, parcels of Jordanian territory to Jordan. In neither case, however, was the territory in question "disputed."

D. ISRAEL'S "PURITY OF ARMS"

Topic	The Case for Israel	What the Evidence Actually Shows
I. DOES ISRAEL ONLY TARGET LAWFUL MILITARY SITES?	(a) [T]he Arabs . . . target soft civilian areas . . . while the Israelis . . . respond by targeting soldiers, military equipment, and other lawful targets. . . . [T]he regular Israeli army has not responded by targeting Arab population centers, such as Amman, Damascus, and Cairo. (p. 75) (b) In general, the casualties among civilians "were remarkably low" during the Six-Day War because Israel made sure that most of the fighting "took place far from major population centers." (p. 93; cf. pp. 142–43) (c) For three-quarters of a century, the Arab-Israeli war has been between Arab nations dedicated to genocidal aggression against civilians on the one hand and the Jewish state determined to protect its civilian population by taking defensive actions directed against military targets	Already during the British Mandate years, the Zionist movement across the political spectrum targeted civilians, and after its establishment, Israel indiscriminately bombarded Arab villages, towns, and cities. Historian Anita Shapira reports that mainstream Labor Zionism and dissident right-wing Zionist factions basically concurred on applying force against Arabs. During the 1936–1939 Arab Revolt, the Irgun engaged in "uninhibited use of terror"; "mass indiscriminate killings of the aged, women and children"; execution of Jews "suspected of informing, even though some of these persons were totally innocent"; "attacks against British without any consideration of possible injuries to innocent bystanders, and the murder of British in cold blood"; and so on. Although Labor Zionism's approach to violence was "more 'civilized' than" the Irgun's, Shapira continues, "they did not differ in essential respects." Comparing the elite Labor Zionist shock troops of the Palmach with the Irgun, she expresses skepticism that the "external differences in framework and patterns of behavior were sufficient to create a different attitude toward fighting or to develop 'civilian' barriers to military callousness and insensitivity." During the Arab Revolt, for example, a British officer recruited squads from Labor Zionist settlements to inflict collective punishment in "merciless raids" on Arab villages: "boundaries of the permissible and nonpermissible" in the assaults on these villages were "vague and intentionally blurred."[22] Mainstream Zionist forces committed multiple atrocities against civilians during the 1948 war as well as afterwards during the "border wars." In 1956 Israel attacked Egypt and occupied Sinai and the Gaza Strip. Regarding its occupation of Gaza, Benny Morris reports: "[M]any Fedayeen and an estimated 4,000 Egyptian and Palestinian regulars were trapped in the Strip, identified, and rounded up by the IDF, GSS, and police. Dozens of these Fedayeen appear to have been summarily executed, without trial. Some were

on the other hand.... [T]he Arab side has consistently, illegally, and aggressively targeted civilians, and the Israeli side has consistently, lawfully, and defensively responded by attacking military targets. (p. 141)

(d) Prior to the establishment of the state of Israel, dissident [Zionist] groups ... did blow up the headquarters of the British colonial government located in a wing of the King David Hotel, killing ninety-one people. ... Dissident groups also killed civilians at ... some other locations, but these deviations were firmly condemned by the Jewish Agency. As soon as Israel became a state, its prime minister, David Ben-Gurion, disarmed these dissident groups by force. ... No further acts of terrorism were committed by the Irgun or Lechi. Ben-Gurion also dismantled the Palmach—the permanently mobi-

probably killed during two massacres by IDF troops soon after the occupation of the Strip.... [T]he day Khan Yunis was conquered, IDF troops shot dead hundreds of Palestinian refugees and local inhabitants in the town.... In Rafah, ... Israeli troops killed between forty-eight and one hundred refugees and several local residents, and wounded another sixty-one.... Another sixty-six Palestinians, probably Fedayeen, were executed in a number of other incidents.... The United Nations estimated that, all told, Israeli troops killed between 447 and 550 Arab civilians in the first three weeks of their occupation of the Strip."[23]

The trigger for the sequence of events climaxing in the June 1967 war was an Israeli "retaliatory" strike in November 1966 against the Jordanian village of Samu in the West Bank. In the largest military operation since 1956, an Israeli armored brigade of four thousand methodically razed 125 homes, a clinic, a school, and a workshop, killing eighteen Jordanian soldiers as well. (One Israeli soldier was killed.) Noting that the toll it took "in human lives and in destruction far surpasses the cumulative total of the various acts of terrorism conducted against the frontiers of Israel," U.S. ambassador to the U.N. Arthur Goldberg declared, "I wish to make it absolutely clear that this large-scale military action cannot be justified, explained away or excused by the incidents which preceded it and in which the Government of Jordan has not been implicated."[24] Oren doesn't state that, during the June 1967 war, to avoid Arab civilian casualties, Israel "made sure" the fighting took place away from densely populated areas. He merely states that, as it happened, "much of the fighting took place far from major population centers." In the course of the June war, Israel executed scores of Egyptian POWs and launched an unprovoked—and almost certainly premeditated—air and naval assault on the USS *Liberty*, killing 34 U.S. Navy men and wounding 171.[25]

22. Anita Shapira, *Land and Power: The Zionist Resort to Force, 1881–1948* (Oxford, 1992), pp. 247–52, 350, 365. See also Tom Segev, *One Palestine, Complete: Jews and Arabs under the British Mandate* (New York, 1999), pp. 386–87, 430–31.
23. Morris, *Border Wars*, pp. 408–9.
24. *United Nations Security Council Office Records*, 1320th Meeting (16 November 1966).
25. Finkelstein, *Image and Reality*, pp. 196–97.

Topic	The Case for Israel	What the Evidence Actually Shows
1. DOES ISRAEL ONLY TARGET LAWFUL MILITARY SITES? *(continued)*	lized commando force loyal to Ben-Gurion's own party: (pp. 141–42) (e) *Israel is the only country in the history of modern warfare that has never dropped bombs indiscriminately on an enemy city in an effort to kill innocent civilians in retaliation for the deliberate bombing of its own civilians. Even when it attacked those parts of Beirut that were home to terrorists, the Israeli air force made great efforts—although not always with success—to avoid unnecessary civilian casualties. Recall that when Israel sought to protect itself against Beirut-based terrorism in 1982, it sent in a team of soldiers—led by then Major General Ehud Barak, dressed as a woman—to target the terrorists themselves in a building then being used as their base, instead of bombing the building from the air, which would have resulted in many more casualties. (pp. 150–51)*	During the 1968–1970 "War of Attrition" between Egypt and Israel, Israel launched attacks on the cities of Ismailia, Kantara, and Suez on the east bank of the Suez Canal, turning them into "empty shells," as scores of Egyptian civilians were killed and 500,000 to 750,000 were forced to flee their homes.[26] Soon after the June war, Israel also began bombing villages in southern Lebanon, and after 1974 without even the pretense of retaliation. In March 1978, after a Palestinian terrorist attack launched from Beirut, Israel invaded south Lebanon, indiscriminately bombing villages, towns, and the city of Tyre, killing some two thousand people, almost all civilians, and creating nearly 300,000 refugees. After the invasion, military correspondent Zeev Schiff glossed an admission of Israel's chief of staff: "The Israeli Army has always struck civilian populations, purposely and consciously . . . the Army . . . has never distinguished civilian [from military] targets . . . [but] purposely attacked civilian targets even when Israeli settlements had not been struck." In June 1982, despite PLO restraint in the face of numerous Israeli provocations, Israel again invaded Lebanon. It indiscriminately bombed and shelled Lebanese villages, towns, and the cities of Tyre, Sidon, and Beirut, as well as—and most mercilessly—Palestinian refugee camps, everywhere hitting civilian sites such as residential neighborhoods, schools, and hospitals. The massive, weeks-long, murderous bombing and shelling of Beirut culminated in early August, when—in the words of veteran Middle East correspondent Robert Fisk—"[t]o call the gunfire indiscriminate was an understatement. It would also have been a lie. The Israeli bombardment . . . was, we realised later, *discriminate*. It targeted every civilian area, every institution in west Beirut—hospitals, schools, apartments, shops, newspaper offices, hotels, the prime minister's office, and the parks. Incredibly, the Israeli shells even blew part of the roof off the city's synagogue in Wadi Abu Jamil where the remnants of Beirut's tiny Jewish community still lived." The carpet bombing and massive shelling of Lebanon's cities, towns, and villages

(f) *Wars waged against Israel are wars of extermination that target its cities and population centers. Its enemies are seeking its total destruction. Israel, in contrast, avoids targeting cities and civilians and does not seek the destruction of any neighboring state. (p. 227)*

SOURCES:
(a) None
(b) [Oren, *Six Days*,] pp. 306–7.
(c) None
(d) None
(e) None
(f) None

and Palestinian refugee camps; the use of cluster bombs and phosphorus shells in civilian areas; the cutting off of Beirut's electricity, water, and food supplies—all this was attested to by innumerable foreign journalists and humanitarian organizations as well as Israeli journalists and soldiers.[27] In the face of this voluminous documentation Dershowitz's lone piece of evidence, which he has repeated on numerous occasions, is the commando raid "led by then Major General Ehud Barak, dressed as a woman." Except that—unless Barak cross-dresses on all his missions—Dershowitz, not for the first time, has his facts confused: this famous Barak mission took place in 1973. One indication of Israel's actual record on respecting Arab life during its many wars is that, according to Morris, "the IDF has progressively become a 'cleaner' army," its record "when it comes to *tohar haneshek* [purity of arms]" having been "far better" during the Lebanon invasion "than in 1948."[28] In July 1993 Israel launched Operation Accountability, a "ferocious Israeli assault on population centers in southern Lebanon," killing some 120, displacing 300,000, and severely damaging more than fifty-five villages.[29] In April 1996 Israel launched yet another invasion of Lebanon, Operation Grapes of Wrath, killing mostly civilians, including two women and four girls inside an ambulance. In addition, Israeli forces shelled the U.N. compound in Qana, killing 102 civilians. "On the basis of all the information available," Amnesty International concluded, "the IDF intentionally attacked the UN compound." All told, some 150 civilians were killed and 350 wounded during the invasion.[30]

26. Martin van Creveld, *The Sword and the Olive* (New York, 1998) (quoted phrase at p. 211).
27. For Israel's depredations in Lebanon, see Noam Chomsky, *Fateful Triangle*, updated ed. (Boston, 1999) (Schiff quote at p. 181), and Robert Fisk, *Pity the Nation* (New York, 1990) (quote at pp. 314–15; emphasis in original).
28. "Benny Morris responds," in "Letters," *Tikkun* (March–April 1989).
29. Human Rights Watch, *Civilian Pawns—Laws of War Violations and the Use of Weapons on the Israel-Lebanon Border* (New York, May 1996); Amnesty International, *Unlawful Killings during Operation Grapes of Wrath* (London, July 1996).
30. Amnesty International, *Unlawful Killings*.

Topic	The Case for Israel	What the Evidence Actually Shows
2. WHAT IS THE BALANCE SHEET OF CIVILIAN CASUALTIES?	(a) Between 1968 and 1990, Palestinian terrorists murdered thousands of innocent civilians, including international travelers, Jews at prayer in synagogues throughout Europe, Olympic athletes, nursery school children, diplomats, and Christian pilgrims. (p. 105)	Dershowitz provides neither source nor basis for any of his calculations. An extreme right-wing, "pro"-Israel website puts the number of victims of "Palestinian terror" between 1967 and 1990 in Israel and the Occupied Territories—including "Israeli civilians and security personnel, and foreigners killed"—at 370, and the number of Jews and non-Jews abroad killed in Palestinian terrorist attacks at 50, for a total of, not "thousands," but 420 dead (including Israeli combatants) over a period of more than two decades.[31] By comparison, Israel killed about five times as many civilians during its one-week-long invasion of Lebanon in March 1978. The basis of Dershowitz's second calculation is equally obscure, but another set of
	(b) Even comparing innocent Israeli civilian casualties with Palestinian civilian casualties reveals that Israel has acted with restraint. (p. 143)	figures will perhaps illuminate Israel's comparative "restraint." From 1947 to the present, the number of Israeli deaths during all its wars and policing operations—1947–1949, 1956, 1967, 1967–1970, 1973, 1982, the first and second intifadas—as well as from all terrorist attacks comes in total to under 22,000, the overwhelming number of them combatants. By comparison, just in the course of Israel's June–September 1982 invasion of Lebanon, between 18,000 and 20,000 Lebanese and Palestinians were killed, the overwhelming number of them civilians.[32]
	SOURCES: (a) None (b) None	

31. See www.jewishvirtuallibrary.org, under "Fatalities in Palestinian Terror Attacks" and "Major Terror Attacks 1952–1989."
32. The Israeli casualty figure was compiled from www.jewishvirtuallibrary.org, www.mfa.gov.il/MFA/MFAArchive/2000_2009/2004/4/Israel+Independence+Day+2004.htm, and Morris, *Border Wars*. For casualty figures during the Lebanon war, see Chomsky, *Fateful Triangle*, pp. 221–23, Fisk, *Pity the Nation*, pp. 255–57, 323, 418.

MUFTI MACHINATIONS

In *The Case for Israel,* Alan Dershowitz devotes many pages to the Mufti of Jerusalem, Haj Amin al-Husseini, who led the Palestinian national movement during the British Mandate years. It is well known that the Mufti personally collaborated with the Nazis. However, Dershowitz makes many claims beyond this fact. On pages 54–60, he writes:

> The SS, under the leadership of Heinrich Himmler, provided both financial and logistical support for anti-Semitic pogroms in Palestine.

> Adolf Eichmann visited Husseini in Palestine and subsequently maintained regular contact with him.

> The official leader of the Palestinians, Haj Amin al-Husseini, . . . was taken on a tour of Auschwitz by Himmler.

> The mufti was apparently planning to return to Palestine in the event of a German victory and to construct a death camp modeled after Auschwitz, near Nablus.

> In 1944, a German-Arab commando unit under Husseini's command parachuted into Palestine in an effort to poison Tel Aviv's wells.

> It is fair to conclude that the official leader of the Muslims in Palestine, Haj Amin al-Husseini, was a full-fledged Nazi war criminal, and he was so declared at Nuremberg.

> The grand mufti of Jerusalem was personally responsible for the concentration camp slaughter of thousands of Jews.

> [S]ome Arab and Palestinian leaders bore significant responsibility for the Holocaust.

Most of these allegations are taken, if not always with proper attribution, from an unsourced opinion column in a right-wing Israeli newspaper: Sarah Honig, "Fiendish Hypocrisy II: The Man from Klopstock St.," *Jerusalem Post,* 6 April 2001.[1] The claim that the Nazis financed the 1936–1939 Arab Revolt is credited by Dershowitz to Benny Morris's *Righteous Victims,* but there isn't any mention of this on the cited pages or any others in Morris's study.[2] It can be found, however, in Honig's column. What does the scholarly literature report about the Honig-Dershowitz claims? None of the major academic treatments of

1. At one point Honig casually asserts: "This is backed by ample documentation from the Nuremberg and Eichmann trials." No further reference is provided although the record of the Nuremberg trial alone comes to forty-two volumes.
2. Benny Morris, *Righteous Victims: A History of the Zionist-Arab Conflict, 1881–1999* (New York, 1999). On p. 165 Morris reports the well-known fact that the Nazis subsidized the Mufti's activities during World War II.

the Arab Revolt—for example, *The Palestinian Arab National Movement* by Israeli historian Yehoshua Porath or *The Palestinian People* by Israeli professor Baruch Kimmerling and University of Washington professor Joel S. Migdal—mention Nazi funding.[3] The major biographies of the Mufti are *The Mufti of Jerusalem* by Palestinian historian Philip Mattar and *The Grand Mufti* by Israeli historian Zvi Elpeleg. Neither of these sources mentions Husseini accompanying Himmler to Auschwitz. Neither of these sources mentions a Husseini plan to build an Auschwitz-style camp in Nablus. Neither mentions a German-Arab commando unit en route to poison Tel Aviv's wells. Neither mentions that Husseini was indicted at Nuremberg. (His name is not even listed in the index to the proceedings of the Nuremberg tribunal.) It is correct that Husseini petitioned the Nazis during the Final Solution not to allow Jews, including Jewish children, to enter Palestine. It is unknown, however, whether his intercession had any practical impact. Mattar found "no hard evidence" that it did, while Elpeleg concluded that "[i]t is impossible to estimate the extent of the consequences of Haj Amin's efforts." Dershowitz cites Elpeleg's book but not this conclusion. Raul Hilberg, the dean of Nazi holocaust scholars, believes it "unlikely" that the Mufti's pleas had any influence. No scholar affirmatively maintains that Husseini "was personally responsible for the concentration camp slaughter of thousands of Jews" or "bore significant responsibility for the Holocaust." Hilberg devotes all of *one sentence* to Husseini's role in his monumental, three-volume study of the Nazi holocaust.[4] Finally, Dershowitz is curiously silent on another initiative emanating from Palestine to collaborate with Hitler. Beginning in late 1940 the dissident right-wing Zionist organization "IZL in Israel" sought an agreement with the Nazis on the basis of a "collusion of interests" between the "new Germany and the reborn *volkisch-nationalen Hebraertum*" and for the purpose of "the re-establishment of the Jewish state in its historic borders, on a national and totalitarian basis, allied with the German Reich." Although the Nazis proved unresponsive notwithstanding repeated appeals, this Zionist initiative did have one noteworthy denouement. A member of this group of would-be Nazi collaborators, Yitzhak Shamir, went on to become the prime minister of Israel.[5]

3. Yehoshua Porath, *The Palestinian Arab National Movement* (London, 1977). Baruch Kimmerling and Joel S. Migdal, *The Palestinian People: A History* (Cambridge, 2003).

4. Philip Mattar, *The Mufti of Jerusalem* (New York, 1988), p. 107; Zvi Elpeleg, *The Grand Mufti* (London, 1993), p. 72; Raul Hilberg, *The Destruction of the European Jews* (New York: 1985), 2:789–90 (citing a Husseini protest to the German foreign minister against further Jewish immigration to Palestine). "Unlikely" comes from a telephone interview with Hilberg on 19 September 2003.

5. Joseph Heller, *The Stern Gang: Ideology, Politics and Terror, 1940–1949* (London, 1995), pp. 77–108 (quoted phrases at 85–86).

Peace Process

We do have a license to advocate outcomes, which
we know would be objectively unjust but subjectively
beneficial to our clients.

Alan M. Dershowitz, *Letters to a Young Lawyer*

A. BACKGROUND

Topic	The *Case for Israel*	What the Evidence Actually Shows
1. DID ZIONISTS AGREE TO PARTITION IN 1937?	(a) *I begin the case for Israel by . . . emphasizing the refusal of Palestinian leaders to accept a two-state (or two-homeland) solution in 1917, 1937, 1948, and 2000.* (p. 6) (b) *[C]ompromise was always seen as a pragmatic necessity by the mainstream Zionists and their leadership. The reality of a Jewish homeland with a Jewish majority population was far more important than the size of that homeland. . . . The developing clash between the Jews of Palestine, led by the pragmatic socialist David Ben-Gurion, and the Muslims of Palestine, led by the uncompromising Jew-hater Haj Amin al-Husseini, was not over whether the Jews or the Muslims would control all of Palestine. . . . Instead, it was—realistically viewed—whether the remainder of Palestine was to be given exclusively to the Muslims of Palestine or whether it would be*	There is no known record of a two-state solution even being mooted, let alone rejected by Palestinians, in 1917. Indeed, right after issuance of the Balfour Declaration, the Jewish state proposed by Ben-Gurion, for example, included not just the whole of Palestine, but all of present-day Jordan as well as wide swaths of Lebanon, Syria, and Egypt.[1] Great Britain's 1937 Peel Commission report recommended the partition of Palestine between a Jewish state, on the one hand, and an Arab state merged with Transjordan, on the other, *not* a Palestinian state *in addition to* Transjordan. Neither the Arabs *nor the Zionist Congress*—Dershowitz gets this wrong too—officially accepted the Peel partition proposal.[2] True, key Zionist leaders rejected the Peel recommendation for tactical reasons, privately lobbying for partition. However, even Zionist leaders accepting partition did so only as the first step toward the total conquest of Palestine. Although Dershowitz ignores it, his main historical source—like all other studies of the period—concludes that both Weizmann and Ben-Gurion "saw partition as a stepping stone to further expansion and the eventual takeover of the whole of Palestine. . . . [Ben-Gurion] wrote to his son Amos: '[A] Jewish state in part [of Palestine] is not an end, but a beginning. . . . Our possession is important not only for itself . . . through this we increase our power, and every increase in power facilitates getting hold of the country in its entirety. Establishing a [small] state . . . will serve as a very potent lever in our historical efforts to redeem the whole country.'" Finally, contrary to Dershowitz, the Peel Report did *not* envisage that Arabs would "remain as part of the Arab minority in the Jewish state." It explicitly recommended that, if most of the 225,000 Arabs currently living in the planned Jewish state didn't voluntarily leave, "in the last resort" their departure should be "compulsory."[3]

fairly divided between the Jews and the Muslims of Palestine, each of whom effectively controlled certain areas. (p. 42; emphasis in original)

(c) As soon as partition into two states or homelands was proposed [in 1937], the Jews accepted it and the Arabs rejected it. (p. 46)

(d) The Jews reluctantly accepted the Peel partition plan, while the Arabs categorically rejected it, demanding that all of Palestine be placed under Arab control and that most of the Jewish population of Palestine be "transferred" out of the country, because "this country [cannot] assimilate the Jews now in the country." (p. 51)

(e) To understand how different the Arab-Israeli conflict would

1. Shabtai Teveth, *Ben-Gurion and the Palestinian Arabs: From Peace to War* (New York, 1985), pp. 34–35. For the official Zionist map circa 1919 staking out similar territorial claims, see Walter Laqueur, *A History of Zionism* (New York, 1972), p. 85, and Simha Flapan, *The Birth of Israel: Myths and Realities* (New York, 1987), p. 17.
2. Avi Shlaim, *Collusion across the Jordan: King Abdullah, the Zionist Movement, and the Partition of Palestine* (Oxford, 1988), pp. 62–64.
3. Benny Morris's *Righteous Victims: A History of the Zionist-Arab Conflict, 1881–1999* (New York, 1999), p. 138; *Palestine Royal Commission Report* (London, 1937), p. 391.

Topic	The Case for Israel	What the Evidence Actually Shows
1. DID ZIONISTS AGREE TO PARTITION IN 1937? *(continued)*	look if the Arab world including the Palestinian Muslims had accepted the two-state solution when it was first proposed (or even for years thereafter), we must briefly return to the Peel Commission Report. If the Arabs had accepted the Peel Commission partition proposal, there would have been a Palestinian state (in addition to Transjordan) in most of what was left of Palestine following the partition of Transjordan. The vast majority of Arabs and Muslims in Palestine would have lived under Palestinian control, and the Arab minority that lived in the land allotted to the Jewish state would have had the choice to move to the Palestinian state or remain as part of the Arab minority in the Jewish state. The same would have been true for the Jews who lived in the Arab state. (pp. 89–90; cf. p. 98 for "Israel accepted . . . the Peel Report" and p. 194 for Jews accepting and Arabs rejecting a "peaceful two-state solution in 1937")	

	SOURCES:	
	(a) None	
	(b) None	
	(c) None	
	(d) [*Peel Report*], p. 141, question to the grand mufti and his answer.	
	(e) None	
2. WHAT WERE THE TERMS OF THE 1947 U.N. PARTITION RESOLUTION (181)?		
(1) WERE JEWS A MAJORITY IN THE PROPOSED JEWISH STATE?	*The Jews were a substantial majority in those areas of Palestine partitioned by the United Nations for a Jewish state. . . . [T]he official U.N. estimate was that the land assigned to the Jewish state contained approximately 538,000 Jews and 397,000 Arabs (a number that included Christians, Bedouins, Druze, and others). (p. 68)*	The 1947 United Nations partition proposal officially included 498,000 Jews and 407,000 Arabs and others in the proposed Jewish state. However, this figure *excluded* 90,000 to 105,000 Bedouins residing within the borders of the Jewish state. Taking this last number into account, the proposed Jewish state would have had roughly equal Arab and Jewish populations or even an Arab majority.[4] In fact, it was impossible to carve out a Jewish state in Palestine without a substantial Palestinian Arab population and thus—in light of the Zionist goal of creating a demographically "stable" Jewish state—without massive expulsion. As historian Benny Morris states: "What happened in 1948 was inevitable. If the Jews wanted to establish a state in Eretz Israel that would be located on an area a little larger than Tel Aviv, a removing of population was needed. . . . Without a population expulsion, a Jewish state could not have been established."[5]
	SOURCES: None	

4. Michael J. Cohen, *Palestine and the Great Powers, 1945–1948* (Princeton, 1982), p. 273n31; Shlaim, *Collusion*, pp. 117–19; Evan M. Wilson, *Decision on Palestine: How the U.S. Came to Recognize Israel* (Stanford, 1979), pp. 112–13.

5. Meron Rappaport, "Interview with Benny Morris," *Yediot Ahronot* (11 November 2001).

Topic	The Case for Israel	What the Evidence Actually Shows
(II) WAS THE PARTITION RESOLUTION JUST?	(a) [T]he state of Israel did not come into existence at the expense of either the Arabs or the Palestinians. The area partitioned for a Jewish state had a Jewish majority that had a right to self-determination vis-à-vis the British (and the Ottomans before them). The land in question was neither Arab nor Palestinian. It had passed from one empire to another, and the time had come for self-determination by the two groups that lived in different parts of it. It was historically, demographically, economically, and legally both a Jewish and an Arab land. (pp. 59–60; emphasis in original) (b) In terms of the division of land, the Jewish state received somewhat more than the Arabs, but only if one counts fully the Negev Desert, which was deemed uninhabitable and uncultivatable. If the Negev is excluded or substantially discounted, the usable land allocated to the Arabs was larger than that allocated to the	The embryonic Jewish state emerging from the British Mandate was imposed by force on, and against the will of, the indigenous Palestinian Arab population. On no generally accepted principles of morality or law could this flagrant violation of the Palestinians' right to self-determination be justified.[6] Dershowitz professes to "know of no situation in history where a state has twice rejected generous offers of statehood." Yet, is there any example in history of a people voluntarily relinquishing a fragment, let alone most, of their country to settlers coming from abroad to colonize it and then drive them out? The U.N. Partition Resolution, giving Zionists title to part of Palestine, appeared to ratify their usurpation as well as "the flouting of a fundamental principle of the [U.N.] organization itself—the imposition of a form of government against the wishes of the majority of the inhabitants" (historian Wm. Roger Louis).[7] The resolution's terms exacerbated this seeming injustice. "[T]he partition resolution awarded 55.5 percent of the total area of Palestine to the Jews (most of whom were recent immigrants), who constituted less than a third of the population and who owned less than 7 percent of the land," historian Walid Khalidi writes. "The Palestinians, on the other hand, who made up over two thirds of the population and who owned the vast bulk of the land, were awarded 45.5 percent of the country of which they had enjoyed continuous possession for centuries." Moreover, "the best lands were incorporated within [the proposed Jewish state]—most of the fertile coastal plains . . . and all the interior plains. . . . These included almost all the citrus and cereal producing areas. Half of the former and the vast bulk of the latter were owned by Palestinians."[8] That a U.N. General Assembly majority approved the Partition Resolution, Louis recalls, was due in no small part to Zionist machination: "[T]he Zionists were able to launch a campaign that left the President and officials at the State Department reeling under a bombardment of letters, telegrams and telephone calls. Truman

Jews. Moreover, much of the land allocated to the Jewish state was originally swamp and desert land that had been irrigated and made fertile by Jewish labor and investment. (pp. 68–69)

(c) Palestinians have been offered a homeland on three separate occasions—in 1937, 1947, and 2000–2001—and each time have rejected the offer and responded with increased terrorism.... I know of no situation in history where a state has twice rejected generous offers of statehood. (p. 159)

SOURCES:
(a) None
(b) None
(c) None

wrote in his memoirs that he never 'had as much pressure and propaganda aimed at the White House as I had in this instance.' . . . Emmanuel Cellar and Sol Bloom in the House of Representatives exerted their considerable influence on Congressional colleagues, the executive branch, the State Department, and in particular on the United Nations representatives from the Philippines, Liberia, and Haiti. Ten Senators sent telegrams to the President of the Philippines, who also received the friendly admonition of Felix Frankfurter and another Supreme Court Justice. . . . The Cuban Ambassador, who remained recalcitrantly pro-Arab, complained that the Costan [sic] Rican vote had been bought with a $75,000 bribe. Niles [a pro-Zionist adviser to Truman] used business connections in an abortive effort to swing the Greek vote. Bernard Baruch let the representatives from China and France know that nothing less than economic assistance would be in jeopardy if they failed to vote in favour of partition. Harvey Firestone brought Liberia to heel. As Robert Donovan summed it up in an understatement in his biography of Truman, intrigue was rife." In addition, "[i]n 1947, there was not yet a solid 'anti-colonial' bloc" in the U.N. Finally, the "overriding Russian aim" in supporting the resolution was not achieving justice but "the disruption of the British Empire."[9]

6. See introduction to this book.
7. Wm. Roger Louis, *The British Empire in the Middle East, 1945–1951: Arab Nationalism, the United States, and Postwar Imperialism* (New York, 1984), p. 445.
8. Walid Khalidi, "Revisiting the UNGA Partition Resolution," *Journal of Palestine Studies* (autumn 1997), pp. 11, 13 (emphases in original).
9. Louis, *The British Empire*, pp. 483n13, 485–86, 491. Against intense Zionist lobbying, the key balancing consideration shaping the Truman administration's decisions in 1947–48 was the Arab, especially Saudi, reaction. Basically, Ibn Saud, the Saudi king, signaled that he wouldn't interfere with the Truman administration's pro-Zionist policy so long as the United States didn't intervene militarily in the unfolding conflict—in the event, this is exactly what happened. On the interaction of these and other factors, see Kenneth Ray Bain, *The March to Zion: United States Policy and the Founding of Israel* (London, 1979), and esp. Michael J. Cohen, *Truman and Israel* (Berkeley, 1990).

Topic	The Case for Israel	What the Evidence Actually Shows
(III) DID ZIONISTS SUPPORT THE PRINCIPLE OF PARTITION IN 1947?	*Israel quickly accepted the U.N. partition and soon declared statehood.* (p. 69) SOURCES: None	Although the Zionist leadership formally accepted the Partition Resolution, its Declaration of Independence, while citing the resolution, made no mention of its provision for not just a Jewish state but a Palestinian Arab one as well: "On November 29, 1947, the General Assembly of the United Nations adopted a Resolution requiring the establishment of a Jewish State in Eretz-Israel." This omission was not an oversight. According to historian Michael Bar-Zohar, Ben-Gurion "deleted any reference to the partition plan" the evening before the declaration was announced.[10] In fact, neither Ben-Gurion nor the Zionist movement generally, accepted the principle of partitioning Palestine. "The partition lines were of secondary importance in Ben-Gurion's eyes," historian Avi Shlaim writes, "because he intended to change them in any case; they were not the end but only the beginning."[11] Accordingly, the Israeli Declaration of Independence didn't specify the Jewish state's borders either: the Zionist leadership, after heated debate, decided against inclusion of the Partition Resolution's borders in the Declaration. "By some twist of vision, historians have generally taken Ben-Gurion's acceptance of the idea of a Jewish state in less than the whole of Palestine as the equivalent of an acceptance of the entire UN resolution," Simha Flapan writes. Yet "Ben-Gurion had always viewed partition as the first step toward a Jewish state in the whole of Palestine, including Transjordan, the Golan Heights and southern Lebanon."[12] Finally, already *before* the Partition Resolution was passed by the U.N. General Assembly, the Zionist leadership had moved to preempt the creation of a Palestinian Arab state. It reached a tacit, secret agreement with King Abdullah of Jordan to divide Palestine between them—which, in the event, was what happened.[13]

B. U.N. RESOLUTION 242

Topic	The Case for Israel	What the Evidence Actually Shows
1. WHAT DID U.N. RESOLUTION 242 STATE?	(a) Note that the resolution [242] does not require Israeli withdrawal from all the territories, only "territories," thus contemplating some territorial adjustments. . . . The elimination of the definite article the was an explicit compromise engineered by the United States in order to permit the retention by Israel of territories necessary to assure secure boundaries. (p. 96; emphasis in original) (b) Israel could have, and should have, implemented the so-called Alon Plan or some variant thereof. The Alon Plan . . . contemplated Israeli withdrawal from the population centers of the West Bank and from all other captured territories except for	Right after the June 1967 war, the United Nations General Assembly met in emergency session. Reviewing these proceedings, Secretary-General U Thant observed that there was "near unanimity" on "the withdrawal of the armed forces from the territory of neighboring Arab states occupied during the recent war" because "everyone agrees that there should be no territorial gains by military conquest."[14] When the General Assembly couldn't reach agreement on a comprehensive resolution, deliberations moved to the Security Council. In November 1967 the Security Council unanimously approved Resolution 242. Dershowitz reproduces in his book (p. 96) the operative paragraph that calls for "[w]ithdrawal of Israel armed forces from territories occupied in the recent conflict." He omits in his rendering, however, the resolution's preambular paragraph, which reads: "*Emphasizing* the inadmissibility of the acquisition of territory by war and the need to work for a just and lasting peace in which every State in the area can live in security" (emphasis in original). The main framer of 242 was Lord Caradon from the United Kingdom. In the Security Council deliberations on the resolution, Caradon explicitly linked these two passages: "In our resolution we stated the principle of the 'withdrawal of Israel armed forces from territories occupied in the recent conflict' and in the preamble we emphasized 'the inadmissibility of the acquisition of territory by war.' In our view, the wording of those provisions is clear."[15] In a symposium some years later, Caradon recalled that, without

10. Michael Bar-Zohar, *Ben-Gurion: A Biography* (New York, 1978), p. 162.
11. Shlaim, *Collusion*, p. 16.
12. Flapan, *Birth*, pp. 31, 34–35.
13. The major studies of this secret agreement are Shlaim, *Collusion*, and Benny Morris, *The Road to Jerusalem* (New York, 2003).
14. United Nations, "Introduction to the Annual Report of the Secretary-General on the Work of the Organization, 16 June 1966–15 June 1967," in *General Assembly, Official Records: Twenty-second Session, Supplement 1A* (New York, 15 September 1967), para. 47.
15. *Security Council Official Records, Twenty-second Session*, 20 November 1967, 1,381st meeting.

Topic	The Case for Israel	What the Evidence Actually Shows
1. WHAT DID U.N. RESOLUTION 242 STATE? *(continued)*	*some unpopulated areas that were deemed necessary to assure Israel's "territorial integrity" within "secure" boundaries as contemplated by Resolution 242. Alon's plan, unlike Resolution 242, drew an important distinction between occupying territory and occupying populations. The Security Council resolution focused exclusively on territories rather than people. But the West Bank comprises cities, towns, and villages, as well as vast expanses of unpopulated land. The Alon Plan would have implemented a "territorial compromise." . . . The Arabs would still complain that their land was being occupied, but Resolution 242 contemplated territorial adjustments designed to achieve secure borders "free from threats or acts of war." (pp. 98–99; emphasis in original)* *(c) United Nations Resolution 242 . . . does not call on Israel to give back all of the territories*	the preambular reference to the inadmissibility of acquiring territory by war, "there could have been no unanimous vote" in the Security Council. Indeed, fully ten of the fifteen members of the Security Council stressed in their interventions the "inadmissibility" clause and Israel's obligation to fully withdraw, while none of the five remaining members dissented from this principle. The definite article was omitted from the operative paragraph ("occupied territories" as against "the occupied territories"), Caradon explained, due to the irregularities of the pre–June 1967 borders, which "were based on the accident of where exactly the Israeli and the Arab armies happened to be" at the time of the original armistice agreements ending the 1948 war. This omission did not, however, undercut the force of the preambular reference: "Knowing as I did the unsatisfactory nature of the 1967 line, I was not prepared to use wording in the Resolution which would have made that line permanent. Nevertheless it is necessary to say again that the overriding principle was the 'inadmissibility of the acquisition of territory by war' and that meant that there could be no justification for annexation of territory on the Arab side of the 1967 line merely because it had been conquered in the 1967 war."[16] To "prove" Caradon supported Israel's official interpretation of 242, Dershowitz cites an out-of-context, single-sentence quote culled from a "reader's letter" to the *Orlando Sentinel* from one "Ricki Hollander" of Brookline, Massachusetts. Beyond the absurdity of using this as the only source on a topic about which countless scholarly studies have been written, the sentence Dershowitz cites merely states Caradon's disapproval of the irregular pre–June borders as final, not his acceptance of territorial annexation, which he emphatically rejected. In the deliberations preceding approval of Caradon's resolution, U.S. ambassador Arthur Gold-

captured during the defensive war of 1967. The compromise agreed to by the Security Council was that Israel would give back "territories"—meaning most but not all. . . . Both Justice Goldberg and Lord Carrington [sic—Caradon] of Britain, the primary drafters of the resolution that was accepted, have stated unambiguously that it did not contemplate withdrawal from "all the territories," recognizing, as Lord Carrington [sic—Caradon] put it, "it would have been wrong to demand that Israel return to its positions of June 4, 1967, because these positions were undesirable and artificial."
(p. 205); (emphasis in original)

berg, acting at Israel's behest, resisted pressures from the Security Council for more explicit language on Israel's withdrawal. The United States repeatedly made clear, however, that it contemplated at most only *minor and mutual* border adjustments. For example, in late October 1967 Secretary of State Dean Rusk told Israeli foreign minister Abba Eban that "our support for secure permanent frontiers doesn't mean we support territorial changes." And Goldberg himself told Jordanian leaders in early November that "some territorial adjustment will be required" but that "there must be mutuality in adjustments," and, on a second occasion, that the United States supported "minor border rectifications" but that Jordan would "obtain compensation . . . for any territory it is required to give up."[17]

In the late 1960s senior Israeli Labor party official Yigal Allon proposed that Israel annex up to half the West Bank. American officials stood firm, however, in their conviction that "the words 'recognized and secure' [in 242] meant 'security arrangements' and 'recognition' of new lines as international boundaries," and "never meant that Israel could extend its territory to [the] West Bank or Suez if this was what it felt its security required"; and that "there will be no peace if Israel tries to hold onto large chunks of territory."

16. Lord Caradon et al., *U.N. Security Council Resolution 242: A Case Study in Diplomatic Ambiguity* (Washington, D.C., 1981), p. 13. For Caradon's position on 242, see also Belabbes Benkredda, "Rethinking United Nations Security Council Resolution 242—The Case for the Status Quo Ante Bellum" (M.A. Thesis, University of Exeter, 2003); for interventions of Security Council members on 242, see esp. John McHugo, "Resolution 242: A Legal Reappraisal of the Right-Wing Israeli Interpretation of the Withdrawal Phrase with Reference to the Conflict between Israel and the Palestinians," *International and Comparative Law Quarterly* (October 2002), pp. 866–72.

17. "Memorandum from the President's Special Assistant (Rostow) to President Johnson (October 24, 1967) (Doc. 487)," p. 942; "Telegram from the Mission to the United Nations to the Department of State (November 4, 1967) (Doc. 501)," pp. 982–83; "Memorandum from the Department of State to the Embassy in Israel (November 30, 1968) (Doc. 506)," p. 998; "Memorandum from Secretary of State Rusk to President Johnson (undated) (Doc. 513)," p. 1012, in *Foreign Relations of the United States, 1964–1968*, vol. 19: *Arab-Israeli Crisis and War, 1967* (Washington, D.C., 2004). The most exhaustive analysis of the U.S. position on 242, supporting the argument presented here, is a State Department study by Nina J. Noring and Walter B. Smith II entitled *The Withdrawal Clause in UN Security Council Resolution 242 of 1967: Its Legislative History and the Attitudes of the United States and Israel since 1967* (4 February 1978).

Topic	*The Case for Israel*	What the Evidence Actually Shows
1. WHAT DID U.N. RESOLUTION 242 STATE? *(continued)*	SOURCES: (a) None (b) None (c) "Not Just Semantics," Editorial [*sic*—"reader's letter"], *Orlando Sentinel*, August 7, 2000.	Referring to the Allon Plan explicitly by name, the United States deplored even the minimalist version of the plan as "a non-starter" and "unacceptable in principle." The full context of the last quote merits quotation, to be juxtaposed against Dershowitz's claims: "The territorial assurances that we have given Hussein are manifestly inconsistent with any proposal that would place 'certain unpopulated areas of the West Bank' under Israeli sovereignty or jurisdiction. The relevance of 'unpopulated areas' to 'minor border rectifications' is, of course, another moot point. (Incidentally, the Jordan Gov't's 1961 maps on the 'distribution of population' and 'population density' show very graphically that the only 'unpopulated areas' on the West Bank lie along the present ceasefire line between Israel and Jordan. . . .) Eban seems to be saying that Israel has suggested to Hussein some kind of variation of the Allon Plan, which we have already indicated is unacceptable in principle both to US and to Jordan. What Eban appears to be asking of Jordan is certainly 'significantly' different . . . from the territorial assurances we have given Jordan."[18] Thus, contrary to Dershowitz's claims, the Allon Plan didn't annex "vast expanses of unpopulated land"; it wasn't consistent with U.N. Resolution 242; and the United States didn't support it. Finally, in private, Israeli leaders suffered no illusions on the actual meaning of 242. Protesting the clause "withdrawal of Israel armed forces from territories occupied in the recent conflict," Abba Eban told Caradon: "The words 'in the recent conflict' convert the principle of eliminating occupation into a mathematically precise formula for restoring the June 4 map. Israel will not reconstruct that map, at any time or in any circumstances." And during a closed session of the Labor Party in June 1968, Moshe Dayan counseled against endorsing 242 because "it means withdrawal to the 4 June boundaries, and because we are in conflict with the SC [Security Council] on that resolution."[19]

2. WAS THE "WITHDRAWAL" CLAUSE OF U.N. RESOLUTION 242 BIASED AGAINST ISRAEL?

[T]he U.N. Security Council . . . for the first time in history ordered a nation to return territories lawfully captured in a defensive war. (p. 96)

SOURCES: None

In fact, Israel was the only country *allowed* by the U.N. to keep territory acquired by war. The boundaries of the prospective Jewish state approved by the United Nations in 1947 allotted it 56 percent of British-mandated Palestine. In the course of the 1947–49 war, Israel expanded its borders, incorporating fully 78 percent of Palestine. It was these forcibly expanded borders that Security Council Resolution 242 effectively ratified in November 1967. In any event, even if it was a "defensive" war—a claim not supported by a single country in the world—Israel could not have "lawfully captured" territory in June 1967, because international law prohibits forcible boundary changes between states under *any* circumstances, including a "defensive" war.[20] An authoritative statement by the World Court has resolved this issue. In its 2004 advisory opinion "Legal Consequences of the Construction of a Wall in the Occupied Palestinian Territory," the World Court repeatedly affirmed the preambular paragraph of Resolution 242 emphasizing "the inadmissibility of the acquisition of territory by war," as well as a 1970 General Assembly resolution emphasizing that "[n]o territorial acquisition resulting from the threat or use of force shall be recognized as legal," denoting this principle a "corollary" of the U.N. Charter and as such "customary international law" and a "customary rule" binding on all member states of the United Nations (paras. 74, 87, 117).

18. "Telegram from the Department of State to the Embassy in Jordan (9 November 1968) (Doc. 312)," p. 619; "Telegram from the Department of State to the Embassy in Israel (13 November 1968) (Doc. 320)," pp. 634–36; "Memorandum of Conversation" (14 November 1968) (Doc. 321), p. 639; "Memorandum from the President's Special Assistant (Rostow) to President Johnson (15 November 1968) (Doc. 322)," p. 641; "Telegram from the Embassy in Jordan to the Department of State (20 November 1968) (Doc. 328)," p. 654; "Information Memorandum from the President's Special Assistant (Rostow) to President Johnson (22 November 1968) (Doc. 329)," p. 655; "Telegram from the Embassy in Jordan to the Department of State (19 December 1968) (Doc. 353)," p. 699, in *Foreign Relations of the United States, 1964–1968*, vol. 20: *Arab-Israeli Dispute, 1967–1968* (Washington, D.C., 2001).

19. Public Record Office, Foreign and Commonwealth Office 17/515, "UK Mission New York to Foreign Office," Telegram No. 3164, 12 November 1967; Daniel Dishon (ed.), *Middle East Record*, vol. 4, 1968 (Jerusalem, 1973), p. 247 (Dayan's statement was leaked to the Israeli press).

20. Sir Robert Jennings and Sir Arthur Watts (eds.), *Oppenheim's International Law*, 9th ed. (London, 1992), 1:702–5, and Sharon Korman, *The Right of Conquest: The Acquisition of Territory by Force in International Law and Practice* (Oxford, 1996), pp. 203–14.

Topic	The Case for Israel	What the Evidence Actually Shows
3. HOW DID ISRAEL AND THE ARAB STATES REACT TO 242?	*(a) Almost immediately upon prevailing over the Arab armies that had pledged and planned to annihilate Israel, the Israeli government agreed to comply with Resolution 242. . . . Israel immediately accepted the principles of Resolution 242. (p. 96)* *(b) Along with most Arab nations, the Palestinians rejected Resolution 242, while Israel accepted it, as it had the Peel Report and the U.N. partition. Once again, the Palestinians and Arabs rejected the two-state solution, while Israel indicated a willingness to take steps that would have led to such a solution. (p. 98)* SOURCES: (a) None (b) None	Israel rejected the consensus interpretation of the withdrawal provision in U.N. Resolution 242. Bent on significant territorial annexation, it initially resorted to diplomatic circumlocutions to avoid outright rejection of 242, claiming, for instance, that the resolution was merely "a list of principles which can help the parties and guide them in their search for a solution because it lists the claims, the main claims, which both parties make against each other, but it has no life of its own." But when Egypt publicly agreed in February 1971 to all the resolution's terms in exchange for full Israeli withdrawal from the Sinai, and a U.N.-appointed mediator called on Israel for a direct response, Israel could no longer hide behind rhetorical evasions. Israel bluntly replied that it "will not withdraw to the pre–June 1967 lines," thereby killing the U.N.-sponsored peace initiative. Jordan had also publicly acquiesced in all the terms of the U.N. resolution by 1971. (Syria's response was more equivocal.)[21] Palestinians were not included in the diplomacy surrounding 242, and the resolution's one oblique reference to them merely "[a]ffirms . . . the necessity . . . [f]or achieving a just settlement of the refugee problem." Dershowitz's claim that 242 called for a "two-state solution" grossly falsifies its content: a Palestinian state was not even a topic of consideration in the diplomacy leading to the resolution's passage. From the mid-1970s, however, the Palestine Liberation Organization (PLO) leadership accepted the terms and language of 242 in the context of U.N. resolutions also affirming the *national* rights of Palestinians to an independent state in the West Bank and Gaza.[22]

C. TWO-STATE SETTLEMENT

Topic	The Case for Israel	What the Evidence Actually Shows
1. WHAT IS THE TWO-STATE SETTLEMENT?	*(a) A two-state solution to the Arab-Palestinian-Israeli conflict also seems to be a rare point of consensus in what is otherwise an intractable dilemma. Any reasonable consideration of how to resolve this longstanding dispute peacefully must begin with this consensus. Most of the world currently advocates a two-state solution, including the vast majority of Americans. (p. 3)* *(b) The current worldwide consensus supports this premise: that there should be two states, one Jewish and one Palestinian, existing side by side. There is no consensus as to the relative size and precise borders to the two states. (p. 65)* SOURCES: (a) None, (b) None	In the mid-1970s an international consensus began crystallizing to resolve the Israel-Palestine conflict. Its core was support for two states in British-mandated Palestine: Israel within its pre–June 1967 borders alongside a Palestinian state in the West Bank and Gaza. Every statement of this international consensus from the mid-1970s builds on U.N. Resolution 242 as well as the Palestinian right to self-determination within the areas of Palestine occupied by Israel in June 1967. A December 1989 General Assembly resolution put forth, inter alia, these principles for resolving the conflict: "The withdrawal of Israel from the Palestinian territory occupied since 1967, including Jerusalem, and from the other occupied Arab territories; Guaranteeing arrangements for security of all States in the region, including those named in resolution 181 (II) of 29 November 1947 [Partition Resolution], within secure and internationally recognized boundaries." (Notice that the resolution includes the definite article before "Palestinian territory.") It passed 151 to 3 (Israel, United States, Dominica). A December 2003 General Assembly resolution "[a]ffirming the right of all States in the region to live in peace and within secure and internationally recognized borders" and "the right of the Palestinian people to self-determination, including the right to their independent State of Palestine" passed by a vote of 169 to 5 (United States, Israel, Marshall Islands, Micronesia, Palau). A January 2004 General Assembly resolution stressing "the necessity for a commitment to the vision of the two-State solution" and affirming the basic principles of 242—"the

21. Finkelstein, *Image and Reality*, pp. 151–65 ("list of principles" at p. 152 and "will not withdraw" at p. 158).
22. Noam Chomsky, *Fateful Triangle: The United States, Israel and the Palestinians*, updated ed. (Boston, 1999), chap. 3.

Topic	The Case for Israel	What the Evidence Actually Shows
1. WHAT IS THE TWO-STATE SETTLEMENT? *(continued)*		inadmissibility of the acquisition of territory by war" and "the right of all States in the region to live in peace within secure and internationally recognized borders"—called for, inter alia, "[t]he withdrawal of Israel from the Palestinian territory occupied since 1967" and "[t]he realization of the inalienable rights of the Palestinian people, primarily the right to self-determination and the right to their independent State." (Notice again that the resolution includes the definite article before "Palestinian territory.") It passed 160 to 6 (United States, Israel, Marshall Islands, Micronesia, Palau, Uganda). Although in practice allowing for "minor" and "mutual" border adjustments, the worldwide consensus on the size and borders of the two states couldn't be clearer: Israel must *fully* withdraw from the territories it occupied in June 1967.[23]
2. WHAT IS THE RECORD OF SUPPORT FOR THE TWO-STATE SETTLEMENT AMONG THE MAIN PARTIES TO THE CONFLICT?	*(a) Israel has long been willing to accept the kind of two-state solution that is now on the proposed "road map" to peace. (p. 1)* *(b) [A two-state settlement] is now the official position of the Palestinian Authority as well as the Egyptian, Jordanian, Saudi Arabian, and Moroccan governments. Only the extremists among the Israelis and the Palestinians, as well as the rejectionist*	For nearly three decades the Palestinian leadership and key Arab states have registered support for the two-state settlement. Israel and the United States have opposed it. In January 1976 a resolution was tabled in the Security Council affirming that Palestinians should have the right "to establish an independent state in Palestine," that "Israel should withdraw from all the Arab territories occupied" in June 1967, and—borrowing the language of 242—that "appropriate arrangements should be established to guarantee . . . the sovereignty, territorial integrity and political independence of all states in the area and their right to live in peace within secure and recognized boundaries." The resolution was supported by the Palestine Liberation Organization (PLO) as well as Egypt, Syria, and Jordan. Israel refused to attend the Security Council session, the Labor government announcing that it

wouldn't negotiate with Palestinians, while the United States vetoed the resolution. In April 1980 the United States vetoed a second Security Council resolution using this same language.[24] In August 1981 King Fahd of Saudi Arabia presented a peace plan calling for "Israeli evacuation of all Arab territories seized during the 1967 Middle East war," "[s]etting up a Palestinian State with East Jerusalem as its capital," and "[a]ffirming the right of all countries of the region to live in peace." Israel reacted by starting preparations to destroy the PLO based in Lebanon.[25] In his analysis of the buildup to the Lebanon invasion, Israeli political scientist Avner Yaniv reports that Yasser Arafat and the PLO mainstream were "visibly engaged in a process of reorientation leading to a far more compromising approach toward the Zionist state than previously," while the United States was increasing pressure on Israel "to deal with the PLO directly." On the other hand, "all Israeli cabinets since 1967" as well as "leading mainstream doves" adamantly opposed establishment of a Palestinian state in the Occupied Territories. The aim of Israeli policy was "weakening PLO moderates and strengthening their radical rivals," thereby "ensuring [the PLO's] inflexibility." To this end, Israel periodically conducted "punitive military action deliberately out of proportion to damage done by PLO attacks" and "raids [that] harmed Palestinian and Lebanese civilians." Ultimately, however, Israel had only two options: "a political move leading to a historic compromise with the PLO, or preemptive military action against it." To fend off the PLO's "peace"

states of Syria, Iran, and Libya, claim that the entire landmass of what is now Israel, the West Bank, and the Gaza Strip should permanently be controlled either by the Israelis alone or by the Palestinians alone. (p. 3; cf. pp. 65, 71–72)

(c) [A]t least until recently, virtually all Palestinian and Arab leaders categorically rejected any solution that included a Jewish state, a Jewish homeland, or Jewish self-determination. (p. 8)

(d) [T]here can be no dispute that until relatively recently the rejection of the two-state solution was virtually unanimous among Palestinians and Arabs. (p. 73)

(e) Israel did manage to make some halting progress in peace

23. U.N.G.A. Resolution 44/42, *Question of Palestine* (6 December 1989); U.N.G.A. Resolution 58/163, *The Right of the Palestinian People to Self-Determination* (22 December 2003); U.N.G.A. Resolution 58/21, *Peaceful Settlement of the Question of Palestine* (22 January 2004).

24. *United Nations Security Council Resolution S/11940*; *United Nations Security Council Resolution S/13911*. For background and details on the January 1976 resolution, see Chomsky, *Fateful Triangle*, pp. 67–68.

25. For the Saudi plan, see Yehuda Lukacs (ed.), *The Israeli-Palestinian Conflict: A Documentary Record, 1967–1990* (Cambridge, 1992), pp. 477–78; Yehoshaphat Harkabi, *Israel's Fateful Hour* (New York, 1988), p. 101, reports that the plan underlying the Lebanon invasion was presented to Prime Minister Begin and cabinet members in September 1981.

Topic	The Case for Israel	What the Evidence Actually Shows
2. WHAT IS THE RECORD OF SUPPORT FOR THE TWO-STATE SETTLEMENT AMONG THE MAIN PARTIES TO THE CONFLICT? *(continued)*	*talks with the Palestinians starting in the early 1990s. Even before that time, a number of senior Fatah figures had been preaching a "two-state" solution, but these individuals had experienced assassination . . . at the hands of other Palestinians. From its founding in 1964 (and even before), the PLO (and its predecessors) had rejected the two-state solution in favor of terrorism, the destruction of Israel, and the transfer out of the Jewish population. (p. 105)* *(f) [T]he United Nations . . . singled out the PLO from among all other representatives of stateless groups for special observer status and other diplomatic privileges. This was done at a time when the PLO rejected the U.N. partition of Palestine, rejected the existence of the U.N. member nation Israel, rejected Security Council Resolution 242, and demanded control*	offensive," Israel chose military action, invading Lebanon. "[D]estroying the PLO as a political force capable of claiming a Palestinian state on the West Bank," Yaniv concludes (as do all serious scholars), was "the raison d'être of the entire operation."[26] Meeting in Algiers in November 1988, the Palestine National Council officially ratified a two-state settlement. Its "political communique" called for the convening of an international conference on the basis of 242 and "the legitimate national rights of the Palestinian people, foremost among which is the right to self-determination"; for "[t]he withdrawal of Israel from all the Palestinian and Arab territories it occupied in 1967"; and for "[t]he Security Council . . . to formulate and guarantee arrangements for security and peace between all the states concerned in the region, including the Palestinian state."[27] In tandem with its escalating repression of the largely nonviolent Palestinian revolt (intifada) in the Occupied Territories, the Labor-Likud "National Unity" government unveiled in May 1989 its own "peace initiative" explicitly barring a Palestinian state in the West Bank and Gaza. Among its "basic guidelines" were that "Israel opposes the establishment of an additional Palestinian state in the Gaza district and in the area between Israel and Jordan" and that "[t]here will be no change in the status of Judea, Samaria and Gaza other than in accordance with the basic guidelines of the government."[28] (The word *additional* refers to the traditional Zionist view that a Palestinian state already exists in Jordan.) In May 1997 the Israeli Labor party, which until then categorically ruled out a Palestinian state, officially recognized "the Palestinians' right to self-determination" and did "not rule out in this connection the establishment of

APPENDIX III **297**

over all of Palestine and the transfer of most Jews out of all of Palestine. (pp. 105–6)

(g) [I]t also follows from the undisputed fact that Palestinian leaders are blameworthy for their repeated rejection of the two-state solution and for the resulting escalation of violence, that the two sides should not be treated in an even-handed manner. To reward rejection and violence with even-handedness is to encourage such conduct. (p. 194)

SOURCES:

(a) None, (b) None, (c) None, (d) None, (e) None, (f) None, (g) None

a Palestinian state with limited sovereignty." However, the platform, on the one hand, was silent on the crucial question of the Palestinian state's borders and, on the other, explicitly stated that "Israel extends its sovereignty over areas that are major Jewish settlement blocs"—nullifying the international consensus.[29] In 2002 Prime Minister Sharon expressed support for a Palestinian state. The Likud Central Committee, however, subsequently passed a resolution stating that "no Palestinian state will be established west of the Jordan River." In addition, as seasoned Israeli commentators have pointed out, the Palestinian state Sharon envisages is based on the South African "Bantustan model," whereby 1.5 million Gazans will be confined "in a huge holding pen," while the wall currently under construction will fracture the West Bank into "three Bantustans."[30] In Dershowitz's imaginative history of this international consensus, "there can be no dispute that until relatively recently the rejection of the two-state solution was virtually unanimous among Palestinians and Arabs"—even if the PLO and key Arab states have registered support for the international consensus since the mid 1970s. In contrast, according to him, Israel "has always favored a two-state solution"[31]—even if until 1997 Labor ruled out any kind of Palestinian state, Likud still opposes one, and Sharon favors a Palestinian state on the "Bantustan model."

26. Avner Yaniv, *Dilemmas of Security: Politics, Strategy and the Israeli Experience in Lebanon* (Oxford, 1987), pp. 20, 22–23, 50–54, 67–70, 87–89, 100–101, 105–6, 113, 143, 294n46.
27. For excerpts from the political communiqué, see Lukacs, *Israeli-Palestinian Conflict*, pp. 415–20.
28. For full text of the "Peace Initiative by the Government of Israel, 14 May 1989," see Lukacs, *Israeli-Palestinian Conflict*, pp. 236–39.
29. For the Labor Party platform, see www.jewishvirtuallibrary.org/jsource/Politics/labor.html.
30. Yossi Verter, "PM loses vote on Palestinian state," *Haaretz* (14 May 2002). Meron Benvenisti, "Bantustan plan for an apartheid Israel," *Guardian* (26 April 2004); see also Akiva Eldar, "Analysis: Creating a Bantustan in Gaza," *Haaretz* (16 April 2004).
31. Alan M. Dershowitz, "Making the Case for Israel," www.FrontPageMagazine.com (1 June 2004).

Topic	The Case for Israel	What the Evidence Actually Shows
3. WHERE DO THE PALESTINIAN AND ISRAELI PEOPLES STAND ON THE INTERNATIONAL CONSENSUS?	(a) *A substantial majority of Israelis have long accepted this compromise* [of a two-state settlement].... *Only the extremists among the Israelis and the Palestinians . . . claim that the entire landmass of what is now Israel, the West Bank and the Gaza Strip should permanently be controlled either by the Israelis alone or by the Palestinians alone.* (p. 3) (b) *Recent public opinion polls taken by Palestinian polling organizations also show that a majority of Palestinians do not accept the two-state solution. As many as 87 percent in one poll were in favor of "liberating all of Palestine."* (p. 72) (c) *Most polls show that an overwhelming majority of Israelis want peace and will give up much in an effort to secure it, while as many as 87 percent of Palestini-*	To document overwhelming Palestinian opposition to a two-state settlement and support for suicide bombings, Dershowitz cites three times the same poll data from a *New York Times* article. All three of his citations of the *Times* are in one way or another wrong. In the March 18, 2002, *New York Times*, Serge Schmemann did report a survey, allegedly conducted by An-Najah National University, containing the data Dershowitz refers to. However, a thorough search found no trace of such a poll at An-Najah.[32] The *Haaretz* article cited by Dershowitz provides no specific data on Israelis' support for the international consensus on a two-state settlement or on Israelis' attitudes to gross human rights violations of Palestinians. On the other hand, although not cited by Dershowitz, extensive, reliable poll data on Palestinian and Israeli attitudes do exist. None of these data even remotely support any of Dershowitz's findings or conclusions. For the period December 2001–June 2004, Palestinians' support for a two-state settlement based on the international consensus ("ending occupation on basis of UN Resolution 242 and establishing the Palestinian State") versus support for "liberating all of historic Palestine" was evenly split at 45 percent to 45 percent, while support for suicide bombings hovered around 63 percent. These percentages reflected a hardening of Palestinian opinion after hopes of an Israeli withdrawal withered and Israeli repression escalated. The anecdotal evidence suggests that during the early years of the first intifada, support for the international consensus was overwhelming among Palestinians, while support for attacks inside Israel proper was virtually nil. Even as recently as February 1999 fully 52.7 percent of Palestinians gave total support and another 22.3 percent middling support to "the idea of establishing a Palestinian state with 1967

ans want terrorism to continue until all of Palestine is liberated. (pp. 108–9)

(d) A recent poll taken at Najab University in Nablus found that "87% of Palestinians surveyed were in favor of continuing terror attacks" and "87.5% were in favor of 'liberating all of Palestine.'" (p. 162)

borders," while even after decades of occupation and repression, only 5 percent of Palestinians supported suicide bombings in March 1996, and as late as March 1999 still only 26 percent approved. Finally, the respected Palestinian pollster Khalil Shikaki points to the consistent finding over a ten-year period that "about three-quarters of the respondents continued to support reconciliation between the States of Palestine and Israel in the context of a two state-solution and a peace agreement between the two sides." His conclusion is that "for short-term needs, high threat perception among the Palestinians elicits a highly emotional and hard-line response," whereas "when dealing with long-term issues, rational thinking prevails among Palestinians, even in the midst of their pain and suffering."[33] Among Israelis, support for

32. Email correspondence between Mouin Rabbani and Dr. Taher Masri of An-Najah National University (12 October 2003). Masri, director of public opinion research at An-Najah, states that a polling center at An-Najah was first established only in July 2003; and the first opinion poll was conducted 17–19 July 2003. Schmemann did not reply to email queries, and an exhaustive search of the Web produced no record of such a poll.

33. The Jerusalem Media and Communication Center (JMCC, www.jmcc.org/publicpoll/results) reports these findings:

	Support for suicide bombings (%)	Support for international consensus/ Support for liberating all of Palestine (%)
December 2001	64	49/40
December 2002	63	46/47
October 2003	62	45/43
June 2004	62	42/46

All other findings reported in the text are culled from JMCC surveys. The World Bank has commended JMCC polls as "methodologically sound" (*Twenty-Seven Months—Intifada, Closures and Palestinian Economic Crisis—An Assessment* [Jerusalem, May 2003], p. 40n77). For Shikaki quote, see Jaffee Center for Strategic Studies, "Palestinian Public Opinion and the al-Aqsa Intifada," in *Strategic Assessment* (Tel Aviv, June 2002), p. 5. For Palestinian opposition to targeting Israel proper during the first intifada, see, e.g., Norman G. Finkelstein, *The Rise and Fall of Palestine: A Personal Account of the Intifada Years* (Minneapolis, 1996), p. 37. In fact, Palestinian public opinion overwhelmingly opposed *any* Palestinian military operations, even against Israeli soldiers in the Occupied Territories.

Topic	The Case for Israel	What the Evidence Actually Shows
3. WHERE DO THE PALESTINIAN AND ISRAELI PEOPLES STAND ON THE INTERNATIONAL CONSENSUS? (continued)	SOURCES: (a) None (b) New York Times, May [sic—March?] 18, 2002 (c) Ephraim Yaar and Tamar Hermann [sic—Hermann], "Peace Index: Most Israelis Support Attack on Iraq," Haaretz, March 6, 2003; Thomas Friedman [sic—Serge Schmemann?], New York Times, March 18, 2002. (d) Thomas Friedman [sic—Serge Schmemann?], New York Times, March 18, 2002.	a kind of two-state settlement close to the international consensus has hovered around 42 percent during the second intifada. Support for the most egregious repressive measures against Palestinians (political liquidations, use of tanks and aircraft, house demolitions) averaged 80 to 90 percent, while nearly half of Israelis polled consistently approved expelling all Palestinians in the Occupied Territories, and nearly a third supported expelling all Palestinian citizens of Israel as well. Unlike in the Palestinian case, these Israeli poll results on the whole *can't* be decisively explained by a hardening of opinion due to the escalating violence and despair of a two-state settlement. Respected Israeli pollster Asher Arian points out that support among Israelis for any kind of Palestinian state stood at only 21 percent in 1987 and 35 percent in 1993, while already in 1991 fully 38 percent of Israelis supported expulsion of Palestinians from the Occupied Territories and 24 percent supported expulsion of Palestinian citizens of Israel. According to other reliable polls, even as late as December 1999 only 6 percent of Israeli Jews fully accepted and another 18 percent accepted at all a Palestinian state on the pre–June 1967 borders (13 percent and 18 percent respectively, for all Israelis, including Palestinian citizens), while even during the early months of the first intifada in 1988, when it was overwhelmingly nonviolent, fully 41 percent of Israeli Jews supported expulsion of the Palestinians.[34]

34. The closest approximation to the international consensus for which poll data are available is Israelis' support for President Clinton's peace proposal in December 2000. Clinton recommended a 94 to 96 percent Israeli withdrawal from the West Bank and a 1 to 3 percent swap of Israeli land for Palestinian land annexed by Israel. Asher Arian's *Israeli Public Opinion on National Security 2003* (Jaffee Center for Strategic Studies, Tel Aviv), p. 33, reported these findings on Israelis' support for the Clinton proposal:

	Establishment of a Palestinian state on 95% of the West Bank and Gaza (%)	Land swap (%)
2001	43	44
2002	40	38
2003	42	45

Arian presents in the 2003 survey, p. 29, these findings for Israelis' support of egregious human rights violations in the Occupied Territories:

	Political liquidations (%)	Use of tanks and aircraft (%)	House demolitions (%)
2001	89	71	No data
2002	90	80	No data
2003	92	79	88*

*Arian reports in his 2002 survey, p. 35, that fully 57 percent of the respondents "thought that the measures employed to ensure quiet in the territories were too lenient."

Arian presents in the 2003 survey, pp. 30–31, these findings for Israelis' support for expelling the Palestinians from the Occupied Territories, expelling Palestinian citizens of Israel, and "encouraging" Palestinian citizens of Israel to leave:

	Expelling Palestinians in Occupied Territories (%)	Expelling Palestinian citizens of Israel (%)	"Encouraging" Palestinian citizens of Israel to leave (%)
2001	No data	No data	50
2002	46	31	53
2003	46	33	57**

**Arian notes in his 2002 survey, p. 27, that already in the early and mid-1990s fully two-thirds of respondents supported such "encouraging," while a June 2004 University of Haifa poll found that 64 percent of Israeli Jews supported "encouraging" Palestinian citizens of Israel to leave. See Yulie Khromchenco, "Poll: 64% of Israeli Jews support encouraging Arabs to leave," Haaretz (22 June 2004), and a 20 October 2004 poll conducted by the Shiluv Institute found that 58 percent of Israelis between the ages of eighteen and twenty-two supported the "deportation of Arabs from Israel" (Americans for Peace Now, Middle East Peace Report [Washington, D.C., 25 October 2004]).

For Israelis' support of a Palestinian state in 1987 and 1993, see 2003 survey, p. 12; for Israelis' support for expelling Palestinians from the Occupied Territories and from Israel in 1991, see Arian's 2002 survey, p. 10; for the December 1999 poll data on Israeli Jews' support for a Palestinian state, see JMCC poll no. 35, "On Palestinian and Israeli Attitudes towards the Future of the Peace Process" ("in cooperation with Tami Steinmetz Center for Peace Research, Tel Aviv University"), p. 5; for Israelis' support for expelling Palestinians in 1988, see Nurit Amitary, "Survey: 41% for transfer, 45% Israel is too democratic," Haaretz (8 June 1988).

DERSHOWITZ v. CHOMSKY

In 1983 Noam Chomsky published *The Fateful Triangle: The United States, Israel and the Palestinians*.[1] Apart from exhaustive research bringing to light a documentary record little known in the United States, the main innovation of the book was to recast debate on resolving the Israel-Palestine conflict. Until then, the terms of debate in the United States typically juxtaposed the "Arab" against the "Israeli" position. Chomsky coined the term *international consensus* to denote a third pole in the debate: the settlement favored by the international community. Registered in numerous forums—most notably, United Nations resolutions—this international consensus supported a two-state settlement incorporating the provisions of U.N. Resolution 242—Israeli withdrawal from the West Bank and Gaza, on the one hand, and Arab recognition of Israel's right to live in security, on the other—as well as establishment of a Palestinian state. Chomsky's main empirical insight, copiously documented, was that the Palestinian leadership and key Arab states had come around to supporting the international consensus for a two-state settlement, whereas Israel and the United States were the major—indeed, before long, the only—opponents of it. Whereas Chomsky had previously given support to a binational state along the lines advocated before Israel was founded,[2] he aligned himself from after the October 1973 war with the international consensus on the grounds that, although far from ideal, it was the only practical basis for a settlement that provided a modicum of justice for all parties concerned. In *Fateful Triangle* he wrote:

> Within the international consensus, there has been little discussion of whether such a settlement—henceforth, a "two-state settlement"—reflects higher demands of abstract justice; rather it has been taken to be a politically realistic solution that would maximize the chances for peace and security for the inhabitants of the former Palestine, for the region, and for the world, and that satisfies the valid claims of the two major parties as well as is possible under existing conditions. One can imagine various subsequent developments through peaceful means and mutual consent towards a form of federation or other arrangements.[3]

While sentiment in Chomsky's political milieu has, in recent years, been shifting toward a "one-state solution" incorporating Israel and the

1. Boston, 1983. In 1999 an updated version was released under the title *Fateful Triangle*.
2. Noam Chomsky, *Peace in the Middle East?* (New York, 1974).
3. Chomsky, *Fateful Triangle*, p. 42.

Occupied Territories, he himself hasn't deviated from support of the two-state settlement in his extensive writings and lectures on this topic since publication of *Fateful Triangle*.

In *The Case for Israel*, Alan Dershowitz states that "the premise of this book is . . . a two-state solution" (p. 2). This "premise" is repeatedly anchored by Dershowitz in what he refers to as the "international consensus" or "worldwide consensus" favoring such a settlement (pp. 64, 65, 69; cf. p. 3). Yet, while using Chomsky's framework and even his coinage, Dershowitz brazenly asserts, in the face of a three-decade-long written record proving otherwise, that Chomsky "reject[s] the two-state solution" (p. 3).[4] As against Chomsky, Dershowitz proclaims that "I've always favored a two-state solution."[5] This will certainly be news to those who've followed Dershowitz's pronouncements over the years. There is no record of him ever having supported an independent Palestinian state or criticizing Israel's opposition to it. In the early 1990s Dershowitz advocated not an independent Palestinian state but "some form of autonomy" for Palestinians.[6] Indeed, in his 1991 autobiography, Dershowitz expressed some doubt whether Israel should in *any* way mitigate its military occupation:

> I think—though I am not certain—that Israel is making a mistake in continuing to occupy heavily populated Arab areas on the West Bank and in Gaza. But the decision to exchange lawfully captured territory (even heavily populated territory) for the promise of peace (even if such a promise were forthcoming) is so complex, so fraught with risk, so unprecedented in world history, so involved with domestic political considerations and consequences, that I, for one, am reluctant to participate in the cacophonous chorus of know-it-all criticism that is currently directed at Israel for its inaction.[7]

4. Although Chomsky has written voluminously on the Israel-Palestine conflict, Dershowitz's preferred reference is Chomsky's public lectures, which can't be checked against Dershowitz's rendering of them—as Dershowitz well knows. The claims of Dershowitz that can be checked against the Chomsky original uniformly lack merit. For example, he suggests on p. 79 of *The Case for Israel* that, in a Harvard lecture, Chomsky misrepresented historian Benny Morris. He quotes Chomsky as falsely asserting, "Benny Morris has shown that the Arab population 'was driven out' by the Israelis" in 1948. Yet just as Chomsky reported, in *Israel's Border Wars* (New York, 1993), Morris states that during the 1948 war "the Palestinians had been crushed, with some 700,000 driven into exile" (p. 410).

5. Alan M. Dershowitz, "Making the Case for Israel," www.FrontPage Magazine.com (1 June 2004).

6. "Invasion Alters Israel's Occupation" (August 1990), in *Contrary to Popular Opinion* (New York, 1992), p. 357; for a similar formulation, see "Why Is the PLO Still So Popular?" (March 1991), in ibid., p. 362.

7. Alan M. Dershowitz, *Chutzpah* (Boston, 1991), p. 232.

In a recent *Haaretz* interview, Dershowitz gave this account of his past views:

> I always thought that Israel made a terrible mistake by not accepting the Allon plan. Israel made a mistake by not making unilateral border adjustments after the war in the spirit of Security Council Resolution 242. Israel and the UN made a mistake in 1967 by not understanding that there is a difference between occupying land and occupying people. Occupying land is okay. Territorial changes after a war of defense are fine, especially in the case of Jordan, which started the war against Israel in 1967. . . . Whoever starts a war should take into consideration that it may suffer territorial changes. On the other hand, occupation of people is always bad. I was always against occupation of people, but not against occupation of land.[8]

The Allon Plan, proposed soon after the June 1967 war by senior Labor party official Yigal Allon, called for Israel's annexation of up to half the West Bank, with the fragmented areas of "dense Arab settlement" exercising in lieu of statehood some form of autonomy or link with Jordan.[9] Contrariwise, the international consensus has called for Israel's full withdrawal to its pre–June 1967 border and the establishment of an independent Palestinian state in the West Bank and Gaza. But unlike Chomsky, Dershowitz has "always favored a two-state solution" based on the international consensus—even if his own written record shows contrariwise.

8. Haim Handwerker, "A paragon, this Israel," *Haaretz* (12 December 2003).
9. For the Allon Plan, see B'Tselem (Israeli Information Center for Human Rights in the Occupied Territories), *Land Grab: Israel's Settlement Policy in the West Bank* (Jerusalem, May 2002), p. 7.

CHARADE

On pages 238–39 of *The Case for Israel*, Alan Dershowitz refers to the "so-called Palestinian right of return" and "claimed right to return" and states that "[t]he time has come—indeed the time is long overdue—to put an end to this right of return charade by so-called Arab refugees."

In December 1948 the United Nations General Assembly affirmed, in accordance with the Universal Declaration of Human Rights (UDHR), the right of Palestinians driven into exile during the first Arab-Israel war to return home.[1] Paragraph 11 of General Assembly Resolution 194(III) "[*r*]*esolves* that the refugees wishing to return to their homes and live at peace with their neighbours should be permitted to do so at the earliest practicable date, and that compensation should be paid for the property of those choosing not to return."[2] The principles of this resolution figure as part of the international consensus among states and human rights organizations for resolving the Israel-Palestine conflict. General Assembly resolutions noting "*with regret* that repatriation or compensation of the refugees, as provided for in paragraph 11 of its resolution 194 (III), has not yet been effected," and requesting "continued efforts towards the implementation of that paragraph" were adopted by votes of 151 to 2 (Israel, Marshall Islands) in December 2001, 158 to 1 (Israel) in December 2002, and 167 to 1 (Israel) in December 2003.[3] A December 2003 General Assembly resolution that "*stresses* the need for resolving the problem of the Palestine refugees in conformity with its resolution 194 (III)" passed 160 to 6 (Israel, United States, Palau, Uganda, Micronesia, Marshall Islands).[4] (All emphases in originals.)

In December 2000 Human Rights Watch (HRW) sent open letters to President Clinton, Prime Minister Barak, and President Arafat regarding the Palestinian refugees. They uniformly stated:

1. Article 13 of the UDHR states: "Everyone has the right to leave any country, including his own, and to return to his country." The International Covenant on Civil and Political Rights (ICCPR), the treaty that gives legal force to many of the rights proclaimed in the UDHR, codifies the right to return, stating in Article 12.4: "No one shall be arbitrarily deprived of the right to enter his own country."

2. *Palestine—Progress Report of the United Nations Mediator* (A/RES/194[III]) (11 December 1948).

3. *Assistance to Palestine Refugees* (A/RES/56/52) (10 December 2001); *Assistance to Palestine Refugees* (A/RES/57/117) (11 December 2002); *Assistance to Palestine Refugees* (A/RES/58/91) (9 December 2003).

4. *Peaceful Settlement of the Question of Palestine* (A/RES/58/21) (3 December 2003).

Since the inception of the international refugee system fifty years ago, three durable solutions have emerged under international law and refugee policy to enable refugees to put an end to their refugee status and re-establish an effective link with a state. These include voluntary repatriation to the refugee's country of origin; local integration in the country of asylum; or resettlement in a third country. HRW calls on Israel, a future Palestinian state, countries currently hosting stateless Palestinians, and the international community to ensure that individual refugees are able to make free and informed choices for themselves from among these three established precedents.

To this end, HRW urges Israel to recognize the right to return for those Palestinians, and their descendants, who fled from territory that is now within the State of Israel, and who have maintained appropriate links with that territory. This is a right that persists even when sovereignty over the territory is contested or has changed hands.

If a former home no longer exists or is occupied by an innocent third party, return should be permitted to the vicinity of the former home. As in the cases of all displaced people, those unable to return to a former home because it is occupied or has been destroyed, or those who have lost property, are entitled to compensation. However, compensation is not a substitute for the right to return to the vicinity of a former home, should that be one's choice.

And again: "Neither the options of local integration and third-country resettlement, nor their absence, should extinguish the right to return; their humanitarian purpose is to allow individual Palestinians to select during a specified period among several choices for ending their refugee status." In a separate statement, HRW noted that it had likewise "defended the right of refugees to return to their homes in Bosnia, Chile, China, East Timor, Rwanda and Guatemala, as well as in other instances."[5]

In March 2001 Amnesty International released a "policy statement" regarding the Palestinian refugees. It stated:

Amnesty International calls for Palestinians who fled or were expelled from Israel, the West Bank or Gaza Strip, along with those of their descendants who have maintained genuine links with the area, to be able to exercise their right to return. Palestinians who were expelled from what is now Israel, and then from the West Bank or Gaza Strip, may be able to show that they have genuine links to both places. If so, they should be free to choose between returning to Israel, the West Bank or Gaza Strip.

5. "Human Rights Watch Urges Attention to Future of Palestinian Refugees" (22 December 2000), www.hrw.org/press/2000/12/isrpab1222.htm; "Israel, Palestinian Leaders Should Guarantee Right of Return as Part of Comprehensive Refugee Solution" (22 December 2002), www.hrw.org/press/2000/12/return1222.htm.

Palestinians who have genuine links to Israel, the West Bank or Gaza Strip, but who are currently living in other host states, may also have genuine links to their host state. This should not diminish or reduce their right to return to Israel, the West Bank or Gaza Strip.

However, not all Palestinian exiles will want to return to their "own country", and those who wish to remain in their host countries—or in the West Bank or Gaza Strip—should be offered the option of full local integration. The international community should also make available to Palestinian exiles the option of third-country resettlement. Whatever solution the individuals choose should be entirely voluntary, and under no circumstances should they be coerced into making a particular choice.

Where possible, Palestinians should be able to return to their original home or lands. If this is not possible—because they no longer exist, have been converted to other uses, or because of a valid competing claim—they should be allowed to return to the vicinity of their original home.

Palestinians who choose not to exercise their right to return should receive compensation for lost property, in accordance with principles of international law. Those returning should likewise be compensated for any lost property.

Amnesty pointed out that it has similarly "supported the right to return of people from countries in all regions of the world, including Bhutan, Bosnia-Herzegovina, Croatia, East Timor, El Salvador, Guatemala, Kosovo, and Rwanda."[6]

6. Amnesty International, *The Right to Return: The Case of the Palestinians. Policy Statement* (London, 30 March 2001).

D. CAMP DAVID AND TABA, 2000–2001

Topic	The *Case for Israel*	What the Evidence Actually Shows
1. DID ISRAEL OFFER PALESTINIANS NEARLY EVERYTHING THEY WANTED AT THE 2000–2001 PEACE NEGOTIATIONS?	(a) *Prime Minister Ehud Barak shocked the world by offering the Palestinians virtually everything they had been demanding, including a state with its capital in Jerusalem, control over the Temple Mount, a return of approximately 95 percent of the West Bank, and all of the Gaza Strip, and a $30 billion compensation package for the 1948 refugees. (pp. 8–9)*	Dershowitz's only evidence for his many assertions listed here consists of the bare text of a proposal by President Clinton reprinted in *Haaretz* and an alleged statement by Egyptian president Mubarak from 1989. Returning to the real world, the international consensus for resolving the Israel-Palestine conflict has called for full Israeli withdrawal from the West Bank and Gaza, allowing for minor and mutual border adjustments. This consensus has included full Israeli withdrawal from East Jerusalem, which all General Assembly resolutions as well as, recently, the World Court advisory opinion have affirmed to be occupied territory. The departure point of Palestinian negotiators at Camp David in July 2000 was acceptance of the international consensus; the departure point of Israeli and U.S. negotiators was rejection of it.[35] In a letter to President Clinton, who presided over the proceedings, Palestinian representatives stated that their aim was implementation of U.N.
DID PALESTINIANS REJECT THIS PROPOSAL AND NOT MAKE A COUNTERPROPOSAL?		Resolution 242 and that "[w]e are willing to accept adjustments of the border between the two countries, on condition that they be equivalent in value and importance." Repeatedly the Palestinian negotiators asked: "Will you
DID NEGOTIATIONS FAIL BECAUSE PALESTINIANS DEMANDED FULL IMPLEMENTATION OF THE RIGHT OF RETURN?	(b) *Barak startled the world by offering the Palestinians nearly all the territory they were seeking. By the time the negotiations ended, Barak had accepted Clinton's even more generous proposal and was offering the Palestinians "between 94 and 96 percent of the West Bank" and all of the Gaza Strip. In exchange for the 4 to 6 percent that Israel would retain for security purposes, it would cede 1 to 3 percent of its land to the Palestinians. This would plainly have*	accept the June 4 border [as the basis of discussion]? Will you accept the principle of the exchange of territories?" The Israeli position was that "[w]e can't accept the demand for a return to the borders of June 1967 as a precondition for the negotiation," while Clinton "literally yells," in response to the Palestinian view that "international legitimacy means Israeli retreat to the border of June 4, 1967," that "[t]his isn't the Security Council here. This isn't the U.N. General Assembly."[36] Measured against the international consensus, the reason the Camp David summit failed was straightforward: whereas the concessions of Palestinians exceeded those required of them, the Israeli position still fell far short of the

satisfied Security Council Resolution 242, which mandated return of "territories," not all territories, captured in Israel's defensive war with Jordan. Few, if any, Palestinian people would remain under Israeli occupation. In addition, Barak offered the Palestinians a state with Arab Jerusalem as its capital and complete control over East Jerusalem and the Arab Quarter of the Old City, as well as the entire Temple Mount, despite its historic and religious significance to Jews. Israel would retain control over the Western Wall, which has no significance for Muslims. (p. 110, emphasis in original)

(c) Arafat did not even offer a counterproposal to Israel's offer [at Camp David and Taba]. He simply rejected it and ordered preparation for renewed terrorism. (p. 118)

consensus. Palestinians were prepared to accept Israeli retention of sizable Jewish settlements in the Occupied Territories in exchange for land of equal size and value in Israel, as well as Israeli sovereignty in East Jerusalem over large Jewish settlements, the Wailing Wall, and the Jewish Quarter of the Old City. Israel, on the other hand, demanded annexation or long-term occupation of approximately 20 percent of the West Bank, *fragmenting it into multiple pieces,* and sovereignty over all of East Jerusalem apart from a few Arab neighborhoods on the city's outskirts. In December 2000 President Clinton put forth his "parameters" for resolving the conflict. He proposed that Israel withdraw from 94–96 percent of the West Bank and Palestinians receive 1–3 percent of Israeli territory as compensation. Regarding East Jerusalem, he called for its demographic and symbolic division along ethnic lines: the Jewish population and religious sites central to Judaism would go to Israel, while the Arab population and religious sites central to Islam would go to the Palestinian state. Both the Israeli and Palestinian teams accepted the Clinton parameters as a basis for further negotiations while neither accepted them unconditionally.[37]

These negotiations resumed in mid-January 2001 at Taba in Egypt. The Israeli side's final offer called for the annexation of 6 percent of West Bank land, which would have still encroached deeply into the Palestinian state, and the leasing of an additional 2 percent, with a maximum 3 percent Israeli land swap of unknown value. Palestinian negotiators adhered to the "minor" and "mutual" formula of the international consensus: a 3.1 percent reciprocal land swap between Israel and Palestinians that would still enable Israel

35. The main sources for Camp David and Taba are Charles Enderlin, *Shattered Dreams: The Failure of the Peace Process in the Middle East, 1995–2002* (New York, 2003), and, specifically on Taba, the *Moratinos Document* by the European Union's special envoy to the peace process, Miguel Moratinos. All parties to the negotiations confirmed the accuracy of Enderlin's account and Moratinos's summary of Taba.

36. Enderlin, *Shattered Dreams,* pp. 185–87, 193, 195, 201–2, 212–13.

37. Clayton E. Swisher, *The Truth about Camp David* (New York, 2004), p. 402, quoting a White House spokesman on 3 January 2003: "Both sides have now accepted the president's ideas with some reservations."

Topic	The Case for Israel	What the Evidence Actually Shows
I. DID ISRAEL OFFER PALESTINIANS NEARLY EVERYTHING THEY WANTED AT THE 2000–2001 PEACE NEGOTIATIONS? (continued)	(d) *Arafat rejected the deal [at Taba] and flew home without offering any counterproposals or amendments. (p. 119)*	to maintain its sovereignty over most of the Jewish settlers in the West Bank. On East Jerusalem, both sides seemed to be edging toward the Clinton compromise. The negotiations were unilaterally suspended by Barak—not Arafat, as Dershowitz falsely claims—in late January, allegedly due to the impending Israeli election, which he lost.[38] Barak subsequently repudiated the legacy of Taba, as did incoming prime minister Ariel Sharon.
	(e) *Yasser Arafat rejected the Barak proposal, making it clear that he would never surrender the right of more than 4 million Palestinians to return to Israel rather than live in the Palestinian state with compensation. (p. 110)*	There is no evidence at all from any sources with firsthand knowledge of the negotiations that Palestinian insistence on implementing the right of return caused the peace negotiations to collapse. Indeed, the indications were that, although Palestinian negotiators insisted that the consensus embodied in U.N. Resolution 194 serve as the basis for resolving the refugee question, as a practical matter, they would acquiesce in a statement of Israel's responsibility for what happened and compensation for all but a few tens of thousands, who would be repatriated to Israel. Barak was categorical, however, in refusing to acknowledge any culpability for creating the Palestinian refugee problem: "[W]e cannot accept historical responsibility for the creation of the problem."[39] Throughout the negotiations, the core of the Palestinian position for resolving the conflict remained constant—that is, the
	(f) *It is the hope of most Israelis that the Palestinians will eventually drop this unrealistic demand [for the right of return], since it was Arafat's refusal to do so that doomed the earlier peace negotiations in 2000–2001. (p. 240)*	terms of the international consensus, although in practice allowing for major concessions on East Jerusalem and the refugee question. Amos Malka, head of Israeli Military Intelligence (MI) from mid-1998 to the end of 2001, stated in 2004: "We assumed that it was possible to reach an agreement with
	(g) *President Hosni Mubarak took a positive first step . . . by declaring that "the Palestinian demand for the 'right of return' is totally unrealistic and would have to be solved by means of financial compensation and resettlement in Arab countries." This, of course, is precisely what was*	Arafat under the following conditions: a Palestinian state with Jerusalem as its capital and sovereignty on the Temple Mount; 97 percent of the West Bank plus exchanges of territory in the ratio of 1:1 with respect to the remaining territory; some kind of formula that includes the acknowledgment of Israel's responsibility for the refugee problem and a willingness to accept

offered at Camp David and Taba—a $30 billion compensation package plus an acknowledgment of "wrongs" done to the refugees, and the right of some refugees to return to Israel. But Arafat walked away, claiming that Barak's offer would not resolve the refugee problem. (p. 240)

SOURCES:

(a) None

(b) Clinton Minutes, *Haaretz*, December 31, 2000.

(c) None

(d) None

(e) None

(f) None

(g) *Jerusalem Post*, January 26, 1989.

20,000–30,000 refugees. . . . [I]t was MI's assessment that he had to get some kind of statement that would not depict him as having relinquished this, but he would be prepared for a very limited implementation."[40] In March 2002 Crown Prince Abdullah of Saudi Arabia proposed, and the Arab League unanimously approved, a plan offering, in exchange for full Israeli withdrawal, not only full recognition but "normal relations with Israel," while it called not for the "right of return" of Palestinian refugees but rather only a "just solution" of the refugee problem. A *Haaretz* commentator noted that the Saudi plan was "surprisingly similar to what Barak claims to have proposed" during the 2000–2001 peace negotiations. Yet, after an ephemeral interlude of evasion and silence, Israel "rejected the proposal with contempt." Deposited in Orwell's memory hole, the occasional subsequent mention of the Saudi plan evoked Israeli ire.[41]

38. There's no dispute that it was Barak who suspended the Taba talks, announcing his decision to Swedish prime minister Göran Persson and U.N. secretary-general Kofi Annan on January 28, 2001 ("PM Barak: Diplomatic Contacts with Palestinians Halted until after Election," www.mfa.gov.il/MFA/Government/Communiques/2001). Although Barak's pretext was the upcoming election, leading Israeli negotiator Amnon Lipkin-Shahak would later state that Taba was never serious about Taba and simply used it as an electoral ploy: "Taba was not aimed to reach an agreement. Taba was aimed to convince the Israeli Arabs to vote" (Swisher, *Truth about Camp David*, p. 403). Once it became clear that he would lose regardless of the Arab vote, Barak bolted from Taba.

39. Benny Morris, "Camp David and After: An Exchange (1. An Interview with Ehud Barak)," *New York Review of Books* (13 June 2002). Compare Enderlin, *Shattered Dreams*, p. 197.

40. Akiva Eldar, "Popular Misconceptions," *Haaretz* (11 June 2004).

41. For text of the Saudi plan, see *London Guardian* (28 March 2002). For its revision on the "right of return," see Suzanne Goldenberg, "Arab leaders reach agreement by fudging refugee question," *Guardian* (29 March 2002). Aviv Lavie, "So what if the Arabs want to make peace?" *Haaretz* (5 April 2002) ("similar," "contempt"); Uzi Benziman, "Distorting the map," *Haaretz* (27 October 2002). For insightful commentary on the Saudi plan, see Uri Avnery, "How to torpedo the Saudis" (4 March 2002), www.counterpunch.org/avnerysaudis.html.

ALAN DERSHOWITZ ON BIGOTRY, DUPLICITY, AND HYPOCRISY

"PEOPLE OF COLOR"-HATING PALESTINIANS AND JEW-HATING JORDANIANS

On page 143 of *The Case for Israel,* Alan Dershowitz writes:

Palestinian terrorists have lynched and blown up more people—including hundreds of people of color—than the [Ku Klux] Klan managed to kill in its century-long reign of terror.

The corresponding endnote reports: "Some of the 273 marines killed by Palestinian terrorists in Beirut were black" (p. 252, chap. 20n5).

Leaving aside the sheer weirdness of attempting to prove that Palestinians have killed more "people of color" than the Ku Klux Klan, and leaving aside that it was 241, not 273, American servicemen, mostly marines, who were killed in the October 1983 suicide bombing, there isn't a jot of evidence—not even serious speculation—that Palestinians were in any way involved.[1]

On page 37 of *The Case for Israel,* Alan Dershowitz writes:

Many of the Jews who lived in what became Transjordan—some of whom had lived there for generations—had been forced to leave because of episodic outbreaks of violence and, by law, the few remaining Jews were forbidden from living in Transjordan.

The corresponding endnote reads: "Jordanian nationality law, Article 3(3) of Law No. 6; and *Official Gazette,* no. 1171, February 16, 1954" (p. 247, chap. 4n13).

On the one hand, carefully compiled Ottoman population statistics do not show any Jews having lived in the area that became Transjordan during the preceding century.[2] On the other hand, the Jordanian nationality law cited by Dershowitz does not address the citizenship status of indigenous Transjordanian Jews at all. According to Article 3(3): "Any non-Jewish person who possessed Palestinian citizenship prior to 15 May 1948 and was normally resident within the Hashemite Kingdom of Jordan on the date this law was issued [16 February 1954]" is considered a Jordanian citizen.[3] As is immediately obvious, the purpose of

---

1. Robert Fisk, *Pity the Nation* (New York, 1990), pp. 511–20.

2. Kemal H. Karpat, *Ottoman Population, 1830–1914: Demographic and Social Characteristics* (Madison, Wisc., 1985), p. 178.

3. Article 3(3) of the Jordanian Citizenship Law . . . of 16 February 1954 (translated from the original Arabic). This writer is indebted to Mouin Rabbani and Anis F. Kassim for clarifying the issue.

the law is to regulate the status of former Arab citizens of Palestine who had become resident in Jordanian-controlled territory as a result of the 1948 war (i.e., West Bankers and refugees) rather than to deprive Jews who were already Jordanian citizens of their existing rights. Furthermore, the law excludes only those Jews who were both Palestinian citizens prior to 1948 and resident in Jordan in 1954, and then only from the opportunity of automatic naturalization—hardly a natural right. The remainder of the 1954 Citizenship Law underscores the reality that Article 3(3) excluded only a specific group of Jews rather than all Jews, and that it was drafted in the context of Jordanian absorption of the West Bank and Palestinian refugees at a time when Jordan and Israel were still formally at war. Indeed, no other article of the citizenship law regulating naturalization explicitly excludes Jews.

ONE (STRANGE) DAY IN SEPTEMBER

On page 257n21 of *The Case for Israel,* Alan Dershowitz reports:

> Estimates vary as to the number of Palestinians killed during "Black September," with some estimates as high as 4,000 (*One Day in September,* Sony Pictures, www.sonypictures.com/classics/oneday/html/blacksept, last visited April 10, 2003), while others cite the figure of 3,000 ("Some Key Dates in the Israeli-Palestinian Conflict," www.umich.edu/~iinet/cmenas/studyunits/israeli-palestinian_conflict/studentkeydates.html, last visited April 10, 2003).

In September 1970 King Hussein of Jordan brutally suppressed a Palestinian insurgency. The range Dershowitz cites for Palestinian deaths during the Black September massacre is accurate. Oddly, however, his first source is the publicity website for a 1999 movie called *One Day in September,* while the second is a chronology appended to a high school syllabus. When this writer publicly noted the anomaly of a chair at Harvard Law School using such references, Dershowitz explained to the *Boston Globe*: **"I'm happy that I don't have to cite inaccessible sources."**[1]

It gets curiouser and curiouser, however. Although citing a range of 3,000 to 4,000 Palestinian deaths during Black September in *The Case*

---

1. Alex Beam, "Another Middle East Conflict," *Boston Globe* (2 October 2003).

for Israel, Dershowitz reports in *Why Terrorism Works* that **"as many as 20,000"** Palestinians were killed in Black September.[2] In September 1972 at the Munich Olympics, eight Palestinians belonging to a faction called Black September killed two members of the Israeli team and took nine others hostage. During a botched rescue operation by Bavarian police, all the Israeli hostages and five of the eight Palestinian attackers were killed. Three of the Palestinians were injured, captured and held for trial. On pages 43–44 of *Why Terrorism Works,* Dershowitz makes this sensational claim:

> Less than two months after the [Olympic] murders, Chancellor Willy Brandt made a secret deal with the Palestinian terrorists. Together they arranged for other Palestinian terrorists to hijack a Lufthansa plane from Beirut carrying eleven German men and a skeleton crew and to hold these Germans hostage, threatening to kill them unless the three Munich murderers were flown to freedom in an Arab country. . . . Feigning terror at the prospect of Germans being murdered on a Lufthansa plane, Brandt gave in to the "demands" of these terrorists. Many observers suspected that the Lufthansa hijacking had been staged by the Brandt government to concoct an excuse for releasing the three terrorists, as a way of avoiding a real hijacking. Until recently there was no proof of this cynical secret deal between the government that had botched the rescue of the Israeli Olympic team and the terrorists who had murdered the Israelis, but it has now been confirmed by both Palestinian and German sources that the Lufthansa hijacking was a sham and that the Germans were all too eager to free the murderers.

This time Dershowitz's source is not the movie *One Day in September* but a subsequent book based on it. His endnote refers readers to Simon Reeve, *One Day in September* (New York, 2000), **"p. 158, citing Jamal al-Gashey, one of the terrorists responsible for the Munich massacre, and Ulrich Wagener [*sic*—Wegener], the founder of the elite German antiterrorist unit GSG-9 (p. 59)."**[3] (The pseudonym *al-Gashey* is given to one of the three imprisoned Palestinians later freed whom Reeve claims to have tracked down.) One problem with relying on books based on movies is that they aren't always the most reliable sources. Typically Dershowitz gets the basic facts wrong. For example, the eleven passengers weren't all German but overwhelmingly non-German, including an American.[4] (The United States would later criti-

---

2. Alan M. Dershowitz, *Why Terrorism Works* (New Haven, 2002), p. 89. Dershowitz repeated this 20,000 figure in his publicity interviews for the book; see, e.g., Suzy Hansen, "Why Terrorism Works," Salon.com (interview) (12 September 2002).

3. Dershowitz, *Why Terrorism Works,* p. 236n11.

4. German Foreign Office, *Political Archives,* vol. B36, no. 578.

cize Brandt for having released the Palestinians, but during the hijack-
ing the U.S. ambassador to Germany pressed the German government
to acquiesce in the hijackers' demands in order to save the American hostage.)[5] Regarding the two personal testimonies to the alleged
Brandt plot, Reeve conceals the whereabouts and even physical identity
of the pseudonymous "al-Gashey," while there's reason to suppose that
Israel long ago liquidated all three Palestinians freed after the Munich
massacre and that, therefore, he doesn't exist.[6] Wegener has asserted
that "my statement in the film 'One Day in September' *can't* be inter-
preted as evidence for an alleged secret deal between the Federal Government and terrorists" (emphasis in original).[7] Every member at every
level of the German government contacted, from surviving senior
officials of the Brandt government to the German Foreign Office and
the Chancellery, dismisses the Reeve claim as preposterous, as do
all knowledgeable German journalists and scholars, Jewish and non-
Jewish alike.[8] But, basing himself on one book, which is itself based on
a movie basing itself on two highly dubious sources, Dershowitz tells
readers that this sensational tale "has now been confirmed." Finally,
in a model of situational ethics, while he castigates for an American
audience Brandt's capitulation to Palestinian terrorists, Dershowitz tells
the German newspaper *Die Welt*: **"There are of course some [German]
people who are deserving of much respect, Willy Brandt, for example."**[9]

5. "Nase abbeissen: Vergebens suchten die Law-and-order-Fans der Union,
die Flugzeugentführung der arabischen Guerillas in Wählersympathie umzumün-
zen," *Der Spiegel* (6 November 1972), p. 25.
6. "Alles hohe Diplomatie: 20 Jahre nach dem Münchner Olympia-Mas-
saker kämpfen die Familien der israelischen Opfer noch immer um Schadenser-
satz aus Deutschland," *Der Spiegel* (31 August 1992), p. 80. Even right-wing
"pro"-Israel websites maintain that all the key Palestinian perpetrators of the
Munich massacre are dead (see Mitchell Bard, "The Munich Massacre," www
.jewishvirtuallibrary.org/jsource/Terrorism/munich.html).
7. Letter from Ulrich Wegener to Gylfe Nagel (29 February 2004). This
writer is indebted to Nagel for making available her extensive research and correspondence on this topic.
8. These include Brandt's minister of interior, Hans-Dietrich Genscher; former Munich mayor Hans-Jochen Vogel (Reeve gestures to Vogel for corrobora-
tive testimony); then-head of the German Chancellery Horst Ehmke; federal
plenipotentiary for Berlin and federal minister Egon Bahr; Parliament member
Hans-Christian Ströbele; Brandt biographer Peter Merseburger; film documen-
tarians and researchers Oliver Storz and Hermann Schreiber; *Frankfurter Allgemeine Zeitung* journalist Rainer Blasius; Professor Michael Wolffsohn from the
University of the German Federal Armed Forces (Munich); and Hans Koschnick,
who represented Germany in talks with Israel after the three Palestinians were
released. This writer has statements from each of them on file.
9. Alan M. Dershowitz, "Alle lieben tote Juden . . . ," *Die Welt* (15 June
2002).

ABETTING TERRORISM

On pages 54–55 of *Why Terrorism Works,*[1] Alan Dershowitz writes:

> The U.N. General Assembly even went so far as to encourage Palestinian terrorism directed against Israeli and Jewish civilians. In 1979, it approved an exception to the international convention against the taking of hostages. The amendment, which was expressly intended to *permit* hostage-taking by Palestinians, went as follows: "The present Convention shall not apply to an act of hostage-taking committed in the course of armed conflicts, . . . in which people are fighting against colonial occupation and alien occupation and against racist regimes in the exercise of their right of self-determination." This formulation then became part of several antiterrorist resolutions, all of which implicitly exempted acts of terrorism committed by Palestinians against Israelis and Jews. (emphasis in original)

The United Nations General Assembly ratified the "International Convention against the Taking of Hostages" on 17 December 1979 (Res. 34/146). There are several problems with Dershowitz's claim that it "encourage[s] Palestinian terrorism." On a smaller, technical point, the passage he cites isn't an amendment but comes right from Article 12 of the Hostage Convention. The larger, substantive point is that he has grossly misrepresented Article 12, the full text of which reads:

> In so far as the Geneva Conventions of 1949 for the protection of war victims or the Additional Protocols to those Conventions are applicable to a particular act of hostage-taking, and in so far as States Parties to this Convention are bound under those conventions to prosecute or hand over the hostage-taker, the present Convention shall not apply to an act of hostage-taking committed in the course of armed conflicts as defined in the Geneva Conventions of 1949 and the Protocols thereto, including armed conflicts mentioned in article 1, paragraph 4, of Additional Protocol I of 1977, in which peoples are fighting against colonial domination and alien occupation and against racist regimes in the exercise of their right of self-determination, as enshrined in the Charter of the United Nations and the Declaration on Principles of International Law concerning Friendly Relations and Co-operation among States in accordance with the Charter of the United Nations.

This article takes note that prohibitions against hostage taking in the context of armed conflict, "including armed conflicts . . . in which peoples are fighting . . . in the exercise of their right of self-determination," already exist. Additional Protocol I explicitly extends the meaning of *armed conflicts* in the Geneva Conventions—and accordingly the absolute ban on hostage taking—to conflicts arising in the course of a people's exercise of its right to self-determination. The plain intent of

---

1. New Haven, 2002.

the Hostage Convention was extending yet further the prohibition against hostage taking, beyond the context of armed conflicts, not to diminish existing sanctions against it. Lest there be any doubt regarding Dershowitz's mangling of the text, the voting record at the General Assembly dispels it. Israel and the United States *approved* the Hostage Convention.[2] To judge by Dershowitz, they both voted "to encourage Palestinian terrorism directed against Israeli and Jewish civilians."

2. For the voting record, see http://untreaty.un.org/ENGLISH/Status/Chapter _xviii/treaty5.asp. Israel affirmed the applicability of the convention's prohibition on hostage taking "in all circumstances," while the United States approved without comment. This writer is indebted to Rafal Szczurowski for clarifying these points.

Index

Abdullah, Crown Prince of Saudi Arabia, 311
Abdullah, King of Jordan, 286
Abed, George, 194–195
Abrahamson, Irving, 63*n*
Abrams, Floyd, 17
Abu Ghraib prison, 41
Abu Sitta, Salman, 5*n*
Ad Dawayima massacre, 263
Afghanistan war, 56*n*
Africa, 63
"Afrocentric demagogues," 70*n*, 224
Agranat, Shimon, 171
Ahmad, Mahmoud el-Abed, 150*n*, 152
al-Akhras, Ayat, 106–107
Alami, Musa, 250
Algeria, 114*n*
Alhamas, Iman, 115–116
Allen, W., 240
Allon, Yigal, 289, 304
Allon Plan, 287–288, 290, 304
Aloni, Shulamit, 140
American Bar Association, 149*n*
American Civil Liberties Union (ACLU), 94, 223
American Friends Service Committee (Quakers), 25

American Israel Public Affairs Committee (AIPAC), 72
American Jewish Committee (AJC), 45*n*
American Jewish Congress, 121
Amiel, Barbara, 41
Amitary, Nurit, 301*n*
Amnesty International, 4, 92–94
 accused of anti-Israel bias, 32, 40, 93, 156, 158
 on administrative detention, 147, 218
 on alleged misuse of ambulance by Palestinians, 129
 on assassinations of Palestinians, 105, 132*n*, 134*n*, 136, 137, 138–139
 on Border Police brutality, 166–167
 on closure and curfew policies affecting Palestinians, 196–199
 on discrimination, 100, 169*n*, 179, 198–199, 211*n*
 on effects of wall construction, 202*n*, 204*n*
 on house demolitions, 169, 173, 178–180, 181–183, 186, 188
 on IDF impunity, 99*n*, 113
 on IDF military support from the U.S., Canada, and Britain, 100

Compositor:	Michael Bass Associates
Indexer:	Herr's Indexing Service
Text:	10/13 Sabon
Display:	Akzidenz Grotesk
Printer and binder:	Sheridan Books, Inc.